MR. TUBA

Mr. TUBA

HARVEY PHILLIPS

Foreword by DAVID N. BAKER

INDIANA UNIVERSITY PRESS   *Bloomington & Indianapolis*

This book is a publication of

INDIANA UNIVERSITY PRESS
601 North Morton Street
Bloomington, IN 47404-3797 USA

iupress.indiana.edu

Telephone orders   800-842-6796
Fax orders   812-855-7931

Publication of *Mr. Tuba* was aided by
the generous support of the Indiana
University Jacobs School of Music.

⊖ The paper used in this publication
meets the minimum requirements of
the American National Standard for
Information Sciences—Permanence of
Paper for Printed Library Materials,
ANSI Z39.48-1992.

MANUFACTURED IN THE
UNITED STATES OF AMERICA

Library of Congress
Cataloging-in-Publication Data

Phillips, Harvey, 1929–2010, author.
  Mr. Tuba / Harvey Phillips ;
foreword by David N. Baker.
  pages cm
  Includes index.
  ISBN 978-0-253-00724-7 (cloth : alkaline
paper) — ISBN 978-0-253-00731-5 (e-book)
1. Phillips, Harvey, 1929–2010. 2. Tubists—
United States—Biography. I. Title.
  ML419.P49A3 2012
  788.9'9092—dc23
  [B]
                                    2012021225

1 2 3 4 5 17 16 15 14 13 12

To Carol

This autobiography is affectionately shared with and dedicated to Carol, my beautiful, loving wife of fifty-five wonderful years. I owe every success to her inspiration, understanding, patience, and encouragement.

To family and colleagues,

past-present-future, for their love, concern, and support through all the years of my life. My cherished life in music was not the result of any planning or ambition; it evolved from a series of unpredictable events and incredibly generous teachers, mentors, colleagues, friends, and family. Their example, support, and guidance inspired every effort to represent the personal and professional integrity so important to developing and preserving our precious, and too often fragile, art of music. May God bless each of you.

HARVEY PHILLIPS

CONTENTS

FOREWORD

HARVEY PHILLIPS AND I got to be really good friends after our first meeting in 1959 on an LP recording of *The Golden Striker: The Music of John Lewis.* Harvey asked me to write a piece for him. In 1967 Gunther Schuller was appointed president of the New England Conservatory of Music and named Harvey his vice president for financial affairs. Harvey and I met in Chicago at a National Association of Jazz Educators reception. Harvey had commissioned me to write a piece for the tuba and asked, "How is that piece coming along?"

I hadn't started it, but I replied, "It's coming along okay."

Harvey asked, "What is it for?"

Well, there was a poster of a string quartet on the wall, so I said, "Tuba and string quartet." So, it became a piece for tuba and string quartet, and Harvey premiered it at Carnegie Hall in a recital series and recorded it for Golden Crest Records. I went with him to the recording session and remarked at his unbelievable stamina. They started recording at nine in the morning and went till seven or eight that evening. The string players were worn out—their fingers were ready to bleed—but Harvey got strong at every take. And when you listen to the recording, it's breathtaking. The piece has had a great life of its own. I think just about every tuba player attending Indiana University has studied or played it under Harvey's tutelage.

I wrote a *Concerto to End All Concertos* for Harvey to perform at IU. We only did it once because of the complex accompaniment, requiring a large jazz band, ballet dancers, a chorus and speech choir, fifteen prerecorded orchestral tuba excerpts, and 33 mm slides of Harvey and me in various artistic poses (imitating Roman and Greek statues and everything in between) projected onto a big screen. The fifteen tapes were scattered throughout the audience to fifteen privileged music students who had been given tape recorders and told to watch for specific cues from the conductor to play their recordings. The piece is a good illustration of the excesses of which both Harvey and I are guilty; it was a spectacular happening.

Without Harvey, I never would have written as much for the tuba. I had not recognized its potential as a solo instrument and collaborator until I heard him play. His sound was very distinct, clean, and clear, which I recognize immediately on any recording he has done. Harvey took away the fear that any composer might have of writing for the tuba. Because of Harvey, there are no limits.

David N. Baker, *Director,*
Smithsonian Jazz Masterworks Orchestra;
Distinguished Professor and Jazz Department Chair,
Indiana University

ACKNOWLEDGMENTS

I THANK Mary Campbell, Rob Teehan, and John Visel for their assistance in editing my manuscript, and Bobbie Ford, Emily Hutchinson, and Marcus Wiggins for their editorial review.

I wish to express my gratitude to:

John W. Ryan, for urging me to write this book. Dr. Ryan became president of Indiana University the same day I became professor of tuba at IU. We first met at the induction ceremonies and our paths crossed at several receptions appropriate to the occasion. It was always pleasant and reassuring to know that the administrative chief office of our university was in the hands, mind, and heart of such a leader. His interest in my activities was always genuine, flattering, and appreciated. It is rare that a person in such a position would take the time and interest to call the professor of tuba on the telephone and ask to take some lessons to learn more about the instrument. I doubt if there are many tuba professors who can list the president of their university as one of their promising students. It is amazing that one with such awesome responsibilities has equal interest in and concern for every member of his university family.

Dean Wilfred C. Bain, who hired me to join the IU faculty. My first year was his twenty-fifth and last year as dean. He demonstrated his magnanimous nature by allowing me to schedule, structure, and host the First International Tuba Symposium Workshop, the first formal event held in the new Musical Arts Center, a major achievement of his administration.

Dean Charles H. Webb, whose magnanimity was shown by his encouragement and support of his faculty and students. He consented to open the First International Tuba Symposium Workshop by performing with me Paul Hindemith's *Sonata for Tuba and Piano*. He often accompanied faculty artists in recital and other solo and chamber music performances. Throughout my tenure he performed with me in a series of solo tuba recitals at New York City's Carnegie Recital Hall.

MR. TUBA

CHAPTER ONE

Growing Up in Missouri

NEWS SPREAD QUICKLY in our small town of Marionville, Missouri. In mid-June 1947, when the preacher of my church heard that I would be "running away with the circus," he drove to our house and asked to speak with my mother and me. As always, Mom greeted the preacher cordially and invited him into our parlor, a room kept prim and proper for the visits of preachers and insurance salesmen, every doily in place and everything clean and orderly. Reverend Gilbert was assigned the most comfortable chair while Mom sat on the front edge of another chair holding a handkerchief in her lap. I sat on the piano bench, in front of our old upright piano.

After friendly exchanges about the weather, vegetable gardens, and everyone's health, Reverend Gilbert took a big breath and extolled lavishly about what a fine young man I was, what a great job I was doing as junior superintendent of the church and as president of the Methodist Youth Fellowship. I enjoyed that part of his visit. But suddenly his manner changed; his voice became dark and ominous and he stated, "From what I hear, this young man is going into a life of sin!" He then continued to express, through combined lecture and sermon, his opinions and what he had heard about the decadent morals of show business people, circus people especially, and how, as an innocent seventeen-year-old youth, I could easily be corrupted by association and temptations.

I was mesmerized by his tirade, but out of the corner of my eye I saw Mom slowly stand and inch crab-like toward the door, so as not to turn her back on the preacher. Then, just as she reached the door and the preacher took another deep breath to continue, Mom suddenly turned, and with a voice and conviction I have heard neither before nor since, said, "Reverend Gilbert, you don't seem to have much faith in Harvey, but I do, and I'd like you to leave now!" I was dumbfounded, as was the preacher, who said no more and left.

Wow, I thought, Mom just threw the preacher out of our house! I didn't know what to say, so I said nothing. I was admiringly respectful of Mom, for although she was obviously deeply hurt by the preacher's words and attitude, she handled the matter beautifully and firmly. I never spoke to her about it, but, throughout my life, I have often thought about my mother's faith in me, expressed that day, and it has given me confidence and the courage to tackle the next thing that needed to be done.

PHILLIPS FAMILY LEGEND

In the summer of 1861, Miles and Mary Phillips (my great-grandfather and great-grandmother) were asked to a meeting at the Shelbyville, Tennessee, schoolhouse near their home. As the meeting was called to order by their member of the state House of Representatives, they noticed rather cool feelings from some of their neighbors. The representative advised the gathering that the nation was in deep trouble over slavery. He noted that two or three states had already withdrawn from the nation and there would likely be more. He wanted to know the opinions of his constituents.

Miles Phillips stated that Tennessee should stay with the union and solve any problems with slavery locally. Several in the gathering expressed different views.

Miles and Mary discussed the safety of their family: Jesse, eighteen; Steve, almost sixteen; John, fourteen; James Anderson, twelve (my grandfather); and Wesley, nine. When they got home from the meeting, Jesse told them he was going to join the Union Army the next day. Early the next morning, Jesse saddled his horse and tied it to the hitching post near the porch. He said he would be leaving after breakfast and asked his mother to fix him a couple of ham sandwiches. Just before breakfast was over, several men on horseback came into the yard. Mary went out on the porch and asked the riders what they wanted. The leader told her he needed to talk to Jesse. Jesse said the man was Bully Smith, leader of a gang that had robbed farmers in the county and left several dead. Jesse, who had a .38 revolver, said, "Mom. Let me kill him now and scatter his gang before they do something to us." She said, "No, son. He just wants to talk to you. Don't shoot anybody."

Jesse went out. Bully Smith offered him a job with his gang, which Jesse declined. Then Bully Smith said, "Okay, Jesse, get on your horse and get out of here." Jesse mounted his horse and started to leave. At that moment, Bully Smith said, "All right, boys, let's give him a good sendoff." The gang shot several times at Jesse. Two bullets hit him in his back and he fell off his horse. He got up to run toward the cedars but collapsed just as he got to the rail fence. The gang rode away at full speed. Miles and Mary ran to Jesse. He looked at his mother and said, "Mom, they got me," and closed his eyes.

PARENTS MEETING

My parents met at a social (party) given by the students of the Marionville Methodist College in early May 1904. My father, Jesse Emmett Phillips (age twenty-two), happened to walk by where my mother, Lottie Amber Chapman (age fifteen), was sitting with some of her friends. Dressed in a suit and tie, he was a handsome young man. After he had passed by, she asked, "Who was tha-a-t?" He was making his own inquiries, asking, "Who is that attractive young lady?"

The following Saturday afternoon he visited her house, with a short buggy ride in mind. Lottie's mother answered the knock on the door and Jesse courteously introduced himself. He told her of his interest in her daughter and said he would soon be going away to continue his studies at Springfield Business College, which would leave little time for him to court Lottie. Lottie's mother was favorably impressed by Jesse, though his visit caught her by surprise. She agreed that he could take Lottie for a very short buggy ride. Thus, their courting was approved, thanks to the old adage about the importance of making a good first impression.

Emmett (Lottie's favored name for him, which stuck) and Lottie's actual first date came a week later. It was an eighteen-mile round-trip buggy ride to a Sunday morning church service at the McKinley Christian Church, attended by Emmett and his family every week. Activities of churches and schools, such as picnics, pie suppers, square dances, and cakewalks, were always good courtship opportunities. Courting at the turn of the century had charm.

While attending Mt. Vernon High School, Lottie dated another young man. One of Emmett's friends wrote him and advised, "If you want to keep your girl Lottie, you had better do something about it." Emmett recoiled like a fired cannon! He packed his belongings, left Springfield, and went directly to Lottie's house. The first thing he said to her was, "Will you marry me?" Lottie replied, "Yes, I'll marry you." The courtship had lasted for eight months. Lottie left high school in the middle of her junior year and Emmett withdrew from Springfield Business College. They married on January 1, 1905, bought a farm with Mom's inheritance from her grandfather, and started a family.

I was born December 2, 1929, at 4:30 AM in a little house on West Tyndall Street in Aurora, Lawrence County, Missouri, and named Harvey Gene. I was the tenth child of ten: six girls and four boys, including Jesse Emmett Phillips Jr. (1910–1928), a brother I never knew because he died from tuberculosis, seventeen months before my birth.

A MUSIC-LOVING FAMILY

Music first came to me from my mother's humming and singing lullabies and church hymns. Music also came from my father, a good country fiddler who inspired occasional family "musicales" with uncles joining in playing guitars, mandolins, harmonicas, Jew's harps, spoons, jugs, washboard, and piano. Refreshments for these gatherings always included apples and apple cider from the cellar, buttered popcorn, popcorn balls, and surprise pitch-in dishes from the womenfolk. A well-laden table of country cooking was enjoyed by everyone.

Sometimes the entire family harmonized voices, with or without instruments. We sang, hummed, whistled, or tapped out rhythms. Inanimate objects could suddenly be transformed into musical instruments. Music heartened spirits and helped our family survive hardships, including the death of a family member and the loss of all property and savings in the Depression of the 1930s.

THE PHILLIPS DEPRESSION FAMILY—1933

When Franklin Delano Roosevelt began his presidency in 1933, we couldn't have known that he would lead us for the duration of the Depression and a second world war. No one knew if his policies would be successful. But what a godsend he proved to be during the hard times experienced by the entire United States, especially by Midwest farmers.

In the Depression, we lost the farm. Like many Depression-era families, we moved frequently. By the age of ten, I had lived in nine houses, all in Lawrence County. We moved as Dad was hired by someone who had bought a foreclosed farm. Only one house had electricity and indoor water. We used outhouses and kerosene lamps, and pumped drinking water from an outdoor well, a bucket at a time.

How our old upright piano survived all those moves is a mystery. Also, since Mom seemed determined to preserve her reputation for having the cleanest house in the county, she scrubbed every square inch of every house we moved into or out of.

Household pets (two cats, two dogs) and our ever-changing collection of farm animals (twelve to sixteen chickens, two to four pigs, two to three dairy cows, one to two beef steers, two draft horses) moved with us.

It takes a farm family to appreciate the importance of homegrown vegetables, chicken, pork, and beef, plus wild nuts and berries, as the major part of the family's diet, keeping us fed, healthy, and happy. Our shopping lists were very simple: flour, coffee, cornmeal, salt, and sugar. The rest we produced ourselves.

Mom and Dad were determined that family activities remain orderly regardless of the length of residency between moves. We were welded together by love and concern for one another, determined that in our moving the only things that changed were the houses, the schools, the teachers, and the neighbors.

1935–1936: ENTERING FIRST GRADE

In September 1935, at age five, I started first grade at the Elm Branch School, a one-room school for the first eight grades. It was a two-and-a-half-mile walk from home. Although I hadn't met many of the other thirty or so students, I knew my sisters Virginia (grade four) and Georgia (grade seven).

On the first day of school, wanting to get better acquainted, the teacher asked the students what their favorite day of the year was. She got lots of Christmases, Thanksgivings, July Fourths, and a few birthdays. When she asked me what my favorite day was, I stood up and said Fool's Day (April 1). The teacher and students laughed, but that was the day my family played tricks on each other. The teacher should have known right then that I was going to be trouble.

At home, I was used to competing in ciphering matches and spelling bees. Just being in school couldn't stop me from competing. This was a problem. When the teacher was teaching the first grade students I felt it was my privilege to answer all the questions before anyone else could. That went on, right through the eighth grade lessons, no matter the subject. The teacher's demeanor finally changed from courteous and patient to angry and annoyed. If she should ask the fourth grade class, "How much is thirteen plus seventeen?", before anyone else could speak, I would shout, "Thirty!" Georgia later explained to Mom, "Old big-mouth Harvey jumped on every answer."

When the teacher finally started whispering to each class, "Old Elephant Ears" (another description by sister Georgia), I heard her and replied to everything—even when she put me in the farthest corner facing the wall. One day the teacher finally lost her patience and spanked me, and I ran off, saying I was going home.

After about ten minutes of rational thinking, the teacher decided that maybe she should have kept me in school and dealt with me through my parents, so she instructed Georgia and another older girl to find me and bring me back to school. I saw them coming from a distance and knew they could outrun me, so I waded out into the creek, clothes and all, until the water was up to my chin.

After Georgia and Virginia related to Mom and Dad all the things I did at school, I got another spanking. For some time I seemed to average two spankings a day, one at school and one at home. There is an old saying, "Spare the rod and spoil the child." Well, I can say without fear of contradiction that *I was not spoiled!*

CHORES BEFORE BREAKFAST

The winter of 1936–1937 was severe. Lots of wintry winds, sleet, and snow. No one knows what cold is until they've awakened with snow in their room and on their bed, and most especially the coldness of a linoleum floor on bare feet, which wakes you up fast. When we went to bed in such weather we treasured the warm flatirons and the multiple numbers of blankets and homemade quilts Mom put on each bed.

Although I awakened each morning at 4:30–5 AM, Mom would already be singing in the kitchen, making breakfast, which always included fresh, hot, homemade biscuits with fresh-churned butter, sorghum molasses, several kinds of jelly, and always some kind of gravy, depending on what meat she fried any particular day. The eggs were always fresh. I knew Dad was already contenting our two cows before milking by talking to them and giving them scoops of bran, which they ate while being milked. My oldest brother, Campbell, was busy chopping a hole in the frozen pond for the livestock, then feeding scratch to the chickens, including our precise "alarm clock" crowing roosters. He would then feed the pigs their slop, kept warm by the kitchen stove.

Meanwhile, I had six box rabbit traps to tend to before breakfast. The traps were placed in fence rows and rock piles and baited with kernels of field corn. When I caught a rabbit, I would prepare it for Mom to soak in salted milk overnight for the next morning's breakfast. Mom would bread and fry the rabbit, which was delicious.

My sister Hazel would often visit with her children Bobby and Wilma Sue, who were near my age. One July day, inspired by Fourth of July fireworks, Bobby and I got Dad's hammers and about twenty of his .22-caliber long-rifle shells. All the shells were smashed to the thinness of a penny.

We loudly protested when none would fire. Mom and Hazel nearly fainted when they saw what we were doing. Dad couldn't understand why they didn't explode.

When Mom, Dad, and Campbell shopped for food in Mt. Vernon, Georgia, Virginia, Wilma Sue, Bobby, and I roamed the stores, deciding how to spend the nickel Campbell had given to each of us. One Saturday afternoon, we noticed men of varying ages in uniforms, with musical instruments, gathering on the Mt. Vernon Courthouse lawn. Chairs and music stands had been set up for them and the cacophony of woodwind and brass instruments warming up got ever more urgent until one of the players stood up and waved his hands for silence. One musician then sustained a single note while all the others tried to play the same note. When satisfied by their efforts, the standing player sat down and there was total silence.

ENTER MAJOR HOMER F. LEE

A tall man with dark sunken eyes and a huge smile then strode to the front of the band, waved a small white stick and, magically, the Freistatt Town Band started to play. I was captivated. It was the first live band I had ever heard. I couldn't believe what I was hearing. When the band finished a selection, people sitting in their parked cars surrounding the town square honked and tooted their horns, while those sitting or standing about applauded and whistled.

The band was from a town close to Monett, Missouri. Its conductor was Major Homer F. Lee, a renowned circus bandmaster and a proud native son of Verona, Missouri, where his family had a farm. Thus went my first band concert and my first experience with Homer Lee. I couldn't have known what a prominent role he would later play in my life.

In the fall of 1939, in the midst of the annual apple harvest, we moved a final time, to Marionville, known as "The Apple Capital of Missouri" and "home of the white squirrels." We had purchased a three-room house on two acres of land in Marionville for $500 down and mortgage payments of five dollars a month. Buying a house in Marionville was the right thing to do. It was time for Dad (fifty-eight) and Mom (fifty-two) to prepare for their senior years, and the location was terrific. The property was at the intersection of Youngblood and Lynn Streets, less than a mile from the town square, on the northwest side of town. Looking west there were no houses to block beautiful sunsets; looking north was a large open field of pasture running up to the edge of a forest some two miles distant. Looking northwest was a forty-acre peach and apple orchard, one of several owned by G. E. Jackson. Looking east or south, good neighbors were a full block away.

Unfortunately, the house was in dire need of maximum renovation, plus the addition of three new rooms and a full bathroom to accommodate our family of six. We couldn't move in until all renovation and new construction was finished. Brother Campbell assisted Dad in jacking up the existing house three feet, making needed repairs, then pouring a new foundation for the completed structure, including the three added rooms. First priority was to get the house under roof and enclosed before winter weather hit us. Dad did all the carpentry, wiring, plumbing, etc., while he continued working most weekdays at the cold storage plant in Marionville.

THE TUBA ENTERS MY LIFE AT AGE TWELVE

As the academic year progressed through the peaceful autumn months of 1941, I looked forward to celebrating my twelfth birthday, with the traditional birthday cake, on December 2. Just five days after my birthday, on Sunday, December 7, Pearl Harbor was brutally attacked by Japan. Our idyllic and peaceful autumn ended suddenly as our country plunged into World War II.

By mid-March 1942, many young men would soon be drafted into the army by Selective Service. Some were able to arrange early graduation from high school and enlist in their chosen branch of military service. The young man who played the old Martin sousaphone owned by Marionville High School graduated early and joined the U.S. Navy.

A short time later, Miss Alice Hardin, our music teacher, called me to her office and said, "Harvey, how would you like to play the bass horn?" I couldn't believe what I was hearing but I quickly responded with, "Gee, thanks, Miss Hardin, I'd love to play the bass horn!" I was very excited. This opportunity would satisfy my yearning to play a brass instrument in the Marionville School Band. The only other band instruments owned by the school were two snare drums, a pair of cymbals, and a bass drum. Since our family couldn't afford to purchase a brass instrument for me, being assigned the old Martin sousaphone was like winning a lottery. No longer would I ask our tolerant and understanding music teacher to let me bring my father's fiddle to school and try to play it with the band. I couldn't realize it at the time, of course, but that bass horn, that old Martin sousaphone, literally held together with baling wire and bubble gum, would introduce me to the instrument that would ultimately provide me with a life in music. I fell in love with the bass horn (tuba, bass horn, helicon, sousaphone); whatever its nomenclature or configuration, it became my constant companion. Playing the tuba at age twelve was fun. It still is!

No tuba method book was available so Miss Hardin told me all she could about how to produce sounds on a brass instrument. She told me not to puff my cheeks, but to anchor the corners of the mouth to form an embouchure and then to "buzz" the center of my lips. Miss Hardin also gave me a two-octave chromatic fingering chart she had written out and she explained the bass clef. My first assignment was to learn the bass part to "Pomp and Circumstance," plus three other short pieces the band would play at commencement ceremonies in June. Miss Hardin gave me parts for the music I would play and said I could take the sousaphone home to practice. She said she would check on my progress in a week and that it might be a while before I could rehearse with the band.

I carried my newly assigned sousaphone home, playing it experimentally all the way. Everyone in my family was surprised when I brought it home, and I was able to demonstrate some of the sounds they could expect to hear when I practiced while seated on the piano bench. They didn't realize how many hours of practice they were going to hear. Nonetheless, there were no complaints. Everyone was happy for my good fortune.

After three weeks of practicing graduation music bass parts, interrupted only by attending school, I started adding hymns from our well-used hymnal. Mom was delighted. From out in the kitchen she would sing along. She knew every note and lyric of those old church hymns. If I played a wrong note or played out of tune, she would correct me: "Now Harvey, that's not right." In that sense, Mom was my first private teacher.

Miss Hardin was pleased with my progress, and by the third week I was allowed to attend band rehearsals. The band managed to do a fairly good performance at the graduation ceremonies. But just a few days later, I received two bits of bad news. First, Miss Hardin was moving to teach at a school in Oklahoma and, second, I would not be allowed to keep the school's sousaphone over the summer to practice as I had planned. It had to be locked up all summer for safety. I couldn't understand the policy but it was made by the Board of Education and that's all there was to it!

A NEW MUSIC TEACHER

After a summer of not practicing, my spirits were lifted considerably when I learned that Major Homer F. Lee would be our new music teacher and that band would meet three days a week instead of two. When I attended the first class meeting for band hopefuls, I was in awe of Mr. Lee, whom I remembered from his Freistatt Town Band concert years earlier. I was told that I would have to audition for the bass horn chair because there was another boy who was interested in the position. On the appointed day of the audition, I walked onto the gymnasium stage (with curtains drawn it became the "band room") and, at Mr. Lee's direction, picked up the sousaphone and awaited further instructions. Mr. Lee said, "Play me a B flat and hold it out as long as you can. . . . Okay, now play it an octave lower." (I preferred playing the upper octave; I liked the way it sounded.) "Now, can you play any melodies on the bass horn?" I played "Rock of Ages."

"What else can you play?" Mr. Lee asked. Although my sound and endurance wasn't what it would have been if I had practiced all summer, I played a few of my mother's favorite hymns before Mr. Lee said, "Okay, son, you're going to be my bass horn player."

Mr. Lee was very kind to me and, because there was no method book, he assigned me the bass parts to the music he knew best, circus music and other band repertoire. The bass parts got more and more difficult as the weeks and years went by. Sometimes they were tricky, calling for multiple tonguing, which no one had explained to me. Actually I think it was beneficial for me not to have yet learned double-, triple-, or other multiple tonguing. It forced me to develop a very fast single tongue.

Once assured of my position in the school band, I made every effort, when the weather was cooperative, to take the old Martin sousaphone home each day. Riding my bicycle with the sousaphone perched on my shoulder, I soon became expert at tacking the bell, as one would tack a sail on a sailboat, to best utilize the prevailing wind.

I was entering my freshman year of high school before I started becoming aware of classical and popular music, swing and jazz. My expanding awareness came primarily from movie background music. In addition to working before and after school and on Saturdays at the Bradford-Surridge Funeral Home, I ran projectors for a local—just reopened—movie house on weekend evenings. I was in awe of the incredible variety of music performed and what effect it had on every film. I was exposed to a kaleidoscope of musical styles that I couldn't have heard from any other source. I first heard jazz from movie "soundies" featuring such well-known bands as Woody Herman's, but most impressive to me was Cab Calloway and his band, mixing vocal and instrumental jazz.

Like other male high school students, I became involved in athletics, especially football and basketball. It was fun to participate. Athletics brought new friends and new outlets for excess energy. In retrospect, while being a high school athlete seemed heroic at the time, the physical injuries sustained (recurring sprained ankles and twisted knees) weren't worth all the disabilities suffered for the rest of my life. As noted by the Pennsylvania Dutch, we are too soon olt und too late schmart!

When the Marionville School Band performed at football or basketball halftime, I played with the band in my athletic attire, while the coach berated or praised the rest of the sports team in the locker room.

By the time I graduated from high school, I was familiar with quite a unique repertoire and, oh yes, I was allowed to keep the sousaphone throughout the summer of 1943 and beyond. This was partly because our band began playing summer concerts on the porch of the Marionville Municipal Building that faced the town square, and partly because Homer Lee paid a visit to the Board of Education and enlightened them as to why I should be allowed to keep the sousaphone at home to practice. Mr. Lee was a very special person, with the biggest and most reassuring smile I have ever seen. At his own expense, he took me to other schools where he taught, to music competitions, and to town band rehearsals.

It wasn't long before the Marionville School Band was noticed and requested, because it entertained audiences. With Mr. Lee's choice of repertoire, his enthusiasm (and patience) for the music, and his special brand of musical showmanship, the Marionville School Band was quite popular at local, county, and district fairs. It was a big deal to be chosen as entertainment for the Missouri State Fair in Sedalia, the hometown of Scott Joplin! Mr. Lee had me join the Sedalia Local 22 of the American Federation of Musicians at age fifteen.

FUNERAL HOME

At age thirteen I was approached by Mrs. Jezebel Surridge, owner of the funeral home, about being a handy helper before and after school and on Saturdays. Seasonally, I would mow grass, rake leaves, shovel snow, or stoke the furnace. I would unpack shipments of caskets and other items for the funeral home. Arrangements were made with the high school that should I be needed to assist an emergency ambulance call, the funeral home would contact the school and I would be ready for pickup when the ambulance came by the school. I was also utilized in a variety of other tasks related to funerals, as well as "babysitting" the funeral home when Mrs. Surridge had social obligations. I was also assigned to execute chickens for dinner by cutting off their heads with a small ax when ordered to do so. Such a variety of work assignments gave me an ongoing association with older people who could observe, evaluate, and appreciate a person of my age being responsible. I did not become a "stick in the mud," however; I maintained some personal quirks that really were my sense of humor coming out in practical jokes.

In that small town—1,251 citizens—the primary business for the Bradford-Surridge Funeral Home was burials and burial insurance. One vehicle served as a hearse for burials and as an emergency ambulance. The driver was always Virgil Anderson, a handsome man in his sixties with a generous amount of neatly groomed snow-white hair. I always enjoyed working with him. He told good stories.

The most bizarre ambulance run I ever made was from Marionville to the insane asylum (now called a psychiatric hospital) 103 miles away. We took an elderly Methodist preacher who suffered psychiatric seizures. After we arrived, a guard, escorting us to the assigned padded cell, took us through a room of some dozen trustworthy patients. He left us there to go check on something. Suddenly one man, I think in his early fifties, accused me of stealing his suit. This announcement was of special interest to the other patients, and if looks could kill I wouldn't be writing this book.

We left after 10 PM and finally got back to the funeral home—in the era of no cell phones and of only police having two-way radios—where Mrs. Surridge gave us the bad news that the reverend had passed away and we would need to go back and get him.

1929 HUDSON SUPER-SIX

Like most country boys, I drove locally at age fourteen and legally at age sixteen. In the spring of 1945, I received an unexpected surprise from Dad. Somewhere in the countryside he had stumbled upon a 1929 Hudson Super-Six four-door sedan with only fourteen thousand miles on the odometer. Dad said the man and wife who had originally owned the car had reputations of being rather racy. Apparently they traveled a lot and they died together suddenly while away from Missouri. Their nearest relatives were an old-fashioned, religious, very successful farm family who frowned on both the reputations of the car owners and automobiles in general. For fourteen years the Hudson Super-Six took up valuable space in one of their horse barns with hay piled on and all around it. The car had been in their way for too long and they wanted to get rid of it. They felt Dad was doing them a favor by removing it.

The car was in mint condition, dark blue and sharp-looking, and had a rear-mounted spare tire. The motor was powerful and quiet with polished aluminum headers. The upholstery was velour, deep and comfortable and immaculate, but it reeked of mildew. I never knew what Dad paid for the car. When I asked him, he would just smile and say, "Oh, I dickered pretty good and they wanted it out of their way."

The only car like it I ever saw had been owned by Al Capone. It was in an antique car collection I saw later on television and it had a $25,000 price tag.

A few years later, after I left home for the circus, Dad cut the Hudson down and made a truck out of it. The velour material of the back seat was saved. It later served as the lining that covered the interior of a handsome homemade padded trunk Dad made for my newly acquired 1920 Conn CC Tuba.

SOLOS ON THE SOUSAPHONE

When Mr. Lee said he wanted me to play a solo on the sousaphone, I responded with, "Aw, c'mon, nobody plays solos on the bass horn."

"Well you're going to play one!" said Mr. Lee. I was fifteen years old at the time. I performed the ever-popular "Solo Pomposo" by Al Hayes at a 1945 District Music Festival held in Springfield, Missouri. Mr. Lee told me that Al Hayes was a pseudonym of Henry Fillmore, a famous circus trombonist and composer. He didn't mention that Fillmore used the pseudonym when he wrote music he considered unworthy of his real name. I made that connection several years later.

The solo competition was adjudicated by Dr. George C. Wilson, Director of Bands at the University of Missouri. Dr. Wilson was considered a major force and influence in college music circles. He was a student of A. A. Harding at the University of Illinois and he worked closely with Dr. Joseph Maddy, founder of the Interlochen Arts Camp. Dr. Wilson liked what I played and encouraged me to perform in other music contests. I performed at several district festivals during my sophomore, junior, and senior years of high school.

In the spring of 1947, at the National Solo Competition in St. Joseph, Missouri, I nearly had a disaster. First, I was totally dispirited after seeing a gymnasium full of bright, shiny tubas and sousaphones lined up on tables. My old Martin sousaphone looked like a war relic, from a lost war! Back at the rooming house, I tried to clean and polish my old, dented, and long-abused instrument as best I could. I washed and flushed the inside with clean, clear water from a garden hose. When I was satisfied I could not clean it any better, we left for the local school auditorium to perform as scheduled. Mr. Lee could tell I was upset by all the fancy tubas. It was the first time I had ever seen a rotary valve. Mr. Lee kept trying to bolster my spirit by telling me, "Remember, Harvey, you play the horn; it doesn't play you!"

Then tragedy struck. Just as my name was called, I blew some air through the horn and got that gurgling sound of water! Quickly I turned the old sousaphone around three times and about a half-gallon of water came gushing out on the floor. My name was called again and, reacting like Pavlov's dog, I walked on stage in a trance with pianist Betty Lou Lewis to play "The Sea Gong." Mr. Lee said I played the best he'd ever heard; I barely remembered being onstage. Dr. Wilson, adjudicating again, evidently was pleased with my performance as well because he awarded me another "first" rating and a scholarship to the University of Missouri. That made me very proud and it also meant a lot to Mom and Dad. I graduated from high school on May 23, 1947, at age seventeen. I went right to work doing farm labor to build up a college account. Now that I was no longer attending school, the sousaphone was again locked up in the high school music room for the summer.

My freshman studies at the University of Missouri would commence in the fall semester. I was excited about attending college, studying music, and playing in the band. It was like a dream. But Columbia, Missouri, seemed a long way from Marionville. I knew I would have to work hard to make my dream come true. Even with a scholarship, it would take a lot of money to pay room and board plus other living and incidental expenses—money our family didn't have. Therefore, I was committed to doing as much farm work as possible over the summer to earn and save money for college. Unbeknownst to me, however, Major Homer F. Lee was seeking employment for me.

CHAPTER TWO

King Bros. Circus Band

IT WAS THE AFTERNOON of Saturday, June 22, 1947, and my dad, brother-in-law Ralph Wilks, and I had just finished putting another wagonload of hay bales into the barn loft. As we replenished our supply of cold well water in a jug hanging on a hook under the wagon, we observed Major Homer F. Lee drive his 1940 black, two-door Ford sedan into the driveway. He drove right up to the gate, got out of his car, and walked rapidly toward the barn. We took a welcome pause in our work to greet him.

As he approached us he was smiling from ear to ear, waving a yellow envelope and announcing excitedly, "Harvey, Harvey, you've got a job with King Bros. Circus!" Like most people in show business, and as a former circus bandmaster, Homer Lee was an avid reader of *Billboard* magazine—especially the circus section. In a recent issue he had noticed that King Bros. Circus bandmaster A. Lee Hinckley needed a bass player for his band. Without my knowledge, Mr. Lee had contacted Mr. Hinckley and, on Mr. Lee's recommendation, Mr. Hinckley agreed to hire me. Mr. Lee said he hadn't spoken with me about such a possibility because I might have been disappointed if the answer had been no. But Mr. Hinckley wanted me to join his King Bros. Circus Band in Waterbury, Connecticut, on Monday,

July 1, only nine days away! The job paid fifty-five dollars a week plus room and board. It was a lot more money than I could earn doing farm work!

After Mr. Lee's brief visit, we continued working till all the hay was in the barn. We also had a lively discussion about what traveling with a circus might be like. As the cons seemed to be winning out over the pros, I took a firm stand and expressed my admiration and total trust of Mr. Lee. That wall of trust was impenetrable. My father and brother-in-law had to concede that Homer Lee was a fine man. At that point I ceased any more thought of doing farm work as a source of money for college.

With my mother's help I commenced preparing for my new venture in show business, circus bands, and a life in music! I was excited but also a bit apprehensive about the unknown. Again, I was comforted that Mr. Lee was strongly in favor of my going with the circus—he felt it was a great opportunity for me to mature and save money for college at the same time.

Travel plans and preparation for my summer excursion continued and progressed rapidly. (Day one: work in the hayfield; days two, three, four, five: pack and plan; days six, seven, eight: travel; day nine: arrive in Waterbury, ready to work.) Luckily, right away Mr. Lee located a used tuba in good condition for sixty dollars; it was a York BB♭ upright, three valves, bare brass finish and with a mouthpiece included. Mom fashioned a "modesty cover" for the tuba out of an old pink and blue blanket neatly secured with extra large safety pins. Mom insisted that we purchase a fiber laundry box so that I could send my laundry home. We located a good strong cardboard box suitable for use as a suitcase when securely tied up with clothesline and I bought a few new clothes and accessories that were required by the circus band: black shoes, black socks, white long-sleeve shirts, and black pants.

ROUTE 66 TO ST. LOUIS AND BEYOND

As luck would have it, a local gentleman, Cyril Williams, who provided taxi service in Marionville ("anywhere in town for a quarter"), came by our house and offered me a ride as far as Binghamton, New York. He had been planning a trip to visit relatives in Syracuse, and Binghamton was on the way. We could also save the cost of overnight stays in motor cabins (this was before the days of motels) and cut down on travel time if we alternated the driving and drove straight through the night. Bus schedules were checked and it was discovered that I could make bus connections from Binghamton to New York City and then on to Waterbury. It was arranged for me to be met at the Waterbury bus station at noon on July 1. Everything looked good!

Driving Route 66 through St. Louis, then Route 40 across Illinois, Indiana, Ohio, and West Virginia, connecting with the Pennsylvania Turnpike, was a real geography lesson. I enjoyed the scenery, especially Pennsylvania, which was absolutely beautiful. I had no camera to record what I was experiencing, but I still have vivid memories of that trip.

Mr. Williams estimated the mileage and travel times generously, allowing for rest and meal stops, or for any mechanical problems such as blown-out tires or overheating. He allowed we might average thirty-five miles an hour on two-lane highways, except for a faster stretch on the Pennsylvania Turnpike. Marionville to Binghamton was estimated at one thousand miles and we planned to arrive at the Binghamton bus station by 4 PM on Sunday, June 30. We made the trip without incident, arrived in Binghamton on schedule, and expressed our mutual thank yous and goodbyes. We had become good friends over the course of our trip.

I took a bus that evening from Binghamton to New York City. I napped in the bus station overnight, positioning myself so I didn't miss the announced Waterbury departure. Except for my tuba (which I kept with me at all times) I checked my other possessions to Waterbury.

Mr. Lee had told me, "Harvey, you will be well cared for. I have the word of my friend, bandmaster A. Lee Hinckley. You will be met at the bus station by members of the band." Right again!

HARVEY G. PHILLIPS, WINDJAMMER

At noon I was met at the Waterbury bus station by a one-legged cornetist, Carl Woolrich, and the drummer, who dressed immaculately but drooled. After introductions, I collected my possessions (tuba, cardboard box, fiber laundry case) and loaded them into Carl Woolrich's huge old LaSalle four-door sedan, one not unlike the "old LaSalle" mentioned in the opening theme of TV's *All in the Family*, sung by Edith and Archie Bunker. Carl lived in his car when traveling with the circus.

We arrived at the circus lot around 1:15 PM. I was delivered with my possessions to the "band sleeper" truck and shown my assigned lower bunk, my home for the next nine weeks. I then met the third cornet player, who told me to leave my possessions on the bunk. He quickly ushered me over to the cookhouse. Since time was short, I was given a couple of peanut butter and jelly sandwiches and a glass of milk to wolf down. We then hurried back to the sleeper so I could put on a clean white long-sleeve shirt, grab my tuba, and rush to the Big Top for the matinee, scheduled to start at 2 PM.

As I stepped onto the bandstand, I barely had time to acknowledge Mr. Hinckley and the other windjammers (circus musicians): three cornets, four clarinets, one trombone, one baritone, one drum, one tuba (me), and one incredible calliope player. There was no time for cordial introductions. I was much too busy to be nervous—that came later. I quickly took my position with the band, folded and tucked the tuba's modesty cover under my chair, and opened the thick bass book placed on the music stand in front of me. I heard the ringmaster welcome the audience: "Children of all ages, King Bros. Circus welcomes you!" . . . etc., etc., and then he blew his whistle to start the show! I caught the downbeat of bandmaster Hinckley and started playing Karl King's "Jungle Queen" with the band. It was traditional to start each circus show with wild animal trainers and their obeying subjects. The tune was perfectly suited to the rhythms of the big cats that presided over the ring. It was my first time playing with all professional musicians and I was amazed at how good the band sounded. The calliope player was superb, filling in missing instrumental parts and amplifying the band sound considerably. Such was the beginning of my career as a professional musician. Playing the tuba was fun and I was being paid to do it—what a life!

I quickly realized how lucky I was to have had the tutelage of Homer Lee during my high school years. I was familiar with a show routine of downbeats, cut-offs, and chords (for bows). I knew many of the bass parts. After all, in high school, in lieu of a method book, they had been my assignments. I had also been taught about most of the important circus composers: Karl King, Fred Jewell, Julius Fucik, Walter P. English, Harry Alford, Henry Fillmore, W. Paris Chambers, C. L. Barnhouse, Russell Alexander,

J. J. Richards, Charley Duble, Edwin Eugene Bagley, and others. In an old-time circus, the band would be on a bandwagon for a morning parade. There would be a concert before both the afternoon and evening shows. Each show would run between two hours and forty-five minutes and three hours. By the time I was in the circus band, there was no morning parade or concert. But very likely, during a show we would play something from each of those composers.

Doing my first show I was reminded of the circus routine I learned from Homer Lee. The consistent music routine replaced the need of a clock for circus people. Each act had its own special music and, by listening, circus people could follow the show's progress from anywhere on the lot. Every segment, act, or transition was started and stopped by the ringmaster's whistle, which he wielded with power akin to that of a traffic policeman. After the opening whistle came announcements and introductions, then a performance accompanied by music, then a whistle followed by a B♭ chord for bows, which was cut off by another whistle. It was a routine repeated for the duration of the show, seldom altered. A change in music signified an alarm to circus people when the safety of the audience was threatened. For example, if a great storm with high winds threatened to lift the huge center poles of the Big Top off the ground and possibly cause the huge tent to collapse, the band would commence playing the trio of Sousa's great march "The Stars and Stripes Forever." It was the only time Sousa's music was played at the circus. This musical alarm brought roustabouts running to pull the guy ropes tighter and secure the Big Top. Once this was done, the regular routine was resumed and roustabout attention diverted to securing the other tents and equipment.

Another feared change in the circus routine was an injury to a member or members of a circus act—a high wire or trapeze fall, for example, or a wild animal attack. (Circus people wisely had the attitude that wild animals can be trained but never tamed!) When any such tragedy struck, the band would commence playing "Twelfth Street Rag" as a signal for the clowns, whatever their state of makeup or costume, to hurry to the Big Top and onto the oval track to divert the attention of the audience, especially the children, from the tragedy. This change in the established routine of music, an unspoken alarm to all circus people, was unnoticed by the audience. Composer Stephen Sondheim dramatically refers to such tragedy with the lyrics and hauntingly beautiful music of his "Send in the Clowns."

Our performance route took us to fifty towns in Connecticut, Rhode Island, Massachusetts, New Jersey, Delaware, Maryland, Virginia, Tennessee, North Carolina, South Carolina, and Georgia.

The cookhouse chef and staff prepared three meals a day for the circus people. When the flag was up, food was served. The most important meal was dinner, served between shows. Immediately following the matinee performance, there was always a rush to the cookhouse. All meals were served by waiters assigned to each table or group of tables. Waiters were tipped a predetermined amount weekly by each person they served. Every eight-foot table was well supplied with peanut butter, jelly, honey, catsup, mustard, steak sauces, sugar, pepper, salt, etc. No limit was ever imposed on the diners and the kitchen never ran out of food. No one left the cookhouse hungry!

The back lot activities of the circus produced a cacophony of radios and conversations in foreign languages. I had never before heard a foreign language. But it was 1947: Europe was still in ruins and show people from all those war-torn countries were coming to America in droves. There were instances when entire families of exceptional performers were recruited from Eastern and Western Europe and welcomed to American circuses. Strangely, they all seemed to get along well together even though many of their respective countries had been at war with each other just months earlier.

Performers who neither spoke nor read English traveled from city to city without maps. The circus had an "advance man" who drove the route as much as a week earlier, painting white arrows on electric and telephone poles, especially at intersections. If there was a danger of following the markings of another circus, a K in a circle, indicating King Bros., was at the bottom of the shaft of the directional arrow.

Time between shows on that first day went quickly, and suddenly it was time for the 8 PM show. My second show was better than the first but there was still much to learn and improve. At the end of that day, I was exhausted. It had been only nine days since Mr. Lee announced, "You've got a job with King Bros. Circus!"

Later, as I lay awake, I reflected on my being hired for nine weeks in the middle of a 36-week season. Except for Mr. Lee's recommendation, I was an unknown quantity to Mr. Hinckley. I then realized just how far Mr. Lee and Mr. Hinckley had extended themselves to give me this unexpected opportunity to become a musician. I made a vow that I would not disappoint them.

I wanted so much to sleep but my thoughts were like dreams, keeping me awake. The electric generator made an intrusive rumbling noise. I felt like a prisoner in a gypsy camp. I was one homesick young man, some twelve hundred miles from home with less than five dollars in my possession. I remembered the words of Reverend Gilbert: "We're going to lose this young man; he's going to the Devil; he's going into a life of sin!" Then I heard the powerful words of my mother: "Reverend Gilbert, you don't have much faith in Harvey, but I do!" It was time to grow up and grow up fast! I was forced to cope with an established adult world of customs, habits, and priorities new to me. I recalled and took comfort in some of the valuable principles I was taught to accept early in life: "Be patient, learn as much as you can with your eyes and ears, before showing how little you know with your mouth!" and "Make every day a learning experience!" and "Always be aware of the needs of others." These axioms (and others) have guided me through many difficult periods.

Finally, at around 3 AM, I realized the only sound now was a steady, comforting drone of the electric generator. Once I was used to it, it became hypnotic and soothing, like the sound of running water. I was sure that if the generator should stop, everyone would immediately awaken and wonder, "What was that?" My body relaxed and I fell asleep, totally exhausted from the events of a very important day in my life. I slept through our journey to the next town, Willimantic, Connecticut (an estimated sixty miles away, with a population of fourteen thousand).

When I awoke it was late in the day and I was the only person in the band sleeper. I freshened up and took advantage of lunch at the cookhouse (the flag was up). There I caught up with other windjammers, who had already made their "approval" visits to and around the town square. To me, every town seemed pretty much the same, but some windjammers made these visits on a daily basis, akin to visiting the shopping malls of today. As for me, I had a burning desire to practice tuba.

UNIQUE PRACTICE VENUES

Mornings are the best time to practice but there was no place to do so without disturbing others. On the back lot, circus people live close together. Suddenly I remembered my experiences of working for a funeral home, and that gave me an idea. I remembered the solitude of the cemetery, and since we were, for the most part, touring the smaller cities of the eastern United States, I thought there should be well-placed cemeteries available for practice. I was right. True, there was no applause, but there weren't any boos either. If a burial was underway, I waited. If one was forecast by a tent and open grave, I positioned myself as far away as possible and quietly played songs from my funeral service repertoire. If the cemetery was deserted, I headed for the very center. I had few problems with this plan except for a couple of sudden rainstorms and, when necessary, getting on and off inter-city buses. Throughout my career, I continued the use of cemetery practice facilities, when available and convenient.

MOM'S FIRST LETTER

On Wednesday, July 9, in Springfield, Massachusetts, I received Mom's first letter, which had been written on July 4. From that day forward, she wrote at least one, and sometimes two, handwritten letters each day. I treasure every letter she sent to me. I keep them in the fiber laundry box.

July 4, 1947.

—Dear Harvey, Just a line to let you know I received the route card. I am sure glad to get it. I will let all the boys know your address. I wish you could be with us today, it won't be much of a fourth without you. Virginia, Ralph, Campbell, Dad and I will spend the 4th together. Be sure to send home all the money you can and I will save every cent for you. It will come in handy for school this fall. You can let the bandmaster read the letter you got from Dr. Wilson if you want to. Harvey, honey, I don't worry about you being led off for I know you are too good a Christian boy for that. I just worry for fear someone might hurt you. Treat those that are not what they should be alright, but always have something to do when they want you to do something. Be good, I love you very much. I will write another letter to you tonight.—Mom

True to my promise and Mom's request, I sent my laundry to her. Each returned box of clean, pressed laundry was accompanied by homemade cakes Mom called blarney stones—small white cakes, half the size of a candy bar, with white icing, rolled in crushed nuts. These cakes were to die for. Each time my clean laundry arrived, the windjammers all lined up for their share of blarney stones. I was the most popular musician in the band . . . till the cake was all gone.

HEY RUBE!

We were midway through the fourth and last show in Bridgeport, Connecticut, when there was an altercation between local yokels and circus personnel, which was known as a Hey Rube. This particular Hey Rube, my first and only, resulted from a liquored-up local tough making comments and a pass at one of the many attractive female circus performers. She had finished her act in the center ring and taken her bow, and was passing by the bandstand on the way to her dressing room when the intrusion occurred. A nearby husky roustabout proceeded to knock the intruder unconscious. The yokel's three cronies worked over him quite a while before he was able to stand. The knockout punch delivered by the roustabout also sobered him considerably. When he got his voice he proceeded to let everyone know he was no one to mess with, that he'd be back with his friends and "destroy this damned circus." The show continued to the end and the audience exited the Big Top.

Meanwhile, an ominous gathering of several hoodlums across the street grew gradually louder and larger. Many had broken pickets off a fence and many others had chains which they liked to rattle . . . between drinks. The roustabouts had ax handles, pick handles, pitchforks, brass knuckles, and other such weaponry. The roustabouts were very quiet; they knew to stay on property leased to the circus, which was their domain. A team of roustabouts rapped on the doors of motor homes and sleepers, telling the occupants to stay inside and be quiet. The circus electric generator was stopped and the circus grounds went dark and quiet. At this point, six police cars, dispatched at the request of King Bros. management, entered the circus grounds unnoticed by the yokels. Suddenly a number of riot police charged the local gang across the street. They made several arrests and dispersed the rest. Through the night the neighborhood was police-patrolled. There was no more trouble and the potential Hey Rube was averted. The electric generator was restarted and the circus was again bathed in light. Everyone slept well.

It was nice to spend Sunday, July 13, in peaceful Pittsfield after the excitement and potentially dangerous Hey Rube in Bridgeport. The roustabouts were disappointed that the rubes didn't invade the circus lot. The police had had all the fun. But, in listening to the old-timers recount their harrowing Hey Rube experiences, I was grateful for the clear heads of our security chief and the roustabout bosses. I know I never wished for another.

Everyone who visits or passes through western Massachusetts would readily agree that it is one of the most beautiful areas in America. That Sunday, I located a cemetery not too far from the circus lot and had a good uninterrupted practice session that lasted most of the afternoon.

I was getting used to exchanging conversations with the windjammers; some were very good players but defined the word "eccentric." With my sense of humor I fit right in and discussions of mundane subjects could become rather lively. The matinee in Pittsfield on Monday went especially well and I was starting to feel the results of performing four to six hours every day. By this time I had played the entire bass book for twenty shows. I was familiar enough with the book to pay more and more attention to intonation, balance, and overall ensemble.

GETTING A NEW TUBA

After the matinee, as I stepped off the bandstand, I was met by a short man with a big smile and definite Italian accent. He introduced himself to me and paid me a compliment. He said, "Young man, you play the tuba very good but you need a better instrument. I have just the right tuba for you. I go home and bring it for you to see." I went to the cookhouse with the other windjammers and we ate our evening meal.

At 7 PM, the Italian man arrived carrying what looked like a brand new tuba case and tuba stand. Inside the case was a BB♭ King Recording Tuba (fixed bell), three valves, gold lacquer. It looked new—there wasn't a dent, scratch, or other mark anywhere on the case or instrument. He was asking $150 for it. I told him I didn't have $150 and besides, we were short on space and I would still have my York upright; there wasn't room for two tubas in the band sleeper. He asked what I paid for the York and I told him sixty dollars. He said he really wanted me to have his tuba. He said he would take the York in trade and I could have the King tuba, the case, and the tuba stand for one hundred dollars.

I am embarrassed to say I knew nothing about what a new tuba should cost at that time. I had never bought one and never expected to. The University of Missouri had tubas for students to use and I would soon be one of those students. Finally, the Italian man said, "Look. I like music. I stay for the evening show. I want to hear you play that tuba of mine. We talk later." He took the tuba carefully and lovingly out of the case and carried it to the bandstand for me.

The first note I played on the King tuba was when I was sitting with the band. A. Lee Hinckley was so impressed that he just about dropped his cornet. He told me the sound projected much better than the upright tuba and wanted to know how I came up with such a great instrument. I told him quickly what the deal was and he said, "Harvey, I'll advance you the one hundred dollars and take something from each of your paychecks. You can repay me at no interest." I bought the tuba with cash. I have always felt remiss in not getting the Italian man's name and address to thank him properly.

BUG BOMBS FOR THE BAND SLEEPER

After my first night in my band sleeper bunk, I noticed little red dots on my neck and arms. I asked one of the clarinet players, who said the sleeper had bedbugs. I wouldn't dare let Mom know about this.

With the circus in Worcester for two days, two weeks later, I had a chance to buy a dozen bug bombs, surplus from World War II. Before the first matinee, I told all the occupants of the sleeper to take what they needed for the show, open up their blankets, and raise their mattresses.

Starting at 1 PM I stuffed every source of fresh air, especially the windows. Then, wearing a breathing mask and goggles, I began to spray each bunk, mattress, pillow, blanket, every surface, and every crack. Then, just before exiting what had truly become a gas chamber, I set the four bug bombs I hadn't used to expend themselves and I closed the door. Later, for a while I wasn't too popular—the sleeper did stink—but there were no more bites.

INTRODUCTION TO FRESH SEAFOOD

The circus lot in New Bedford was alongside a variety of neighborhood stores and eateries. As I strolled through the crowded streets between shows, I took special interest in a takeout seafood store. Through the window I noted a customer pointing to what looked like lumps of lard the size of golf balls. The clerk placed a dozen lumps in his deep-fry basket and eased it into the bubbling grease. I expected them to melt. I was wrong. They came out a golden brown and were packed for taking home. I couldn't contain my curiosity and entered the fish market to order some. I got in line; there were at least a dozen customers ahead of me. When I reached the front of the line I ordered a half dozen fried and asked what I was about to eat. "They're scallops," said the clerk. He then recommended some sauces to try with the scallops. I bought a small bottle because I didn't recognize it as among those on our cookhouse tables. They were delicious. I still cannot quite explain the taste I experienced eating my first scallops. Up to then the only fresh fish I ever ate were catfish and perch out of our Missouri creeks. Lobster, shrimp, crabs, crawfish, snails, clams, oysters, and squid were all fresh seafood I had yet to experience.

When I returned to the back lot to prepare for the evening show, a gentleman with a sousaphone showed up and wanted to sit in with the band. His name was Mac McConnell; his sousaphone was Pan American (second line Conn); his home was in Astoria, Long Island; his employer was Con Edison. Every summer, as part of his vacation, he liked to be around circuses and to sit in with circus bands with his sousaphone. Most of the windjammers knew him. He became a good friend. After I moved to New York City, I was often invited to a family dinner at his house. I accepted whenever I was able to do so. Later, when I performed with the Ringling

Circus, Mac would always visit us when we played Madison Square Garden—but he never tried to sit in with that band!

A TRUCK DRIVIN' MAN

In Framingham I was approached by the wagon master and asked if I would like to make an extra five dollars a week by driving one of the trucks from venue to venue. I told him I had never even driven a pickup truck and he said, "Why, there's nothing to it. The trailer follows wherever the cab goes—you just have to give it a little more room to make tight turns. Come on over here and I'll show you what there is to driving a truck." I went with the man. He explained the gears: compound, four forward gears and reverse. ("This can get tricky but you won't need to back up very often.") Then he explained the brakes. Simple: for the cab there was a brake pedal next to the clutch; for the trailer there was a lever on the steering wheel that activated the air brakes. He met me between shows in Athol, Greenfield, and Meriden so I could practice driving the semi-truck while he gave me instructions. He was a good teacher but I was still apprehensive. When Sunday rolled around and I was preparing to drive my truck from Meriden, Connecticut, to Asbury Park, New Jersey, a roustabout asked if he could ride with me. I said OK. I was scared but I had taken a liking to the wagon master and sympathized with his shortage of experienced truck drivers.

My truck cab was a vintage 1939 Chevrolet. The motor seemed to run smoothly enough but the right side of the cab was severely damaged to the extent that the right passenger door couldn't be opened. The right door window was shattered safety glass, permanently up. With a flatbed semi-trailer I would be hauling the blues—blue-painted unreserved bleacher seats from opposite ends of the Big Top. Effectively, I was hauling a significant load of strapped-down lumber. Quite an assignment for a first time semi-truck driver just seventeen years old!

Between shows in Asbury Park, I just had to visit the famous boardwalk and see the Atlantic Ocean. It was a beautiful day and I was impressed with the city and the beaches. While strolling up and down the boardwalk I entered a room full of pinball machines, photo booths, and something I had never seen before, a machine where you could close the booth door and for fifty cents record your voice on a 45 RPM record. I inserted fifty cents and made a recording for Mom and Dad, including my singing "Always," and sent it home. (This song by Irving Berlin had been Wendell Wilkie's theme, with special lyrics, of course, during his run for the presidency in 1940.) At the time, I had no way of knowing what Asbury Park would bring to me just five years into the future. It was there that I was destined to meet my wife for a lifetime.

After my first frightening Sunday drive—from Connecticut to New Jersey—my driving seemed to improve but I was never completely comfortable. I regretted making such a commitment. The extra inconvenience just about wiped out my visits to cemeteries to practice my tuba and I couldn't help but feel I was an accident waiting to happen. Nonetheless, the tour was going smoothly until we got into the Blue Ridge Mountains of Virginia. They were a challenge for all the drivers. In 1947, driving was mostly on two-lane roads. There were some frightening moments and, contrary to the wagon master's earlier remarks, I did have to back up more times than I liked. For two weeks, by being "old lady" careful, I pulled my rig onto the circus lots at the proper place of delivery, at a manageable time. I then took off my truck-driving hat and put on the cap of a windjammer.

With another Sunday drive we entered the state of Virginia, going from Cambridge, Maryland, to Culpepper. The wagon master always checked my truck and trailer personally, so I usually gave cursory examinations. The drive from Culpepper to Front Royal was treacherous. Nerve endings were getting frayed. The next town was Luray, a short thirty to forty miles from Front Royal. I and the roustabout who had been a passenger with me before left early in the morning, as usual. It was a beautiful day until we started our descent down a mountain and I discovered we no longer had air brakes. The air hose had come loose! It took only a couple of pumps on the foot brake and the cab brakes were no more. This meant I was steering a loaded lumber truck with *no* brakes, a runaway!

We were careening down the narrow two-lane road at ever-increasing speed; my passenger was praying, cussing (in that order), and fighting the door, trying to open it and jump! I had my hands full; it was either into the mountain (in which case the load of lumber would have crushed the cab along with the occupants) or over the guard rail and off the mountain, an unacceptable option. I fought the curves and hoped we didn't turn over or meet another vehicle. These thoughts kept going through my mind, as did the welfare of my passenger (still praying and cussing). Meanwhile, it was all I could do to steer the missile we had become. As busy as I was trying to control the truck, I was mindful of what would happen if we met an oncoming car.

God was with us that day! We made it to the bottom of the mountain and sped on level highway for about one hundred yards before starting up another grade which slowed the truck to a stall, at which time I pulled as far to the right as possible, locked the compound gear in position and, now thoroughly limp and weak, stepped out of the cab. My passenger fell out of the truck, sobbing uncontrollably while hugging me and blessing me for saving both our lives. We sat beside the road for some time, waving and/or explaining to other circus drivers what had happened. We waited for the circus mechanic, who was always the last truck in line, to aid breakdowns. I was embarrassed to have achieved hero status with one roustabout, the mechanic, and the wagon master. Despite my triumph over near-catastrophe—or perhaps because of it—I swore never, ever, to attempt driving another semi-truck, or any vehicle with air brakes.

A few days later the wagon master took me to one side and explained that King Bros. Circus was slowly replacing old and damaged cabs with new ones. Would I be interested in driving the new cabs as they arrived and until arrangements could be made to dispose of the older cabs? I wouldn't be pulling a trailer or using air brakes, just getting the new cab to the next venue, still at an extra five dollars a week. I accepted his offer. It was a great deal for me. Now I could drive around in each town, just like a tourist.

I became friends with a young Greek wrestler who was all muscle, wavy hair, good looks, and happy smile. He was visiting relatives who were performers in the circus. He was put to work as a mark in the audience to accept the challenge of our mean-looking pro wrestler who, at the end of the show, would enter the center ring and offer five hundred dollars to any man from the audience who could last three minutes in the ring with him. My Greek buddy, planted in the audience, would accept the challenge. Heroically, with only seconds to spare, he would defeat our professional wrestler to the screaming delight of the audience, women especially. It was a good way to end the show; everyone was happy.

AN EMOTIONAL FAREWELL

My final days with the circus went routinely and quickly. The venues were enjoyable and friendships deepened as each performance passed and my departure drew closer. Suddenly we were in Charleston for my final performance with the King Bros. Circus Band on Saturday evening, August 30, 1947, after exactly nine weeks of touring. Before I departed the back lot for the final time, I was able to present to Mr. Hinckley and the other windjammers a final allotment of blarney stones, boxed and sent especially by Mom for them to share. Playing my last two shows brought my total number of shows to 106 and my total performance hours to 212. I could only guess at how many hours I practiced in cemeteries.

For my "homecoming" I purchased a suitcase to replace the cardboard box. I also bought a suit and tie to wear when my folks met the train in Aurora, Missouri. I had matured considerably. It had been weeks since I had conversed with anyone even close to my young age, still seventeen.

As I departed, I knew I would miss my circus friends but I was also homesick and anxious to see Mom and Dad. Unfortunately I could be home only a few days before leaving for the University of Missouri in Columbia.

It just so happened that down the road from Ralph and my sister Virginia's farm lived a young man who was also entering the freshman class at the University of Missouri. His name was Marion Masters and he was majoring in agriculture. He and his parents had been searching for a room he could rent in a private house convenient to the campus. We pooled our resources of contacts and the Department of Music located for us a small basement room with bunk beds and shower in a rather large house owned by an elderly lady. The landlady retained the first floor living room, dining room, kitchen, bath, and master bedroom. She rented the second floor containing three generous bedrooms and two full baths to six male students.

It was a stately house and made a good impression. I negotiated a lower rent for myself in exchange for keeping the premises clean. I agreed to sweeping walks, raking leaves, shoveling snow, emptying wastebaskets every day, mopping when there was mud on the floor, and stoking the furnace. I soon realized I was much too generous with my time and totally unfamiliar with how infuriatingly spoiled young male students could be.

Nonetheless, I stuck to my word. I was a full-time student, taking eighteen hours of credits, much too much for a servant, janitor, and housekeeper. I was keeping up with my classes and assignments but I wanted more time to practice the tuba.

Strangely enough, my favorite class was English, which I abhorred in high school. The English teacher made the language and definition of words an enjoyable challenge. I was anxious to attend her classes and to converse with her after class. I still spoke with a slight Ozark twang but I had lost much of it from traveling with the circus.

Music theory class was at 8 A M every weekday. I loved music theory and ear training classes. I also liked the teachers. Piano proficiency was tough and, for me, it took too much time away from my chosen instrument. But I soon came to appreciate the importance of being familiar with the piano keyboard. Every afternoon, we had either concert band or marching band. I enjoyed every moment with both bands and thought Dr. Wilson was terrific. I also enjoyed my private tuba lessons with him on the new Conn sousaphone assigned to me by the school. I finally had a method book. The book, by Walter M. Eby, organized the basics of articulations, scales, arpeggios, slurs, and other technical considerations.

The Christmas break approached at accelerated speed. Like many other music students, I had kept so busy with studies and practicing my instrument that the break came as a welcome surprise. I was ready for the recess and anxious to see Mom and Dad. I was now the last of their ten children still living with them. Once home, I realized how much weariness had built up from my college routine. I moped around until Mom asked if I would play a few hymns for her; she said she had missed hearing them. Of course I complied, on my King tuba, and we soon got into Christmas songs. Between that and the food Mom prepared, it's a wonder I went back for the second semester.

Suddenly it was New Year's Day, 1948, Mom and Dad's forty-third anniversary. With some regret I left almost a week early for the second semester because I knew there would be sidewalks to clear and as-yet-undiscovered housekeeping tasks to tend to. I also wanted to practice tuba in a way I couldn't practice at home. I wanted to impress Dr. Wilson with improved performance.

Soon, I started palling around with Daniel Henkin, a clarinet player from Kansas City. We would get together and play our own brand of Dixieland, just tuba and clarinet.

Around Valentine's Day, I was surprised to receive a telegram from Merle Evans, famous bandmaster of the Ringling Bros. and Barnum & Bailey Circus. He was offering me a job with his band! He heard about me from A. Lee Hinckley and others in the King Bros. Circus Band. I wasn't sure who I should talk to about receiving a job offer from Merle Evans, but I knew I had to discuss it with Dr. Wilson. At first he couldn't believe it. When I showed him the actual telegram, he expressed great concern for my well-being and tried to assess my options. He came to the conclusion that it would be a big mistake for me to go with the circus. To sum up his thoughts and recommendations, he said, "Don't do it, Harvey—you'll never finish school and you'll never amount to anything! Stay in school—finish what you've started." I mentioned my situation to Dan Henkin and got the same reaction almost word for word.

I took another look at the telegram. Mr. Evans wanted a yes or no answer right away. It was a "lightning bolt" opportunity, there only for an instant before it would be taken away forever, seized by someone else. I had heard so much about the great circus bandmaster Merle Evans and I was stunned by his offer. At a loss, I called Mom and Dad to tell them about the decision I had to make. I told them what Dr. Wilson had advised me to do. Almost immediately Mom wisely said, "Why don't you call Homer Lee? Maybe he'll know what you should do."

I promptly called Mr. Lee and told him about the telegram. He got very excited and said, "What! I don't believe it! Merle Evans! Read it to me!" I read the telegram over the phone and Mr. Lee's response was, "Oh, Harvey, you go with Merle Evans. Why, this is your chance of a lifetime!" I trusted Mr. Lee's opinion, so I sent an acceptance telegram to Mr. Evans. I said my goodbyes to Dr. Wilson and Danny Henkin. I said an emotional goodbye to my English teacher. With feelings of relief, I returned my set of keys to our sweet old landlady.

In 1987 I was invited back to the University of Missouri, where I hadn't finished my freshman year. I was given an honorary Doctor of Humanities degree.

CHAPTER THREE

Traveling with the
Greatest Show on Earth

I WAS APPREHENSIVE, but I hoped I could be successful with bandmaster Merle Evans and his band. This was no small-town circus I would be joining—it was the Greatest Show on Earth!

Once again, I was "running away" with the circus, only this time there was no preacher's visit to contend with. Mom and Dad, with Mr. and Mrs. Homer Lee, gave me a proper send-off from the Missouri Pacific Passenger Station in Aurora. I was excited and anxious to be making music again with professional musicians. We would have two weeks of rehearsals in Sarasota, Florida, three full days of travel between Sarasota and New York City, then another week of rehearsals in Madison Square Garden. The Ringling Bros. and Barnum & Bailey Combined Shows, the Greatest Show on Earth, was scheduled to open in New York City's Madison Square Garden on April 7, 1948. Then on to Boston and the world!

I was met at the Sarasota train station by circus drummer Red Floyd. Red was truly a legend to drummers the world over and, as time would tell, one of the most unforgettable people I have ever known. Once I had my tuba and other luggage in Red's Chrysler Town and Country station wagon, he said, "We'll leave your tuba at the American Legion Hall where we rehearse tomorrow morning at 9 o'clock. Then we'll pass by the trailer park and meet the other bass player, Reuben Clinton 'Johnny' Evans—no relation to Merle." Red then said, "Johnny is a terrific bass player, one of the best ever. He has only one problem. He never gets along with other bass players, so be careful." As Red finished this surprise bombshell, we arrived at Johnny's trailer. I enjoyed meeting Johnny. He asked questions about my trip, my hometown, my folks, and my experience. He seemed to be satisfied with my answers and was quite pleasant. Johnny said, "I look forward to tomorrow's rehearsal." I agreed.

From Johnny's we drove to the Cypress Inn and Red introduced me to Merle Evans. Merle asked me about Homer Lee and A. Lee Hinckley and spoke highly of them. He couldn't have been more congenial. He said, "Well, now, Junior, you're going to have a roommate tonight, a good friend of mine, Dr. A. A. Harding from the University of Illinois." I told Merle I would be proud to meet Dr. Harding, that my band director at the University of Missouri, Dr. George C. Wilson, had been one of his students. Dr. Wilson always spoke reverently of his teacher.

Dr. Harding was a down-to-earth gentleman and very friendly. I enjoyed hearing his stories, including how he received the entire Sousa Band library for the University of Illinois archives. I slept well.

THE FIRST REHEARSAL

I didn't need an alarm clock the next morning; I was up at 6 A M. I showered, dressed, then had breakfast in the restaurant. Since the American Legion Hall was only a few blocks away, I walked there from the Cypress Inn. I timed myself to arrive at the hall no later than 8:30 to warm up for the 9 A M rehearsal. About a block from the hall I began to hear instruments warming up (trombones, euphoniums, clarinets, and horns), all playing scales and arpeggios. Suddenly I heard the addition of an incredible tuba sound warming up. It was Johnny Evans on his vintage Holton sousaphone. I couldn't believe what I was hearing—the sound, range, technique, scales, arpeggios, slurs, and articulation all blew me out of the water. I wondered what I was doing there. I swallowed hard and cautiously proceeded on to the hall. I took my King recording tuba out of the case and checked it over but I didn't play even one note. What could I play after hearing Johnny Evans warm up?

I sat in the back of the room with my tuba, waiting for Johnny Evans to take one of the two tuba chairs. Once I knew where Johnny chose to sit, I felt safe in taking the chair next to him. We greeted each other with "Good morning." After the band tuned to concert B♭, played by principal clarinetist Everett Gavin, and the room was quiet, Merle Evans formally introduced his friend and special guest, University of Illinois bandmaster Austin A. Harding. Merle then introduced me to the band and, scared to death, I politely acknowledged his introduction. I picked up my tuba and watched for Merle's famous "casual" downbeat. We warmed up with a semi-pop tune entitled "Cuban Pete." It had lots of syncopation and Latin rhythms. After we had played through it, Johnny reached over, squeezed my leg, and said, "Hey kid, don't you worry about a thing; everything's going to be just fine." And so it was.

Johnny and I became fast friends. And what an education I received playing on the same music stand with him, one of the greatest tuba players of all time. I was in awe of Johnny Evans. I don't recall everything we played in those first Sarasota rehearsals but just sitting next to Johnny, listening and learning, caused my playing to improve more than it did over any other equal period of time in my entire career. Johnny never held anything back when it came to helping me with the tuba or other concerns.

Throughout our association, I made a point always of showing Johnny my respect, admiration, and gratitude.

Starting with those first 1948 rehearsals in Sarasota, Johnny Evans took me under his wing as a surrogate father or older brother. I know he cared about my well-being. Without any formal acknowledgment of our relationship, I became an apprentice to his mastery of technique and musicianship, applying his concepts six hours a day. There was no other place I could have had such an experience. I have never heard another tubist play more cleanly or precisely than Johnny. When I asked him how we could be such good friends with his reputation for not getting along with other bass players, he bristled, then growled, "Hell, Harvey, they never gave me anybody who could play!"

Johnny and I employed the following routine when we played with the band: (1) We would both play introductions. (2) Johnny would play the first strain *flawlessly*. (3) I would play the repeat. (4) When there was no repeat, we would both play. (5) We would reverse or adjust the routine when appropriate. One of the most meaningful compliments I ever received was when Joe Browning, one of our trumpet players who had played with Sousa, had to leave the bandstand for a period of time and on his return observed, "I was listening to the basses and I couldn't tell which one of you was playing." I could hardly get my cap on after that.

As rehearsals progressed, I listened and learned, and I gradually began to feel more confident about my tuba playing. Finally, Sarasota rehearsals were finished. A date and time was announced for our departure to New York City. I was upset by the bad news that personal domestic problems would prevent Johnny Evans from doing any of the six-week run in Madison Square Garden. He would return to the band in Boston. Next came the good news! Merle Evans hired the great Bill Bell as Johnny's replacement for the New York City run. Talk about mixed emotions! (See Appendix for a list of 1948 Ringling Band personnel.)

THE CIRCUS TRAIN

The Ringling Bros. and Barnum & Bailey Circus traveled via 120 double-length railroad cars split into four sections. Our particular work classification determined our assignment to the appropriate section. Each of the sections traveled with freight train specifications including the speed and priority of track access. Circus trains had to pull off onto rail sidings to let scheduled passenger and commercial freight trains pass. The first section included sleeper cars, cattle cars, flat cars, etc. It transported cookhouse personnel, tents, and equipment. The cookhouse was always the first tent to be raised and put into service. Also in the first section was the power center, including electric generators, the Big Top, chain-driven trucks, work elephants, menagerie tents, sideshow tents, and roustabout crews to raise and service most of the tents in advance of those who would need them. The second section included the menagerie, show elephants, horses, and other animals, plus the roustabouts and trainers needed to get them safely to the particular venue for that day. The third section transported the reserved seats, bleachers, rigging, wardrobe, and other personnel for concession stands, etc. The fourth section transported the owners, managers, administration, and performers (band, clowns, acrobats, etc.). The band car included staterooms for some of management's upper echelon—the circus police chief, for instance.

CARD TRICKS

The first night after we departed Sarasota for New York City, drummer Red Floyd gave me a lesson in dealing with people and life—and cards. I was sitting on my third-level top berth tossing playing cards into my hat at the opposite end. Red noticed what I was doing and, after watching awhile, said, "Hey, Junior, you're pretty good with those cards—do you know any card tricks? They always fascinated me." I was happy to climb down and show him my half-dozen tricks. He seemed impressed and asked me to show him how to do them. I showed him tricks and he said he would practice.

The next morning I was dressed and relaxing in my berth when Red came shuffling down the aisle in pajamas, robe, and slippers, carrying a large mug of black coffee. As he approached he said in his distinct gravelly voice, "Say, Junior, I remembered some card tricks I used to do as a dealer in New Orleans. Would you like to see them?"

"Sure," I replied. Several of the other musicians heard what Red said and started gathering around. They were familiar with Red's talents and expertise, apart from the drums. Red was putting on a show for me but others crowded around to quietly observe "Junior's lesson."

I had never seen anything like it. His first trick was to take a deck and split it between red and black. He shuffled them thoroughly five or six times and asked me to cut them. They were still all black and all red. He explained what he called "shuffle through," how to appear to have mixed the cards but actually have kept them the same. He proceeded to do one trick after another, including the "old shell game," which I never won. For a finale, he shuffled the cards and had me cut them. He then dealt five poker hands, and his was always the winning hand. I couldn't believe what I thought I was seeing! His hands were so fast they seemed hardly to move at all. I asked him to deal in slow motion. I was surprised to see him deal from the second card, third card, bottom of the deck and middle of the deck. Each card seemed to be right where he wanted it to be. The guys enjoyed my baptism. Red Floyd had quite a reputation. He cautioned me never to play cards with strangers, and I never did!

One of the new acts that caught my eye was a Mexican family of unusual abilities. The youngest son had broken and continued to break a record of four complete somersaults before being picked up by the catcher. I was delighted to note that the young Mexican sister was very friendly and inviting. She didn't speak English so I asked Tony Ramiros, the first clarinetist, if he could teach me a little fast Spanish. I asked for, and he taught me to say, the following: "Usted es muy hermosa."

To which she replied, "Gracias, Señor."

Next, my turn again: "¿Me gustaría platicar por un momento." As I was talking to her, I felt her brothers' eyes burning into my flesh. I eventually became friends with them, but I never tried to speak to the girl again.

LEARNING ABOUT WILLIAM J. BELL

As we approached New York, I started learning about William J. Bell from the other musicians. At forty-five, he was a legend to everyone who knew him or knew about him. As an eighteen-year-old circus band tuba player, I was amazed by his achievements.

When Bill Bell was eighteen years old, his reputation was so widely known and admired that, in 1921, John Philip Sousa personally summoned him to join his famous band as principal tuba! Merle Evans and others would tell me about how Bill Bell liked to sit in with the circus band when they played in the Olympia Hippodrome and how he always visited his circus friends when they were in New York City.

Comments made to me included: "You've got to meet Bill Bell." "You've got a treat in store." "What a wonderful guy." "You'll like Bill Bell. He's terrific!" "Arturo Toscanini chose Bill Bell for his NBC Symphony Orchestra in 1937; he could have had any tuba player in the world but he knew Bill Bell was the greatest." "Did you know that he won the Cincinnati Symphony Orchestra in 1924 by playing just four measures for Fritz Reiner? He played the opening of Wagner's *Faust Overture* and that's all it took." "Why, it was this same four measures that Arturo Toscanini had him play five times because it was so beautiful!" "Bill Bell is a great singer. He sang 'When Yuba Plays the Rhumba On the Tuba Down In Cuba' with Leopold Stokowski and the New York Philharmonic!" "Yes, and he both narrates and plays 'Tubby the Tuba' at children's concerts." "Bill Bell loves to play band music." "After leaving the Sousa Band for the Cincinnati Symphony, he played summers with the Goldman Band." "He also played with Frank Simon's Armco Band while he was in Cincinnati. And he plays with the Asbury Park Municipal Band." "Bill Bell is a great teacher. He has his own studio and he teaches for Juilliard and the Manhattan School of Music." "Have you ever been to Gilhooley's or McSorley's Old Ale House or the Carnegie Tavern with Bill Bell? You must do that—it is an unforgettable experience." I heard so much about Bill Bell I thought I might faint when I finally did meet him.

Our fourth section of the train from Sarasota, Florida, arrived in Jersey City, New Jersey, one week before the Madison Square Garden opening. I followed the lead of the other bandsmen and checked out of the train's band car and into New York's Forest Hotel. It was on 49th Street (between Broadway and Eighth Avenue), a short distance from the Madison Square Garden stage door. I had my tuba with me in the hotel room. I noticed that the faulty plumbing pipes in the walls moaned and groaned each time someone used the hot water. I decided to join in with my tuba and very softly sought the pitches I heard from the water pipes. No one ever said anything and I enjoyed the challenge.

The next day the band was assembling for a 2 PM rehearsal. Added to the basic circus band personnel were five extra musicians required by Local 802—the American Federation of Musicians union. The band was assembled in the hallway outside the band room, waiting to start our first New York rehearsal, when a large gentleman carrying a tuba approached from the end of the hallway: obviously Bill Bell! From the reaction of the other musicians, there was no doubt that someone important had arrived. Everyone was smiling and shaking hands, flattered that Mr. Bell remembered their names. I stood back, nervous and anxious, until Merle called me over and made a formal introduction. We had a pleasant conversation and Merle said, "Well, now, I'm happy I could get the two of you together."

During rehearsals preparing for our opening in Madison Square Garden, Mr. Bell lived up to his reputation. He was the greatest, most wonderful, most ordinary, most friendly, most cordial person one could ever hope to meet.

Mr. Bell's presence seemed to brighten the day for everybody. He gave me a warm greeting, a handshake, and a friendly smile. I was entranced by his gracious manner. Respectfully I handed the "first tuba" book to him but he politely and firmly refused it, saying, "No, no, Harvey, you're Merle's principal tuba player. Besides, I will need to send a substitute for most of the shows." He spoke most highly about Bill Rose, one of his very best Juilliard students. Bill Rose started subbing the next day. We became good friends, with respect for one another.

Mr. Bell was fully aware of my background, as related to him by Merle Evans. After one of the shows he asked me to meet him at 9:00 the next morning at the Carnegie Hall stage door on 56th Street. I would get to hear a New York Philharmonic rehearsal that started at 10 AM, and I needed to arrive an hour early so the orchestra personnel manager, Maurice Von Praag, could place me in a curtained box overlooking the stage. I had to be settled and out of sight before the orchestra and conductor were onstage. I was told to stay quiet. I could view the stage through the parted drapes of the box. I felt very privileged to be living such a secret. For the first time in my life I witnessed a professional orchestra assemble, warm up, rehearse, and perform. As an audience of one, I was impressed and inspired beyond description. It left me with a feeling of pride and respect that has lasted a lifetime.

PREPARING FOR MADISON SQUARE GARDEN OPENING

Preparing for opening day, several hours of rehearsals were devoted to music written especially for production numbers (Grand Entry—Spec—Aerial Ballet—Finale). Meanwhile, a dirt floor covering the entire arena was installed and packed down to a depth of one foot. Next came the installation of complex rigging, put in place and secured for high wire, flying trapeze, aerial ballet, etc. All animals were cared for and well fed every day. The logistics of the world's largest traveling circus were incredible to fathom.

The Army Corps of Engineers came to the circus every year and traveled with us. They would have a team observing and taking notes on how orderly the circus could move four trains; feed twelve hundred people three times a day, plus sixty elephants and more than one hundred head of horses; and set up two performances, and do the same thing the next day some 150 or more miles away, in rain or other bad-weather conditions. They were always amazed at the efficiency of the circus.

During my first visit to New York City, in 1948, I not only met Mr. Bell and Bill Rose, but I also met dozens of other important New York City musicians. Many were great circus music fans and/or alumni of the Sousa Band; all were friends of Merle Evans. Celebrities and famous musicians came to the circus and enjoyed sitting close to the band as much as seeing any part of the show. Almost every day at the matinee, famous drummers—sometimes the entire percussion section of the New York Philharmonic—came to admire the incredible playing of Red Floyd. Red, who had been struck by a car in New Orleans, breaking his right arm and elbow, played the right style for each number. His smooth drum rolls were heard throughout the Garden and he caught every trick in three rings and two stages, even catching elephant droppings. Drummers were amazed to learn that Red's snare drum was almost as deep as a field drum, with sixteen-gauge gut snares and size-twenty-two sticks. Red's drums were especially made for him by the Leedy Drum Company.

Leedy also made the forty-eight-inch-diameter bass drum played by Rollin E. Sherbundy. Sherbundy was a marvel at playing bass drum and twenty-two-inch mounted cymbals. We could play galops unending and he never lost time.

Each day I would awaken around 9 or 10 AM, take a shower, and get dressed for the day. I sometimes ate a light breakfast and lunch but usually settled for a hearty brunch at one of the fabulous and famous NYC delicatessens. I loved exploring the city, discovering and uncovering old and new gathering places. Restaurants, parks, colleges, universities, museums, theaters, and concert halls were targets of curiosity. I learned about unique and ethnic neighborhoods. Marionville had none of this. After the matinee, around 5:00, I would return to the Forest Hotel and relax for a couple of hours. I was always up and ready to play the next show at least a half hour before it started. After the evening show I rarely ventured far from the Forest Hotel.

We left New York on May 10. I was pleased Johnny Evans was able to return to the band in Boston. He was a little rusty for the first two shows but the same old Johnny from the third show on. Boston is so full of American history that mornings were generally taken up with sightseeing. After Boston we traveled to Washington, D.C., for five days. The nation's capital is always impressive, especially seeing it for the first time: the White House, the Capitol, monuments (quite a number have been added since 1948), all other grand government buildings, and world history being made by the minute. It is simply overwhelming.

Many VIP band visitors came daily, mostly between shows. These visitors included military band conductors, past and present, as well as players from the service bands, most notably Tony Zavarella (tuba) and Charlie Owens (drums). Tony was in the U.S. Army Air Corps; there was no separate U.S. Air Force at that time. Charlie was with the Marine Band. Both had toured with the Cole Bros. Circus and were allowed to sit in with our band. Tony had been a sparring partner of Jack Dempsey's when the former champ toured as an exhibition for Cole Bros. Tony was also a resource of information about Gabe and Jess Russ, brothers who were both tuba players from Cleveland. Gabe Russ toured with the Sousa Band and Jess worked for the H. N. White Company, manufacturers of the King line of brass instruments. Charlie Owens had an incredible career, including twenty-two years in the Marine Band (retiring at the rank of Sergeant Major), twenty years with the Philadelphia Orchestra (retiring as principal percussionist), and a subsequent appointment to the University of Michigan faculty.

Our 1948 tour stops included six days in Philadelphia and five days in Pittsburgh. There were always lots of musician visitors in these two cities, mostly Sousa Band alumni. One frequent visitor was Donald S. Reinhardt, trombonist and creator of the pivot system employed by many brass players. We played back across Pennsylvania, into New Jersey, and up to

Poughkeepsie, New York, and throughout the New England states. During the last half of June and the first half of July, we played several of the cities I had visited one year earlier with the King Bros. Circus. We did a cluster of small cities surrounding Albany, then traveled west to Ohio, Michigan, Indiana, Illinois, Wisconsin, Minnesota, Iowa, Nebraska, Missouri, Colorado, Utah, Montana, Washington, and Oregon.

No matter where we were, Merle wore a diamond ring on his left hand. He played cornet with his right hand while he conducted the band, with his back to the band, watching everything that happened in the circus performance. At least three times someone from the audience approached Merle and tried to take the ring off his finger. In each instance, one of the roustabouts or another circus employee would come to Merle's aid. The ring was pulled off his finger once but it was never lost. I don't know the carats in the diamond but it was the largest diamond I ever saw. It was purchased by Merle in the mid-1920s and was worth a fortune.

SHOOTING CRAPS ON THE RAILS

There were certain people in the circus who liked to gamble. They represented all departments, from roustabouts, ushers, and performers to management. So, on occasion, when we were in a town for more than one day, they would make a craps table out of blankets laid across the empty rails next to the band car. There might be as many as twenty people shooting craps until daylight. Bill Hall, the band car porter, had a reputation for spicy chili and great sandwiches. The gamblers liked to set up next to the band car, where they could order food and use the restroom.

Red Floyd, in addition to being an incredible drummer, was a professional gambler. Every so often he would leave the game, "to use the restroom" or "get a cup of coffee," at which time he would frequently hand me—already in my bunk—a wad of bills: "Hey Junior! Keep this for me until tomorrow!" Then he would get a sandwich and return to the game. Some people are poor losers and give the winners a hard time, but Red could turn out his pockets and say, "This is all I got! I had a few lucky runs but it's all washed out!" On some evenings he would give me as much as $1,300 to hold for him. When we stopped in Los Angeles the gambling "table" would be visited by movie stars, and some lost a fair bit of money (mostly to Red). Red also ran all the betting pools on sports teams. His wife was head of the wardrobe department. With their combined incomes they did very well!

At each venue our circus cars were stored on freight sidings, leaving the open tracks to passenger trains and commercial freight trains. In 1949 the circus's Chicago venue was Soldier Field. Chicago has one of the largest railroad yards in the country, and accessing the circus trains properly required walking a considerable distance.

One night about midnight, I was returning from a downtown jazz club and decided to take a shortcut to our band sleeper. The shortcut required climbing onto the coupling between parked freight cars, jumping to the ground between trains, then onto another coupling, and so on, until I reached my destination. On this occasion, just as I was crossing over, standing atop a coupling, a rail yard freight engine slammed into that particular string of cars. This created a chain reaction that moved amazingly fast from car to car and the entire line of coupled cars started picking up speed. To keep from falling under the wheels of the moving train, I had to dive to the ground next to another train, which I also had to climb over. I narrowly escaped losing an arm or leg, or worse. Finally, still shaken up from my experience, I reached the haven of our fourth-section band car and fell into an anxious, fitful sleep.

BIG BLUE

The Ringling Bros. and Barnum & Bailey Circus, living up to its billing as "the Greatest Show on Earth," was full of interesting characters. One of the most memorable was Big Blue, the six-foot-five boss of all roustabouts. He was a handsome man with a complexion so black that it looked blue when the sun reflected off it—hence his nickname. He ruled his domain fairly and squarely. He seldom resorted to street language, and then only to make a point that would be understood by his roustabout subjects. Big Blue was articulate and spoke with authority. His primary assignment was to supervise lacing together huge sections of canvas, forming the three largest tents on the ground, then raising them in juxtaposition each day: Big Top, Menagerie, and Sideshow. All tents had to be erected timely, no matter the weather or show ground conditions. Big Blue wore dark blue pinstriped suits with a tie and stickpin, a gold watch chain across his vest, gray spats on his well-shined shoes, and, to top it all off, a matching bowler hat. He was impressive. He would stand out in any crowd and stop conversations when he entered a business establishment.

One day, by chance, the fourth section of the circus train was parked on a railroad siding alongside and overlooking the circus lot. It was early morning and the Big Top was being raised under Big Blue's instructions. He sang and chanted orders to his work crew of roustabouts. His voice resonated clearly under a cloudless sky and the relentless heat of the unfiltered summer sun. As I passed by the private car of John and Henry Ringling North, I overheard their two maids having a conversation. One maid lustily said to the other, "My, my. Would you look at that Big Blue? Ain't he sump'n!" The other maid, of course, agreed. I wasn't asked for my opinion, but I understood their passionate expressions and agreed, too.

1948 TOUR HIGHLIGHTS

Traveling through the Rocky Mountains for the first time was a mind-blowing experience. Playing two shows a day with Johnny was most enjoyable and I looked forward to each performance. After Portland, Oregon, we spent two days en route to San Francisco and on the way came down and around Mt. Shasta. The day was clear and at one spot we could look down and see the other three sections of our circus train. It is interesting to note that in 1948 there were only three indoor venues the Ringling Circus could play: Madison Square Garden, Boston Garden, and the San Francisco Cow Palace (our venue for the next four days). All other performances were under the Big Top.

After San Francisco we moved on to Santa Barbara for one day and then to Los Angeles for eighteen shows over nine days. The proceeds of one of the shows we played in Los Angeles were donated to a Hollywood charity, a children's hospital that was being built. Many Hollywood movie stars contributed their talent to attract maximum income for this very special performance. Harry James conducted the band with Merle Evans; Burt Lancaster performed the act he had done when traveling with a circus; Red

Skelton, a one-time circus clown from Indiana, performed, and the great tenor Lauritz Melchior sang the songs of the circus Spectacular. Many other movie stars rode the floats featured in the performance, including Ava Gardner and Harry James's wife Betty Grable.

Among others participating were Gary Cooper, Buster Keaton, Bing Crosby, Rosalind Russell, Walter Pidgeon, Greer Garson, Lucille Ball, Elizabeth Taylor, Van Johnson, Danny Kaye, and Gregory Peck. This one show raised more than $175,000 for the hospital.

In the last three months of our 1948 season, we performed 246 shows in fifty-seven cities in the West. Each show ran at least two hours. We stopped everywhere from San Diego to Nashville.

We had been on a very intense tour and I was amazed at how tolerance and understanding reigned over our living and working so closely for extended periods. I think a partial explanation is the fact that our work and our passion were one and the same and we recognized this similar attitude in one another, with mutual respect and admiration. There were no egos to massage.

As we crossed the hot and dry southwestern states, we kept our metal window shades open, enjoying the fresh air moving through the car. We seemed to be taking turns occupying the vestibule between cars by some unwritten schedule. Suddenly our quiet conversation was interrupted by porter Bill Hall's well-known voice yelling to tell those inside the car to look out the windows on the north side of the train. What we saw was incredible. Lined up neatly and orderly were hundreds, if not thousands, of surplus items from World War II. There were jeeps, trucks, tanks, airplanes, howitzers . . . if it was metal and prone to rust, it was there. We reasoned that the desert provided the uninterrupted amount of space needed for such storage, and protection against vandalism or theft, due to its remote location and safeguarding against rust with its hot, dry atmosphere. What an impressive sight!

I observed that traveling with the circus was like being paid to take a ten-month sightseeing tour of the United States of America. My fellow bandsmen had made many such tours and they acted as experienced guides. I could sleep in the same clean, comfortable bed every night in our semi-private railroad sleeper. If I wished, I would be served as many as three delicious, nutritious meals each day. The circus offered round-trip bus service to and from the train and the show grounds, where I had two three-hour sessions of my favorite activity—making music. I was also permitted to watch two exciting performances. All of this would have been a bargain if it were free of charge—but I was being paid! It felt almost criminal. Even worse, I developed a hidden talent for knock and gin rummy (taking inspiration from Red Floyd, who taught me to remember cards) and managed most weeks to send my entire salary home to Mom for saving.

The major highlight of the 1948 tour for me was playing Ponca City, Oklahoma, on October 3. Ponca City is some eighty miles from Conway Springs, Kansas, home to my sister Sue, her husband Gabe, and their four children. Sue arranged for Mom and Dad to visit and travel with them to Ponca City to see the circus and spend the day with me. I arranged free passes for the matinee performance and met them at noon at the entrance to the Big Top. I showed them around the lot. They got to meet Merle, Johnny, Red, and most of the other bandsmen, as well as several of the clowns and other performers. None of them had ever seen anything like the Ringling Bros. and Barnum & Bailey Circus—only small carnivals at Fourth of July celebrations. Everyone was impressed. I had dinner with the family after the matinee and promised Sue, Gabe, and the kids that I would visit them after the circus season ended.

When the season was over in November, I took a train to New Orleans with connections to Springfield and Aurora. The first weekend after my return to Marionville I made contact with some of my old high school buddies. We got together and tried to have some fun, but it just didn't work. We were no longer on the same wavelength. Our goals and priorities were foreign to one another. We were still friends but not associates, and certainly not buddies. I was happy to have more time with Mom and Dad and to have another Thanksgiving dinner with family.

KEEPING MY PROMISE TO SUE

On the Saturday after Thanksgiving I left for Conway Springs to visit Sue and her family, keeping my promise made in Ponca City. I didn't call ahead because I wanted to surprise them. They had recently moved to a modest farmhouse, where they tended to the usual farm chores for their landlord. Gabe also had steady work away from the farm.

When I arrived at the bus station in Conway Springs, I asked a taxi driver if he knew where Gabe Estes lived. He said yes but he couldn't drive me there because of the deeply rutted road conditions. However, railroad tracks ran just back of the house and he could get me within a mile of the farmhouse. I would have to walk the last mile between the rails. This was good enough for me so I engaged the taxi to take me to that railroad intersection. I trekked with my suitcase down the tracks and arrived via the backyard. It was good timing; I arrived before dark and before supper. Like Mom, Sue was a great cook.

I spent ten joyous days visiting with Gabe, Sue, and their children, but I was itchy again to be back home in Marionville with Mom and Dad. I looked forward to being with them for Christmas and New Year's Day, their forty-fourth wedding anniversary.

While at home following the 1948 circus season, I had Mom and Dad to myself, except for a very few visitors. It was a special time but I didn't realize just how special. It turned out to be the last Christmas season and New Year's Day wedding anniversary celebration I would enjoy at home with my parents. They were both sharp and had good memories and good senses of humor, and they were obviously still very much in love.

I asked Dad one day, "What did you think of Mom the first time you met her?"

"I thought she was an angel from Heaven and the greatest woman in the world."

"What do you think of her now?"

"Same thing."

ANOTHER CIRCUS SEASON, 1949

When it was time, I returned to Sarasota, where the band boarded the train for the trip to New York City and the start of a new season in Madison Square Garden. After the travel experiences of the 1948 season, another trip on the circus train was old stuff. The choice of a New York City hotel for 1949 was the Sharon Hotel on West 46th Street. Small, clean, and private, it was next door to the Paramount Hotel, which housed Billy Rose's

Diamond Horseshoe nightclub featuring his Long-Stemmed Roses chorus line. I was never in the nightclub but I did enjoy *Diamond Horseshoe,* the movie made about it.

Just around the corner on Broadway was the entrance to the Paramount Theater, which, in addition to showing movies, presented live performances of the most popular swing bands and their featured vocalists. The Paramount is where Frank Sinatra gave his debut performance in New York City.

Johnny Evans couldn't do the 1949 season and Merle hired a second tuba player named Bob Beatty. Bob was a player with popular polka bands of the upper Midwest, à la Lawrence Welk. He was no Johnny Evans. And Merle, being an astute bandmaster, changed the seating for the band. He separated the tubas, putting one on either side instead of seating them together. This prompted me to play everything, not alternating strains as Johnny and I did for the 1948 season. Bob Beatty was accustomed to playing in small groups in enclosed dance halls. His sound didn't project as needed for playing with the circus band, under a tent, out of doors.

Bob was a decent sort of fellow and I enjoyed knowing him. He had many stories to tell about his polka band experiences. One I remember well was his relating how the polka band moved from town to town. A special trailer was built to tow behind a car. In this trailer would go music, music stands, and instrument cases, including a set of drums. Bob was paid extra for pulling the trailer and took on the responsibility of packing the musical instruments and other equipment. He had to be particular to get it all in. The last thing he did was to secure his tuba with strong rope atop the trailer. One day he'd been driving for quite a time when he happened to look into the rearview mirror and saw his tuba fifty feet behind the trailer, still attached to the rope, bouncing up and down and taking up the entire two-lane highway. Fortunately he had not met another car but unfortunately his tuba was destroyed. I missed Johnny but, very importantly, what I had learned from him allowed me to please Merle. It also forced me to develop maximum endurance and a performance style of my own. I felt prepared to cover the tuba chair in Johnny's absence.

During the 1949 run of the circus at Madison Square Garden, William Bell visited the band several times and we often had lunch or dinner together. More often than not we met at the Carnegie Tavern. The food was always good and the service unmatched by any restaurant I had yet experienced. To be a luncheon or dinner guest of Mr. Bell was always memorable, but to enter the Carnegie Tavern with him was to experience a stoppage of time for an instant while all the waiters, from wherever they were in the restaurant, would say, "Hi, Bill," "Hi, Mr. Bell," or whatever greeting they had for him. No matter how crowded the restaurant, there would always be a table for Mr. Bell, even if one had to be set up instantaneously.

His fellow musicians in the New York Philharmonic also held him in the highest regard. If you were with Bill Bell, you couldn't help but feel proud and important or, at the very least, self-conscious! I have never known any musician more beloved by colleagues than Bill Bell.

Several times he repeated his invitation for me to come to New York City after the 1949 season to spend Christmas Eve through New Year's Day with him and his family in their Larchmont, New York, apartment and, as he put it, "Take some tuba lessons and get to know each other better." I promised Mr. Bell I would return to New York to visit him on December 23, 1949, through January 2, 1950. As long as I knew him, I always addressed him as Mr. Bell.

Three of Mr. Bell's students played "musical tuba chairs" in 1949: Abe Torchinsky left the NBC Symphony Orchestra for the Philadelphia Orchestra, Joe Novotny followed Abe at NBC, and Bill Rose followed Joe in Houston. They had been freelancing in the summers. As my career progressed, these great tubists became my good friends and colleagues.

DEMILLE VISITS THE CIRCUS

Perhaps the most exciting and interesting visitor of the 1949 season was famed film director Cecil B. DeMille. He was known for innovative and realistic presentation of subjects captured on film and had just completed *Samson and Delilah*. We were pleased and excited that the great Cecil B. DeMille would direct a movie about the circus. *The Greatest Show on Earth* starred Jimmy Stewart, Cornel Wilde, Charlton Heston, Betty Hutton, and Dorothy Lamour. DeMille joined the circus to study and experience every aspect of circus life. He worked sixteen hours a day to "get the feel" of the circus. While the circus was in Madison, Wisconsin, on his sixty-eighth birthday, he spent twelve hours with his circus friends on the ground (observing, asking questions, taking notes) plus another four hours high up in the Big Top tied in a bosun's chair, noting camera angles and lighting effects. The movie was a masterpiece, illustrating the love and commitment of circus people to their art and to one another.

At the end of the 1949 season in early November, I returned home to Marionville and spent almost a month with my family, including an unforgettable family Thanksgiving feast. On December 2, my twentieth birthday, I started serious practice on my King recording tuba, preparing for my trip to New York City. At the end of the circus season I had left my Conn sousaphone and trunk in the care of Joe Land, responsible for band uniforms and equipment. It would be in Sarasota waiting for the next season's rehearsals. Mom and Dad had wanted me home for Christmas but they knew it was important that I go to New York City and spend some time with Mr. Bell. I promised to return to Marionville in January. We could enjoy being together for another six weeks before I reported to Sarasota for the 1950 season rehearsals.

I traveled by train from Missouri to New York City, arriving at Pennsylvania Station in the early afternoon on Friday, December 23, with a suitcase and encased King BB♭ recording tuba. I struggled to a taxi stand and loaded my possessions into a Checker cab and rode to the Sharon Hotel on West 46th Street, close to Broadway. I was checked into the hotel by the same clerk who worked the desk in April and May when I stayed there for the Madison Square Garden run of the circus. Once I got settled in my hotel room, I called Mr. Bell to let him know I had arrived. He welcomed my safe arrival and instructed me to meet him the next day at 4 PM at the Carnegie Tavern. We would take a taxi to Grand Central Station and a commuter train to Larchmont. I assured him I would meet him on time.

Having made contact with Mr. Bell, I wanted a peaceful, restful sleep . . . but only after visiting the nearby Gaiety Delicatessen for one of its famous "takeout" two-inch-thick, thinly sliced kosher pastrami sandwiches on rye, with mustard on the side, one huge new pickle, and two bottles of celery tonic. I had my pastrami feast in the hotel room. I then slept a sleep most people can only dream about.

I awakened early the next morning. At 10 A M I called Wayne Lewis, a trombone and euphonium player friend of Merle Evans and other musicians in the circus band. Wayne owned a music store on West 48th Street, close to the Sharon Hotel. Since it was Christmas Eve, I called Wayne at his home. I told him Mr. Bell had invited me to spend the holidays with his family in Larchmont and then have some tuba lessons. My first lesson was scheduled for Saturday, January 6, at 6 PM in Mr. Bell's uptown studio on 121st Street. I told Wayne I was concerned about the first lesson because I would be without practice since leaving Missouri for New York on December 20. I expected to return to the Sharon Hotel around noon on January 2, and did he know where I might be permitted to practice? Wayne chuckled and said, "Harvey, with your circus chops, you'll be okay. You can use one of my teaching studios in my store for no charge. My store hours are 9–9 weekdays and 9–6 on Saturdays; the store is closed Sundays. You can keep your tuba in my studio after you return from Larchmont on January 2." I was speechless. I accepted his offer and thanked him for his generosity. He warmly responded, "It's Christmas." I arranged to store my instrument in the Sharon Hotel trunk room and reserved a hotel room for my return on January 2.

With my suitcase in hand, I met Mr. Bell at the Carnegie Tavern as scheduled. He welcomed me to New York City and asked about my parents and other family members. The conversation put me at ease. Being with Mr. Bell was always comfortable. On the train I told Mr. Bell about my conversation with Wayne Lewis, and he was delighted to learn of the arrangements made for me to practice in Wayne's music store. Mr. Bell held Wayne Lewis in high regard. We enjoyed a lively conversation during our ride to the Larchmont station and then walked the few blocks to the Bell apartment. Mr. Bell showed me to a guest bedroom off the kitchen, where I left my suitcase. I then had the pleasure of meeting Mrs. Bell; I soon learned to call her Aggie. After a delicious dinner was served, we sat in the living room admiring the Christmas tree and other beautiful Christmas decorations and listening to recordings of Christmas carols.

The next morning I discovered that not only was it Christmas Day but Mr. Bell's birthday as well! Aggie was already preparing the special late afternoon Christmas dinner requested by Mr. Bell: baked ham and everything that goes with it. One very special dish, an absolute favorite of Mr. Bell, was baked giant butterbeans. It was an incredible meal! After birthday cake and other desserts, we collapsed into comfortable chairs. After a while, Mr. Bell stood up and, from a cabinet, withdrew a sheet of manuscript paper. In a focused, transfixed state, he began to write music. When he was finished he called me over and explained that I now had two of the tuba excerpts I needed to learn: the overture to *Die Meistersinger* and the bear solo from *Petrouchka*.

Every day between Christmas and New Year's, Mr. Bell and I would take an early afternoon walk in the village of Larchmont, purchasing items Aggie requested for the New Year's Eve party. As their house guest, I always found something to contribute to the occasion: flowers, boxed candy, tree ornaments, etc. As the date of the party approached, Mr. Bell would step into the local liquor store and buy cases of champagne—some by the magnum (the equivalent of two bottles of champagne) and jeroboam (the equivalent of four bottles). On the afternoon of New Year's Eve, shaved ice was delivered and poured over the champagne, filling a large bathtub.

Everyone enjoyed the celebration. Many of the Bells' guests were faithful friends, going back to Mr. Bell's early years in Iowa and Ohio and on through his relationships with the Sousa Band, Cincinnati Symphony, Goldman Band, NBC Symphony Orchestra, New York Philharmonic, and the Asbury Park Municipal Band, founded by two of his friends, Arthur Pryor and Simone Mantia.

By Tuesday morning, January 2, 1950, life had returned to normal. I had been the Bells' house guest for ten days. They had treated me as a family member and were great hosts. I tried to respond in kind by being a polite and worthy guest. But I now desperately needed to prepare for my first tuba lesson with Mr. Bell, still scheduled for January 6 at 6 PM.

Mr. Bell and I took an early morning commuter train from Larchmont to New York City. He had a morning rehearsal in Carnegie Hall and I returned to the Sharon Hotel. Once settled in my hotel room, I called Wayne Lewis and arranged to have a practice studio from 2 to 9 PM. I would reserve more time when I arrived at his store that afternoon. I practiced no fewer than six hours each day to prepare for my first lesson with Mr. Bell.

Mr. Bell had given me directions to his studio at 419 West 121st Street. He said, "Why, it's simple. Take the IRT Subway from 42nd Street to 116th Street at Columbia University. My studio is about a six-block walk from there." The fact that there were two west-side IRT subway lines must have slipped his mind.

GETTING TO MY FIRST LESSON WAS AN ADVENTURE

On January 6, I left the lobby of the Sharon Hotel with my encased tuba and walked five blocks to the 42nd Street Times Square subway station, then down two flights of stairs to the IRT subway line platform, following Mr. Bell's directions. I boarded the IRT train and got off at 116th Street, struggled up two flights of stairs with my tuba, and discovered that nothing looked like Columbia University. I was at 116th Street in Harlem. An attractive black woman showed interest in the large case I was carrying, so I took the opportunity to ask her how to get to Columbia.

She said, "Columbia University is up on the hill, through Morningside Park. I wouldn't walk through that park at this time of day for anything—there are people in there that can hurt you! What you need to do is go back down the stairs here, take the subway to 96th Street, get on the right train, and get off at 116th Street and Broadway. That's where you're supposed to be."

I thought of hailing a taxi, but there weren't any available. And I wasn't about to climb up and down more long flights of subway stairs with the tuba. So I struck out on foot and walked through the park toward Mr. Bell's studio. I would have been better off if I had followed the lady's advice; it was a long walk. I was a half hour late for my 6 PM lesson.

I apologized for being late and told Mr. Bell I had taken the wrong train. He said, "Well, that's all right, old thing, you're my only student tonight. Let the tuba get warm and then we'll have our lesson."

While waiting for the tuba to defrost, Mr. Bell introduced me to Tante Lena Wanner, who, at age seventy-four, lived in the apartment and managed the studio. She took an interest in every student. She weighed over 300 pounds. Mr. Bell knew her from Prohibition days, when she made bathtub gin and home brew. Mr. Bell paid the apartment rent and taught in the living room as needed. He was a kind and generous man.

When the combined warmth of friendly conversation and room temperature had taken off the winter chill, Mr. Bell took on a more professorial demeanor and said it was time to start the lesson. I was nervous and although I had prepared both *Die Meistersinger* and *Petrouchka* from the handwritten manuscript he gave to me in Larchmont on Christmas Day, I didn't get to play them during that first lesson. Mr. Bell knew I was exhausted from anxiety and walking many blocks carrying my awkward and heavy tuba case. Being considerate, he started the lesson by referring to his observations of my playing from when we had played together with the circus band.

Positive: He said he liked my sound and was impressed with my technique. And he was pleased I didn't have any of the most common bad habits: puffing the cheeks, pulling back the corners of the mouth (smiling), or using excessive pressure on the mouthpiece.

Negative: "I did observe, however, that your approach to both the upper and lower register is the opposite of what I do and teach." I was opening my mouth for the upper range (I wanted to get a "big sound" in the upper range) and I was closing my mouth for the lower range, relaxing the lips and pulling away from the mouthpiece (like many trombone players).

Solution: I asked, "What do I need to do?" His response was, "Change it. Do what I tell you. Approach all aspects of playing the tuba with order and logic. That is why I endorse the pivot system for tuba." I had heard some of the circus brass players discussing the pivot system but, not wanting to be presumptuous, I had never participated in their discussions.

Needless to say, my first lesson with the great Bill Bell was very important to me. I listened attentively to everything he said. I didn't want to miss anything and I wanted to retain as much as possible. Mr. Bell continued to speak distinctly and, when it was appropriate, he would pick up my tuba to illustrate a point. I refrained from asking questions. I didn't want to divert his train of thought. Somehow I sensed that all my unasked questions would be answered in due course. Mr. Bell was on a roll; everything he said and demonstrated was logical, clear, precise, and understood. He gave me much to think about. He instilled confidence in my approach to the tuba, to music, and to life.

The following account is a compendium of my first lesson, subsequent lessons, and more than twenty-three years of close association (1948–1971) with William J. Bell. Any activity with Mr. Bell was a lesson. His logical considerations and attitude guided my every performance and responsibility. I found that every element of my being was an attempt to perpetuate, honor, and represent extensions of Mr. Bell's pedagogical thought. What I learned from Mr. Bell has been attested to and enhanced by sixty-plus years of performances, observations, and discussions with many of the world's greatest musicians, including many outstanding brass players and brass pedagogues.

BRASS INSTRUMENTS—BASIC TECHNIQUES

Brass instrument techniques and musical nuance are the result of physical and intellectual application.

PHYSICAL:
(1) Posture
(2) Mouthpiece Placement—Embouchure
(3) Breathing: Source—Support—Control
(4) Tone Production—Syllables
(5) Articulations
(6) Projection
(7) Dynamics
(8) Range
(9) Endurance.

INTELLECTUAL:
(10) Logic.

Endurance and note placement must be understood and accepted; they must become natural reflexes in playing the tuba. Once these basic skills are mastered, a lifetime of technical refinement follows. As technical skills are developed and mastered, intellectual artistry, musicianship, individual interpretations, and nuance are possible and expected.

Mr. Bell's explanation and demonstration made logical sense to me. It allowed me to place each note on the tuba confidently over a three-plus octave range and over a full range of dynamics. Mr. Bell urged me to adopt the pivot system and I started feeling and hearing positive results immediately. Once this became my natural approach to playing the tuba, technical issues no longer interfered with my playing music. I had no need to experiment with another search for the right embouchure. I never considered any other approach until I started teaching a lot and had to deal with one homemade bad-habit system after another.

Bill Bell really made me think about how I played the tuba. His teaching encouraged order and logic, to practice with a plan and a balance of techniques. It sounds like a simple matter, but it took several hours of concentrated practice to change to Mr. Bell's pivot system. His gentle but firm guidance changed my approach to the instrument.

For the second lesson, he gave me a copy of his *Daily Routine* of scales and arpeggios, a copy of *Arban's Complete Method* (for bass clef instruments—transcribed by Charles Randolph and Simone Mantia), and Marco Bordogni's *Vocalises-Book I*—transcribed for bass clef instruments by Joannes Rochut. Mr. Bell spoke about the purpose of each book. He made sweeping articulation assignments, including *Characteristic Study No. 1* in Arban and the first four Bordogni vocalises. He explained that there were no published collections of either band or orchestra excerpts and suggested that I get a book of manuscript paper and copy every excerpt as they became available to me. Finally, he asked me to play the two excerpts he gave me on Christmas Day, *Die Meistersinger* and *Petrouchka*. I had practically memorized both excerpts and received some help from Wayne Lewis, who heard everything I played when I practiced in his store. Mr. Bell suggested I should listen to recordings of both composers (Wagner and Stravinsky) whenever possible. He referred to the tremendous output of repertoire from these particular composers. When the lesson was over, Mr. Bell congratulated me for having played a good lesson.

Then he said, "Son, if you're going to have a career in New York, you must get yourself a CC tuba!" This shook me up. I had no ambition for a career in New York. As far as I was concerned, the circus band was my career. I had heard many glamorous stories about Bill Bell, about the bands and orchestras he played in, but I never dreamed such a life would be possible for me. When I asked, "Where can I get a CC tuba?", his response was, "I haven't the vaguest notion!" My third and last lesson before returning home to spend a month with Mom and Dad was scheduled for January 18. My stay in New York was dipping into my savings more than I had estimated it would.

A CC TUBA FINDS ME

Bill Bell had a student named Fred Marzan. Every month or so Fred would hitchhike to New York from Pittsburgh to take a tuba lesson from Mr. Bell. He would usually arrive late Friday afternoon, stay overnight, and take his lesson on Saturday morning, as early as Mr. Bell would tolerate it. Fred would then spend the rest of Saturday visiting pawn shops and junk stores in downtown Manhattan. He was looking for quality instruments that he could buy cheap and sell at a quick profit. Fred never failed to locate instruments. He was always able to cover his hotel and lesson expenses.

On one of his visits, in a Manhattan junk shop, he spotted a tarnished tuba that he managed to buy for forty-nine dollars. After cleaning the instrument and adding new pads and corks, he found it was a small silver-plated 1920 Conn four-valve CC tuba with an eighteen-inch bell, in excellent condition. He sold the tuba to Abe Torchinsky for $175. About once a month the Philadelphia Orchestra performed in a subscription series in New York. Mr. Bell and Abe would try to meet for lunch at the Carnegie Tavern. It was on one of those occasions, a spring day in 1950, when Mr. Bell made a plea for a kid from the circus who was having trouble finding a CC tuba. Abe said, "Well, I'll sell him the one I got from Marzan but he'll have to come to the Academy to get it."

I made an appointment with Abe the next day, took an early morning train to Philadelphia, and tried it out in one of the practice rooms, but I couldn't tell anything about it. I didn't know anything about a CC tuba but I bought it. I had to be back in New York by 2 PM for the circus. As it turned out, it was the perfect size for a brass quintet, pit orchestra, and almost every gig I later had. No fellow musician or conductor ever complained.

Rehearsals for the 1950 season of the circus were in Sarasota, Florida, as usual, and again we rode the circus train from Sarasota to New York. We disembarked at Jersey City and took a train from there into Pennsylvania Station and then a cab from the station to the Sharon Hotel, which would again be my home for the six-week New York City run of the circus.

In May 1950, before leaving New York to start our annual tour, Merle Evans summoned the circus band (minus the five New York City extras) to the Capitol Records recording studios on 46th Street, just east of Seventh Avenue, for a commercial LP recording.

We recorded three hours on each of three mornings. The music we recorded included "Gentry's Triumphal March" by Fred Jewel, "The Storming of El Caney" by Russell Alexander, and other circus repertoire. At the time, I couldn't possibly imagine that my second recording session would be a year later with the New York Philharmonic brass section conducted by Leopold Stokowski!

DECISION TO MAKE—LEAVING MID-SEASON 1950

The circus tour continued throughout the summer of 1950, and in mid-August we were playing in Indianapolis when I received the following telegram from William Bell: "Have scholarship at Juilliard—live in my studio—come to NYC ASAP."

To say that I was surprised and delighted would be an understatement. But I was also immediately concerned because Merle had a reputation for not looking too kindly upon musicians who left in mid-season, mostly due to the difficulty of finding suitable replacements.

I carried the telegram around for a few days while I worked up the courage to talk to Merle. After much consideration, I finally scheduled a meeting with Merle between shows. At the appropriate time, I rapped lightly on the door of his red wagon. He invited me in and, once we were seated, he asked what I needed. Saying nothing, I simply handed the telegram to him and awaited the expected explosion. After a long silence, Merle looked up smiling and said, "Well, Junior, I think you should be with Bill. We'll work something out." I breathed a sigh of relief, thanked him for understanding, and shook his hand. Years later I suspected a certain amount of collusion between Merle and Mr. Bell.

Merle approved my calling Arnold Jacobs, principal tuba with the Chicago Symphony Orchestra, to inquire if he could recommend a replacement for me. Mr. Jacobs replied positively and asked that I call him again in two days. Meanwhile, the old-timers in the band were pleased and impressed that I had obtained Merle's blessing to leave in mid-season. I called Mr. Jacobs in two days and he recommended Mac MacDonald to replace me for the rest of the circus season. Mac was a terrific player; a few months after replacing me he won the principal tuba position with the Pittsburgh Symphony Orchestra. This first contact with Arnold Jacobs was the beginning of a lifetime friendship—it seemed that any time I was in Chicago as the years went by, on tour or giving a clinic, Arnold always showed up at my events.

I left the circus in Madison, Wisconsin, taking the train to Milwaukee, then to St. Louis, and on to Aurora, Missouri. I didn't stay at home very long. I got home at the end of August and left for New York in time to register for fall classes at Juilliard.

On reflection I couldn't believe how much I had changed in just two years with the circus. Maturity came about by my learning to accept assignments and responsibilities while living and working closely with experienced musicians old enough to be my father or grandfather. They were great resources for counseling. I couldn't be a kid while playing an adult role of equal responsibility with such senior musicians.

I heard Merle Evans's expression about me many times: "Gee, Junior, you're the oldest young guy I've ever known." Playing with the Ringling Bros. and Barnum & Bailey Circus had been an incredible experience. People today don't understand the quality of the musicians in the top circus bands at that time. We really had some terrific players—windjammers, we were called—and Merle Evans was in a class by himself as a band conductor. In Gene Plowdon's biography of Merle, *Maestro of the Circus,* Merle included a "Hall of Fame Circus Band" selected from the musicians he directed for more than fifty years. I was deeply honored to be listed as Merle's first chair tuba player. Second and third were two of my greatest heros, Johnny Evans and Bill Bell, both former members of the Sousa Band.

After Merle retired, the windjammers organization celebrated a special week of rehearsals and concerts honoring him. I was very honored when

Merle asked me to deliver a luncheon address. A few weeks later I was asked to perform with fellow alumni of the Sauter-Finegan Orchestra, at Town Hall in New York City, on the same day as Merle's luncheon in Sarasota, Florida. I was in a quandary. I called Merle and told him about the conflict. Merle immediately said that I should go where I would be performing. He said, "Harvey, you have to do Sauter-Finegan. You can do me next year." But he died shortly after that. I never got to honor Merle in such a formal setting. To this very day, I have a knot in my stomach thinking about what I missed. It was no consolation that the Sauter-Finegan Orchestra "Revisited" was successful and a lot of fun.

When I think back on the touring I did with the circus, I know now that I made some significant connections with musicians without realizing it. No matter the city or town, it seemed there were ex-Sousa musicians coming to say hello to Merle and other friends in the band. Some were curious to know about the eighteen-year-old tuba player. I felt like my performances were being auditioned almost every day. When I came to New York as a Juilliard student and freelance musician in September 1950, I had already made the acquaintance of a number of musicians. What I didn't realize was that much of the profession in New York was managed or controlled by ex-Sousa bandsmen, and that I had established a reputation through my two and a half years with the circus band playing all styles of music.

PREPARING FOR NEW YORK CITY, 1950

On Tuesday, August 22, I arrived at the Frisco Depot in Aurora, Missouri. I was met by my brother-in-law Ralph Wilks, my sister Virginia's husband. Making conversation on the way to Marionville, Ralph expressed amazement at the metamorphosis I had undergone since we were putting up hay in his barn in June 1947. That was the day Homer Lee came to tell me I had a job with King Bros. Circus. Ralph asked questions about my circus experiences and seemed fascinated by my answers. I doubt if he believed all I told him. In his place, I doubt if I would have believed it either, but it was all true.

Mom and Dad were awaiting our arrival when we pulled into their driveway a short time later. After hugs and a warm reception, Mom brought up a subject she had obviously given much thought to. She said, "Harvey, honey, I've been thinking about your going to New York and I think you should buy some new clothes. Ralph and Virginia have offered to take us to Springfield on Saturday morning for a shopping spree." I assured Mom the same thoughts had crossed my mind and I confessed to having studied men's fashions in *Esquire*.

Ralph and Virginia picked us up on Saturday at 7:30 A M as promised and we headed for Springfield. The stores opened at 9:00. We went directly to a men's fashion store. It was a new experience for me, going back and forth between the dressing room and full-length mirrors, modeling men's suits, sport coats, slacks, and sweaters for three-way decisions among Mom, Virginia, and myself. Ralph spent the day with his friends at the Farm Bureau. Yea and Nay were placed in two separate piles, with a third pile for reconsideration. Mom took a real interest in making sure I bought the best possible clothes. She said, "I want you to look good for Mr. Bell and Juilliard." It was the only time I have ever enjoyed shopping for clothes.

The final tally: two suits (top of the line), one sport coat, two pairs of slacks, two sweaters, four ties (two matching, two contrasting), two hats (one gray, one brown), two belts, one pair of suspenders, two pairs of shoes, one pair of gloves, two scarves, four shirts (two white, two colored), a bathrobe, one pair of pajamas, six sets of underwear, a cashmere overcoat, a "Dick Tracy" raincoat, and a box of initialed handkerchiefs. It was expensive, but I had saved every nickel I earned with the circus. At a nearby luggage store I purchased an ample Samsonite suitcase. Within six months of my arrival in New York City, I would have to purchase complete sets of tuxedo and tails at Herman's on Sixth Avenue, recommended by my new musician friends.

CHAPTER FOUR

Juilliard, Studying with William J. Bell

I ARRIVED IN NEW YORK CITY by train during Labor Day weekend 1950 and took a taxi to Mr. Bell's uptown teaching studio. Tante Lena was still there, as was Eric Hauser, with whom I would share the back bedroom while attending Juilliard. It was a utilitarian apartment/ studio. I took one good look at the back bedroom and immediately started considering plans for making it more comfortable.

The morning after I moved in, I spoke to Eric about doing some minor redecorating, at my expense, of course. Eric cordially allowed that I could do whatever I wanted to do, as the room had needed redecorating for too long. I went to Tante Lena about my proposal. As expected, she was delighted, especially when she heard I would paint the walls and install new linoleum and custom-made venetian blinds to replace the dirty old window shades. She was even more delighted when I paid two months' rent in advance. I went right to work, scrubbing the walls and floor and measuring everything. Over the telephone I ordered the linoleum and the custom-made blinds, to be delivered in one week. I visited the local hardware store and bought paint, paintbrushes, spackle, putty, several grades of sandpaper, and the minimum tools I expected to need as a bona fide resident of Apartment 1-E. When visitors smelled fresh paint, they wanted to see the room. They were surprised to see burgundy walls and a white ceiling along with matching yellow-green venetian blinds and linoleum. OK, so it wasn't stylish, but it had character to spare! I was finished with decorating our room.

BUGGED IN NYC

Like every apartment in New York City, the studio had its share of cockroaches. Remembering my decisive victory over bedbugs three years earlier, I decided to take similar action. Knowing Mr. Bell rarely taught on Sunday, I planned my attack for Saturday, after midnight. Using damp towels around the doors, I sealed off our bedroom from the rest of the apartment and set off several bug bombs in the kitchen. After some twenty minutes I was surprised to hear Tante Lena screaming. I rushed into the room where she slept and was shocked to see that the floor was covered with a cockroach carpet. Hundreds of them—more like thousands—were lying on their backs and kicking their legs in the air as they reacted to the chemicals released by the bug bombs. We were victorious for a while but the unreachable unhatched eggs and the social life of New York City cockroaches defies destruction and assures perpetuity. Ask any New Yorker.

Eric Hauser was a gentleman in his sixties, a former horn player and a fine musician. Sadly, he was a melancholy alcoholic, gradually going blind. Like Tante Lena, he was another adopted and grateful ward of Mr. Bell. He did the shopping for Lena and ran errands for Mr. Bell. A veteran of World War I, Eric looked forward to receiving his government check each month. One can only guess what that meager monthly offering meant to him.

Eric was extremely proud of having played horn in the New York Symphony under such conductors as Damrosch, Mengelberg, and Furtwangler. Through our conversations and Eric's reminiscing about his life's experiences, my respect for him grew. I soon realized I had much to learn from him.

Eric was usually quiet and passive. Though an alcoholic, he was still able to communicate and was generally pleasant and happy. In the circus I had experienced many types of alcoholics. Those like Eric are the easiest to tolerate: ever conscious and harmless, with a fixed happy smile like he had just remembered savoring a blissful experience. He kept a lidded tankard full of Ballantine ale around the clock, or so it seemed.

I ingratiated myself with Eric by seeing that the refrigerator always had at least two to four quarts of Ballantine on the lower shelf. For hours, Eric would sit on the edge of his bed listening to me practice, commenting on how he thought my practicing was going. "Now, Harvey," he might say, "I think Bill would want it a little more relaxed and the dynamics a bit more exaggerated, both ways. Now hold back on the bear solo, be in charge, don't let it rush, hold back—there, that's the way." Or, "Play *Die Meistersinger* again. Take charge from the first note, articulate firmly and blend with the basses; keep the notes full and tenuto throughout."

Playing for Eric was like having a coach, with Mr. Bell as the trainer, teacher, and mentor. "Coach" Eric selected his musical heroes with great care and consideration. He was a good storyteller, with a calm, matter-of-fact manner. He transported me out of that small and stuffy room to one great concert stage after another. No one (or so it seemed) had ever given Eric the admiration and attention he needed and deserved.

Per Mr. Bell's instructions, I spent as much time as possible trying to develop proficiency on the CC tuba purchased from Abe Torchinsky. It was a tough assignment. I had to continue playing my King BB♭ recording tuba on all professional engagements while exclusively practicing the CC tuba. I felt secure reading music on the BB♭ tuba but I was very insecure reading music on the CC tuba. I never thought it would be so confusing. I sold my Conn BB♭ sousaphone and trunk to a string bass player who doubled on tuba. I persevered in following Mr. Bell's persistent instructions to learn CC tuba well enough to perform equally on the BB♭ and CC.

While living in the studio, I enjoyed the tremendous bonus of witnessing Mr. Bell's teaching of other musicians, both student and professional players, mostly tuba but sometimes trombone or euphonium. He sometimes disciplined his students severely. His most persistent requirements were rhythmical precision with constant subdivision. One day, a young euphonium student was having a lesson and his rhythm was not good. He rushed or dragged, depending on the range he was playing in. Mr. Bell said, "OK, you play, I'll sing, we'll both march." He stood up and starting singing the melody of the march being studied while the student played his euphonium part. They marched in the living room, into the dining room, around the table, and back into the living room . . . repeat and repeat again. The student couldn't rush or drag as Mr. Bell sang and counted the cadence. He adopted the manner and persistence of a drum major. Some thirty minutes later Mr. Bell sank exhausted into his chair. The student packed his instrument and left for home with strong suggestions from his teacher that he start using a metronome and subdivide habitually. I'm glad Mr. Bell didn't have a whistle. I'm doubly glad the studio was on the first floor with no one living below. After a short breather and a long, cold Presbyterian, Mr. Bell was ready for his next student. I realized how blessed I was not to require such discipline.

I listened to everything Mr. Bell said and I adored and respected him deeply, and I am forever proud to be one of his devoted students. The circumstances of my being in New York City were due to his often-demonstrated personal interest in my well-being. Spending time with him in any activity allowed observations and lessons in both life and music. With all the time we spent together, official private tuba lessons consisted of perhaps a dozen sessions where I played and he critiqued. Some scheduled lessons were spent playing duets, technical studies and vocalises, and orchestral excerpts, and discussing various technical considerations. These included musical phrasing, clear tone, creating and projecting tonal colors through the instrument, blending, balancing, controlled vibrato, relative intonation, and one of his favorite criticisms: failure to subdivide consistently.

My study with Mr. Bell was based on logic, acceptance, application, results, and improvement. I soon discovered that friendly, seemingly casual, suggestions were to be taken just as seriously as any other instruction. There was seldom an order to do a particular technique his way only! Mr. Bell didn't like raising his voice above conversational level, whether in criticism or compliment. He enjoyed speaking about his youth touring with the Sousa Band, and all his many friends and their escapades together. Just walking down the street having conversation, I learned about the music business.

I had several important lessons with Mr. Bell before I began studies at Juilliard. He prepared me for the required entrance audition before the entire brass faculty, mostly members of the Philharmonic and N B C orchestras. All students, including those with full scholarships, were required to play an entrance audition. Mr. Bell had me prepare his transcription of J. S. Bach's "Air" and "Bourrée." At the audition I had the special pleasure of meeting Fred Geib, a great tuba player and great teacher. Mr. Geib died in 1950, a short time after I met him.

VOLUNTEERING WITH BANDS AND ORCHESTRAS

When I first arrived in New York City in mid-September 1950, I had no performance assignments other than private lessons with Mr. Bell and eventual assignments by Juilliard. Having grown accustomed to playing my instrument for a minimum of six hours a day, I was not happy about this situation. I wanted to keep playing my tuba six or more hours a day. I faithfully commenced each practice session with the *Bell Daily Routine* of scales and arpeggios, always pushing the outer limits of the tuba's full range. I wanted to maintain the chops I had developed in the circus band.

I put into practice two maxims I have lived with most of my life:

(1) *Always think big. It takes no more energy than thinking small . . .*
    (A big idea can be refined and, if necessary, reduced in scope; a small idea cannot easily be enlarged.)
(2) *You cannot be sure you're doing all you can do unless you're overcommitted.*

Mr. Bell suggested I make contact with Hunter Wiley, director of bands at Columbia University. It was conveniently close to Mr. Bell's uptown studio, so that very day I strolled over to the Columbia University band rehearsal hall and introduced myself. I received a cordial and enthusiastic invitation to rehearse and perform concerts with his band any time it was possible for me. Hunter Wiley was much younger than I expected. He also played solo euphonium and second trombone with the New York City Ballet Orchestra.

I next visited the Seventh Regiment Armory, suggested by George Black, principal tubist with the Seventh Regiment Band. George was a fan of the circus band and a close friend of Bill Bell. Conductor George F. Briegel had met me when he visited Merle Evans at one of our circus performances in Madison Square Garden. I was invited to attend rehearsals every Tuesday evening.

Highly recommended was the Young Men's Hebrew Association Orchestra on East 92nd Street, conducted by Maurice Levine. The orchestra met every Sunday morning for intense rehearsals of important standard orchestral repertoire. The volunteer orchestra consisted mainly of professional musicians who performed in Broadway pit orchestras and wanted to keep their orchestral chops in good shape. Personnel was augmented by talented students from the Manhattan School of Music and Juilliard. The orchestra rehearsed adventuresome programs—important fare for a young circus band tuba player. It also provided opportunities to make influential new friends. From my perspective, every note I played served as a mini-audition. Later, to repay Maurice Levine for the opportunities I enjoyed when I first arrived in New York, I volunteered my services for an important concert and received a gracious acknowledgment from him.

A couple of the brass players who attended the 92nd Street Y rehearsals asked if I was available to rehearse Thursday evenings with the Gotham Brass Ensemble, conducted by David Simon in the WNYC studios. Live concerts were sometimes scheduled for radio broadcast. This was my first opportunity to play brass chamber music. It was good experience.

Occasionally I also rehearsed with another brass ensemble of younger students conducted by Simon Karasik somewhere on lower 2nd Street above a Jewish restaurant. Rehearsals were followed by a pizza party. I enjoyed every opportunity to play my tuba.

THE NATIONAL ORCHESTRAL ASSOCIATION

The most important performance activity I took on was the National Orchestral Association, which met for rehearsals every Monday, Wednesday, and Friday from 4–7 PM. Conducted by Leon Barzin, Wednesday rehearsals were broadcast over the *New York Times'* FM station, WQXR. Barzin was a proud man and a visionary who observed that the majority of musicians filling the rosters of American symphony orchestras were European-born and -trained. Obviously, many gifted young American musicians were not being sufficiently trained to win symphony auditions. Barzin decided to do something about it. He resigned from his position as principal violist with the New York Philharmonic (1925–1929) to devote his efforts to that cause. He was friends for several years with Mary Flagler Cary, whose father was chairman of the board of the New York Philharmonic. Together, Mary Flagler Cary and Leon Barzin organized a board of directors and in 1930 founded the National Orchestral Association.

The early mission of the National Orchestral Association was to train American musicians in orchestral technique, traditions, and repertoire, developing their ability to perform in a major orchestra, regardless of their race or gender. More than any other single person, Barzin opened the door of opportunity for important changes in orchestral personnel. It was at the National Orchestral Association that I may have first met Gunther Schuller, who became a lifelong friend and associate. Gunther was a devoted fan of Leon Barzin.

Barzin presented numerous concerts at Carnegie Hall, providing students with opportunities to refine their techniques and perform with many world-renowned soloists. In addition to training orchestral musicians, there were numerous other initiatives including a conducting program and performances fostering the careers of American composers.

The success of the National Orchestral Association inspired many similar training programs. Furthermore, the National Orchestral Association was one of the first arts organizations to present instrument demonstration concerts for schoolchildren, giving the first such concerts as early as 1947. These concerts enriched the lives of thousands of young American students and were a successful model for orchestras and other ensembles (including the New York Brass Quintet).

The NOA headquarters was a complete floor of the New York City Center, used for rehearsals and broadcasts. There was an office for Leon Barzin which doubled as a studio for instrumental section rehearsals for musicians not involved in the current repertoire. Donald Trump made one of his most successful real estate investments by purchasing the air space over City Center. Trump benefited from his acquisition but so did City Center.

When the National Orchestral Association played repertoire with an important tuba part, it also served as an audition for me—especially since many of the faculty coaches also played first desk positions in the New York City Ballet Orchestra. In fact, concertmaster Hugo Fiorato was also concertmaster and personnel manager of the ballet orchestra, of which Barzin was director of music. In this way, playing with the National Orchestral Association gave me an inside track for the New York City Ballet tuba position.

ENTERING JUILLIARD

The Juilliard School of Music was an awesome and imposing place when I reported there for freshman entrance exams. Juilliard was located at the intersection of Broadway and 122nd Street, with its main entrance on Claremont Avenue (parallel to Broadway). Diagonally across to the left was the famous Riverside Church, also known as the Rockefeller Church. On the peak of a high gable, a bronze statue holds, at the ready, a herald trumpet directed at Columbia University's International House. Legend claims the trumpet will sound when a virgin exits the International House. Brass players fear the trumpeter will lose his chops before he uses his chops. His trumpet remains silent.

Across Claremont Avenue to the right was an attractive neighborhood park. The tidy little park had well-placed gingko trees interspersed with patches of grass and paved concrete, with benches thoughtfully arranged. Starting in the spring and continuing into the fall months, it was a grand place for mothers to stroll with baby carriages, for adults to read books, for children of the age for skipping rope or playing hide-and-seek or tag. There were constant choices for action with new rules and new games being discovered or made up at the moment. At twilight time neighborhood parents knew where to start looking for their puberty-age children. Conscientious groundskeepers, carrying three-foot-long poles with six-inch spikes to clean and clear the grounds of paper scraps and other debris, agreed it should be called "Cherry Park."

I auditioned before the brass faculty and registered for class assignments on the first day of the fall semester. I made note of the routine for reserving a practice room and located the student lounge and cafeteria. I also noted the locations of the administration offices. As my studies proceeded at Juilliard, I became increasingly impressed by the performance levels of students on their respective instruments, both in rehearsals and in practice rooms.

Once the first semester began I was assigned to the second orchestra, conducted by Frederik Prausnitz, assistant dean. Scheduled for performance on my first concert was *Billy the Kid*, by Aaron Copland. Wow, my first experience with ⅝ and ⅞ rhythms and my first time playing with an orchestra! I enjoyed every rehearsal. The Literature and Materials of Music (music theory) class to which I was assigned was taught by Vincent Persichetti. Ultimately, Professor Persichetti would play a significant role in my life's commitment to music and the tuba.

Juilliard was crawling with world-famous teachers and student potential. Piano Class was taught by Gordon Hardy. Composer William Schuman was president of Juilliard and, later, head of Lincoln Center. Norman Lloyd, a composition teacher, later became director of the Martha Baird Rockefeller Fund. Hearing and performing their compositions gave me personal contact and lasting friendships with each of them. I admire their achievements. Two other outstanding faculty for whom I had tremendous respect were Margaret Hillis, choral director, and Jean Morel, a wonderful musician who conducted the first orchestra at Juilliard. He also conducted performances of French operas at the Metropolitan. In rehearsal he usually had a cigarette dangling from his mouth and he had a tremendous "French vinegar" (sour) sense of humor. He could be quite caustic to student goofs and impropriety.

I had a memorable experience with Jean Morel early in my first years at Juilliard. I had left my tuba in the orchestral rehearsal room. When I returned to pick it up, I noticed that Jean Morel was conducting the orchestra in a rehearsal of the *Oberon* overture and, for some reason, there were no basses present. Now, I had played the band transcription of *Oberon* on tuba so many times I knew the part inside out. Johnny Evans and I used to play it for fun during warm-ups with the circus band. The transcription is a full tone lower than the orchestral part, which meant that the fingerings for the band part on BB♭ tuba and for the orchestral bass part on CC tuba were the same. So I pulled out my tuba and started playing along with the orchestra from memory. Not loud, but certainly loud enough for the conductor to notice.

Jean Morel completely flipped, but in a good way. He had the other students applaud. And from that day forward I believe I played every professional recording he conducted that included the tuba. He never yelled at me. Also, for a time I became the object of student whispers and finger pointing.

One evening I arrived at Juilliard for a practice session. I entered my reserved practice room, turned on the light, took off my overcoat, positioned a music stand and chair, took the cover off my tuba, opened my briefcase, put my music on the stand, and suddenly had no interest in practicing. I was about to rehearse again the first published tuba solo, "Rocked in the Cradle of the Deep" (1879). It was a sea chantey melody with variations, typical of the meager solo literature for tuba. I sat there for perhaps half an hour staring at my music. Then I packed up my tuba, put on my coat, and left the school.

THE LAUNCH OF A LIFELONG PROJECT

The next morning, after theory class, I asked Vincent Persichetti for an appointment. He suggested we meet at 1 PM in his office. His desk was in a rather large room of desks assigned to members of the theory and composition departments. When I entered the room, it was deserted except for Dr. Persichetti. He called me over to his desk, which had a chair in front, facing him. He invited me to be seated and asked what he could do for me. I proceeded to pour my heart out about the solo literature for tuba. When compared with the libraries of solo material for other instruments, the tuba came up short. It was upsetting to hear other instruments practicing great music by master composers while the tuba was stuck with "Beelzebub," "Asleep in the Deep," "Rocked in the Cradle of the Deep," "Down in the Deep Cellar," "Solo Pomposo," etc. While these works are entertaining and offered the young tubist performance challenges, none had the artistic stature of music performed by other instruments.

Dr. Persichetti listened attentively to my concerns. He then cleared his throat and very tutorially said, "Harvey, I have two things to say to you. First, I want you to know that all the music ever written belongs to you as much as it belongs to any other musician. I am a composer and I speak for composers who cannot speak for themselves. I speak for Bach, Handel, Mozart, Scarlatti, and others. They all want you to play their music. They want you to play it well, in the right style and with serious purpose. So if you hear something you want to play on the tuba, take it; play it. It belongs to you. The second thing I have to say to you is,"—and here he injected a bit of sarcasm in his voice to make a point—"so you want better music to play on your tuba. Well, let me ask you, Harvey, do you think violinists are going to do anything about it? Do you think flutists are going to do anything about it? You're the one who wants better music for the tuba, so you're the one who has to do something about it." We sat in silence long enough for me to soak up his declaration. I had just experienced perhaps the most important music lesson of my life. I was given a mission to develop, improve, and expand literature for the tuba. Everything he said made perfect sense.

Thus, in 1951, while a Juilliard freshman, I started organizing my lifelong goal to generate, acquire, and perform music of every genre for the tuba. It was a mission with many facets, inadvertently assigned to me by Vincent Persichetti. I dedicated myself to seeking, adapting, transposing, and commissioning works that featured the tuba. Other important facets of my mission were to change the public and music industry images of the tuba.

Most effective in elevating the tuba to equal stature with the other brass instruments was the emergence and success of the New York Brass Quintet, the first successful brass chamber music ensemble. It became evident that the future of the tuba was its relationship with composers and their acceptance and enthusiasm for the tuba as a solo and chamber music instrument.

New "mutual respect" relations with composers came to be evident. Ultimately, solo clinics, recitals, and brass quintet performances transformed super players into super pedagogues (Arnold Jacobs), and brought the tuba into true prominence.

JOHNNY APPLESEED OF THE TUBA

When I look back on my lifelong mission to gain a better life for the tuba, I remember constant efforts to stimulate composers to write music that featured the tuba. I am proud to be considered and sometimes referred to as a latter-day "Johnny Appleseed of the tuba." I knew that composition seeds planted in the minds of composers would someday germinate and bear fruit.

As I started my quest, I felt a need to review the history of the tuba and the priorities of composers before and after its evolution and development. What makes brass instruments a family is the like manner by which they produce sound: the projection of an airstream through the lips (causing them to vibrate) into and through a cup-shaped mouthpiece (of appropriate size) inserted into a given length of tubing which provides for a desired center of pitch and range. The tubing into which the mouthpiece is inserted may be cylindrical—producing a brighter tone (trumpet, trombone), or conical—producing a more mellow tone (cornet, horn, euphonium, tuba). Predecessors and early versions of modern brass instruments were limited to a particular overtone series suitable to outdoor usage for signaling, such as bugles and hunting horns, animal horns, and large conch shells. With the exception of the trombone, which has maintained the same configuration for centuries, early brass instruments were not chromatic. Generations of composers did not consider brass instruments worthy of indoor performances with courtly orchestras made up of strings, flutes, woodwinds, harpsichord, clavier, or organ.

The first predecessor of the tuba was the serpent (from the end of the sixteenth century into the beginning of the nineteenth century). The earliest serpents were made of wood covered with leather. To facilitate access to the tone holes, the instrument was curved into the shape of a serpent. Its limited range of notes and dynamics prevented broad composer acceptance. The serpent could not compete with nor balance sounds with other instruments. It was most successful when used in unison to enhance the bass voices of vocal choirs. Both Haydn and Beethoven used the serpent in military music.

Second came the ophicleide, an enormous improvement over the serpent but doomed to be out of favor once the tuba became established. Patented in France in 1821, the ophicleide resembled an enlarged metal bassoon with tone holes, covered with padded keys. A chromatic instrument played with a cup-shaped mouthpiece, the ophicleide was still no match for the upper brass and a section of three trombones. Also, the tone quality and dynamic range varied, depending on how many tone holes were open or closed. Nonetheless, composers Mendelssohn, Berlioz, and Wagner wrote important parts for the ophicleide in some of their major orchestral works.

As late as 1912, the Paris Opera had an ophicleide. In the last fifty years, as the tuba has become more popular, it has stirred up renewed interest (by instrument historians) in the serpent and the ophicleide, resulting in the gatherings of serpent and ophicleide cliques.

INVENTION OF THE VALVE

The invention of the valve was the single most important development in making the tuba a chromatic instrument. Available information about a workable valve dates back to 1815 and Prussian-born horn player Heinrich Stolzel. The valve, and its adaptation in clusters of three to five, made possible the birth of the tuba.

In the early nineteenth century, brass instrument makers throughout Europe and the United States were pursuing ways to improve their products. Today, in the early twenty-first century, the search continues with the addition of several countries, most notably Japan and Russia, joining in this never-ending quest.

Between 1815 and 1835 much experimentation led to various types of valves, added one at a time to the open horn and cornet. Chromaticism was ultimately made possible by adding a cluster of three valves, making possible seven valve combinations, each with appropriate lengths of tubing to lower the pitch of the open horn by a half step. In effect, one instrument had seven bugles, each with a full range of overtones. Additional valves provided for added lengths of tubing for lower notes and alternate valve combinations for improved intonation. For instance, for a CC tuba the valve combinations can be:

C: 0
C♯: 1–2–3D♭: 1–2–3
D: 1 and 3
D♯: 2–3E♭: 2–3
E: 3
F: 1
F♯: 2G♭: 2
G: 0
G♯: 2–3A♭: 2–3

A: 1–2
A#: 1B♭: 1
B: 2
C: 0

Clifford Bevan, who wrote the definitive history of the tuba, says, "There is only one instrument in the modern orchestra of which we know the precise date of birth. Prussian Patent 19 was taken out on 12 September 1835 by Wilhelm Wieprecht and Johann Moritz of Berlin for the bass tuba."

Vaclav Cerveny, a Bohemian (Czechoslovakian) instrument maker, invented contrabass tubas in BB♭ and CC in 1834. There is no patent known.

Hector Berlioz said that a tuba, playing its lowest notes, doubled an octave higher by another tuba, "takes on amazing richness and resonance" and in the middle and upper registers "the tone is impressively noble." And it blends perfectly with trombones and trumpets.

With such endorsement from Berlioz, the tuba quickly displaced the ophicleide in the symphony orchestra. Important ophicleide parts, including Mendelssohn's famous *Midsummer Night's Dream Overture*, were assigned to the tuba. To the present day the tuba holds a principal (solo) chair in the modern symphony orchestra.

The New York Philharmonic, America's first symphony orchestra, was founded in 1842, only seven years after the tuba was invented. From conversation with the historical offices of the New York Philharmonic, we know of two tuba players doubling contrabass: Charles Preusser (1854–1855) and Charles Dillhard (1855–1867).

RESEARCH AND JUSTIFICATION

In my original and subsequent conversations with Dr. Persichetti, I repeatedly expressed frustration that while over a century had passed since the invention of the tuba (1835–1950), we still had no serious solo repertoire. Later, in a cursory review of that period of history, I developed a better understanding of this void of solo tuba repertoire. Throughout the nineteenth and into the twentieth century, solo repertoire for all brass instruments, not just the tuba, suffered from lack of both composer and player awareness of solo and chamber music potential. I reflected on the unprecedented impact the tuba had on bands and orchestras during those early years. I thought about how slow communication was from one country to another, from one composer to another, one conductor to another, one instrument maker to another, one player to another. I thought about what tubists of those early years had gained for the art and profession of music. I thought about what a family of chromatic brass instruments in sections of trumpets, horns, trombones, and tuba(s) did for the orchestra and for bands. Basic instrumentation of the modern symphony orchestra evolved from repertoire established by the most respected composers.

I decided that I needed to know more about the state of solo and chamber ensemble literature using the tuba. It appears that more often than not tuba solo music was written by tuba players to play for other tuba players to hear. After "Rocked in the Cradle of the Deep," other sea chanteys followed. And polkas with variations were the order of the day, for tuba and also for trumpets and other brass instruments. There was no crop to harvest, to pluck and pick.

Mr. Bell seems to be the first tubist to transcribe selected masterworks of great composers for his instrument: Beethoven's *Variations on a Theme by Handel (Judas Maccabeus)*, "The Jolly Farmer" by Robert Schumann, and "Air" and "Bourrée" by Johann Sebastian Bach. For most of these melodic transcriptions he continued the brass soloist's established routine of adding a series of variations to be performed with piano or band accompaniment. These efforts by Mr. Bell to provide tubists with music by master composers were not unnoticed.

And while we must tip our hat to Fred Geib and other tubists for their compositional efforts, they generally go unnoticed by our musician colleagues. Before 1950, the worthiness of the tuba as a solo instrument was inevitably compared with transcriptions of music written for other instruments. In my humble opinion, we too often came up short.

The most important solo for tuba with orchestra (and narrator) prior to 1950 was "Tubby the Tuba," by American composer George Kleinsinger and lyricist Paul Tripp, written in the early 1940s and recorded in 1947. Capitol Records proudly credited narrator Danny Kaye but made no mention of the fine tuba playing of Hollywood tubist George Bouje. This recording did more for our instrument than we could ever imagine—or admit. Written as a children's record, it introduced the tuba to countless young "unprejudiced" ears. And, it was the first and most popular children's record—ever. I have performed "Tubby the Tuba" many times. My best narrators were the composer himself and Gene Shalit, a host and film critic on NBC's *Today Show.*

OPPORTUNITIES FOR SOLO TUBA

In my research up to 1950 I located no serious compositions written for solo tuba (no concertos, no sonatas). I believe it is fitting for tubists to study and perform the four wonderful horn concerti by Mozart and the two challenging horn concerti of Richard Strauss (written for his father, who said they were impossible). Tongue in cheek, I explain to my horn-playing colleagues that both Mozart and Strauss were clairvoyant. They knew there would someday be tubas to play their concerti. Seriously, young student tubists benefit immeasurably from listening to the excellent recordings and live performances of the world's greatest horn virtuosi.

In the mid-1980s I was invited to appear as a featured soloist at the highly regarded summer Mozart Festival in Vermont to perform Mozart horn concerti. In addition to recital repertoire performed in the summer theater, concert manager Melvin Kaplan asked me to organize and conduct a pops concert performed by multiple tubas and euphoniums. The core of a group I put together was the Colonial Tuba Quartet (Mary Ann Craig and Jay Hildebrandt, euphonium, and Gregory Fritze and Gary Bird, tuba, former graduate students of mine). To this solid personnel we added another twelve instruments or so, including Mark Nelson, Andrew Seligson, and Michael Salzman. I rehearsed and prepared them. A near-capacity audience enjoyed the casual concert presentation. We were on a ferryboat that went from Vermont to New York. In the middle of the lake the boat cut its engine and we floated, under mostly a moonlit sky, made all the more appreciated by a light rain which did not dampen the enthusiasm already established.

My research supports the concept that no important solos were written for tuba primarily because few tubists believed enough in their own instrument. Since I started following the advice of Dr. Persichetti, I have approached dozens of composers with success. When people ask me about the future of the tuba I tell them, "The future of the tuba will be determined by the composers."

I believe it is important that a library of music for solo tuba with established chamber ensembles be developed. In this way, the importance of the tuba as a solo instrument is endorsed by a string quartet, brass quintet, woodwind quintet, saxophone quartet, percussion trio, or other. Patrons of these chamber ensembles will then have the opportunity to hear solo tuba in performance. All composers want to hear their music in formal concert settings.

THE FIRST FAMOUS BRASS PEDAGOGUE

No organized pedagogy for brass existed until cornet-trumpet virtuoso Jean-Baptiste Arban (1825–1889), on the faculty of the Paris Conservatoire, produced his complete method for cornet and trumpet (ca. 1868). To this day, the *Arban Complete Method* and its transposition for bass clef instruments by trombonist Charles Randall and trombone-euphonium virtuoso Simone Mantia are considered biblical by every brass player and teacher.

Jean-Baptiste Arban, born in Lyon, France, was probably the first brass virtuoso to write his own solos. He established the pattern of solo with variations. Several of these solos are published in the back of his *Complete Method for Cornet and Trumpet.* When he established a cornet class in 1868, the cornet was most often used as a secondary instrument by trumpeters, trombonists, and horn players. One of his goals was to prevent the disappearance of the trumpet, whose use and popularity were waning.

AMERICA'S SUPERSTARS

Patrick S. Gilmore (1829–1892) emigrated from County Galway, Ireland, to Boston at age twenty. He was a cornet player and founded his first Gilmore Band at the age of thirty. Improvements of the brass family of instruments inspired the formation of countless military bands around the world. Gilmore became the most important band conductor of the nineteenth century. He presented the first promenade concert in America, in Boston, and created Gilmore's Concert Garden, which became the first Madison Square Garden, in New York City.

Gilmore liked the configuration of the military band, and, relying on the availability of suitable personnel, the 1880 instrumentation of Gilmore's famous band was: one piccolo; two flutes; two oboes; six first, three second, three third B♭ clarinets; two E♭ clarinets; one A♭ piccolo clarinet; one E♭ alto clarinet; one B♭ bass clarinet; two bassoons; one contrabassoon; five saxophones (soprano, alto, tenor, baritone, and bass); four French horns; five cornets; four trombones; one euphonium-trombone; one tenor horn; four bass tubas; one euphonium; one flugelhorn; one pair of timpani; two percussion: bass drum, cymbals, side drum, gong, bells, triangle, glockenspiel, tambourine, etc. Literature available to my research made no reference to salaried band members.

Gilmore, referred to as "America's First Superstar" in the biography written by Rusty Hammer, wrote songs and performed for some of Thomas Edison's earliest recordings. In his later years, John Philip Sousa was a rival, but always an admirer of Patrick S. Gilmore.

John Philip Sousa (1854–1932), born in Washington, D.C., was the son of a trombone player in the U.S. Marine Band. His father enlisted him in the Marines at age thirteen after he tried to run away to join a circus band. After 1880, he conducted the Marine Band under five presidents. When he organized a civilian band, the first concert was two days after Gilmore had died. Sousa established his touring band as perhaps the greatest band of all time. He toured for forty years. The last piece he conducted was "The Stars and Stripes Forever," with the Ringgold Band in Pennsylvania. The musicians who toured with Sousa held him in high esteem.

SOUSA'S MOST FAMOUS BRASS SOLOISTS

Herbert L. Clarke (1867–1945), who gained prominence in the Gilmore Band, became a famous cornet soloist with Sousa. It is estimated that Clarke performed more than 15,000 solos during his career. Arthur Pryor (1870–1942), who encouraged Clarke to write his own cornet solos, is best known as a trombone virtuoso. Sousa referred to Pryor as the best brass instrument soloist he ever had appear with his band. Simone Mantia

(1873–1951) emigrated with his family from Italy when he was seventeen. He played euphonium in many famous bands, and then was principal trombonist in the Metropolitan Opera Orchestra for more than thirty-five years.

COMPOSITIONS FEATURING TUBA

As well as seeking established composers who might be induced to write good parts for tuba, I also sought fledgling composers. I knew that many of the profession's most admired and productive composers started writing great music when they were very young.

Composers who had not yet written for solo tuba might be taken to lunch or, time permitting, invited to visit my studio for a demonstration and discussion. These sessions started lifelong personal relationships with some of the most influential people in the music profession. I tried to encourage all tuba players and tuba students to follow my lead and approach composers with whom they came in contact to write for their instrument—to plant seeds, à la Johnny Appleseed.

Major works by highly respected composers, *Concerto for Bass Tuba and Orchestra* (1954) by Ralph Vaughan Williams and *Sonata for Tuba and Piano* (1955) by Paul Hindemith, strangely enough, were voluntarily written by the composers. These works were a windfall for tuba players. Having these two important compositions provided a powerful reference when approaching other composers.

JUILLIARD PROJECT

In addition to trying to generate more and better compositions for solo tuba, I decided to undertake another project that would broaden my musical horizons. I decided to have one-on-one practice sessions with every string, woodwind, brass, and percussion instrument. I wanted to learn as much as I could about matching intonation, timbre, articulations, blend, and balance. I wanted to mirror the gradations of articulations available to the mallet instruments and drums from the vibraphone or marimba sticks of wood, leather, hard rubber, soft rubber, and felt. As a tuba player, I already had one-on-one experience with brass instruments, but I knew I still needed to explore articulations and nuances with all instrumentalists, particularly studying jazz traditions to which I had not yet had much exposure. It seemed that different music disciplines had special considerations, especially articulations and style. Dr. Persichetti sometimes helped me recruit some of the best and most cooperative student musicians to assist me in my project. I got the impression that, as a composer, he had traveled this road himself.

Often, carrying my tuba and briefcase, I made the rounds of practice rooms, listening for instrumentalists who seemed to know their instrument and who practiced with purpose. When I heard such a player, I listened long enough to work up the courage to rap lightly on the practice room door. When the door opened, I talked fast, like a Fuller Brush salesman, to say what I had to say before the student could interrupt. I quickly apologized for the interruption, complimented the person on what I had heard, introduced myself, explained what I was trying to achieve and asked if he or she would be willing to help me. By making such approaches late in the evening, more times than not, the musicians were about finished with their planned practice sessions and curiosity would win them over. If we became intrigued with our mutual efforts, we would compare schedules and try to arrange another session. This was often the case. I looked forward to each session.

I met many of Juilliard's most serious, most talented, most articulate, and most self-disciplined students through this project. However, I noted that some player/instrument pairings seemed at odds when it came to music making. Some were slow learners who needed more time to season their ability to match timbre and intonation. Others had to set ample technique aside while learning to blend and balance. Still others were able to hear but unable to cope technically. Musicians, like athletes, have physical limits that cannot be overcome. But, also like athletes, their desire and determination can be so focused that they may ultimately be rewarded with career opportunities.

Every now and then, I would encounter a player who was so in control of his or her instrument that player and instrument seemed to mutate into one entity, never at odds technically or stylistically, letting or making music happen appropriately. Such players were destined for a rewarding career in music. I learned a great deal from each one-on-one session.

Occasionally a practice room door was opened by a charming young lady, reassured that it was indeed safe to practice evenings in Juilliard. An invitation for Coke or coffee and getting better acquainted was usually accepted. Later, as I was walking down the hall with some of my brass player friends, a young lady passing by might say, "Hello, Harvey." My friends would then inquire, "Damn, Harvey, how do you know all of these women?" I never told them.

CHAPTER FIVE

Freelancing 101

IT IS DIFFICULT to reconcile that, having had such limited exposure to music for seventeen years, at age twenty I was a Juilliard freshman studying tuba with the great William Bell. I was also a busy freelance musician in New York City, the Big Apple, having a ball! By listening attentively I came to appreciate the finer stylistic concerns of each musical situation I encountered. Everything I was called on to play as a freelance musician was judged by composers, conductors, and other musicians dedicated to authentic interpretations. I listened closely to their discussions as well as their performances. I learned to appreciate, understand, and enjoy why each particular style of music was considered so special. For freelance musicians, coping with all musical styles was essential if they wished to remain on the "call lists."

Active tubists in New York when I arrived included Bill Barber, Karl Bedurke, William Bell, George Black, Don Butterfield, Philip Cadway, Al Corrado, Fred Exner, Fritz Geib, Doc Goldberg, Major Holley, Tex Hurst, Herb Jenkel, Harry London, Jay McAllister, Giovanni Manuti, Joe Novotny, Joe Park, Fred Pfaff, Bill Rose, Joe Tarto, Abe Torchinsky, Vincent Vanni, Giovanni Volpe, and Herb Wekselblatt.

I personally never called a contractor, personnel manager, or conductor soliciting opportunities for myself. Rather, I made a point of making the personal acquaintance of each tubist. I knew early opportunities would come in the form of serving as a substitute player.

FREELANCE BEGINNINGS

I started my first steady job in March 1951, with Bernie Mann's All-American Band at the Roosevelt Hotel supper club. (Bill Bell had recommended me.) For thirty years Guy Lombardo and his Royal Canadians had appeared regularly in the Roosevelt. In 1951, Guy Lombardo made the decision to tour with his orchestra in order to bolster his international popularity. While Lombardo was out touring the United States and Canada, Bernie Mann replaced Lombardo at the hotel. The name "All-American Band" was a friendly international departure from "Royal Canadians." It was a remarkable group whose original personnel were: Saxophones: Red Press, Aaron Sachs, Frankie Sokolof, David Carr, Irving Frank; Trumpets: Chuck Genduso, Irving Applebaum, Sonny Dunham, third trumpet and fourth trombone (replaced by Walter Robertson); Trombones: Billy Rausch, Leon Cox, Eddie Bert; Tuba: Harvey Phillips; Guitar: Steve Jordan; Piano: Irving Joseph; Drums: Sid Bulkin. Through those musicians, I began to learn the New York jazz scene. First stop: Charlie's Tavern.

Located on Seventh Avenue between 51st and 52nd Street, Charlie's Tavern was part of the huge Roseland Ballroom building which took up an entire city block. (In 1956 the ballroom moved one block north.) From Broadway all the way east on 52nd Street to Fifth Avenue was a nonstop row of jazz clubs. Across the street from the Roseland Ballroom on Broadway were Nola's rehearsal studios. Big bands often rehearsed there. It was a good part of town for networking and meeting other musicians. Charlie's was a natural spot for jazz musicians and swing band players to meet.

I heard many stories about the largess of Charlie. He had a soft spot for musicians down on their luck and it was not uncommon for him to slip them twenty bucks out of his pocket or out of the cash register. Nobody ever saw him write down any records of his loans or gifts of money. All the bartenders who worked for Charlie had the same temperament. Charlie never forgot a name or a face.

Well-known instrument technician Bob Giardinelli had a shop on the second floor above Charlie's. This strategic location ensured Bob's success as an instrument repairer, but so did the fact that he was well-liked by the musician community and always willing to go the extra mile. There were several occasions during my freelancing days in New York when I had an early morning rehearsal or recording session and something would break on my instrument. I would telephone Bob at his home and he would meet me at his shop at 8 or 8:30 AM to fix my horn so I could make my gig. He did it out of friendship.

MOONDOG

In 1951, when I was playing with Bernie Mann's All-American Band, most nights the last set ended at 2 AM. So I would often walk over from the Roosevelt Hotel to Charlie's Tavern, open until 4 AM.

It was 2:30 on a balmy mid-April morning and I was walking up Sixth Avenue. The streets were almost void of traffic. Between 42nd and 50th Streets there were no lit businesses at that hour. It was so quiet I could hear the sound of my shoes on the concrete sidewalk. As I crossed 44th Street on the west side of the avenue and stepped up onto the curb, I was startled when the silence was broken by the chanting of vocal sounds accompanied by tastefully balanced beating of small drums. Daytime traffic noise would have rendered the sounds inaudible.

The sounds came from the set-in entrance to an electronics store. They were being produced by a lone bearded musician sitting in the lotus position with drums in his lap. He was a striking figure, obviously tall, clothed in robes fashioned from khaki Army blankets held in place by a sash. This garb was given added theatrical effect by a Viking helmet with two horns. Later, when I saw him standing on a street corner, he was wearing soft leather sandals laced to the knees and held a six-foot-long spear. My initial fear quickly abated so I stopped and listened for a good ten minutes, until the performance ended. As the bearded performer started packing his instruments, I noticed he was blind. Curiosity prompted me to introduce myself. As a fellow musician, I couldn't help but wonder why he would be performing at such a late hour on darkened Sixth Avenue. He told me his telephone number and, because we were both tired, asked me to call him the next day between 3 and 4 PM.

I called him as suggested and was invited to his apartment. His room was full of 78 RPM records, for which he would reach up to a shelf and count tabs, and never fail to get the record he wanted. He told me that oftentimes he couldn't sleep, but he couldn't play in his small apartment, so the street gave him a venue. He told me his birth name was Louis Hardin, but he was well-known to New York musicians as "Moondog." He played homemade percussion instruments and chanted in coffee houses.

Moondog's address at the time was 101 West 44th Street, Room 3, which was close to where I had first heard him perform. He explained to me that in 1929, the year I was born in Aurora, Missouri, he was living in Hurley, Missouri, on a farm with his family, only eight miles away. He told me that as a child, he made Fourth of July firecrackers out of gunpowder from shotgun shells and a cup of powder exploded and took his eyesight.

Somehow he wound up in Greenwich Village, and the family he was living with then decided that the only way he could make a living in New York was to become a street performer. They dreamed up the Moondog costume and mystique and he became very popular. There were times when he simply would stand on the street holding his spear and pleasantly responding to people who showed an interest in him. He never asked for money but I don't think he ever turned any down, either. When I encountered him on the street, I frequently stopped and talked to him and we soon became good friends. I would say, "Hello, Moon!" He would reply, "Harvey, how you doing, man?" He would often reach under his robe, take out some music or poetry, and say, "I've been keeping this for you. Let me know what you think."

He married a Japanese girl who would write down what he dictated. He had a lot of pride in himself and really wanted to be considered a composer and author as well as a performer. He wrote poetry and chant. He had no agent but somehow became so well-known that he recorded with Columbia Records. I was once asked to do a recording with Moon but I couldn't because I was in Puerto Rico at that time. Moondog eventually moved to Germany and died there in 1999.

THE NEW YORK FREELANCE BUSINESS—A WAY OF LIFE

When World War II ended, swing bands rode the crest of the music business. Swing was believed by many to be perfect music. The three major broadcasting behemoths—NBC, ABC, and CBS—not only broadcast the famous swing bands but also had musicians on staff. New York City and the surrounding environs were teeming with venues employing bands which were broadcast over radio throughout the nation. Many hotels maintained active ballrooms or intimate lounges featuring solo pianists or combos with two to six musicians, sometimes with a salon (not saloon) singer. Some hotels became famous through the artist or artists they featured. A few became infamous for the same reason.

From 1935 to 1945, supper clubs and ballrooms were very popular, but the situation quickly changed. One important factor influencing change was the tape recorder, allowing extended uninterrupted recording time, better sound, and corrective splices. Another important factor was the long-playing record. At 33⅓ RPM, it was possible to have sixteen minutes of music on each side instead of three minutes on each side of a 78 RPM record. This was a boon to record companies and to classical performances. The sophistication and improvements made in electronic duplication gave new direction to the recording industry. Another factor was television, which had both bad and good influences. Instead of going out to spend an evening in a ballroom, people were staying home and watching television, often shows that rejuvenated the careers of vaudeville performers.

The cost of touring bands became very expensive and many of the more popular swing band leaders settled down for long stays in major cities. More and more, smaller combos became the rage. Cost became a deterrent to new bands being formed. Innovative performers wanted to improvise and play new music or standard music more adventurously. Breaking new ground were Charlie Parker, Dizzy Gillespie, Thelonious Monk, Art Tatum, Roy Eldridge, Tad Dameron, Miles Davis, John Lewis, Hal Overton, and Gunther Schuller. Meanwhile, trios and quartets played in clubs that usually didn't even have a dance floor. Audiences came, ate dinner, listened to music, and went home.

To get an echo effect, Buddy Williams in Philadelphia utilized a section of three double-bell euphoniums, instead of a section of trombones, in his dance band, the Golden Echoes. Abe Torchinsky was his tuba player. Euphoniums were mostly members of the Philadelphia Orchestra. They were enterprising musicians who wanted to involve themselves in music outside their work with the orchestra. Unfortunately, their maestro, Eugene Ormandy, frowned upon such activities and negated any future membership in a dance band.

The music industry was in constant change, some from within, some from without. It became more difficult to get sufficient bookings to salary a big band. Agents like Willard Alexander (who would later manage, or mismanage, the nineteen-piece Sauter-Finegan Orchestra) were shocked by the closing of ballrooms and theater venues throughout the country. The trend was not believed at first and perseverance prevailed for a time. My busiest time as a freelancer in New York was from 1952 to 1970, and most of the musicians I worked with were jazz players.

The classical scene and the jazz scene consisted of different sets of musicians. I suspect that some players allow themselves to be frightened by unfamiliar styles. In general, it was rare to find a jazz player who could play convincingly in the classical idiom or vice versa. But those few players who could cross freely between the stylistic worlds found themselves in demand as freelancers for recordings and live performances.

1951—NEW YORK CITY BALLET

I played in the New York City Ballet Orchestra from 1951 to 1971. To me, it was the best job in the city, because it allowed me freedom and flexibility. The seasons were short, running from April through May and October through November. And of course there was *Nutcracker* season around Christmas, which was busy but lucrative (sometimes requiring as many as three performances a day). The total was about twenty-four weeks per year. The periods of downtime allowed me to take other gigs like the ice show, rodeo, circus, and opera. Also, most nights we presented three or four short ballets rather than a full-evening ballet and I would often be required only for one or two of the ballets on the program.

The non-*Nutcracker* season consisted of classical ballets: *Cakewalk,
Western Symphony* (both by orchestrator Hershy Kay and commissioned
by the choreographer George Balanchine), and Stravinsky's *Card Game*
and *Firebird.* Also, we played *Seven Deadly Sins* (by Kurt Weill, composer of
The Threepenny Opera), *Prodigal Son* (Prokofiev), and *Age of Anxiety* (Bernstein). Hershy Kay was commissioned by Balanchine to write *Stars and
Stripes,* which was almost a full evening of ballet danced to Sousa marches.
When the "Stars and Stripes Forever" march appeared in the ballet, the
extended piccolo solo was orchestrated by Hershy Kay to be played instead by the tuba. Carmine Fornarotto, trumpet, recalled how surprised
the ballet orchestra was at the first reading. "Harvey took off on the tuba,
jumping, trilling, and all. We just about fell off our seats. And gave Harvey
a thunderous round of applause."

During performances in the ballet orchestra, I would have long sections of rest. For example, I had three short cues in *Midsummer Night's
Dream*—the overture, the wedding march, and one other short piece—and
the rest was all tacet (I did not have anything to play). I would sometimes
fill the time by writing poetry. Here's one that survived:

ALMOND JOY—NUTS TO YOU

*Oh, what a joy it is to play
The Nutcracker Ballet everyday
And not considered part of my wage
I sit where I cannot see the stage
I have to sit next to the drums
They keep me awake till my entrance comes
They play so loud, crash boom! Crash bang!
They're fondly called the Volpe gang!
On my left with his big fat tone
Sits my good friend George with his bass trombone
Though his act is sometimes tough to follow
Giving their best shot are Uber and Swallow
Beside the bones the trumpets sit
They see the stage best from the pit
But ahead of them about four paces
The horns blast notes back in their faces
The clarinet section's another treat
Just watch the way they tap their feet
They kick each other on the shins*

Then claim to be the best of friends
Marilyn stands to saw her box
While the Duke looks at her like a fox
Yes, we're the luckiest in the land
To be part of this contra band.

When my poetic muse deserted me, I found other ways to entertain myself and my colleagues. Arnie Goldberg, the timpani player, sat next to me, and sometimes I would pretend to unscrew his timpani heads while he was in the middle of a long, sustained roll. He didn't know if I was actually unscrewing them or just pretending, but as he was powerless to stop me without interrupting his timpani roll, he had no choice but to trust that I was just joking around (most of the time, I was).

Other times (in rehearsals only) I would play along very softly with another instrument's solo. A favorite was an extended first horn solo in Stravinsky's *The Fairy's Kiss.* It was all in fun. Sometimes in rehearsal, Leon Barzin would grin and throw his baton like a dagger at me. His aim was always perfect. Sometimes I was lucky enough to catch it. Once, I threw it back to him and he caught it just as neatly. Barzin could do more with a baton than any conductor I ever worked for.

Interplay, with music by Morton Gould, was a popular modern ballet in our repertoire. It had a slow "finger snapping" blues motif that held the ogling attention of the audience's first row. Since I was seated directly underneath the stage overhang, I had no view of the stage. David Uber could see the stage, so I asked him, "What's happening during that jazzy blues?" Dave replied, "Two ballerinas are doing slow splits right above your head; too bad you can't see it."

For the next performance of *Interplay* I brought in pieces of an old canvas window shade. I told no one about my intention but I instructed Dave to give me a precise cue when the dancers started their slow splits. On Dave's cue I slowly started tearing a strip of the canvas window shade. The front rows of the audience on our side of the pit gasped and stared open-mouthed at the stage. A couple in the front row leaned over and looked into the pit but couldn't discern where the ripping sound originated. For the enjoyment of our colleagues, when the mood was right, we would repeat our coordinated sound effects when that particular ballet was programmed at City Center.

These gags might not have gone over so well in some other orchestra pits, but at that time the New York City Ballet was like a family. In the City Center, we were all in somewhat close quarters. Musicians, dancers, managers, etc., were all forced to share a relatively small space—and we all knew each other and got along very well. The sense of humor of Leon Barzin and George Balanchine helped cultivate a relaxed but no less dedicated professional atmosphere.

Some of the best gags were reserved for the final performance of a ballet season. On one such occasion, Barzin's expensive conductor's baton was replaced with one extended by a long piece of thin white rubber hose. Barzin, always a good sport, pretended not to notice that his baton was drooping like a piece of cooked spaghetti and conducted much of the final ballet with it. On another such occasion, Bizet's *Symphony in C* was scheduled last on the program. Since there is no tuba in the Bizet, I was in the balcony to watch the performance. The intermission seemed excessive but as the house lights dimmed an elderly man was helped into the pit and onto the podium. The audience began to murmur, "It's Toscanini! It's Toscanini!" The old man was the spitting image of the famous conductor, but it wasn't him. It was George Balanchine dressed in white tie and tails with makeup doing a great imitation of the Maestro. He conducted the entire *Symphony in C* and never revealed his true identity to the audience.

It was the opening of the ballet season and the first time to play *Card Game* and *The Fairy's Kiss*. I remembered Mr. Bell's wise recommendation that since no books of excerpts for tuba were published I should always have a notebook into which I could copy interesting parts for my instrument. During my first years in New York I was never without it. Stravinsky was such an important composer for ballet that I wanted to be sure I didn't overlook anything. After our dress rehearsal of *Card Game* and *The Fairy's Kiss*, I placed the tuba parts on the floor alongside my chair, to claim later for copying them. After putting my tuba away, I remembered the parts but they were nowhere to be found. On the verge of panic, I then noticed that alongside the wall of the pit floor was a half-inch-wide crack. I felt there was hope but I couldn't confirm it until I got two of my stagehand friends to take up an eight-inch-wide floorboard with hammer and crowbar. Voila! I learned later that we were lucky to find them because there were no extra parts available from the publishing house.

THE NEW YORK CITY OPERA

The New York City Opera shared the City Center with the New York City Ballet. As mentioned previously, the New York City Ballet was only in season for twenty-four weeks of the year and the New York City Opera ran during part of the ballet's off-seasons. Many of us played in both the ballet and opera orchestras, although the two organizations were administratively separate entities. I became principal tubist with the opera orchestra from October 1951 to October 1952 while Herb Wekselblatt was called back to duty with the Navy Reserve in the Korean War. Herb later covered the New York Brass Quintet for me during my time in the Army: November 4, 1954, to September 14, 1956.

As fledgling opera and ballet companies, both had to be very watchful of their budgets to the extent that not all orchestra parts could be covered by the correct instrument. For the opera this meant covering stage parts from the pit and for the ballet it meant tuba covering contrabassoon solos in *Age of Anxiety, Till Eulenspiegel,* and, of special interest to me, the famous contrabassoon solo in *Peer Gynt.*

The musicians used to say that the ballet made money and the opera spent it. When we sat down to negotiate raises, it would invariably end up with one more musician being hired instead of the entire orchestra receiving a minuscule raise.

I was hired by the Metropolitan Opera for five performances of *Wozzeck* in 1961, to play the onstage tavern scene that comes early in the second act. One morning I arrived for rehearsal, which was starting with the second act, and John Clark, bass trombone player, asked me if I could cover the pit tuba part being played by Joe Novotny until he arrived. Joe had overslept. I knew the part so there was no problem. Joe and I were of similar size and wore horn-rimmed glasses. So, in the confusion of the stage tuba's not being in place, Joe arrived in the pit but I had to walk onstage, chastised for being late by the conductor, Karl Böhm. It was no problem for me because it was a minor infraction and I was warmed by the applause of the brass players in the pit.

We had a real sense of camaraderie in the New York City Opera low brass section. I remember in particular a performance of *La Traviata* with a visiting conductor who shall remain nameless. At the first rehearsal, before we had played a note, the Maestro told me not to play the "tutti" introduction to the overture, to leave it to the trombones. I suppose he was worried about balance, but it is somewhat offensive for a musician to be told that he is too loud before he has even picked up his instrument. This conductor created further hostility with the musicians by his behavior in rehearsals. So we exacted our revenge on opening night, the performance attended by critics and society in evening dress. The conductor must have known he was in trouble when the trombones never lifted their instruments in response to his opening downbeat and I played the introduction on tuba.

As the performance pressed on, Dave Uber had a fistful of pennies which he would slide off his stand one at a time during quiet moments in the score. If a dropped coin attracted the attention of the conductor and he looked our way, we were all innocence.

ORCHESTRA MANAGER FABRONI

I do not use the word "notorious" lightly, but Joseph Fabroni certainly deserves the description. He was one of the biggest contractors in New York City, handling all the RCA Victor classical recording sessions, and the New York City Opera and various pickup orchestras as well. I believe he was born in Italy. He was short and thin and resembled a ghost. When he tried to smile, it looked like it hurt. He was known for not giving his musicians any slack: if he hired you for a recording, you'd damned well better be there or he wouldn't call you again.

Fabroni played second violin in the *Voice of Firestone* Orchestra. As a violinist he was not above playing footsie with other contractors, which is to say they hired one another when they could.

I stayed on Fabroni's good side for the most part, but I had my round with him over a performance of *Rigoletto* which took place on October 1, 1956. I hadn't performed the opera before, and I knew that the New York City Opera had fourteen hours of rehearsal to put it together. But Fabroni didn't call me. In fact, I met him on the street at 5 PM, just three hours before the opening night performance. He asked me to call him as soon as I got home and he would give me all the details. I told him that I didn't know the opera. I went home and called Fabroni, and he said to come to the City Center. When I got to the theater, trumpeter Ted Weis and trombonist Dave Uber were waiting for me in the pit to talk me through the part. *Rigoletto* is full of little tuba solos and tricky changes in tempo that I would have learned if I had been called for the rehearsals.

As we frantically talked through the impromptu rehearsal, time was ticking down before the start of the opera. Fabroni approached me wearing his most ghoulish smile and said, "Everything all right, boy?"

"No!!" I said.

"What's the matter?"

I replied that if he had wanted me to play this opera he should have engaged me for the rehearsals. Fabroni just shrugged, and said, "You called me, boy. I didn't call you!" With such cheek, I had to laugh. It was typical of Fabroni. Fortunately the performance went well.

AN ASIDE

The first recording session I did in New York City after the 1950 album with Merle Evans was with the New York Philharmonic brass section conducted by Leopold Stokowski in 1951. The RCA Victor recording was called *Early Italian Music* and featured the music of Gabrieli and his contemporaries. I am not credited on the official personnel list, but you can clearly hear a second tuba in some of the antiphonal sections. For that recording I used the King tuba that I had bought from the unknown Italian man while I was on tour with the King Bros. Circus. I wish to this day that I had gotten his name and address so I could have sent him a copy of the LP and thanked him for his kindness.

Recording sessions came fairly frequently and I've long since lost track of how many albums I played on. In one two-week period I played on two recordings by jazz drummers: one by Joe Morello and the other by Gene Krupa (this was his last album). Before one recording session, I was at a musician hangout, Joe Harbor's Spotlight. (Joe had been a bartender at Charlie's Tavern before starting his own place, which attracted classically oriented musicians.) I ran into a string player I knew and asked him if he was on the upcoming session and what the repertoire was. He said he was and that we were recording *Lulu*. I thought immediately of the song "Lulu's Back in Town," then of "Don't Take Lulu." I arrived to find Berg's twelve-tone opera on my stand, which was not quite what I had been expecting.

THE VOICE OF FIRESTONE

The Voice of Firestone was started in 1928 as a weekly radio broadcast featuring symphony orchestra and great opera singers. The program was the brain child of Harvey Firestone, Jr., and his mother, Idabelle Firestone. The opening and closing themes of the show were composed by Idabelle Firestone. After twenty years of weekly radio broadcasts over NBC, the show in 1948 was the first program to be simulcast on both radio and television. In 1951 I was called by David Kulini, contractor for the *Voice of Firestone* Orchestra. He asked if I would fill in for Herb Wekselblatt until his return from fulfilling an obligation to the U.S. Navy. I agreed to do so. The orchestra rehearsed only on the day of the broadcast. It required musicians who knew the repertoire and were excellent sight-readers.

Sometimes we had to transpose in a hurry, usually down a tone for soprano soloists (especially an opera diva singing something not usually in her repertoire) and up a tone for bass voices. Cold weather could influence the range of vocalists. Such decisions were usually made between the rehearsal and broadcast, when a featured singer might need to change the key of a particular work. Also to be admired was the incredible ability of conductor Howard Barlow to memorize each of the musical selections. He never used a score in rehearsal or performance.

The Voice of Firestone broadcast every Monday at 8 PM. The announcer was a gentleman named Hugh James, who had a special quality in his announcer's voice. The orchestra featured many star musicians: principal cello Frank Miller (later principal cellist of the Chicago Symphony), concertmaster Oscar Shumsky, principal clarinet Daniel Bonade, second clarinet Jimmy Abato, principal flute Fred Wilkins, principal horn John Barrows, and first trumpet Bob Cusumano. I played with *Voice of Firestone* for only one year. On the Monday following Herb Wekselblatt's return I started performing with Paul Lavalle's Band of America, also broadcast every Monday evening over NBC. The tuba section during my tenure included, in addition to myself, Don Butterfield, Joe Tarto, Harry London, and Al Corrado.

MISSING CLASS AT JUILLIARD

I had acquired a full-time performing career, and so the fact that I was also a full-time student at Juilliard caused a number of conflicts. Nearly every week I was summoned to the dean's office. Frederik Prausnitz, an assistant dean, would complain about my having missed a rehearsal or piano class, or some other shirking of my studies. One day I missed orchestra rehearsal, but I wasn't required to play since the program didn't call for my instrument. Prausnitz's response was that I should have attended the rehearsal because I could learn by listening to the music of Mozart and Beethoven.

Vincent Persichetti was upset with me when I missed his class until he heard why: I had been playing a concert at Town Hall with conductor Milton Rosenstock. The concert featured the dance music of Mexican composer Silvestre Revueltas, *Redes* and *Homage to Garcia Lorca,* which had prominent solo tuba and solo cornet parts. The featured dance artist was Jose Limon. Persichetti was an admirer of Revueltas, who was Indian. He had been to visit his family in Mexico. At the next meeting of the class, Persichetti made an announcement regarding my absence and proclaimed, "If any of you have an opportunity to play the music of Revueltas, you are automatically excused from class."

An English horn player, who played for *The Voice of Firestone* and the New York City Opera, and who as a youngster began his career in the Radio Orchestra in Mexico City, told me the reason the instrumentation was so odd in Revueltas's music was that he was given each morning a list of the musicians who would play his music that night.

In 1951, still my freshman year, the Philadelphia Orchestra needed a tubist to finish out the season. I was recommended by Abe Torchinsky, their tubist. But the Juilliard Orchestra had a concert, including Mahler's *Symphony No. 2,* which I was required to play. I felt I'd been to the dean's office enough that I didn't want to push it too hard. But I was disappointed not to have the experience of playing with Philadelphia.

Early in the summer of 1951 I was invited to spend a weekend with Mr. Bell and his family at Asbury Park, New Jersey, where he had rented a cottage on the beach for the season. Being an inveterate host of his many friends, he and Aggie entertained other cottage guests plus impromptu come-and-go guests over the summer. He had committed himself to performances with the Asbury Park Municipal Band until the season ended on the Sunday of Labor Day weekend.

Being with Mr. Bell and his family was always a pleasure and an adventure. The humor and rapport of the family made a visitor feel at home. As I basked in the warmth of the Bells, the sun, and the beach, I remembered my first visit to Asbury Park as a windjammer with King Bros. Circus. I thought about making another recording for Mom and Dad, but never got around to it. Asbury Park would be the setting for an important event in my life the following year!

SUBBING FOR BILL BELL

As my second year of studies at Juilliard began, one of my first major assignments was subbing for Mr. Bell with the New York Philharmonic for two weeks while he presented solo performances and clinics in Ohio.

This was my first experience playing with a great professional orchestra. I was challenged. But my greatest fear was that I might in some way let Mr. Bell down. This fear was mollified when the incredible trombone section—Gordon Pulis, Lewis Van Haney, and Allen Ostrander—treated me with respect and assistance, for which I was grateful. The main work for tuba on the series of three concerts was de Falla's *The Three-Cornered Hat,* conducted by Dimitri Mitropoulos. He was inspiring and respected by musicians around the world. My nerves were settled by the encouragement I received from the entire brass section; I was not nervous and I played well. The next week Maestro Efrem Kurtz was guest conductor. For the life of me I cannot remember what works were programmed.

On his return Mr. Bell thanked me and said he had many good reports about my playing. He also said that Mr. Von Praag wanted to see me about a job. When I reported to Mr. Von Praag he informed me that Maestro Alfred Wallenstein had attended the Sunday afternoon performance of the de Falla and called to inquire if I would be available to join the Los Angeles Philharmonic. It was a flattering offer, but I explained to Mr. Von Praag that I was attending Juilliard on a scholarship with Selective Service deferments to complete my education. The alternative was being drafted into the Army during the Korean War. Maestro Wallenstein telephoned me and said he understood my situation and should it change, to let him know.

The position was given instead to Herb Jenkel, who had played with the Cincinnati Symphony and the NBC Symphony Orchestra. Jenkel had been the inspiration for George Kleinsinger's most famous composition. Kleinsinger had noticed Jenkel sitting backstage during a performance and asked, "Why aren't you out there playing?" Jenkel replied, "There's no tuba in this piece. We don't play a lot." Kleinsinger took pity on the plight of the tuba player and, with librettist Paul Tripp, wrote a charming piece for solo tuba, narrator, and orchestra which gives the tuba its deserved solo voice. Thus was born "Tubby the Tuba."

Other orchestras that offered me a position during my career were the Minneapolis Symphony, the Metropolitan Opera, the Boston Symphony Orchestra, and the Philadelphia Orchestra. The only ones I auditioned for were the Minneapolis and the Met, where only five tubists showed up in New York.

I thought I was in musician heaven as a freelance player because there was so much variety, which dissuaded me from putting all my performance eggs in a symphony orchestra or opera basket.

BLIND AUDITION ON BROADWAY

On the fifth floor above Mr. Bell's teaching studio/apartment lived Tilly Knoesel Kennedy with her mother Tante Marie, sister of Bill Bell's studio manager, Tante Lena. Tilly was a businesswoman with offices in downtown Manhattan. I had a standing invitation to watch television with her. One day in mid-January 1952, during a cold New York blizzard, we were watching *Texaco Star Theater* when the telephone rang. Tilly answered and I heard her say, "Yes, he's here. Harvey, it's for you."

I couldn't imagine who would know I could be reached at Tilly's apartment. The gentleman on the other end of the line said, "Harvey, this is Sol Gusikoff, the contractor for the Shubert theatres. William Bell gave me this number and recommends you highly. I need you tonight for a performance of *The King and I* at the St. James Theatre. The storm has shut down the Long Island Railroad and our regular tuba player, Bill Barber, is snowed in. The show is about to start and the tuba part is very important. Are you available to cover the part? How quickly can you get to the theater?"

I told Mr. Gusikoff I would get to the theater as quickly as possible but it would be difficult to get a taxi at 121st Street and Amsterdam Avenue. I hung up the telephone, explained to Tilly, ran down four flights of stairs, put on a tux, overcoat, and scarf, bagged my King bell-front tuba and walked the half block to Amsterdam Avenue. I stood in the cold, blowing snow for about ten minutes when I spotted a car turn onto Amsterdam Avenue from 125th Street. It was a taxi with roof light on, signifying it was empty. I crossed my fingers and it reached me before anyone else flagged it. I waved for the cab to stop and loaded my tuba and myself into the back seat. I told the driver why I was in a hurry and he said, "Sir, with the streets like they are, I ain't in a hurry for nobody. Now you sit back and relax. We'll get there."

We did indeed arrive at the theater and as I entered the stage door, I discovered three people waiting for me. Two took care of my coat and tuba cover while the third person guided me to the basement, through a labyrinth of hanging costumes, leading me to the pit entrance. The show had already started. I quietly climbed into the pit and got as comfortably settled as one could expect. As I looked around seeking help, the flute player sitting next to me pointed at the tuba book. I then realized he had turned the tuba pages as the show progressed. Suddenly it was panic time as he pointed to a part marked "TUBA SOLO" while closing the thumb and fingers of his left hand, indicating the number of measures left before I was supposed to play: five . . . four . . . three . . . two . . . one . . . TUBA SOLO. Fortunately, it went well, as did the rest of the show. Sol Gusikoff was impressed and often mentioned my bailing him out of a difficult situation.

In mid-April 1952, I received another, rather strange, call from Sol Gusikoff. He asked if I could meet him the next day a little after 5 PM at the Blackburn Theatre. "Use the stage door and wait there until I call you," he said, "and bring your tuba. I want you to meet someone."

The next day I found the theater and entered the stage door. I was surprised to find the theater dark except for one bare incandescent light bulb providing gloomy light for an upright piano, a pianist, and a girl singer. I could barely hear a conversation between the singer and people sitting in the middle of the darkened theater. Quiet conversation continued from the theater as the pianist and singer packed their music and left. I waited patiently for Mr. Gusikoff to call my name. After about ten minutes, I heard, "Harvey, are you back there?"

"Yes, Mr. Gusikoff." He told me to bring my tuba to center stage. I did as I was told and he asked me to play *Die Meistersinger* overture. I played it and he next requested the bear solo from *Petrushka*. I complied and he then asked if I could play a popular song. I played "All The Things You Are."

"Very good, Harvey; now wait for us." Two gentlemen came on stage with Mr. Gusikoff and he said, "Harvey, I want you to meet Richard Rodgers and Oscar Hammerstein." I was speechless!

Richard Rodgers was very affable and said, "Sol told us all about you. You play very well." Oscar Hammerstein was less affable but very pleasant. I would see Mr. Rodgers a lot over the next twenty years.

COLONEL HOWARD

In 1952 I received a call from my friend, U.S. Air Force tubist Tony Zavarella. Tony said there was an opening for tuba in the band and he had recommended me to the officers and musicians. Tony knew of the deferments I received from my local (Missouri) draft board to attend Juilliard, which were good for only four years. If I enlisted in a military band, I could avoid being drafted into the infantry. It sounded like a good plan to me. Tony wanted to arrange an audition for me with Colonel George Howard. I discussed this with Mr. Bell and Joe Novotny, who agreed that I had nothing to lose. So I called Tony to go ahead and schedule a date and time when I could play for the Colonel. When it was arranged, Joe happened to be on tour in Washington, D.C., with the NBC Symphony Orchestra and invited me to share his hotel room to save expenses.

On the day of the audition, I reported to the USAF Band headquarters in Bolling Field at 11 AM as scheduled and was escorted to the band rehearsal hall. I had allowed myself a good half-hour to warm up. The Colonel arrived on time with the band librarian ready to fetch anything he might wish to hear. Already on the stand were tuba parts for "The Stars and Stripes Forever," "The Russian Sailor's Dance," "Fingal's Cave," the *Oberon* overture, the *1812 Overture, La Forza del Destino, The Magic Flute, Rienzi,* and some other military band staples. Colonel Howard chose some passages, seemingly at random, and I know I played them well. He even hummed and sang along with some of the parts.

As the audition seemed to be winding down, Colonel Howard suddenly asked for the opening of *Rienzi.* I was happy to oblige. Up to now, other than his requests and mumbled approvals, he had made no comments about my playing. Now, all of a sudden, he said, "It's out of tune."

I said, "I'm sorry, Colonel, but I played it in tune." He asked me to play the opening again. I did so. This time he got even more vocal and accused me of playing a wrong note. I then suggested he sing the passage and I would be pleased to play it however he sang it. The audition was over.

As we exited the rehearsal hall and stepped out onto the porch, quite a crowd was waiting to go to lunch with Tony and me. Tony said, "Well, Colonel, is Harvey going to be with us?" The Colonel retorted, "He has no respect for an officer. My comments were to see how you would react." I said, "That's kind of childish, isn't it?"

Some years later, when I was playing with the Goldman Band, an Air Force Colonel showed up during intermission. It was Colonel Howard. Jimmy Burke, our cornet soloist, said, "Colonel Howard, I'd like you to meet our principal tubist." Colonel Howard turned white and said, "That was such an unfortunate incident."

In future years I appeared often as guest soloist with the United States Air Force Band, conducted by Colonel Arnald Gabriel, who became conductor and commanding officer following the reign of Colonel Howard.

MOVING OUT

By the fall of 1952, I had started to become restless living in one half of a room and keeping the kind of schedule I kept. There was no social life to be had in such living quarters. I remember standing at the bar in the Wellington Hotel one night, drinking ginger ale and discussing that situation with Mr. Bell, Louis Van Haney, David Uber, and Hunter Wiley. I excused myself and walked up Broadway, stopping in every resident hotel and apartment complex along the way. When I got to 101st Street, I found the Whitehall Hotel, clean, with reasonable rates, a short city bus ride to the Juilliard School.

After living in the Whitehall for a few months I moved into a furnished upscale apartment with trombonist Ed Erwin. The apartment was one block from a subway express stop in Jackson Heights, Long Island. John Rossi, horn, visited frequently. He was a good friend to Ed and me and a dynamite cook. We had a walk-in kitchen closet containing almost every spice, arranged in alphabetical order. Sometimes to relax we'd boil some water and make "tea," testing the strength and flavor of each spice selected. We became connoisseurs of herbal tea and learned what spices would enhance certain dishes.

We were all busy freelancers as well as students and often played gigs together. In September, John Rossi and I were hired for the band at the San Gennaro Festival in Manhattan's Little Italy. The band was led by Salvatore Minichini. Streets for some ten blocks were arched over with multicolored lights. A statue of San Gennaro, patron saint of Naples, was carried down various streets on a platform. People ran out from apartments and pinned paper money on the statue for the church (and also for the Mafia, as we found out later). We strolled behind the statue, playing Italian songs, excerpts of operas—some unfamiliar and difficult—and some martial music. It ran all day, beginning at 9 AM, one hour on, one hour off, with two hours for lunch and for dinner. Then at 8 PM we played a concert on a platform. You needed a lip of iron. Minichini had gallon jugs of homemade wine on the platform, which the musicians enjoyed at breaks. At the end of the concert, at midnight, there was one jug left, but when we went to get it, it was gone. John cursed all the way home on the subway. As he was telling the story to Ed, I uncovered my tuba, pulled out the gallon of wine, and gave it to him. He kissed me!

CHAPTER SIX

Carol

THROUGH MUCH of the summer of 1952, I performed as a replacement for Mr. Bell with the Asbury Park Municipal Band, conducted by Frank Bryan. The proud traditions established in the 1930s by conductors and legendary co-founders Arthur Pryor (trombone) and Simone Mantia (euphonium) were carried on. My teacher, William J. Bell, was a close friend of both Pryor and Mantia and loved playing with the band. Bill Bryan (the conductor's brother and band manager) had no trouble recruiting top freelance musicians from New York City.

The concerts were always challenging. Rehearsals were not in the budget, so good sight-readers were always in demand. Like most band programming, each concert started with a spirited march to get the adrenaline flowing. Also featured were major orchestral works transcribed especially for band. Other featured numbers could be Broadway medleys (Victor Herbert, George M. Cohan, Richard Rodgers, etc.) and descriptive medleys (*Battle of Little Big Horn,* circus music, waltzes, galops, trombone smears, characteristic pieces, etc.). Circus music had an excitement and flavor all its own. And there was always a soloist, usually a cornet player like Armando Ghitalla, but sometimes there would be a trombone, euphonium, or occasionally tuba, when William Bell was so inclined! Whatever the musical menu, programs of one-and-a-half hours were always well received by loyal and enthusiastic audiences.

MEETING CAROL—LABOR DAY SUNDAY 1952

Popular diversions on weekends included the beach, the board-walk, and the Asbury Park swimming pool, located diagonally across from the concert pavilion. It could not have been more convenient, especially when the surf was rough and the temperature soaring. The swimming pool was high priority for tourists, younger members of the band, and local residents.

The Asbury Park Municipal Band season was ending on the Sunday of Labor Day weekend. This last concert always had a good turnout of loyal local followers, bolstered by musicians' wives, family members, and girlfriends invited to enjoy a last respite before resuming school and work schedules. Some bandsmen spent the day with their guests, relaxing and swimming at the beach or in the pool, advertised as "The World's Largest Swimming Pool."

I was alone for the afternoon and chose to relax at the pool. I arrived around 2:00. I swam for a half hour or so and as I prepared to climb aboard one of several sunbathing floats, I heard someone shout, "Hey, Harvey!" It was fellow bandsman Jack Urban, a trumpet player and Juilliard student. Our conversation was interrupted by a beautiful girl who swam up and, admonishing Jack, said, "Hey, I thought we were playing tag!" Jack then introduced me to Carol Dorvel, his guest for the weekend. She was there with Elsie and John Richardson, her sister and brother-in-law. We were about to continue our conversation when Carol said she wanted to resume playing tag. As she swam away, she temptingly purred over her shoulder, "Harvey, you want to play?" I tried to hide my enthusiasm as I was told the rules of the game. She scared me. With her white rubber swimming hat pulled down tight over her hair and without makeup she looked as young as fifteen. She was actually just two months shy of eighteen.

That night, before the concert began, I saw her arrive with Elsie and John. She had wonderful long hair, halfway down her back. She was perfectly attired. Her makeup was minimal and perfect. She was easily the most beautiful and desirable woman I could ever have imagined. When I could sneak a peek at her while playing my tuba, I did so. Maybe I was afraid she would disappear. She didn't.

As Carol remembers it, "The concert was in a pavilion on the beach. I sat on a railing. A breeze was blowing and it was a beautiful night. I watched Harvey in profile, dressed in musician's summer attire, a white jacket and black bow tie, which bobbed up and down as he played. After the concert we went to Oscar's Bar, a tradition with bandsmen and their guests. Harvey was sitting at the bar and offered to buy me a drink. 'Thanks,' I told him, 'I already have one.' Later he initiated conversation and asked if I would like to attend the next day's *Voice of Firestone* broadcast at NBC's Center Theater followed by dinner at Gallagher's Steak House. I accepted. When I told Elsie, John, and Jack about accepting a date with Harvey, Jack uttered a warning: 'You'd better watch that guy; he's wild!' So, the next evening for the broadcast and dinner, I brought Elsie and John along to help me tame this 'wild guy.'"

That night in Asbury Park, Ed Erwin, John Rossi, and I made the traditional visit to Oscar's Bar, toasting another successful season of band concerts. We paid our respects to Bill and Frank Bryan as well as members of the audience who attended the celebration. We engaged in conversations with our friends but, because of busy schedules the following day, we agreed to depart early, staying about forty-five minutes. We were in Ed's car and as we departed Asbury Park, I told them about the date I had arranged with Carol. They both congratulated me; Carol had not gone unnoticed by the other bandsmen.

Driving home, the car radio was tuned to a favorite station and everything was normal until new sounds from the radio stopped all conversation. It was a big, swinging band with incredible instrumentation and orchestration, featuring percussion, harp, every combination of woodwinds, and a tuba that was given a melodic line rather than just playing woofy whole notes. We had never before heard such a sound and we were awestruck. It was the Sauter-Finegan Orchestra, given birth in April 1952, in the studios of RCA Victor. The recordings were being broadcast for the first time. Over the next couple of days I made inquiries and confirmed that the tubist was Bill Barber. I learned later that Joe Novotny had played on some of the recordings.

Bill Barber told me the band would be doing its first continental tour booked May to October in 1953. Neither he nor Joe could do the tour and both had recommended me. The band would be rehearsing to prepare for the tour. I made certain I was available. Musicians were eager to play in the band but not all applicants could meet the challenges. The five woodwind chairs all required multiple doubling of instruments. The harp and tuba were featured in unusual solo capacities. Besides a drummer, there were two other percussionists, to play mallet instruments, finger cymbals, and an endless list of other percussion instruments.

For over a decade Bill Finegan and Eddie Sauter had shaped the music of a dozen top-flight orchestras. Sauter wrote originals for Benny Goodman and was responsible for most of Benny's famous arrangements. He also wrote for Artie Shaw, Woody Herman, Red Norvo, and Ray McKinley. Finegan wrote countless scores for Tommy Dorsey and served as the musical genius behind the Glenn Miller Orchestra.

Finegan was in Europe arranging and studying with Nadia Boulanger when he suggested in a letter to his long-time friend Ed Sauter that they set up their own group and do things they had always wanted to do.

Their respect for one another made their partnership unique. The theme song they chose and collaborated on was the very American "Doodletown Fifers," a tune from the Revolutionary War. But mostly, each wrote in his own style. RCA gave them loose rein as they created a unique repertoire that challenged the status quo. No other orchestra of that period had the instrumentation or the creativity to match the genius of Ed Sauter and Bill Finegan. Billy May, Nelson Riddle, and others were impressed and influenced by Sauter-Finegan.

I had given very specific instructions to Carol for Monday evening—Labor Day. She was to meet me at the Center Theater stage door on Sixth Avenue and 47th Street at 7:30 PM, a half hour before the broadcast began. She arrived late, unexpectedly accompanied by Elsie and John. I had to go to the box office for two more tickets, which were free but sometimes hard to come by, since the *Voice of Firestone* NBC broadcasts were very popular. I came back from the box office with three tickets in hand for my guests and quickly arranged for a staff person to escort them to their seats. I still had to call Gallagher's and tell them my reservation would be four people instead of two. I sat down in my orchestra chair a bare two minutes before conductor Howard Barlow gave the downbeat to start playing the famous theme, thus prompting announcer Hugh James to welcome the radio, television, and theater audience to *The Voice of Firestone.*

As Carol remembers it, "After the broadcast and dinner at Gallagher's, we went to Harvey's and Ed Erwin's apartment in Jackson Heights. We put music on the hi-fi, had some dessert hors d'oeuvres and sat on the balcony talking. He showed us a big closet in the kitchen full of spices in alphabetical order. The apartment was immaculate. Then we went home to 186 Claremont Avenue in Manhattan. I believe we dated a couple more times, then Harvey just disappeared. During that year, I kept telling my brother-in-law, 'Why don't you have a party and invite that tuba player?' I remember going to the circus, knowing he played it, and looking over to see him in the band."

Carol attended the circus but never came by to say hello. We were both living in New York at the time. I was in Jackson Heights; she was in Manhattan. Carol impressed me the first time around but, quite frankly, I thought she was much younger than she was. On Tuesday morning, the day after she attended the *Voice of Firestone* broadcast, I continued my attempts to identify the personnel of the Sauter-Finegan Orchestra.

Joe Novotny invited me to come with him to an RCA Victor recording session at Manhattan Center to meet Ed Sauter and Bill Finegan. I was very excited to meet these men, who had well-deserved reputations as two of the great arrangers. The recording session was terrific and the two co-leaders invited me to their upcoming rehearsals in Carroll's Drum Studio. This made good sense because the arrangements called for a great variety of drums and percussion.

The band, which included Harvey Estrin, Joe Ferrante, Joe Venuto, and Mundell Lowe, was incredible, and the tuba parts, for once, were challenging and musically interesting. Going on tour with Sauter-Finegan was one of the first times I felt like the tuba was treated with the sensitivity and respect shown to other solo instruments. I felt like a caged bird allowed to fly free for the first time.

The tour started with a week of performances at Frank Dailey's famous Meadowbrook Supper Club in New Jersey, then Hartford, Boston, Rhode

Island, and New Hampshire. Other stops on the tour included Buffalo, Youngstown, Akron, Cleveland, and cities in Michigan, Wisconsin, and Iowa. We also had two weeks at the Blue Note in Chicago. Arnold Jacobs was there almost every night—he either didn't have a concert with the Chicago Symphony or, if he did, he came after his concert. We stayed at the Croydon Hotel, which was a famous musician hotel noted for its wall beds. You could have space to relax during the day and then pull the bed out of the wall when you needed to sleep. On our first night, I went up to the roof, where they had lounge chairs for tanning. I took the padlock off the door, took it to a locksmith, and had a key made for it. When we came home late at night, if we wanted to watch the sunrise we could go up on the roof and sit on the lounge chairs.

For most of the tour, we were in a rented bus which seated about forty people. There was ample room for personnel and there was a truck that had all our equipment in it. We had more percussion instruments than most colleges or universities have today.

Mousey Alexander was our tour drummer. The Sauter-Finegan Orchestra had some famous drummers during its New York days, including Don Lamond, but they were mostly too busy to come on tour. Mousey was no slouch, though; he had been playing with Marian McPartland before he joined our tour, in Buffalo. He drove a little MG with a trailer that was specially made for his drum equipment. Mousey wasn't a great sight-reader and struggled at first until Eddie and Bill took him aside and said, "Don't even try to read the music. Just play what you think it should be." After that he was perfect.

Everybody who played with Sauter-Finegan will tell you that it was the height of his professional career. The quality of the arrangements and the musical integrity of both Ed Sauter and Bill Finegan were unparalleled. Unlike many arrangers who try to imitate other successful writers, Eddie and Bill were both 100 percent original. With Sauter-Finegan you felt that you were in on something very special.

Gil Cohen, bass trombone, attended many rehearsals and was scheduled to do the tour but had to pull out at the last minute. So I spoke to Bill and Eddie about my roommate Ed Erwin, who was subbing with the New York Philharmonic at the time, and they invited him to come to rehearsal the next day. When I got home, I told Ed and he had no commitments the next day, so he came to rehearsal. That's how Ed Erwin came to be involved in the group.

Almost anything we played would have been considered avant-garde to a regular dance-hall audience. Our booker, Willard Alexander, was the major booker of swing bands in the 1930s, 1940s, and 1950s. His office booked us into ballrooms, which were all over the United States at that time, but the ballroom audiences usually wanted more traditional dance music than what we offered. We should really have been booked as a concert orchestra and not a dance orchestra. The audience might try to dance but usually ended up standing in front of the stage, listening. They would occasionally request polkas or other dance music that was not our style. In some instances it would be obvious that there was no hope of connecting with our audience so, in desperation, we might do a set performing some of Alec Wilder's octets with me playing bassoon parts. Ray Shiner had brought them along, just for our own amusement. This was the first time I played Alec Wilder's music.

Upon our return to New York City, I finished a two-week engagement with Sauter-Finegan at the Band Box followed by some "run out" single engagements. On our return, I received a call from Jay McAllister, tubist of the Radio City Music Hall Orchestra, who had covered some of my freelance engagements. Jay said he heard I was leaving the Sauter-Finegan Orchestra and that he was interested in taking my place, that he was fed up with his job. I was delighted; Jay was a favorite colleague and a terrific tuba player. I gave him recordings I'd made of some of the more interesting and difficult tuba parts, so he wouldn't have to sight-read everything.

I got a job offer from Stan Kenton, who was adding the tuba to his band, in 1954. I was a fan of Kenton but I couldn't accept because I knew I was going in the Army.

Remembers Carol, "The summer of 1953, while Harvey was on tour with Sauter-Finegan, I went with my sister Elsie and her husband John to Alabama to visit John's parents. We were in a place called the Log Cabin. I was introduced to Bob Dabney, whose father was a wholesale grocer. He was maybe twenty-three or twenty-four, bald, with a catfish mouth. He wanted to take me out in Alabama. There was no way that I was getting in a car in Alabama. He was coming to New York and asked if I would show him the town. I said sure.

"He stayed at the Plaza. His aunt came in four days later. We hit everyplace in town—the Four Seasons, Sardi's, the Stork Club, etc. We ate at Lindy's one night. We took a cab to Rockefeller Center, two blocks away; we were going to go to the Rainbow Room but it was closed. The flags around the skating rink were blowing in the strong summer wind.

"During that summer, the talk was of the Sauter-Finegan Orchestra. They were the rave. I said, 'I hear they're at the Band Box, which is downstairs next to Birdland.' He said, 'Or, do you want to go someplace romantic?' Pee Wee Marquette, a dwarf, stood in front of Birdland greeting customers. It was about 9:30. We listened to Sauter-Finegan and had drinks at a small table. All night I was looking at the tuba player, trying to remember his first name. At 2 A M, the band was on a break at a table just behind us. We got up to leave. Halfway up the stairs to Broadway I turned around and said, 'Wait a minute, Bob.' I walked back to the table. The name came to me: 'Harvey.' He stood up and said, 'Monument 3–8927.' Harvey couldn't remember my name, but had memorized my telephone number. He asked about Elsie and John. I said, 'Why don't you call us sometime?'"

Two of the people I was sitting with were Fred Exner and his wife. He was the tubist with the Guy Lombardo Band.

Carol says, "I was told that after I left, Fred's wife said, 'I hear wedding bells,' predicting our marriage. Harvey called the next day, and the next day and the day after that. We went out every night."

The ballet season restarted the very next week. Carol came with me to my engagements, whatever they might be. One date in particular was a recording session with Stokowski at the Manhattan Center on 34th Street. I told her that nobody was ever allowed at a Stokowski recording but, if we could get there early, I could put her behind a column in the balcony and she could stay there and listen if she didn't make any noise. I gave her a signal to meet me at the elevator when I would be through. Stokowski never saw her.

One of the pieces being recorded that night had no tuba. Stokowski didn't rehearse. He started on the upper left and went all the way through, no stops. He would take the time to go into the recording booth and listen and make notes, then come out and, talking to the orchestra, fix the things he wasn't pleased with. He'd take a break and then we would play top to bottom again, no stops. Usually that take was what was released.

Joseph Fabroni, the contractor, was sitting at a little table next to the door, making notes. I walked up to him. They were getting ready to start another piece, so we whispered to avoid interrupting the recording. "What do you want, boy?"

"I have nothing in the other piece. I'm going."

"Jesus Christ, boy, don't you know the Maestro, he does everything over again?" He had just saved me from missing the second take of my piece. I had to tell Carol to go down to the New Yorker Hotel lobby and wait for me.

DON'T MARRY THAT MAN—HE'S TOO OLD FOR YOU

In January I received a call from NBC asking about my availability to do *The Lucky Strike Hit Parade* with Raymond Scott's band. I was needed to play on an arrangement of "When Yuba Plays the Rhumba on the Tuba Down in Cuba." It was a duet feature for solo tuba and voice. The singer would be Dorothy Collins, a regular on the show and the wife of Raymond Scott. The rehearsal and broadcast times were open on my schedule so I booked it. I called and told Carol about the booking and she called all her many aunts, people she worked with, and other friends. She told them to watch the *Hit Parade* broadcast, because the man she was going to marry (news to me, she hadn't let me in on it) was being featured on the show, performing with Dorothy Collins. What neither of us knew was that the *Hit Parade* choral director, Gene Lees, was made up as a bald, mustachioed old Cuban tuba player in a very amusing way while I played the tuba off camera. I found out about Carol's embarrassment the very next day. I was told her telephone just about rang off the wall with everyone advising her, "That man's too old for you! Don't you dare marry him!"

Remembers Carol, "They all thought the bum was my fiancé, and the looks I got at work were really wild. I kept saying, 'That's not him! That's not him!' . . .

"From the time we started our almost daily dating I was impressed with how many people knew Harvey. In just about every city block there would be three or more people greeting him. It boggled my mind. I was born and raised in New York and if we met a neighbor downtown it was an occasion."

MARRIAGE PROPOSAL AND ACCEPTANCE

In Carol's words, "We were having dinner on Thursday, February 18th, 1954, at the Sheraton Hotel on 56th and Seventh, prior to a ballet performance, when Harvey looked at me and said, 'You can't go to work tomorrow.'

"'Why?'

"'If we're going to get married Monday we have to get blood tests and a license tomorrow.'

"This was his proposal. I went home and told Mom and Dad. The next day, we went to get the license and blood test."

From City Hall we walked over to Wo Kee's in Chinatown and had lunch, then walked up Mulberry to Grand Street to Ferrara, an Italian bakery that supplied many New York restaurants. We had espresso and cannoli. Carol was always impressed with how many friends I would meet and greet on the street. Between Broom Street and Houston Street I pointed out a little man crossing the street about two blocks away. Carol said, "I suppose you know that man." I replied, "Of course, that's Adolph." She had a good laugh, thinking I was kidding, until we were close enough to say hello and have a brief conversation. Adolph worked in one of the offices in the musicians union and had been a violinist at one time.

I picked Monday evening for the wedding because on that holiday weekend the New York City Ballet was doing a performance on the afternoon of Monday, February 22, Washington's birthday, and I had Monday and Tuesday nights off. I called the Roosevelt Hotel and reserved the Bridal Suite for three nights.

As Carol tells it, "I had to get a dress and a church to get married in. My sister Elsie and I went shopping on Saturday and I bought a dress at Henri Bendel. The dress was ankle-length and powder blue because that was the one that fit! I got shoes to match at Andrew Geller. I tried to book the Riverside Church on Claremont Avenue, where I attended regularly, just two blocks from Mother and Dad's apartment, but they had let most of their staff off for the holiday weekend and couldn't accommodate us. We called Christ Church Methodist on 60th Street and Park Avenue and they were able to schedule us."

There was no time to send out invitations. I invited the ballet orchestra and anybody I knew who I met on the street. I would say, "What are you doing at 7 PM Monday? Want to go to a wedding?" They'd say, "Whose?" I'd answer, "Mine."

We had a candlelight service. The chapel of the church was all blue mosaic tile, inlaid with gold, which serendipitously turned out to match the color of Carol's wedding dress. The church was full. Arnold Goldberg, timpanist and later manager of the New York City Ballet Orchestra, came and took beautiful three-dimensional slides and photos of our wedding. Ed Erwin was my best man. Carol's matron of honor was her sister Elsie, who also gave us a reception in her apartment. After the reception, Carol and I went to the Roosevelt Hotel to check into the Bridal Suite. As we were about to enter the elevator, the door opened and Fred Exner and his wife stepped out. They had been sitting at the table with me the night Carol and I met for the second time; Fred's wife had predicted, "I hear wedding bells." When we told them we were at the Roosevelt Hotel to claim our reserved Bridal Suite, they were surprised and delighted.

After we were married, we moved into Carol's parents' apartment in New York for a short time; then we took an apartment in Ridgefield, New Jersey. It was just across the George Washington Bridge, about half an hour from midtown Manhattan. Luckily most rehearsals or recording sessions would go from 10 AM to 1 PM, or 2 PM to 5 PM, or 7 PM to 10 PM, which usually allowed me to miss rush hour traffic. If I had a morning rehearsal, for example, I would leave at 9 AM when everyone else was already at work.

Carol had worked as a secretary for Salmon Management, a real estate company, while we were dating. She quit her job once we were married and usually came with me to recording sessions and other gigs. Friends and colleagues quickly got accustomed to seeing us together.

From the time I first met Carol, I became aware of the outgoing nature of her family. Her mother and father, Anna and Alex Dorvel, brother Arnold and wife Joy Dorvel, sister Elsie and husband John Richardson, and of course a flock of aunts and uncles, kept a close eye on Carol. Over the years

I enjoyed being adopted by the family. John and Elsie opened their house, hosting many parties and celebrations of my musician activities. There were parties with Manny Albam, Ed Sauter, Hoagy Bix Carmichael, New York Brass Quintet, John Carisi, and Alec Wilder. In my memory it seems like one big nonstop party with John and Elsie, Arnold and Joy, hosting at their respective homes. Knowing them was to love Carol. Other memories include hosting John and Elsie and their month-old infant, Leslie, in our apartment in Maryland. To be cuddly safe, she was assigned the bottom drawer of our bedroom chest of drawers. There were many other instances that helped to cement our thoughts and concerns of one another.

CHAPTER SEVEN

Chamber Music,
New York Brass Quintet

WORLD WAR II ENDED in August 1945. By the fall of 1946, Juilliard, like many other conservatories and college and university schools of music, was crowded beyond capacity by returning servicemen taking advantage of the GI Bill. Few schools were prepared for such a windfall. Juilliard, with only two orchestras and no wind ensemble or band program ("band" was a four-letter word), could not offer sufficient performance opportunities for the abundance of brass players, including seventy trumpets! An enterprising trombone student named Julian Menken became aware of the early music for brass published by Robert King Music and took it on himself to acquire copies. He then organized a large New York Brass Ensemble (NYBE) and prevailed upon his friend Samuel Baron, a renowned flutist finishing a graduate degree in conducting, to coach and conduct the group. Baron, with his enthusiasm for chamber music, was perfect. Earlier he had founded the New York Woodwind Quintet.

As Baron molded the brass players into an outstanding ensemble, Menken began booking concerts, often sharing programs with the New York Woodwind Quintet. In addition to concerts, Menken booked a number of radio broadcasts and two LP recordings that are historic. The first NYBE recording on the Esoteric/Counterpoint label presented *Seven Can-*

zoni of Giovanni Gabrieli and won a Grand Prix du Disque in Paris. The second recording on the Period Records label was also praised by critics and presented Gabrieli's *Sacrae Symphoniae* (multiple antiphonal choirs) conducted by Samuel Baron. The larger antiphonal works of Giovanni Gabrieli were masterpieces of the Renaissance but the known library of large brass ensembles was not sufficient to sustain series of concerts. Nor were there supporting audiences or sponsors for unknown ensembles.

From 1950 to 1953, several outstanding members of the NYBE were leaving Juilliard to accept important orchestra and teaching positions. The future of brass chamber music was uncertain. In the meantime, Julian Menken had conversations with Robert King and joined his in-depth research of early brass music and literature. Their successful efforts are well documented.

Robert Nagel, trumpet, an icon and original member of the NYBE, never lost his dedication to the music he became so expert at interpreting. Nagel and Sam Baron agreed that the bulk of brass chamber music being discovered was in four parts, but by having a tuba double the trombone part one octave lower, the music took on a richer sound. They also noted that the New York Woodwind Quintet was maintaining a steady schedule of demonstration concerts in elementary through high schools, under the auspices of Young Audiences, Inc. A brass quintet, with two trumpets, horn, trombone, and tuba, would fill a void in demonstration concerts. But four things had to happen before a brass quintet could be successfully marketed: (1) an authentic library of early, classical, and modern repertoire had to become available via tireless research, inspiration, and sometimes expensive commissions; (2) musicians selected for the quintet would have to be dedicated to brass chamber music; (3) audiences needed to be won over by heretofore unheard brass chamber music; and (4) agents and managements must be convinced of the group's viability and future.

Robert Nagel, who was teaching at Yale University at the time, started thinking about who would be in a brass quintet that he was forming. He chose an outstanding student, John Glasel, for second trumpet. He also chose two colleagues from Little Orchestra Society, Frederick Schmidt, horn, and Erwin Price, trombone. New York Brass Ensemble tubist Bill Barber had first consideration but his busy freelance schedule and recent commitment to a full-time public school teaching position took him out of the loop of rehearsal possibilities.

In 1950 I acquired a CC tuba at my teacher's insistence. He urged that I switch from BB♭ to the CC tuba. Being more comfortable with the BB♭ tuba, I was slow to make the change. It was at this precise time that Bill Barber asked me to cover a rehearsal with the New York Brass Ensemble. I checked my calendar and said yes. I thanked him for the opportunity to play with the NYBE and asked if the tuba parts were available for study in advance. He said he had no idea as to who had the music, but he knew all the music would be at the rehearsal. He then gave me a couple of names with telephone numbers on the chance that one of them might have the parts or know where they could be found. I called both numbers several times without any luck. I arrived at the rehearsal studio a half hour early, so I could at least study the tuba parts minimally. Unfortunately the music didn't arrive until ten minutes before the rehearsal was scheduled to start.

I was excited; it was my first opportunity to perform with the NYBE. I was also apprehensive, since this would be my first appearance with the CC tuba exclusively. Up to now I played most professional engagements on my Conn BB♭ sousaphone (in the circus band) or King BB♭ recording tuba (in the Bernie Mann and Buddy Williams dance bands). I only used the CC when there was ample time and opportunity to prepare the music in advance. I played a couple of scales, generally warming up with everybody else. I was given a folder marked TUBA and rifled through the parts. In a quick study of the music, near panic set in as I realized my uncertainty of sight-reading and instantaneously choosing correct valve combinations between the BB♭ and CC tubas. Now I knew why Mr. Bell suggested that I put the BB♭ aside until I had thoroughly learned and felt comfortable with the CC. I had thought it was an impractical consideration with my busy schedule of engagements on the BB♭.

Sam Baron was conducting and coaching the ensemble. The first two pieces were fairly easy, though not without transposing problems for me. Sam and the ensemble were understanding and patient. Then Sam called up Gabrieli's *Canzona Per Sonare No. 2,* which the other players could probably have played from memory. Not me. I had never seen it. I was embarrassed, and the harder I tried to concentrate, the more confused I became.

It was the longest hour I have ever experienced. The other players were amused by my struggle. I swore it would never happen again. It didn't.

Robert Nagel, who was there, recalled, "He didn't do too well. But we were impressed with his good tone, technique, musicianship, and determination. We asked him to join the New York Brass Quintet (NYBQ)." I joined. The NYBQ was the only professional concertizing brass quintet anywhere.

The year 1954 was a halcyon one for the quintet. It proved to be the year the group resolved once and for all the proper name of the New York Brass Quintet. The New York Brass Ensemble became the title used for brass ensembles exceeding a group of five players. If Juilliard had had a wind instrument or band program, there might never have been a New York Woodwind Quintet, New York Brass Ensemble, or a New York Brass Quintet. But Juilliard didn't have those things, which left the door open for innovative thinking and discovery.

By 1954 Bob Nagel had chosen the New York Brass Quintet personnel, players who could sustain a good livelihood apart from the quintet, who enjoyed the challenges of brass chamber music and saw potential for that medium, who made time for rehearsals, and who had a good stage presence in formal concerts and before schoolchildren and their teachers. The rehearsals often started at 10 or 11 PM, after commitments to ballets, operas, symphonies, recordings, or television engagements had finished.

The pioneering work of Leon Barzin and his National Orchestral Association concerts for schoolchildren inspired Nina Collier to found Young Audiences, Incorporated. The quintet was fortunate to join her roster because it gave us a venue to perform and perfect our repertoire. Between 1954 and 1958 the NYBQ presented more than four hundred lecture demonstration concerts in schools throughout the East Coast, often five concerts a day, for a week or more at a time. These were some of our earliest concert experiences together. Young Audiences became a good base of income for the quintet and performing our repertoire many times helped us to blend, balance, and improve our concert routine.

Commitment to school demonstration concerts for Young Audiences, Inc., often required quintet members to sacrifice important higher-paying freelance recordings and concerts. Nonetheless, gratification started to materialize as composers became aware of this new chamber music outlet for their compositions. A trickle of new works became a flood as the New York Brass Quintet and composers sought each other out.

We experimented with and learned approaches to teaching that we may never have considered otherwise. I remember one special concert in Baltimore in 1954 which we performed for an audience of handicapped children. We planned an intermission halfway through in case the children would tire. We also wanted the kids to have individual hands-on contact with the instruments. I had noted a little girl I estimated to be eight years old waving her arms when we played. When we took intermission, I walked down and said to her, "My, you're a good little conductor." She replied in a voice of a much older person, "Oh, I'm not conducting. I'm dancing, because I never could walk."

Most impressive to me was a group of five or six deaf children who seemed to enjoy the concert. Through their teacher, I invited them to hold the bell and feel the vibrations of the tuba while I played "Pop Goes the Weasel." The teacher asked the children if they would like to sing it with me. Not only were they game to sing along but, by some unknown alchemy, they sang it in pitch as well.

I'd have kids come up to try to play the tuba. Some would produce a terrible sound. I'd say, "You seem to have some potential for the tuba." If a kid produced a gorgeous sound, I'd say, "This person shows too much talent. He should try trumpet or trombone."

Sometimes if a kid could make a good sound on the tuba, I'd teach him to play quarter notes in march tempo and I'd have the other members of the quintet start in with the trio section of "The Stars and Stripes Forever." It didn't matter if the kid was playing actual pitches or not—it still sounded like he was playing along with the group. Then I would say to everyone, "Wow! See how easy it is to play the tuba?"

We once played in Philadelphia at a very exclusive high school, and we spoke of playing "tower music," referring to the trumpeters in ancient times who would play from the top of a tower to reach the most citizens and pass news. Some of the best examples of this come from German composer Johan Pezel. The students laughed every time we talked about tower music.

We later learned that the restrooms at this historic school were contained in a tower at each end of the building. "Tower music" to them was toilet music!

The bulk of our repertoire was from the Renaissance with transcriptions of the baroque. Most of this music was researched and adapted to modern brass instruments by Robert King, a Boston baritone player who in 1940 dreamed of touring with his Boston Brass Quartet. His dreams were dashed by Selective Service following America's entrance into World War II. Disappointed, but possessing New Englander savvy, King began publishing the early brass music he had researched with his own music publishing company in his hometown of North Easton, Massachusetts. His first publication was *Music for Queen Mary* by Henry Purcell.

The *Sonatine for Brass Quintet* (1951) by Eugene Bozza was premiered by the NYBQ at Castle Hill in Ipswich, Massachusetts, on August 6–7, 1954, in a series of programs shared with dancer Geoffrey Holder and his Jamaican Drummers. The *Sonatine*, a catalyst for inspiring new compositions that leveled the playing field for all brass instruments, was especially beneficial for the tuba. It required equal agility, technique, rhythmic precision, and tonal control from each player. Composers were challenged by this newly discovered high level of brass chamber music playing. They were also impressed by the endurance required and sustained by five brass players performing full concert programs, compared with the endurance required of brass players in the bulk of symphonic repertoire. Composers recognized this new potential for extended brass technique and exploited it in their new brass quintet compositions. Robert Nagel has chronicled some one thousand works written for the NYBQ since the Bozza *Sonatine* was premiered. The NYBQ music library and other archival materials are on deposit with the Yale Music Library.

In the early years of touring and concertizing, the NYBQ often relied on two specific works to contrast Bach and Handel transcriptions (and the early music of Gabrieli, Pezel, Holborne, Purcell, Gottfried Reiche, Anthony Holborne, and Tielman Susato). These two works were *Quintet No. 1 for Brass Instruments* by Victor Ewald (obviously influenced by Tchaikovsky), a great feature just before intermission, and, as a concert closer, the Eugene Bozza *Sonatine,* which featured technical and dynamic fireworks that left audiences breathless. Attending brass players and composers were impressed that the quintet could play such a piece at the end of a full evening's concert. They were not accustomed to hearing from brass such musical nuance, technical precision, endurance, balance, and blend. After one concert, I overheard someone say, "Those guys are just a bunch of show-offs!" A critic of one of our performances said we were musical alchemists, turning brass into gold.

For thirty years, from 1954 to 1984, the N Y B Q concertized throughout the United States, Canada, and Europe. There were many rehearsals, many premieres, many concerts, many recordings, and many tours. This "brass chamber music icon" has inspired and encouraged continued growth in numbers of ensembles and numbers of loyal supporting audiences. The future looks bright for brass chamber music.

Before the N Y B Q—the first-ever brass quintet—there was no viable ensemble for the tuba. The result of our success was to stimulate the writing of music using tuba. Our success also influenced colleges and universities that didn't have a full-time tuba professor to create full-time positions for tuba so they could have a faculty brass quintet. This elevated brass instructors to the level of artists in residence. From 1960 to 1975 full-time college teaching positions for tuba grew from one (Rex Conner, University of Kentucky) to more than one hundred, in virtually every state. I don't think there has ever been as dramatic an increase in employment for any instrument.

When the New York Brass Quintet gave a concert on a college campus, each quintet member also gave a master class and clinic on his particular instrument; I gave my first master class with the N Y B Q. These sessions generated interest and activity within the host institution. In visits with the dean or department head or sometimes the college president, bolstered by support from awakened colleagues serving on the faculty, I made the case for the college hiring a full-time tuba professor.

The call to serve in the Korean War was omnipresent. So, in 1954, while the quintet was performing concerts in Baltimore, my friend Paul Lavalle arranged an audition with the Navy Band for me. I knew that I had entered my fourth and final year of deferment from Selective Service and I was likely to be drafted unless I enlisted in a military band. The Navy Band seemed like a good choice.

While I was scheduled to audition for the Navy Band, Leon Barzin, following the guidelines for service band recommendation, wrote the following letter:

To Whom It May Concern:

I am glad to recommend Harvey Phillips as an outstanding musician who has had experience in all fields of performance, including services for the Barnum and Bailey Circus.

His sight reading ability is excellent.

His technique is good.

He played the tuba for the NY City Ballet.

He grasps new ideas very quickly.

He has played under my direction for 7 years.

He works hard and is very cooperative.

Very truly yours,

Leon Barzin

Musical Director, The National Orchestral Association, Inc.

I went to the Navy Yard in Washington, D.C., and auditioned for Commander Brendler and his assistant, Warrant Officer Townsend. I remember that after having played all of the "warhorse" band transcriptions, they brought out a special arrangement of *Till Eulenspiegel,* adding sight-reading to the audition requirements. When the audition was over, Commander Brendler encouraged me to enlist in the Navy as soon as possible and said that the principal tuba position would be reserved for me. I have a copy of a letter from Paul Lavalle to Commander Brendler congratulating him for having acquired my services with the Navy Band.

I had four months to join the Navy, after which the Selective Service Board was free to send me a notice of induction. I was busy with the New York Brass Quintet and other freelance activities so I didn't enlist right away. It was a mistake that, had circumstances played out differently, could have proved catastrophic.

PRECEDENT-SETTING ENGAGEMENTS

During that summer of 1954, the New York Brass Quintet presented several concerts in the Castle Hill Series, hosted at the Crane Estate in Ipswich, Massachusetts. It was a grand old house, with many bathrooms and gold-plated faucets. As we looked out from the terrace, all we saw was the green ocean. The terrace had been constructed and elevated in such a way that the nearby roads and cars were invisible.

Also in 1954, Elaine DuPont commissioned a work for the Brass Quintet for the procession and recession of her wedding. The wedding was in the garden at the DuPont estate in Hyannisport, Cape Cod. The night before the wedding, there was a party on the beach featuring a small jazz group called Les Six, including the jazz trumpet playing of John Glasel. Carol and I had checked into our motel and were on our way to the beach party when I got lost, so I pulled into the driveway of an impressive mansion, drove up to the front door, got out of the car, and rang the bell. A rather dapper gentleman properly attired in a smoking jacket said, "Can I help you?" I asked if this was the DuPont estate.

"No, this is the Phillips estate."

"Well, that's my name, too."

"Where is your home?" he asked.

"Missouri," I said.

He said, "Well, we'll have to talk tomorrow at the wedding." Then he gave me directions to the DuPont estate. We enjoyed the beach party immensely. It was a truly authentic New England clambake. They had scooped a hole in the beach, lined the hole with stones, built a fire, and, when the stones were hot, alternated layers of seaweed, lobsters, seaweed, potatoes, seaweed, corn on the cob, seaweed, clams, and mussels. The mound was then covered airtight with canvas. It was fantastic.

The next afternoon, we played for the wedding, followed by the wedding reception. A hardwood dance floor was installed on the lawn. Dance music was provided by the Meyer Davis Orchestra. Wedding gifts were displayed in the multiple garage area and heavily guarded by Pinkerton.

As a concertizing chamber ensemble, we were given opportunities to meet and converse with some of America's wealthiest families. Music has a curious way of equalizing the social lives of audience and artist together.

That first year, 1954, Young Audiences kept the New York Brass Quintet busy until mid-June when school finished. We did concerts in August at the Crane estate. We also played at other important venues in the Boston and New England area that summer. Many friends that we made would later come back into our lives. Some would be board members at the New England Conservatory when I went to work there in 1967.

After we finished that busy summer, Carol and I took a trip to Marionville, Missouri, to visit my parents. We left around the last two weeks of August. It was a very important trip because Carol had not yet met my parents, although we had been married for six months by that time. It was also Carol's first airplane ride. I knew Carol and I knew my parents, so I couldn't see any way they wouldn't get along. Sure enough, they fell in love with each other right away.

DRAFTED!

While we were in Missouri, a notice of induction arrived at Carol's parents' house. Carol's mother read it to me over the phone. I was to report to the reception center in Newark for a physical examination and possible induction into the Army. My deferments were up; I was being drafted! I thought I had a standing offer of employment with the Navy Band and all I had to do was show up at the Brooklyn Navy Yard with the paperwork that Commander Brendler had given me and I would enlist in the Navy and be shipped off to the Navy Band. So I thought.

When we returned to New York, I scheduled a visit to the Navy Yard and arranged an interview. When I arrived and expressed my desire to join the Navy, I was given the standard form with a list of questions. The last instruction on the page was to check a box for "I have/have not received an induction notice from my Selective Service board." I dutifully checked the proper box and I was told by the lieutenant in charge that unless I could bring a letter of release from my draft board, there was no way they could accept me. I had been drafted and it was too late to enlist. I contacted my draft board in Missouri but they were not keen on granting me a letter of release.

I had only a few weeks before I had to report to Newark on November 4 at 5 AM for my Army physical, and, if I passed, I would go straight on the bus to Fort Dix, New Jersey. As the date approached, I called Bill Barber and asked him if he could cover the New York City Ballet performances for the coming Friday, Saturday, and Sunday, because I had to report for my Army physical on Friday morning. My plan, I explained to Bill, was to fail the physical and celebrate all weekend. But if I passed it, he would have a job with the New York City Ballet Orchestra for the next two years. Carol and I tried everything we could think of to sabotage my health, including staying up all night before the physical. But, lucky for Bill Barber and unlucky for me, I passed the exam and was transported by bus to Fort Dix, along with other draftees. Herb Wekselblatt subbed for me in the New York Brass Quintet while I was in the service, which was fair because I had held a few of his jobs (at *The Voice of Firestone* and New York City Opera) while he had been called back to the service a few years earlier.

At Fort Dix I commenced infantry training. Our drill sergeant was, like most, a veteran of Korea, and had been highly decorated. I suppose the higher-ups wanted some of his greatness to rub off on us recruits. He was one of the only understanding Army people I talked to. He didn't play mind games with his squad, which some other drill sergeants did. He was very fair, regardless of the age of the recruit. And he was certainly well-equipped to train infantry! Duck walking, jogging in the early morning, twelve-mile marches, crawling under live fire—we were put through all the standard paces.

Because of my single semester of ROTC experience at the University of Missouri, and also because I was twenty-four and most of the draftees were eighteen, I was entrusted with the position of squad leader, which included the duty of marching groups of recruits around. In an effort to depart from the standard marching songs, I started humming a certain melody that I knew but couldn't remember the name of. My troops eventually learned the melody and would hum it with me as we marched. We got "thumbs up" from various majors and colonels as we marched by—"That is a really spirited group!" they would say. Later I phoned Carol to ask if she remembered the name to the tune. She said, "Oh, that's the Russian Army Song." I tried to stop the song, but my squad had all learned the tune and liked it because it was such a stirring melody—why did I suddenly dislike it? At this point I thought it wise to keep my mouth shut, so I was overruled and the squad continued to sing. I tried my best to look patriotic as we marched.

It was a difficult time for Carol and me. It was the first time we had been apart since we were married in February of that year. It was more difficult for Carol than for me because I was kept busy through basic training and she was left alone. After two weeks, it was possible for her to visit me every weekend but I worried about her driving alone. The first time she drove to see me she had just gotten her driver's license the previous week. She had to leave at 4 AM to be at the Fort by 6:00 so we could spend the day together, and by the time she made the seventy-mile return journey it was already dark. I had asked her to pick up my check from the ballet, which hadn't been ready when I left. So, back in New York City the same night as the first round trip, she stopped and picked up her mother and headed to the City Center. Entering Central Park on 59th Street, they were pulled over for rolling through a stop sign. Carol burst into tears, having already been wound up from the stress of the long drive. This in turn caused Carol's mother to burst into tears. The poor police officer, confronted with these two wailing women, and noticing Carol's newly acquired driver's license, decided to let them off with a warning.

I had made it known to my Army superiors that I wanted to get into a band, but I was rebuffed by an uncooperative Orderly Room staff who insisted that I had failed the recent auditions. That was not true. I had not played an audition because they had already finished when I arrived. But I was unable to convince anyone otherwise and attempts to persuade people of my qualifications fell on deaf ears. I had Carol call Paul Lavalle, conductor of the Band of America, and ask for his assistance. Paul had set me up with the Navy Band audition that summer and I hoped he would come through for me again. He called a friend, a general in the Pentagon who was in charge of all music in all the services, and this general found that the United States Army Field Band had an opening for a tuba player.

He called Major Whiting, conductor of the band. Major Whiting agreed to take me on, a draftee, based on my reputation and the recommendation from Paul Lavalle.

The Army allowed us a week's pass for the Christmas holidays and we spent our time at Carol's parents' apartment. At that time, the Sauter-Finegan Orchestra was performing at the Statler Hotel across from Pennsylvania Station. We went to visit the band and it took some time for the band members to recognize me. None of them had seen me since I'd played with them on the 1953 tour. Back then I weighed 210 pounds; now I had dropped to 184 pounds, with a thirty-two-inch waist and size forty-two suit. As soon as the guys recognized me, they laughed so hard that the music had to stop.

Carol and I went with some of the guys in the band across the street to a nice bar and ordered drinks, and they wouldn't serve me without an ID because, being so trim, I looked under eighteen. I had just turned twenty-five. They served Carol although she was five years younger than I was.

THE ARMY FIELD BAND

I reported to the Army Field Band the last week of January 1955. I had finished the required eight weeks of basic training. On contacting the headquarters for the Army Field Band in Fort Meade, Maryland, I was given a list of the band's tuba players by rank. The highest-ranked tuba player was Paul Pickens. Paul invited us to canvas his area for an apartment and was very helpful. He and his wife invited us to dinner at their Glen Burnie apartment after we finished looking at housing in the area. Carol and I will never forget that dinner, a platter of soft-shell crabs and everything that went with them, including a beer called National Bohemian, or National Bo, now extinct. It was a feast and a proper introduction to soft-shell crabs, which we had never eaten. We have eaten quite a few since then.

The next day we met Robert (Bob) Pallansch, another tubist in the Field Band, who would become my stand partner. He went out of his way to show us around and had even inspected some locations in advance for us. We looked in the College Park area and several locations before finally settling on a garden apartment at 1355 Langley Way in Hyattsville, near Silver Spring, Maryland, not far away from Bob. From that location we were able to carpool to Fort Meade with another tubist, Bruce Butler.

At my first official rehearsal with the Field Band, Major Whiting announced that today there would be section rehearsals led by principal chairs. He then assigned people to run them. Immediately after introducing me to the rest of the band, Major Whiting said, "Private Phillips, you will run the sectional for basses and tubas." I was the only private in the band. I looked up the row of my section and saw arms filled with stripes; everyone there was a staff sergeant except Paul Pickens, who had three stripes up and three stripes down and a diamond in the middle, which meant first sergeant. In our sectional, the very first thing I did was apologize for having been given this order, which put me in an awkward position. But I added, "Since I have been given the responsibility to rehearse the section, I must do so regardless of any difference in rank." So I ran the rehearsal and we all got along well.

The Field Band, founded by Major Chester E. Whiting, is the touring unit of the United States Army; its motto is "The Musical Ambassadors of the Army." It tours more than any other service band. We were on tour almost constantly, but rarely longer than two weeks at a time. And we had annual concerts, like our performance for Senator Theodore Green of Rhode Island, who was in his nineties and hosted an authentic clambake for the Field Band every year. The band often toured outside of the country, but not while I was a member. In fact I think the farthest west I traveled with the band was Kansas. Our concerts were very entertaining and very popular. All the main service bands in Washington had the personnel to assemble a wide variety of ensembles: orchestras, brass quintets, saxophone quartets, Dixieland, big band, and marching bands. This meant we could put together a show for any occasion while on tour.

The Army Field Band had four buses and trucks of equipment. I rode in the first bus. Frequently we would pass a midwestern farm with pigs lying around, and I would open a window and yell, "Sooie, pig!" They would stand up and run for the barn, thinking it was time to be fed. Somebody in one of the trailing buses always asked, "What is it about an Army bus that scares a pig?"

One time, Bob Pallansch was driving Carol and me to a concert at Fort Meade when a car with four men in it came very close behind Bob's car, then went around, getting as close to the front of our car as it could.

Ahead of us, it did the same thing to the driver of another car, hitting its rear bumper. That car flipped over. There were five people in that car. Three died. Bob, who had worked part-time at a fire house with its rescue squad, stopped the car, and while we tried to help the injured, he went to the fire house in Laurel, Maryland, to report the accident. The assistant conductor from the Field Band stopped when he saw us, and asked if we were involved in the accident. Finding out we were not, he said, "We must leave; we have a concert to do."

Carol and I were so happy in the Field Band that I almost re-enlisted when my two years were up because we were having so much fun. But I wanted to get back to New York and take up where I had left off. I was due to get out on November 4 but I got an early release to attend the Manhattan School of Music, which began classes on September 17, 1956. So I spent a total of twenty-two months in the Army instead of four years in the Navy as originally planned.

Ron Bishop, a tuba player from the Eastman School of Music, said, "It took four tuba players to replace you in the Field Band, Harvey: myself, section leader Burt Clark, Willis Traphagan, and Dick Foley."

RETURN TO NEW YORK

The day after I arrived in New York, I started playing the annual National Rodeo Championships with the Jimmy Cimera Rodeo Band out of Chicago. It was a three-week run and paid very well. During this run with the rodeo band I was called for Leonard Bernstein's *Candide,* which ran from December 1, 1956, to February 2, 1957. I was able to do *Candide* because the New York City Ballet, which usually had a Christmas season in New York, was on tour in Japan. There were thirty musicians in the pit for *Candide.*

Early in the story is a song about money that appears four times. Each time, on the turnaround, David Jandorf, first trumpet, was featured in a solo à la the Sousa Band's Herbert L. Clarke. He always played the solo very well and slyly looked at his colleagues to be certain they had noted his performance. One Saturday evening, following a sumptuous dinner at Barbetta's restaurant, I decided to embellish his solo by playing it with him each time. Conductor Samuel Krachmalnick said, "It blew the whole orchestra away, including me. They started stomping on the floor. The whole band went wild. I'll never forget it and neither will anybody who was in the orchestra." Hershy Kay, who orchestrated *Candide*, thought I should leave the part in. I thought once was enough.

As soon as I was settled in my performance commitments, I made personal courtesy calls on my tuba-playing friends and colleagues, starting with Don Butterfield and other members of the Radio City Music Hall Orchestra. As I approached the 50th Street stage door, I noticed several musicians in conversation. Don Butterfield saw me coming and came to greet me, to welcome me back to New York. Tubist Bill Stanley, whom I had not yet met, was standing holding his tuba in its gig bag. When Don introduced me to him, he quipped, "Well, it's all right if you come back to New York as long as you don't take any of my gigs." This prompted Don to pull Bill over and growl into his face, "Bill, you'll soon learn that Harvey doesn't take gigs; he makes gigs!"

I couldn't believe the number of concerts booked by the New York Brass Quintet. My schedule got busy very quickly and my sub list got more complex every day.

On October 5, 1956, I was invited by National Orchestral Association Concertmaster Hugo Fiorato to be the brass coach for that organization. I was honored to follow long-time brass coach Dick Moore, associate first horn with the Metropolitan Opera.

Once, in a heavy ballet season, I was engaged by three companies for one night. For the Martha Graham Dance Company at the Mark Hellinger Theatre on Broadway, I played only the first ballet of four, by Erik Satie. The show started at 7:30. The New York City Ballet at City Center started at 8:15 and I played only one of its ballets, the first. At 9 PM I went to the Metropolitan Opera House to play the last ballet of the American Ballet Theatre's evening performance. The doorman at each theater had a taxi waiting for me when I exited the theater. I covered all the tuba parts at all three ballet companies and I was happy there were no program changes.

Going to Dayton for a series of clinics sponsored by the Conn Corporation, I was met in the airport by Jim Klapp, my host for the week. He passed me twice in the airport. He told me he was looking for an old guy, because of my resume. He said, "You're about a tenth of the age I expected!"

CHAPTER EIGHT

A New York Professional

AFTER MY DISCHARGE from the Army, Carol and I took an apartment at 42-25 80th Street in Elmhurst, Long Island, one block away from Elmhurst Hospital. A lot of musicians had apartments in that big building. The owner and manager of the building was very musician-friendly. If someone came to complain about musicians practicing at all hours of the night, he'd tell them to move. He said, "I've never been stiffed by a musician."

New York musicians often said, "If you want to learn the art of music, go to Juilliard. If you want to learn the profession and business of music, go to the Manhattan School of Music." I had the good fortune to attend both schools, but my motivation for enrolling in the Manhattan School of Music was so I could leave the Army in time for the start of the 1956–1957 concert season, which began in mid-September. After completing four years of music studies at Juilliard, I didn't feel like I was in dire need of academia. By the time I returned to New York, I had more than twenty gigs booked already, including the rodeo, ice show, the New York City Ballet, and the New York Brass Quintet.

British pianist-composer-comedian Donald Swann, together with Michael Flanders, had a successful show, *At the Drop of a Hat,* on Broadway for two years. Swann also was the primary arranger for the Hoffnung Festival in England in 1955. Swann had sublet a garden apartment convenient to the theater. Arnold Black, violinist and theater contractor, called and told me Donald Swann had inquired about my availability, so he could hear a work performed that he was writing, *Two Moods for Tuba and Piano*, which had been requested by famous cartoonist and British tuba player Gerard Hoffnung. While we were rehearsing and trying things out in his apartment, he finished the composition. A week or so later I made a second visit to Donald's apartment. He sadly informed me Hoffnung had passed away.

Donald and I played the piece several times and I suggested that the Chamber Music Library publish it. The first movement was meant to be humorous, but I suggested that out of respect for Gerard Hoffnung we slow the tempo and make it into an elegy. The mute, which Hoffnung called "a whopping big cork," was used throughout the elegy. The second movement was a scherzo that changed keys every few measures. On my first solo recital LP, I included *Two Moods for Tuba and Piano*. It's still fun to play.

Hoffnung's widow sent me a box of his cartoons featuring the tuba.

CLARK GALEHOUSE—GOLDEN CREST RECORDS

I first met Clark Galehouse, founder and president of Golden Crest Records, through John Barrows. John had recorded a solo LP and another with the New York Woodwind Quintet, all music by Alec Wilder, for Golden Crest. At the time, Clark Galehouse had a company that pressed records for all the major labels. First and foremost, Clark Galehouse was a musician who, in addition to performing as a saxophonist, also did arrangements, most notably for jazz violinist Joe Venuti. His other major activity was recording performing ensembles at music conferences, opening up a potential for major music educators and their ensembles. He established a new market for soloists and chamber ensembles, which could not exist before the advent of 33⅓ LP recordings.

In 1957 the New York Brass Quintet produced its own LP titled *The New York Brass Quintet in Concert*. Our intention was to market this recording as a demonstration for concert bookers to understand the variations of programs. Before we could market it, opportunity came to record *Two Contemporary Composers* (Alec Wilder and Don Hammond). As things

worked out, in negotiating *Two Contemporary Composers,* Clark also agreed
that Golden Crest Records would release *The* N Y B Q *In Concert,* as well as
a solo recital album by each member of the New York Brass Quintet. Alec
Wilder and I had become good friends by this time and arrangements were
made to record his *Sonata No. 1 for Solo Tuba and Piano,* resulting in my first
Harvey Phillips in Recital L P. This recording was very popular with the Japanese and Scandinavian tubists. Keith Brown followed with a solo album for
trombone, John Glasel did a jazz album with his Brasstet, and John Swallow did a solo recital recording. Once I started doing recordings with Clark
Galehouse, we developed a close friendship, resulting in several recordings
of solo tuba. That simply could not have happened without Clark's support.
Clark also made possible *The Burke-Phillips All-Star Concert Band, Volumes
1 and 2,* two of the finest band recordings ever made.

MANAGING A FREELANCE CAREER

Don Butterfield and I were by far the busiest freelance tuba players in New York and subbed for each other many times. Philip Cadway (an
A B C staff musician), Bill Barber, and I also passed jobs back and forth, but
we never had the opportunity to play together. We were all versatile players,
comfortable in the various styles of music, including classical and jazz. In
the freelance world, an instrument like the tuba is severely handicapped
and penalized if the player can't cope with every style of music. In other
words, if 90 percent of your training and activities comes from playing with
a symphony orchestra, it is very unlikely that you will be called at the last
minute to play recordings of Dixieland music, bebop, avant-garde, or aleatoric compositions. I strove to be able to accept every gig with confidence
regardless of the style of music. I can't think of anything more damaging
to a freelance career than receiving a phone call and having to say, "No, I'm
sorry. I can't play that kind of music."

I was also very conscious of the importance of putting my best foot
forward. At every performance there might be someone who had never
seen or heard me before and was weighing me as a potential colleague in
the music world. Therefore I considered every gig an audition and tried to
conduct myself accordingly. I knew that people pass judgment on what

they hear but also on what they see: habits, personality, neatness, a show of respect (or lack thereof), as well as musicianship.

It was important for me to maintain good relations with the contractors and conductors for whom I played, because my schedule required frequent use of substitutes. Whenever I had a conflict, I would have my substitute come to rehearsals and sit next to me. Not many other musicians did this because it amounted to playing rehearsals free; I gave my pay to the sub. But the sub had the opportunity to observe how I played and interacted with the brass section and other musicians. If we went out for lunch or dinner after rehearsal, he got a chance to socialize with the brass players. All of this greatly increased his chances of fitting in with the ensemble and doing well on the performance.

This practice earned goodwill from conductors and contractors that ultimately proved far more valuable than the money I paid the subs for attending rehearsals. Eventually, contractors would just call me when they needed a tuba, knowing that if I couldn't do it, I would ensure a quality sub. (Occasionally they would call and ask when I was available for a certain recording date and they would schedule the date for that time.)

An instrument as large as the tuba, tuba mute, string bass, or harp can be a problem moving from one studio to another and, in busy downtown New York, arriving on time. Over the years I had lockers in Carnegie Hall, the City Center, New York State Theater, Manhattan Center (RCA Victor), and various other locations. For most concert works and recordings, I used my 1920 Conn CC tuba. Sometimes—if I was recording with Jackie Gleason/George Williams, I would use a Martin BB♭ recording tuba and leave it in a large instrument locker at the City Center or New York State Theater for as long as a week. I shared with Lou Waldeck my locker and access via combination lock, 9988, the last four digits of my home telephone number. Busy freelance bass players and harpists contracted with men who made a living by being responsible for their having the right instrument at the right concert or recording session. The tuba is a little more transportable.

I developed the habit of entering in my datebook the telephone number of the recording booth in each studio and carrying a list of telephone numbers of any nearby pay telephones. In those pre-cell-phone days, this allowed me to get in touch with personnel managers in case I was running late or had some emergency. This saved my bacon on more than one occasion!

In 1964, I did an LP with Billy Byers entitled *Impressions of Duke Ellington*. The personnel was first class, the arrangements were great, and the camaraderie perfect. Sometimes Billy, Pat Williams, or Quincy Jones would leave a recent release LP at Jim and Andy's Bar with a recipient's name attached. In 1968, I decided to visit Jim and Andy's, which in the interim had moved from 48th Street and Sixth Avenue to west of Broadway on 55th Street. When I entered the bar, the bartender said, "Oh Harvey, haven't seen you in awhile!"

"Well, I moved to Massachusetts a year ago."

"I've got something I've been holding for you." He reached behind the cash register and handed me an LP left for me by Billy Byers. Not only had they kept it for three years but they kept it in spite of the move. Such was the loyalty and appreciation of establishments we frequented.

One of the first regular engagements I took on after my return to New York in 1956 was *The Bell Telephone Hour,* which ran from 1940 to 1966. Like *The Voice of Firestone,* it began as a radio broadcast, then was simultaneously produced on radio and television. I received a call from Bill Trone, who was manager for the Bell Telephone organization, informing me of the retirement of *The Bell Telephone Hour* tubist, Fred Pfaff, and inviting me to audition. Five tubists were given the opportunity to audition by performing one Monday night broadcast during September and October. I was the last to play an audition broadcast, and I was notified the following week that I had won the position. The orchestra paid very well; it was only one day per week but paid almost as much as a whole week in the New York City Ballet Orchestra.

The first time I played the opening theme under the baton of Donald Voorhees, I was scared to death because the tuba played the very first note with the timpani and triangle, to emulate a telephone sound. At first, the broadcast was played on the Carnegie Hall stage (on the New York Philharmonic's night off). Rehearsals usually started at 2 in the afternoon and the broadcast was at 9 PM. Sometimes the show was live and sometimes taped.

Playing on *The Bell Telephone Hour* provided, among other opportunities, ten years of playing with and getting to know the legendary Harry Glantz, who had been first trumpet for Toscanini's NBC Symphony Orchestra. Harry set such a high standard for trumpet playing that he gave a trumpet player with the talent of Bud Herseth something to reach for and exceed. Like Roger Bannister's running the four-minute mile, he made new heights of trumpet playing possible. Just listening to him was an education. I have always said that a university school of music should hire such outstanding artists after they retire from performing and make them available to students.

There was a particular *Bell Telephone* program that featured Jascha Heifetz as the violin soloist. In the middle of the rehearsal, conductor Donald Voorhees stepped down from the podium, walked over to the piano, and, without music, accompanied Heifetz. This was a surprise to the orchestra but typical of the incredibly gifted conductor. Donald Voorhees was one of the few conductors at that time who was neither born in Europe nor trained there—he was from Allentown, Pennsylvania.

After I left the circus to go to Juilliard, I played the circus each New York season, at Madison Square Garden—from 1951 through 1967, except for the years in the Army Field Band and the year of Merle Evans's retirement, 1960. The circus came for six weeks, April into May, while the New York City Ballet wasn't performing. The Musicians Union Local 802 required that the circus hire five New York musicians for the season. I was one of them. Merle would have hired me anyway.

PRIVATE TEACHING

I started teaching privately in New York in 1956, shortly after leaving the Army. By 1958, I was teaching tuba at the Manhattan School of Music, and I taught at the Hartt School at the University of Hartford, a post that I held for about four years. I also taught at Yale University while the New York Brass Quintet was in residence there, from about 1960 to 1967.

Teaching in New York was more of a luxury than an obligation. I rarely taught more than three or four students a week in New York plus the handful at Hartt and Yale. Sometimes my Hartt and Yale students would have to come to me in New York because my schedule didn't allow me to leave the city. In 1957 I took advantage of the opportunity to rent a studio in Carnegie Hall, at a time when its demise was threatened. Sconces were being removed from the walls by a contractor, who told me I could take a couple. I still have them.

It took an artist of the stature of Isaac Stern to champion Carnegie Hall's salvation. Often I would rent the use of my studio for private teaching. It also provided a convenient place for the New York Brass Quintet to rehearse.

The two-room studio I rented from Carnegie Hall was on the fourteenth floor in the front addition and was accessible from the 56th and 57th Street elevators. It also served as the headquarters for my contracting and for Mentor Music Inc. (BMI), a publishing company started by Robert Nagel and myself. At the same time, John Glasel, a quintet member, started Chamber Music Library (ASCAP). Identification of the studio and its activities prompted the title Brass Wind Music Studio.

The first piece of Alec Wilder's I brought in to be published by Mentor was *Sonata No. 1 for Tuba and Piano.* I also had Gunther Schuller's *Concerto No. 1 for Tuba and Chamber Orchestra,* subtitled *Cappricio,* written so it could be performed by two pianos. Bob's eyebrows went up when I brought in music from other composers. I was hoping Mentor Music Inc. would be a publishing company for brass chamber music and solo literature. Bob and I settled; I asked him to buy my 50 percent of the company. I asked that the Wilder *Sonata No. 1 for Tuba and Piano* come back to me so that Alec's compositions would be published together.

Charles Colin, an enterprising brass teacher, became a major publisher of study materials for brass instruments. He founded annual brass instrument workshops—the New York Conference for Brass Scholarships. He also rented out teaching studios.

I had an ongoing interest and concern for composers having control over their compositions with a known company or under their own names. For instance, later, I wanted Tubists Universal Brotherhood Association (TUBA) to publish music featuring tuba, paying the composer 10 percent more than big publishing companies would pay and asking composers to write program notes for each composition. These program notes would be available for any TUBA member to access for his or her recital performances.

When *Marat/Sade* opened on Broadway, I was called for rehearsals and the recording of the production's music composed by Richard Peaslee. We met at the Martin Beck Theatre and I asked him if he had written any brass quintets, and who published the music he wrote for the New York Shakespeare Festival. He said the Shakespeare Theatre published it. I suggested that he publish his own music and consider a distributor. So, using my lawyer, Joseph Taubman, the two of us started Magellan Music, later changed to Peaslee Music, Inc. Once the company got going, I bowed out. I had negotiated that any company with which I was involved could have international distribution.

One unfortunate feature of the Carnegie Hall studios was a transom over each door leading to the hallway. Jimmy Burke, famed cornet soloist, was a clinician for Leblanc Holton Company. Soon after we had moved into our quarters, Jimmy received a special cornet for a left-handed player. It was decoratively inscribed and gold-plated, one of a kind. Jimmy unpacked the instrument and admired it, but was too tired to try it out. He said he would reserve that pleasure for the next morning and left it in the studio. That very evening our studio was broken into, entered through the high transom. A typewriter, money, and Jimmy's cornet were stolen. Nothing taken was ever found. The first thing I did after discovering the loss of Jimmy's cornet was to bolt on ¾-inch plywood, closing the transom forever. Nothing else was ever stolen from the studio.

I always enjoyed teaching very much. I was busy enough that I didn't have to rely on teaching as a source of income and this allowed me to choose my private students. I did get a lot of one- or two-lesson students really only interested in name-dropping; they would take one or two lessons from William Bell, Arnold Jacobs, myself (or other professionally well-placed teachers) just so they could list the names on their resumes. These types were easy to spot; they came and went. I preferred, and welcomed, serious students who were genuinely interested in long-term development and responded well to my teaching, and had motivation and commitment.

HARTFORD AND SPRINGFIELD

I oftentimes played concerts with the Hartford and Springfield symphonies. I usually was able to attend at least the dress rehearsal, but sometimes not—such was my schedule. When I had dates in Hartford, Carol and I would stay overnight at the Canton, Connecticut, home of her brother Arnold Dorvel and his wife Joy. On one such occasion, I'd had a horrendous schedule all that week in New York, and we drove directly to the Dorvels' house. I dressed for the concert (tuxedo and black bow tie), but needed to rest. The weather was terrible, with ice and snow and high winds. I asked Carol and Joy to please wake me after a half hour so I could get to the concert hall in time. The concert was scheduled for 8:00, and the hall was a fair distance from the house. I was exhausted and slept soundly and neither Carol nor Joy could interrupt their conversation long enough to keep track of the time for me. I finally woke up on my own, looked at my watch, and found that I had fifteen minutes to get to the hall.

I knew I couldn't possibly make it, but I had to give it a try. Luckily the traffic was minimal on the drive into Hartford, but the roads were so slick with black ice that I couldn't drive with any kind of speed. I arrived at the hall a few minutes after the scheduled start time, left my car illegally parked in the only spot left, and ran in with my tuba, which I had kept in the front seat near the heater so it would be warm and ready to play.

The orchestra had just started, so I had one of the stagehands get a chair and a music stand. In the meantime, I said "Pssst" a few times to get the attention of Bert Turetzky, principal bass, who was positioned in the upper corner of stage left. I whispered to Bert to have the music passed to me, since the stage layout prevented me from getting to the tubist's chair without walking through the front of the orchestra. I played just off the front of the stage, with my bell pointing toward the center of the orchestra. This was very disconcerting for conductor Fritz Mahler, who heard the sound of my tuba but couldn't tell where it was coming from. To make matters worse, the second movement opened with a tuba solo. Poor Fritz didn't know where to look to give his downbeat. When I felt enough time had elapsed between movements, I simply started playing and he followed me.

One evening in 1959, I was scheduled for a concert in Springfield, Massachusetts, which was almost three hours away from New York by car. I had arranged a ride with a husband and wife horn players and an oboist and had made plans to meet them at the Scarsdale train station at 5 PM after a busy afternoon of recording sessions. I boarded the train at Grand Central Station, relaxed into my seat, and the next thing I knew I was being shaken by the conductor of the train, telling me we had reached the end of the line and I would have to get off. So I took my tuba and asked him, "Where are we?"

He said, "North White Plains, New York."

"What happened to Scarsdale?"

"That was two stops back!"

Hmm. That was a problem. I went to the pay phone and called the Scarsdale station and paged my ride. Nobody answered the page so I knew they had gone on without me. I called friends who lived in White Plains but either they weren't home or I caught a wife who was home alone with no transportation, so no luck there. My next effort was to go to the cabstand and see if there was a cab driver who would drive me to Springfield, which was about 115 miles from White Plains. I found one driver who offered to make the trip for seventy-five dollars. So I told him I would give him what I had, fifteen dollars, and he could get the rest of the money as soon as we arrived in Springfield.

We drove to Springfield and arrived at the concert hall at about ten minutes to 8. By the time I got inside and unpacked my tuba, the orchestra was onstage ready to play and the conductor, Robert Staffanson, was about to walk out to start the concert, which began with the overture to *Candide*. He saw me enter and said, "Oh thank God, Harvey; we thought something had happened. We're glad you made it."

Ben Snyder, personnel manager, came over to say the same. I said, "Ben, would you please pay the cab driver?" as the conductor and I walked onstage together. After thirty-five or forty minutes, we finished the first half and I walked backstage, only to see the cab driver still standing there. I said, "What are you doing here?"

He said, "That son of a bitch won't pay me!"

Ben Snyder motioned me over. He said, "Harvey, this cab driver wants sixty dollars!"

I said, "Yes, that's right."

"Well, didn't you take the cab from the train station?"

"Yeah, I did, from White Plains, New York!"

Ben paused. "I'll go to the box office."

Later, I received a check as payment for the concert, which I endorsed and sent back, feeling guilty. Ben sent me a new check and said, "Harvey, the story is worth sixty dollars." He later told me he often told the story as an example of commitment and professionalism.

These stories illustrate the perils of such a busy schedule. I had just as much jazz and commercial work as I did with orchestras and the New York Brass Quintet, and these worlds sometimes overlapped. It was not uncommon for my day to include recording sessions or orchestra rehearsals during the morning and afternoon, symphony concerts in the evening, and playing in jazz clubs after the symphony concerts until early the next morning.

DICK CARY'S LOFT SESSIONS, 1956–1959

Dick Cary was a jazz pianist, arranger, and composer who maintained a loft apartment on Sixth Avenue at 28th Street. He had the second floor. On the third floor was Hall Overton, a composer and pianist who understood all styles of music. He was highly respected by both jazz and classical musicians. We had a group that met at 8:00 every Monday night at Dick's apartment, or as close to 8:00 as the musicians could manage. I was often late due to *Bell Telephone Hour* broadcasts or other commitments. We played experimental music that various composers (primarily Dick Cary) would write. We would usually take a break about midnight and at 2:00 go up to Hall Overton's loft, where Thelonius Monk would come in, sometimes with a drummer or bass player. We'd play as late as 6:00 in the morning. I remember sometimes Carol and I would leave in these early morning hours, before the sun rose, stepping out onto Sixth Avenue into silence and falling snowflakes. It was eerie to be out in New York City with no taxicabs or cars. We sometimes had trouble getting home.

In addition to frequent jingle recordings for producers Scott Taylor, Morris Mamorsky, Billy VerPlanck, and others, I played on a variety of jazz and classical recording sessions. One of the most important recording gigs I did was *The Golden Striker*, a suite of pieces by John Lewis, all for brass. Nesuhi Ertegun, who was intrigued by unusual music, took it for Atlantic Records. John Lewis and I hired the players, and John and Gunther Schuller, who played horn, took turns conducting. That's when I first met David Baker, who was traveling with George Russell's band. He would become my friend and later my colleague at Indiana University. He was playing bass trombone at that time and had just been named "Most Promising Jazz Trombone Player" by *Downbeat* magazine.

My recording session work encompassed a wide range of formats, including several television productions and films. My first score for television, I believe, was a documentary about the presidency of Harry S. Truman. I played on a film score by Laurence Rosenthal, *Requiem for a Heavyweight*, and one by Quincy Jones, *The Pawnbroker*. I also remember *The Eisenhower Years, How the West Was Won*, and *Odds Against Tomorrow* (starring Harry Belafonte and Robert Ryan), scored by John Lewis and featuring the Modern Jazz Quartet. *Victory at Sea* was a T V documentary about the naval battles of the Second World War between the U.S. and Japan. Richard Rodgers was the composer and Robert Russell Bennett did the orchestration.

Recently, I received from pianist Dick Hyman a copy of a film I'd nearly forgotten called *Leader of the Band*. The soundtrack, which I played on, was scored by Dick Hyman, and the movie featured Steve Landesberg as the conductor of a very bad high school band, whose troublemakers were the tuba section. It was fun to see New York's best freelance musicians pull their slides out or push them all the way in to sound like a bad high school band, then to experience the improvement of the band through the film, culminating in its winning a music competition.

I also played Fox Movietone newsreels under Jack Shaindlin, who was the conductor for the ice show at Madison Square Garden. Shaindlin, who had been a silent movie piano player, had collected in file cabinets music he had written appropriate for a plane crash, a ship going down, a storm, etc., as background for newsreels. He would say to Harry Shulman, before we started recording, "Okay, Harry, let's fake another tuneup." We recorded for newsreels on 105th Street.

I remember one time we recorded music for a disaster and the next day I recorded for Perry Como at the RCA studio on 24th Street. I also played on all the Perry Como Christmas TV programs, in the Ziegfeld Theatre on Sixth Avenue. I played many recording sessions for Cinerama films, which were in their heyday in the late 1950s and the 1960s. *How the West Was Won* was a Cinerama film. These were big-paying dates because we started at 9:00 in the morning and would sometimes continue until 2:00 the next morning. We recorded on the tennis court of an estate in Oyster Bay, Long Island. The night before the first day we recorded, the woman of the house heard somebody in her bedroom, took a gun her husband had given her, and blew him away. It turned out to be her husband. One of our trombone players, Jack Satterfield, mistakenly drove up to the main house instead of the tennis court and policemen questioned him and examined his trombone case.

I substituted for Phil Cadway, an awesome tubist, on *Your Show of Shows,* starring Sid Caesar and Imogene Coca. I was called several times when a tuba was needed by *Your Hit Parade.* NBC *Bandstand* had a big band on each week; the Sauter-Finegan Band hired me to do the show when it was its turn to be on.

I also did some choice Broadway shows, including *Kismet* (presented at the Mark Hellinger Theatre) and *Candide* (at the Martin Beck Theatre), but I eventually left both shows to go back to the New York City Ballet once it started its next season. At the New York City Center, I performed revivals of *South Pacific, The King and I, Camelot,* and others. When I left *Kismet,* the other musicians told me that the contractor, Morris Stonzek, would stop using me for recordings. I took care of having someone ready to replace me. I chose an older gentlemen named Joe Park who had played the Roxy Theatre until it closed. The week following my departure from *Kismet* I was called for four recording sessions conducted by Andre Kostelanetz, contracted by Morris Stonzek.

I remember a recording session with Victor Borge. We were recording *Rhapsody in Blue* with a freelance orchestra. During rehearsal, a gentleman came from the opposite end of the studio, walked up behind Borge, stepped up on the podium, pushed Borge to the side, took the baton, and started conducting for a few measures. Then he gave the baton back to

Victor Borge and walked out. Borge knew who it was, of course, but asked the orchestra, "Who was that?" It was Jackie Gleason, who at the time was the highest-salaried actor at CBS and whose hit show, *The Jackie Gleason Show,* was in its prime.

I played on a lot of recordings of instrumental pop music released as "Conducted by Jackie Gleason." He was always sitting backward on a chair when I was there. George Williams, who also did arrangements for Gene Krupa, did the arrangements and conducted. He was called "The Fox" because his arrangements were so clever. The first Gleason recording I became familiar with was the incomparable, beautiful stylization of Bobby Hackett with strings, *Music for Lovers Only.* The reason Bobby Hackett was replaced by Pee Wee Erwin on later recordings was because of some misunderstandings about his featured position. Other albums, such as 35 *Mandolins,* would take on a Gleason touch. *Lover's Portfolio* had different ensembles playing something for every mood, from Dixieland ensemble to the perfect cocktail piano of Bernie Leighton. I played in two of the groups. When Gleason went on his splurge weekend parties, via private train to Miami, the Dixieland band was indispensable. One of his excesses is demonstrated by an album called *Aphrodisia,* featuring twenty-four trumpets, horn quartet with tuba, and a rhythm section with bass, piano, and drums. The trumpets sometimes play four groups of six and sometimes six groups of four, resulting in surround sound. We recorded "That's a Plenty," up-tempo, in unison, with clarinet, trombone, cornet, and tuba. Cornetist Charlie Shavers said he had never before been cut by (had to take a back seat to) a tuba player.

Jackie Gleason's recordings were especially memorable for the players because of drummer Jimmy Crawford. Jimmy would show up early and play a simple swing pattern on the sock cymbal and narrate as everyone walked in: "Well, folks, we're here in the studio to do this recording session, and here's Harvey Phillips with his tuba; he's wearing a nice shirt today, and hey! there's Charlie Shavers with his trumpet; he's getting his valves oiled up, and wow, we're almost ready to start!" and so on. Everybody was happy and grinning because of Jimmy's routine, and you can almost hear this happiness in the way we played. Those remain in my memory as some of the most enjoyable recording sessions in my career.

In addition to the almost constant barrage of classical recordings, I played on jazz albums led by many great New York musicians. Some that come to mind include *Pee Wee Erwin's Dixieland Eight,* a series with Quincy Jones and Billy Byers, Freddie Hubbard's first album, two albums with Rahsaan Roland Kirk, J. J. Johnson's *Concerto for Dizzy Gillespie,* Gene Krupa's last album, Gil Evans's *New Bottle Old Wine* (featuring Cannonball Adderley), and Joe Morello's *It's About Time.*

The golden age of recording was the mid-1950s to the 1960s, until the Beatles came along and changed everything. I feel the Beatles were geniuses, in a class by themselves in many respects, but they were such a success that every record label started looking for the next Beatles, a quartet they could make a lot of money on. It was certainly attractive to the record labels on a financial level—four musicians were much cheaper than a twenty-piece band. And so this spelled the demise of the big band as the foremost popular ensemble, and caused a general decrease in the amount of recording work available in New York City. Eventually, many of the top writers moved to the West Coast and got involved in Hollywood.

It was not unusual to do three recording sessions in a day and work with the same string, woodwind, brass, and rhythm sections. Only the section leaders would change. One of the most highly regarded lead trumpet players was Bernie Glow. When it was discovered that Bernie had an incurable illness and was forced to give up playing, many of the leaders and arrangers he had worked for would include a little "Bernie Glow solo" (played by one of the other trumpets), so he would still have an income. Such unpublicized generous concern for a colleague was not unusual.

Perhaps the most admired freelance horn player in New York, John Barrows, never loaned money. If someone asked John to lend him twenty dollars, John would take out a twenty-dollar bill and say, "No, I won't loan you twenty dollars, but I'm more than happy to give you twenty dollars." Musicians who worked together had an unwavering code of genuine concern for each other.

John Barrows used to tell his students that if they wanted to hear the first horn solo in *Till Eulenspiegel* played perfectly fifty times in a row, they should go to Chicago's Orchestra Hall and hear Phil Farkas play it backstage forty-nine times and then one more time onstage with the orchestra. Phil's emphasis as a teacher and player was on accuracy, intonation, and repetition.

Barrows had an uncanny ability to color sound, and he was a great influence on my tuba playing. I've always felt that the most subtle adjustment of pitch is not a change of pitch, but a change of color.

In 1960 John and Jim Buffington, out of concern for horn-playing colleagues, organized a horn club known as the Valhalla Horn Society. The name Valhalla is found in Wagner operas and, strangely enough, in Rockland County, New York, where John was living. Jim Buffington telephoned to tell me about the club and invite me to his apartment for a meeting. The founding members were nine horn players and one tuba. I couldn't have been more honored. Other horn players joined the club later. We looked out for each other. When John passed away in 1974, I commissioned Indiana University composer Bernhard Heiden to write a work for solo tuba with the Valhalla Horn Choir of nine horns. I included it on an L P recording, *Tribute to a Friend*.

My affinity for horn prompted me to commission (I believe) more works for tuba and horn than any other person.

One of the greatest musicians I have ever worked with was much-admired lead trumpet player Raymond Crisara. I remember a recording of Spanish bullfight tunes, *Corrida*, which included a famous trumpet solo assigned to another trumpet player, who was having difficulties. Finally, he deferred to Ray, who polished off the solo in one take.

In a string of recording sessions conducted by Robert Russell Bennett it was discovered that a fourth trumpet was needed for an upcoming session. One of the other trumpet players went to Ray and asked if it would be possible to hire one of his students, who needed a break, for that session. Robert Russell Bennett is very soft-spoken, as is Ray Crisara. Ray said that would be fine. So the young man arrived and took his place in the section. Rehearsing the section, Bennett said politely to Ray, "Ray, at letter C the trumpets are a little heavy. Take it down a dynamic." In the silence of the moment, the new young man playing fourth trumpet said, "It's marked fortissimo." I never saw the young man again. Such disrespect was never tolerated.

The N B C Symphony Orchestra was created in 1937 for world-renowned conductor Arturo Toscanini, then in his seventieth year. Over the next seventeen years Toscanini and his orchestra maintained a rigorous schedule of concerts, broadcasts, and recordings, with tours in the United States and South America. When Toscanini retired in 1954, at age eighty-seven, concerned orchestra musicians formed a committee to discuss options for the future with N B C management. N B C expressed no intention of continuing the orchestra without Toscanini. The orchestra committee then recommended that the orchestra be registered as a cooperative organization and incorporated in the state of New York as the Symphony of the Air. Toscanini died on January 15, 1957, just two months before his ninetieth birthday. A short time after his death, I was engaged to perform with the Symphony of the Air in a memorial concert honoring Toscanini in Madison Square Garden. There was no conductor and no music stand because Toscanini never used a score. There was only a spotlight on the podium.

HELPING A BELL STUDENT

In 1959 the New York Brass Quintet traveled to Montreal, Canada, for a series of concerts. The concerts were well attended by resident musicians and the news media. In fact, it was in these concerts that I was first referred to as "the Paganini of the tuba," in print, in a review. This title was picked up by *Newsweek* magazine. Important to note is a conversation I had on that occasion with the tubist of the Montreal Symphony Orchestra. We had a pleasant chat and he informed me that he was resigning from the orchestra and moving to France at the end of the concert season but didn't want the management to know of his plans, for personal reasons. I made a mental note of this information. Strangely enough, shortly after my return to New York, I received a call from William Bell, asking me if I knew of any orchestral openings for tuba, as he had a young student he thought was ready for such an assignment. The student's name was Robert Ryker. I suggested he have Mr. Ryker give me a call. I spoke to an executive friend at Local 802 and confirmed the policy followed by most American Federation of Musicians locals. This policy was to audition members of a jurisdiction's local before hearing anyone else audition for a full-time position.

I suggested that Ryker contact the current tubist to confirm that he was indeed leaving the orchestra and that he had not informed the management or local union. If this was confirmed, then Ryker should immediately move to Montreal, establishing a residence, and quickly join the musicians union, so that when the opening was announced he would be a full-fledged member of the Montreal AFM local. It took three months to establish full union membership. Ryker followed my advice and was successful in winning the position.

Later, in 1966, Ryker wanted to audition for the Boston Symphony, but the audition dates were in conflict with the Montreal Symphony Orchestra's schedule. The orchestra had a concert which included Bela Bartok's *Concerto for Orchestra* and the opening of the Montreal Opera season with a performance of Verdi's *Aida*. When Ryker asked conductor Zubin Mehta's permission to audition in Boston, Mehta was upset but informed Ryker that the only way he would allow him to audition in Boston would be if he could get Harvey Phillips to cover his Montreal Orchestra assignments.

Ryker phoned me, told me of the conversation with Mehta, and asked if I would be able to spend four days in Montreal. I had four recordings and three performances scheduled in New York City. I felt some kinship with the Boston Symphony so I told him I'd be able to cover his concerts and opera with the Montreal Symphony but I couldn't afford to do it for less money than I would have earned in my New York commitments. Ryker paid me around $750. He placed second in the audition in Boston, which was won by Chester Schmitz.

In 1957 I began accepting some of the numerous requests I received to serve as personnel manager (contractor) for a diverse assortment of performers, conductors, producers, and record companies. I engaged from one piano accompanist to a full symphony orchestra and everything in between. Before engaging musician personnel I prepared a Projected Musician Personnel list and met with the conductor, producer, or other responsible person in charge. I verified if any commitments had been made to certain musicians. If so, I entered them on my personnel list. I then confirmed all other details of the engagement, including venue, date, time, dress, repertoire, and any other pertinent information. I projected a full personnel list in pencil. As musicians accepted the engagement, their penciled names were inked over.

I always engaged my concertmaster first, then principal players and section leaders. This approach gave me the opportunity to discuss seating assignments with section leaders and principal players. A worthy contractor knew musicians and how to contact them; he knew what position a woodwind or brass player usually played—or wanted desperately to play; he knew which violinists could serve as concertmaster; he knew which violinists to place in the first and second sections and in what order to seat them; he knew musician dispositions; he knew how to make a schedule and how to do payrolls; and he knew important details such as where, when, and how to file contracts with the musicians union. A contractor earned his double scale.

I think I was one of the few brass players who truly recognized the importance of arranging chairs for first and second violins, violas, celli, and contrabass. A musician colleague may recognize the superior playing of one violinist over another, but couldn't always recognize subtle leadership qualities and the stigma of inside or outside seating at shared stands in the string sections. It was a task that orchestra personnel managers must live with. Keeping peace among 103 musicians can be difficult. I conferred whenever possible with my concertmaster and took on the responsibility (blame?) for where each string player sat. On the phone as I was hiring them, I told them where they would sit, so there would be no shocks when the musicians assembled for the first rehearsal. Woodwinds, too, could sometimes be a challenge. Brass players are the easiest to work with. None of them ever took me to task for the positions I assigned them in the orchestra.

In 1959, I became personnel manager of the Symphony of the Air, and in 1961–1962, I assisted Leopold Stokowski in establishing his American Symphony Orchestra. A primary activity of the Symphony of the Air was the Empire State Music Festival summer concert series founded by the orchestra in Ellenville, New York. The orchestra also presented concert series in Carnegie Hall. The orchestra did many recordings and concerts with conductors Leopold Stokowski and Alfred Wallenstein.

Stokowski broke his hip at Christmastime in 1960, while playing with his young children. The Symphony of the Air had recordings scheduled between Christmas and New Year's, which had to be canceled. Two months later, in February, Stokowski conducted a performance of *Turandot* at the Metropolitan Opera. His entrance onto the podium was pure Stokowski showmanship: using two canes, he strolled slowly and erect, down the aisle, through the audience, to the orchestra pit, and stepped onto the podium. The audience went wild.

A few weeks later, Stokowski conducted the Symphony of the Air at Carnegie Hall. The orchestra had finished tuning and quietly awaited the Maestro's appearance. We waited for the house lights to dim and a spotlight to splash the stage for the Maestro's entrance. I was to follow him. He entered regally with his two canes and, after taking a few steps onto the stage in view of the audience, turned slowly and ceremoniously passed the canes to me and continued his stroll to the podium. Another victory for Stokowski! The audience cheered. He had won them over and the orchestra hadn't yet played a note.

The Symphony of the Air performed many new compositions, including, on an Ellenville concert, Stravinsky's *Agon,* which was brand new in 1957 and was written at the request of George Balanchine, the great choreographer. I believe *Agon* is the only twelve-tone composition by Stravinsky in the concert repertoire. It is quite dissonant at times, and some in the audience, showing their bad manners and lack of musical élan, may boo—as they did at this particular performance. Having just conducted the complete work, Maestro Stokowski stayed on the podium and politely waited for the boos and applause to fade. Then he turned to the audience and said, in a normal speaking voice, "You must hear it again." Whereupon he turned to the orchestra and again performed the entire work. This time, there were no boos. I am certain that if he had heard any negative noise, he would have conducted it a third time.

Once, at a rehearsal of the New York Philharmonic, Stokowski became involved with lengthily rehearsing the woodwind section. He finally started conducting the ensemble tutti. Percussionist Bert Brodkin, with triangle in one hand and striker in the other, had dozed off past his entrance and when Stokowski, not hearing the sound, said "Triangle!," Brodkin stood straight as an arrow and responded with, "Louder, Maestro?"

Stokowski wrote a concise letter of recommendation in 1978 when Indiana University was considering upgrading my rank to "distinguished professor." It read: "Harvey Phillips is Mr. Tuba U.S.A."

I especially recall one discussion about the American Symphony Orchestra with Stokowski, which took place when he was in his eighties. He was sitting at his desk, with thinning white hair and unbridled optimism, telling me that in ten years time he planned to have the best orchestra in the world.

In reviewing possibilities of personnel, I mentioned a young violist, Samuel Rhodes, whose Carnegie Recital Hall debut I paid for. He was outstanding but with little orchestral experience. The Maestro gently laid his hand on my arm, smiled, and said, "I will give him experience."

While in Aspen for the summer of 1962, I chose to resign my position with Stokowski and his American Symphony Orchestra. I felt I was overextended and in conflict with my duties for the Symphony of the Air. Stokowski responded with a brief note thanking me for previous assistance and regretting my resignation.

The Little Orchestra Society had scheduled a performance of Gunther Schuller's *Symphony for Brass*. The orchestra was conducted by Pierre Monteux at Town Hall. The score called for two euphoniums and one tuba. I got a call from Gunther about performing on the piece and I reminded him that the Orchestra Society had its own tubist, Bill Stanley. Gunther said he had John Swallow for euphonium 1. I started giving Gunther the names of euphonium players I knew, and he said I didn't understand: he wanted me to play the euphonium 2 part. I accepted the schedule of rehearsals and performances and was happy to learn that henceforth the *Symphony for Brass* would be performed with one euphonium and two tubas.

The next time I played with the Little Orchestra Society, some twenty-five years later, it was the Ralph Vaughan Williams *Concerto for Tuba and Orchestra* at Alice Tully Hall.

My career was given a forced rest in June of 1959. The New York City Ballet Orchestra had just finished two recording sessions of Hershy Kay's ballet orchestrations, *Western Symphony* and *Stars and Stripes,* in a hotel ballroom at Broadway and 76th Street. We were on our way to the City Center for an evening ballet performance. Personnel manager George Michelmore was driving principal violist Jack Bronstein's car with David Uber and myself as passengers; I sat in the rear seat. It was a beautiful day and there was little traffic. We turned south onto Columbus Avenue and stopped at the traffic light at 60th Street, in the right lane. Suddenly we were struck in the rear by a large refrigerated meat truck leased from Hertz. The truck driver was obviously trying to keep up with the staggered traffic light system. Jack Bronstein's prize vehicle was demolished.

I was thrown up to the ceiling and into the back of the front seat. I was taken to see Dr. Kurzner, an orthopedic surgeon, for examination. He diagnosed severe whiplash and back injuries. I was hospitalized and put in double traction for two weeks followed by twenty-two months wearing a back brace and a neck brace.

After three months, Dr. Kurzner okayed my return to performing on my tuba but instructed me not to carry it. Carol carried my tuba from one recording session to another. Recording engineers would help me get settled in a chair and place a music stand in front of me, and Carol would take the tuba out of its cover and set it in my lap. The recording engineer then adjusted the microphone and we were in business for another three-hour recording session. Carol never complained about a bruised hip from carrying my tuba. She enjoyed witnessing musicians at work and play. Carol and I have had a remarkable life together, sharing recording sessions, rehearsals, concerts, events, and unpredictable occasions around the world. Before children, during children, after children, good times, bad times, it doesn't matter. With Carol, life is a ball.

My court case came to jury trial five years after the accident. On the recommendation of a trusted ballet orchestra colleague, the law firm of a former New York City police commissioner, George P. Monaghan, was engaged to represent my interests regarding injuries resulting from the accident. Unfortunately for me, the attorney assigned to my case was young and inexperienced. Dr. Kurzner, the orthopedic surgeon who treated my injuries, presented my case well in court. He described the back and neck injuries I suffered in the accident and gave his medical prognosis for future complications and treatment. Lewis Waldeck, also a tubist, as well as a colleague and neighbor, testified in court about professional engagements I had diverted to others because of my injuries and prolonged treatment.

The judge sat back in his chair, with his feet on his judge's dais, giving short, snippy instructions to witnesses and to my attorney. After listening to witnesses and my attorney's representation of my case, the judge requested a meeting of the attorneys in his chambers. The jury left as well. When the attorneys returned, the smiling Hertz attorney flashed five fingers to those who had accompanied him to court. The judge announced the settlement amount to be $5,000, not enough to pay for my hospital stay, let alone doctor bills, attorney fees, and lost earnings, plus other incalculable and miscellaneous expenses. The jury never returned.

GOLDMAN BAND

During the summer seasons of 1959 and 1960, I performed with the Goldman Band. Edwin Franko Goldman (1878–1956) was born in Louisville, Kentucky, and studied cornet and composition at the National Conservatory in New York City. He was solo cornetist with the Metropolitan Opera Orchestra from 1899 to 1909. In 1911 he formed the New York Military Band, renamed the Goldman Band in 1917. In 1918 the Goldman Band presented its first season of summer concerts at Columbia University.

In 1923 Goldman's most famous composition, "On The Mall," was premiered in the newly constructed Naumburg Bandshell in the Central Park Mall. It proved to be the most popular number played in the band's concerts; it was sung, whistled, hummed, and always enjoyed by the audience. In 1924 the Guggenheim Foundation began underwriting the Goldman Band's summer concerts. Two of Goldman's publications, *The Amateur Band Guide* and *Aid to Leaders* (1918), helped inspire the founding, in 1929, of the prestigious American Bandmasters Association (ABA). Goldman served as its first president. Two additional books, *Band Betterment* (1934) and *The Goldman Band System* (1935), guided the structure and development of America's unparalleled high school and college band programs.

With his vision, influence, and leadership, Goldman could not have come at a better time. With the death in 1932 of musical icon John Philip Sousa, the success of talking movies, and the impact of the Great Depression on instrument manufacturers and town bands throughout the country, it was time for new leaders to step forward. Edwin Franko Goldman—and others inspired by his vision, persona, and the ABA—together provided the necessary leadership. He was one of a group of band giants which included Sousa, Pryor, A. A. Harding of the University of Illinois, William Revelli of the University of Michigan, and, over the years, noted conductors of the major service bands in Washington, D.C.

The most prestigious award given by the American Bandmasters Association is the Edwin Franko Goldman Citation. I received it, in 1996, for doing more than 250 clinics in schools and at the Music Educators national conference.

The Goldman Band in its prime was the pride of New York City and for most of its tenure maintained a musician personnel typically American— that is to say, countries of major immigration to America were represented in the band. Goldman was fiercely loyal to his musicians. And enthusiastic audiences were equally loyal to the band and its charismatic conductor. Through the years when there was no television and no air-conditioning, audiences enjoyed band concerts in the park, light summer breezes, and escaping the stifling heat of confining city apartments.

From mid-June through August, the Goldman Band performed five nights a week in Central Park and one night each week in Prospect Park, "The Central Park of Brooklyn." Programs were published in the *New York Times*. Musicians had to be on their toes. The band had only one rehearsal—for the season's opening concert. The musicians did a lot of sight-reading, as there was no budget for additional rehearsals. At a time when citizens were unafraid to frequent the park, concerts started at dusk.

THE BURKE-PHILLIPS ALL-STAR CONCERT BAND

In 1960, Jimmy Burke (renowned cornet soloist with the Goldman Band for more than twenty years) and I were featured soloists and clinicians at the Burlington Music Festival in Vermont. Over lunch we were discussing the current state of professional civilian bands with which we had performed as soloists and/or section players. We lamented the 1956 demise of Paul Lavalle's Cities Service Band of America and the positive influence of its Monday evening broadcasts over NBC. Members of American town bands, as well as college band faculties, students of all ages, and people who just enjoyed good band music, looked forward to every broadcast.

The Goldman Band was one point of our discussion. We were concerned that after the death of Edwin Franko Goldman the quality of the band had declined. Younger talent was needed to maintain the musical integrity of the band. Jimmy and I, and a few others in the band, felt we were pulling a heavy load.

Daydreaming, Jimmy said, "How fantastic it would be to have a band with no weak sections!"

I said, "Let's do it. We couldn't tour or concertize with such a band but we could make recordings. I'm sure my good friend Clark Galehouse would help us record such a band." Jimmy agreed to the project and started a dream list of repertoire he wanted to record. We enjoyed the challenge and pleasure of selecting an entire band of great musicians who loved and admired one another. We agreed that Jimmy would conduct and choose repertoire. I would play tuba and contract our chosen personnel. We would both play solos, with Hunter Wiley as guest conductor. On the back of an envelope I listed our dream band personnel, with very few alternates. We agreed to share the costs of production. We recorded two LPs for Golden Crest Records.

At his own request, playing last chair trumpet was Harry Glantz, principal trumpet for Toscanini in the New York Philharmonic and NBC Symphony Orchestra. I called Al Gallodoro, considered to be the world's greatest alto saxophone player, and Jimmy Abato, who was also great. The rumor for years was that they didn't get along, because they were never seen on the same recording sessions. I called Al first, and told him what we were doing. After he committed to the project, I said, "By the way, we want Jimmy Abato to share the first part with you." He said, "Jimmy Abato!" There was a pregnant pause. "I haven't worked with him in years! Boy, this will be a treat!" Phew! I did the same thing with Jimmy, being stealthy about it and telling him at the end of our conversation that he would be working with Al Gallodoro. He said, "Al Gallodoro! Wow, he's my hero!" So much for rumors. All the players I called expressed similar delight at being included.

Instead of recording in a studio, Clark Galehouse recommended and booked a movie theater with great acoustics in Huntington, Long Island. Each LP was recorded in six hours: 8:30–11:30 on successive Saturday and Sunday mornings to accommodate musicians committed to theater matinees or other gigs. We had to be out of the building before noon so the movie could begin. A good half hour of the first session was everyone greeting each other and having orange juice, coffee, and doughnuts or Danish pastries. We didn't despair about the lost time; the superb quality of the recordings reflects the rarified atmosphere that was established. Contrary to many LPs, which condescend to list musician personnel on the back of their album covers (if at all), musician personnel in the Burke-Phillips All-Star Concert Band are listed on the front of the recording's jacket in big letters.

One of the recordings presents an incredible transcription of Rimsky-Korsakov's *Scheherazade*, sight-read at the end of the second session. The piece is about twelve minutes long and we had only fifteen minutes of time left to record. The famous solo violin double stops, played by two trumpets in the transcription, were quickly rehearsed by Robert Nagel and Raymond Crisara. We then started at the beginning and played straight through to the end. Just as the minute hand reached 11:30 so did the reverberation of the last notes. We had finished it. I have never heard a more exciting performance of *Scheherazade*. It only goes to prove that experience, expertise, musicianship, and camaraderie are sometimes worthy substitutes for rehearsal time.

Equally thrilling was the second recording of the Burke-Phillips All-Star Concert Band, which was a year later. The only change in personnel was the addition of one percussionist. The recording consisted of a transcription of Berlioz's *Roman Carnival Overture* and the Jimmy Abato performance of the Tchaikovsky *Violin Concerto*, transcribed for solo clarinet and an all-clarinet choir, led by guest conductor Lucien Cailliet. (Lucien later wrote a piece for solo tuba and wind ensemble called *Le Pioneer*, dedicated to me.)

In 1959, a classic recording, *The Golden Striker,* was released, written, and orchestrated in the style of Giovanni Gabrieli. The musicians on this recording have often appeared in projects motivated by John Lewis of the Modern Jazz Quartet, and John inevitably involved his close friend and associate, Gunther Schuller. This recording should be in every collector's library. A spinoff from this recording was the film score of *Odds Against Tomorrow.*

Recording *Odds Against Tomorrow* led naturally to founding Orchestra U.S.A., organized to cope successfully with all styles of music. Gunther Schuller calls the thirty-member Orchestra U.S.A. a third-stream orchestra, a term he invented to mean doing both classical and jazz in various amalgamations. Personnel chosen for this orchestra combined the talents of great classical players who could feel at home in the jazz idiom and great jazz players who could successfully fit into the classical style. The core of Orchestra U.S.A. included the New York Woodwind Quintet and New York Brass Quintet and other gifted players such as Phil Woods, Charles Russo, Herb Pomeroy, and Eric Dolphy. Besides playing tuba with Orchestra U.S.A., it has been my pleasure to assist Gunther Schuller and John Lewis as executive vice president. I worked with attorney Joseph Taubman on the business and legal affairs of the orchestra.

I wanted to find rehearsal space for the ensemble. After looking around and finding only an expensive top-floor loft on 79th Street, I called Artie Shaw and explained what we were trying to do with the orchestra. I told him that I had found a rehearsal space but did not have enough money to pay the lease, and I asked him if he could help us. He met me at the loft on 79th Street and approved of the room. Artie Shaw's office paid the rehearsal hall expenses directly. Not only did we rehearse Orchestra U.S.A. there, but we also made it available for Arthur Weisberg's Contemporary Chamber Music Ensemble. Orchestra U.S.A. recorded four LPs. The selected personnel for each came from a pool of qualified musicians, based on their availability.

CLINICS

Performing clinics and solo recitals became a constant extracurricular activity for me. One of the early clinics I presented was sponsored by the Olds Instrument Company when they made their first CC tuba. I borrowed Sammy Green's car (he was my stand partner in the Goldman Band that summer) so Carol and I could drive to the Pennsylvania Music Educators Association meeting in Reading. A new Olds CC tuba was being shipped there. When it arrived, the packing crate was opened onstage, with great ceremony, and then I presented an impromptu clinic-recital on the new tuba. Orin Sepp, eastern representative for Olds, set up the clinic; he was also very helpful with my proposal that Olds add an orchestral CC tuba to its product line. Olds was the first manufacturer since the early 1930s to produce an orchestral CC tuba. They produced only one. Olds, like other American manufacturers, was more interested in producing instruments for secondary school bands than in meeting the need for professional quality instruments. Unfortunately, Olds ceased musical instrument production shortly after the debut of its CC tuba.

I performed many clinics with the New York Brass Quintet and some while a member of the U.S. Army Field Band. But it wasn't until around the fall of 1959 that I started performing solo clinics regularly for the Conn Corporation. By 1964 I was doing twenty to thirty solo clinics annually. Factoring in one travel day in each direction, that amounted to a minimum of sixty days a year on the road for clinics alone! Solo clinics were great for opening doors and reaching new audiences. For example, an appearance at the Chicago Midwest Clinic might lead to ten or more bookings with the bands of music educators attending that conference.

Performing new works I had commissioned helped spread awareness of new solo repertoire for the tuba, including Warren Benson's *Helix* for solo tuba and wind ensemble, Gunther Schuller's *Diptych* for brass quintet and concert band, Alec Wilder's *Elegy* for solo tuba and brass choir, Thomas Beversdorf's *Concertino* for solo tuba and symphony winds, Bernhard Heiden's *Concerto for Solo Tuba* (scored by the composer for either symphony orchestra or wind ensemble), Eddie Sauter's *Conjectures* (subtitled *Harvey Phillips, Tuba*) for solo tuba and wind ensemble, and significant other solos for tuba with band accompaniment.

Composer Harold Farberman recalls that he composed a piece for the quintet to record with a tuba part "fit for a Phillips." He added later, "While

Harvey played it beautifully, what seemed so effortless to him has proved the opposite to other tuba players who've tackled it. "

In 1965, I was appearing again as a tuba clinician for the Midwest Conference, at the Sherman House in Chicago. This year's conference included a special band comprising clinicians and performing music educators. Circus bandmaster Merle Evans, who retired in 1965, was conducting a concert of circus music. Forest McAllister, publisher of the magazine *School Music News*, served as announcer and ringmaster, in proper attire. There was no rehearsal. Meanwhile, I was keeping a dinner date made with Arnold Jacobs in the excellent seafood restaurant located in the basement of the hotel. We were enjoying our meal when Arnold casually inquired, "Harvey, what time is your concert?"

"Oh," I said, "The concert doesn't start till 8:00." Alarmed by my response, Arnold said, "It's five minutes to 8 now!" I then noticed my watch was not working.

Hastily, I thanked Arnold and apologized as I exited the restaurant and ran for the elevator. I had to go to my eighth-floor room and retrieve the white fiberglass sousaphone that the Conn Corporation wanted me to play in the concert. Fortunately, the lobby and elevators weren't crowded, since all the hotel guests were in the main ballroom waiting for the concert to start. There is no incognito way to enter a filled-to-capacity hall carrying a white sousaphone and arriving after all other members of the band have been introduced. The clever stalling tactic of Forest McAllister worked out perfectly with the timing of my entrance as the last to be introduced with, "Oh yes, the late Harvey Phillips." One would think we had rehearsed it that way. The closing number on this program was Sousa's "The Stars and Stripes Forever" and featured Mr. Bell and me playing in unison the famous piccolo solo in front of the band.

In 1966, I had completed a series of clinics in Wisconsin, followed by one in Hattiesburg, Mississippi. I asked a high school band director in Wisconsin to send the music to Hattiesburg but the student he assigned didn't send it. And to top it off, when I arrived at the New Orleans airport, my luggage didn't. I rented a car.

Two college band members, in band uniforms, standing at attention and holding sousaphones, were standing along the highway near Hattiesburg. I stopped and asked them why they were there; they said they were there to make contact with Harvey Phillips. When we got to the clinic they selected music out of their library for me to play. Euphonium player Rich Matteson, also a soloist with the band, said that if I didn't have to wear a tuxedo at the concert (because mine hadn't arrived) then he didn't either. He never wore one again.

Over the years, I made several appearances at the Chicago Midwest Band and Orchestra Clinic, at the Hilton Hotel, always in December. I did clinics on a fairly regular basis for the New York State Schools of Music Association, the Texas Music Educators Association, and the Texas Bandmasters Association.

In 1961, William Bell retired from the New York Philharmonic to accept an appointment from Dean Wilfred C. Bain to the Indiana University School of Music. Replacing William Bell in the Philharmonic was Joseph Novotny, who resigned from the Metropolitan Opera to accept the New York Philharmonic's tuba chair. I was invited to audition for the Metropolitan Opera. I had already been performing in the stage band of *Wozzeck* at the Met, and was also a member of the New York City Opera Orchestra. I auditioned for nine Met conductors; each wanted to hear how I sounded in the operas he conducted.

I signed a contract with orchestra manager Felix Eyle, stipulating that my principal chair salary would be the same as the first oboe, making one fewer negotiation for me. I immediately started having second thoughts. I called Carol and told her I had signed the contract but I felt like I had just joined the Army. I thought about the Met schedule and was concerned that I would ultimately lose the privilege of variety I enjoyed as a freelance player. I notified Mr. Eyle that I would be resigning from the contract I had signed. He said it was not within his power to negate such an agreement but he would pass on my intentions to Maestro Erich Leinsdorf. Throughout all of this negotiation, the Met was on tour. A few days later, Eyle called to inform me that he had spoken with Maestro Leinsdorf, who said I would be allowed to send "deputies" to other operas if I would guarantee performances of Wagner and Strauss. Fearing there might be trouble brewing with all of this, I made an appointment to meet with Al Manuti, president of Local 802, and the son of Giovanni Manuti, tubist at the Met for forty-five years. Al Manuti assured me he understood my situation and would support my decision. I next received notice from Eyle that if I would agree to do all the Wagner, I would be allowed to send deputies to Strauss. I still wanted out of the contract.

Eyle said, "Why don't you want to work at the Met? Everybody wants to work at the Met."

I replied, "I don't want to be in the opera business. I want to stay in the music business." It was a flippant response but it had the result intended. I was very pleased to learn that Herbert Wekselblatt was called for the position. Herb and I often spoke of how different our lives would have been had I stayed with the Met.

FUNNY ASIDES

Across the street from the stage door to the old Met was a bar frequented by some of the Met Opera orchestra players. The horn players could march directly from the bar to their chairs in the pit, without missing a beat, and discreetly pick up their horns and start playing their next entrance.

One time, Carmine Fornarotto, who played trumpet in the New York Philharmonic, and his wife gave a party. About 11:15 Carmine and I went out for pizza. I asked the pizza seller if we could also buy a half-dozen empty boxes and some cardboard, for weight. Back at the apartment, Marie Fornorato screamed each time she opened a box and it was empty. Finally, thinking she might faint, I went back into the hallway and brought in the boxes with the pizza inside.

Many of our parties were at the home of John and Elsie Richardson (Carol's sister), who lived in Armonk, New York. John was a fine trombonist whose position with IBM included responsibility for entertainment for IBM's annual corporate 100 Percent Club banquet. John had ongoing contact with many musicians and entertainers. John and Elsie were great hosts and their home a great party house. There were many memorable incidents. One was at a party for Hoagy Bix Carmichael, son of composer Hoagy Carmichael. Several guests arrived at the same time and the foyer was crowded as they hung up their winter coats. The president of Local 802, John Glasel, arrived with his wife Maryanne at the same time Hoagy Bix arrived and he turned to introduce himself. "Hi, I'm Hoagy Carmichael." Maryanne replied in her distinctive New York accent, "Sure you are. And I'm Marilyn Monroe." It was a great way to start a party. Many of our musician friends had homes in the Armonk–Greenwich–White Plains–Bedford area.

Peter Sexauer was attending the IU School of Music and taking euphonium lessons from family friend William Bell. One day close friends of the Sexauers, passing through Bloomington on a trip west, stopped to look up Peter and say hello. Answers to a few questions got them to the School of Music offices. The visitors walked up to the inquiries window just as Dean Bain arrived to open a file cabinet and retrieve a file. When asked by a secretary, "Can I help you?" the visitors responded, "We're wondering if you have a Sexauer in this School of Music." Dean Bain, quick and of good humor, responded for the secretary by saying, "Sex hour? Hell, we don't even give them coffee breaks!"

UNEXPECTED OPPORTUNITIES

In 1966, I received a telephone call from the Boston Symphony personnel manager, Rosario Mazzeo, in Tanglewood. He informed me that K. Vinal Smith was retiring from his position as tubist with the Boston Symphony. Maestro Leinsdorf, who had left the Metropolitan Opera to be music director of the Boston Symphony, had asked him to contact me and negotiate a salary. I told Mr. Mazzeo I would need some time to discuss such a major move with my wife and other associates. He said he understood but would appreciate my getting back to him as soon as possible.

I was concerned about giving up a well-established freelance career and I soon decided to pass up this opportunity. I still find it rather strange that one year later, in 1967, I would give up a full-time freelance performance career and accept an administrative position with Gunther Schuller at the New England Conservatory of Music, across the street from Boston's Symphony Hall.

CHAPTER NINE

On Tour with the
New York Brass Quintet

ONE TIME IN 1954 the New York Brass Quintet was in Boston to do children's concerts in Brookline, Massachusetts, for a couple of days. We had an afternoon off and went to Harvard to their little recital hall to rehearse and perform. There was an older gentleman in the hall who turned out to be music publisher Robert King. That's when we first met him. He was very taken with the group because he had organized a euphonium–tuba quartet in the late 1930s. He and his friends would go into the mountains of New Hampshire to rehearse. They intended to tour. Then the Japanese attacked Pearl Harbor and their plans were all smashed. He had done a lot of research into Purcell's, Holborne's, Gabrieli's, and other Renaissance composers' brass works. He became an ardent fan of the New York Brass Quintet and gave us a catalog of his publications, which was very helpful. After the quintet became popular, he sold a lot of music.

The last concert of the New York Brass Quintet was in North Easton, Massachusetts, in 1984, in his church. We let him choose the program. I replaced Toby Hanks for that concert.

Before the New York Brass Quintet agreed to exclusivity, I played in several brass quintets, including the Metropolitan Brass Quintet. At a school concert in Brooklyn with this group, after our first selection was announced, one player decided it was time to check his instrument to see if there was any water in it. He pulled out and checked each of his slides, which took some time. So, as soon as he was through and ready to play, I started pulling my slides and winked at the other players, who followed my lead and made a big production out of emptying their instruments. It became a big joke for the high school audience. I told them, "Let this be a lesson to you. If you ever play in a brass quintet, make sure you empty your slides before going onstage." Needless to say, that musician managed to control his nervous habit of emptying his slides onstage from that point on.

One day, I received a call from trombonist Arnold Fromme, one of the original enthusiastic Juilliard musicians who helped organize the New York Brass Ensemble. He was helping organize another brass quintet and asked if I would play tuba in the group; if I wasn't available, they would take bass trombonist Gil Cohen. I had just pledged allegiance to the New York Brass Quintet and had to say no to Arnold. So he formed his new quintet with a bass trombone instead of tuba. This became the remarkably successful American Brass Quintet and it caused to be created an important library of brass quintet music with that combination of instruments.

Our vows of exclusivity were important to the growth of the New York Brass Quintet. We were all busy freelancers and realized that maintaining the quality of our ensemble required commitment and the undivided attention of each player.

Keith Brown, trombone, was with the NYBQ for only one year, leaving in the fall of 1959 to join the Philadelphia Orchestra. His playing had a profound effect on the other members of the quintet. It was a very productive year that brought about major decisions. Also, ironically, at the same time, Hunter Wiley, who had played second trombone and solo euphonium with the New York City Ballet Orchestra, announced he was leaving to join the faculty of the University of Tampa. First, I spoke to the personnel manager of the New York City Ballet Orchestra, George Michelmore, who played bass trombone and sat next to me in the orchestra. He was familiar with John Swallow's playing and agreed that I could offer him the position. Then I spoke with Bob Nagel of the New York Brass Quintet. Bob also was familiar with John's performance and agreed that I would call John about joining the N Y B Q. Once I knew that both positions were open and being offered to John, I called his home in a Chicago suburb to tell him we wanted him in New York for two positions that started at the same time and did not conflict with each other—and the sum of the two positions paid in excess of the Chicago Symphony position which he had just lost.

His wife, Wendy, answered the telephone and didn't believe it was me and thought it was a crank call. She hung up without talking to me. When John arrived home, she told him about the call. He phoned me immediately and cordially accepted. The following week he moved his family into a Long Island apartment. His first assignment was a recording with the quintet titled *Two Contemporary Composers:* two difficult works by Alec Wilder and Don Hammond.

Concert bookings for the quintet increased dramatically, but lucrative freelance engagements could no longer be sacrificed for school demonstration concerts. So, amicably, we left Young Audiences, Inc., to other newly formed brass quintets. Maintaining the N Y B Q's high level of performance now required scheduled rehearsals, formal concert engagements, and concert tours. It was time to seek the booking services of professional management.

Helpful to these bookings would be an "in concert" L P recording that presented sample concert repertoire of this "new" brass chamber music, unknown to community concerts. Having no record company connections at that time, we decided to produce our own master tape on speculation. In the spring of 1959 we engaged long-time friend Bobby Blake, a recording engineer with studios on the ninth floor of Carnegie Hall, convenient to my rehearsal and teaching studio. The results of this collaboration were enhanced enormously when Clark Galehouse, president of Golden Crest Records, agreed to remaster and release this N Y B Q *in Concert* (Golden Crest 4023) recording, featuring Robert Nagel and John Glasel, trumpets; Frederick Schmidt, horn; Keith Brown, trombone; and Harvey Phillips, tuba.

The second recording made by the N Y B Q was *Two Contemporary Composers* (Golden Crest 4017), with Robert Nagel and John Glasel, trumpets;

Frederick Schmidt, horn; John Swallow, trombone; and Harvey Phillips, tuba.

Columbia Artists Management, Inc., (CAMI) was the largest booking agency for music artists in New York. CAMI was very good at promoting new artists and new chamber ensembles. The strategy was simple. If a presenter wanted to book one of the "name" artists, CAMI pressured the presenter also to book a new, not yet widely known artist or ensemble. This usually paid off well for all concerned. CAMI was very organized for booking programs for presenters of "community concert" series across the United States.

To acquaint presenters with new artists and ensembles, CAMI arranged each spring to have promoters from different regions of the country come to New York City and hear the proposed new crop of musicians perform. There might be a showcase audition before one hundred presenters from the Northeast region one day, then one hundred from southern mid-America on another day, and so on. The New York Brass Quintet was selected for this important exposure and planned American tours based on bookings received from these "showcase" auditions.

After the quintet was no longer on CAMI's roster, I continued to be listed as one of its three brass soloists. We were Maurice Andre, trumpet; Barry Tuckwell, horn; and Harvey Phillips, tuba.

FIRST AMERICAN TOUR

In 1960, the New York Brass Quintet decided to embark upon an extended tour of the United States. Carol was with me on that first tour. The quintet became a sextet with her membership. She was a very keen critic of the group and kept a close eye on details such as how we walked on stage, how we bowed, how we talked to patrons, what people said about us during intermissions, etc., as well as critiquing our performances. We learned that having this extra set of eyes and ears was very important to evaluating the success of our touring ensemble, a lesson we have tried to pass on to other groups and to our students. On that first national tour, Bob Nagel, John Swallow, and I, while riding in the same car, created a very important educational handout for the many clinics and master classes we were asked to present at schools. The handout was an outline for discussing brass instrument techniques for performance.

Just the word "brass" seemed to scare our elderly female contingent of concertgoers. Carol reported from the lobby that the older ladies would often remark, "Let's sit in the back row—brass is so loud." We would come out onstage and the first twenty rows of the theater would be empty and the audience would be clumped together in the back. So we would play everything very softly, just nice, polite, quiet music. Even if we did the Ewald *Brass Quintet* to close out the first half of the concert, we would render a very subdued version.

At intermission Carol would overhear the ladies: "Wasn't that wonderful! Not loud at all!" They would then position themselves in the front rows for the second half, at which point we would take great delight in pulling out an exciting opener that would just nail them to their seats. They had come with a certain expectation and we didn't want to disappoint them. They were surprised by our range of dynamics and often found themselves enjoying the "loud" music.

One of the first people to recognize the importance of Gunther Schuller's *Symphony for Brass and Percussion* was conductor Leon Barzin. Barzin volunteered to conduct rehearsals and possibly a debut performance if Gunther would recruit the musicians. Proving the legend about musician traffic on Carnegie Hall's famous corner, 57th Street and Seventh Avenue, Gunther told me he literally stood on the street corner and recruited an excellent group of players to rehearse at the National Orchestral Association rehearsal hall on 56th Street. I think this endeavor prompted a lot of curiosity and excitement among brass musicians. I also seem to recall that a bootleg recording resulted from this initial effort. Only in New York.

Two of Gunther's early compositions to capture the attention of conductors and music directors were *Seven Studies on Themes of Paul Klee* for symphony orchestra and *Symphony for Brass and Percussion*.

Gunther gave the NYBQ the first movement of *Music for Brass Quintet* (commissioned by the Elizabeth Sprague Coolidge Foundation) about five days before Christmas. We immediately started rehearsing, with Gunther in the room. He would hear something he wanted to remark on or he would have something to interject, and then he would return to composing the second movement, which we received the day after Christmas. It was a busy time and it was difficult to schedule rehearsals. But we somehow managed to do so. We received the third and final movement January 11 at Pennsylvania Station just before boarding the train to Washington, D.C. The third movement had to be rehearsed in the Library of Congress without Gunther's assistance. The premiere was performed at the Library of Congress on January 13, 1961.

Gunther said he could write anything for the NYBQ because we liked to be challenged. His "Little Brass Music," for brass quartet, one trumpet, was dashed off, completed on the day of performance for a birthday party honoring composer Stefan Wolpe. Wolpe, popular among his colleagues, attended a private concert in Carnegie Recital Hall in the discomfort of a stretcher on wheels. The entire concert comprised works by friends and students of Wolpe. "Little Brass Music" is, in my view, as near perfect as any composer could write. It's exactly the right length; nobody will leave hating twelve-tone music; it's a challenge; and it's fun to play. We rehearsed it in my studio on the fourteenth floor of Carnegie Hall, above the Carnegie Recital Hall, right until it was time for us to play. Somebody let us know when it was time.

Fred Mills, who played trumpet in the Canadian Brass for twenty-four years, always said that in Indiana I held open house for students, former students, and musicians wandering through the Midwest. On one of his visits to the TubaRanch, he reminisced that he met me when he was a student at Juilliard. He said, "At the National Orchestral Association, when you were brass coach, you would whisper to a musician who made a mistake so it could be corrected and he wouldn't be embarrassed. You never acted too professional to help and nurture young people who were becoming musicians."

Mills went on, "Once in 1963 you phoned and said, 'I need to borrow your piano.' You came in with John Barrows, pianist Gil Kalish, and Alec Wilder. You all took over my living room with readings of Alec's *Suite for Horn, Tuba, and Piano No. 2*. These fantastic musicians were playing. Wilder was smoking a pipe, looking at the score, and nodding. What an experience! It struck me as just another day in your life."

DRIVING ACROSS AMERICA

Touring always involves copious amounts of driving. After performing a concert in Garden City, Kansas, the NYBQ left early the next morning for a long, lonely stretch of road en route to Wichita. We pulled into a gas station restaurant to have lunch. On the wall of the restaurant was a pay telephone which began to ring impatiently. The lone gentleman who was working there pumping gas, cooking, and serving meals eventually answered it. After he said, "Hello," there was a pause while he received some kind of instructions. Then he turned and yelled at us, "Is there a Harvey Phillips in the restaurant?" The other members of the quintet just about fainted. But it was Gunther Schuller on the phone, wanting to discuss some details for one of our New York projects. I hung up the phone just as lunch was served and sat back down to dumbfounded looks from the other quintet members.

Gunther had found me by calling the Kansas State Highway Patrol, telling them of the route we were traveling, and inquiring if there was any place to eat that would be about three-and-a-half to four hours outside of Garden City. The State Police identified two such places, both with pay telephones, and shared the numbers on file. Gunther called the first number on the list and struck oil. To this day, the quintet members swear I somehow arranged the whole thing. How could I have possibly known in advance which gas station we would stop at in the middle of rural Kansas?

On the same tour, as we left Wichita for our next concert engagement, I told the other members of the quintet that since we had the evening free, I would like us to visit my sister and her family in Conway Springs. I said they lived on a farm seven miles south of town and I had visited there in 1948 when I was home from the circus. Now, I knew that my sister and her family had since built a beautiful house in the town of Conway Springs and that nobody had lived on that farm for some time. But just to have fun with the guys, I took them out to that old farmhouse and told them Sue would have dinner ready for us.

The farmhouse looked like it was ready to collapse. My fellow musicians looked at me incredulously. I said, "I'll go and see if I can find Sue; she's got to be here somewhere." I stepped out and yelled for Gabe, her husband. But, of course, no one showed up. I somehow enticed the guys out of the car to help me look around the farm. I opened up the big barn doors and hollered into the darkness, "Sue! Are you in there?" I think I almost had them convinced that they still lived on the farm and were just around the corner. Finally the guys began to notice the obvious signs that nobody had lived there for years. My response was, "Boy, I sure must have gotten turned around." I then proceeded to take them into town, where we met Sue and her family for a wonderful visit. When I recounted our visit to the old farm, Sue said if only I had let her know she could have come from the barn with a shotgun and a jackrabbit. The evening included dinner and an impromptu musicale with Gabe getting his guitar and Sue singing and demonstrating a flapper's dance. The rest of us sang and played our instruments and other instruments that were there. It was a good party.

In Emporia, Kansas, we stopped at a highly recommended steak house. It was small and intimate and managed by Kansas State University graduate students. They had a huge St. Bernard that sat just outside the restaurant. When we first drove up, we thought it was a statue but, no, it was a real St. Bernard. His name was Joe. They served enormous steaks in this place and they had a note on the menu, "Save the bone for Joe," which we did. He was very happy to get it.

From there we went up to Laramie, Wyoming. I was met by a dear friend I hadn't seen in a long time. He wanted to take us for a steak dinner before the concert and we obliged. We imagined they would have great steaks in Laramie and we weren't disappointed. After our sumptuous meal, we just barely made it to the concert hall in time to put on our tuxes and assemble our instruments and go out onstage to perform. We didn't realize right away that we were now seven thousand feet above sea level, higher than we had been in Kansas. So we were out of breath and full of steak. It was one of the toughest concerts I've ever performed; we started Victor Ewald's *First Quintet* and I needed three or four breaths to get through the first phrase! As our stomachs began to digest the steak through the second half, the concert became more bearable to play and we managed to survive to the finish.

In Portales, New Mexico, we stopped at a steakhouse just outside the town where the evening's concert was to take place. We were all famished and looked forward to the meal, which took awhile to prepare. We passed the time by chatting about the tour and only gradually came to the realization that we were running out of time and had to make the difficult choice between making our concert on time or enjoying our dinner. They brought out the beautiful steaks and we had only fifteen minutes to spare. Luckily, we were able to have it both ways. We told the kitchen to put them back on the grill when we returned and left Carol as collateral as we dashed off to play the concert. When we returned, the steaks, freshly reheated and still delicious, were waiting for us. As was Carol.

I was never too fond of driving long distances and I had a trick for getting out of long hauls. I would close my right eye and nod my head while keeping my left eye opened and focused on the road. I was alert and driving safely but, to the person in the front passenger seat, it looked like I was dozing off. He'd notice this and, with an effort to conceal his alarm, would suggest very casually, "Hey, let's stop, Harv. I think I'll drive for a while." I would say, "OK, that's fine." I would get in the back and go to sleep.

Once while touring Iowa and Nebraska, we had a long trip ahead of us to our next day's booking and decided to do our extra driving after the concert. So, I called the motel that we had booked and told them we would only need the room for eight hours, to change clothes. Of course the changing of the desk clerk may have left some wrong ideas as we poured out of the car. I checked us all in, and we left the lobby for a large double room—the brass quintet guys and Carol. We had time for a little relaxation before departing in tuxedos for the concert. After the concert, we returned just long enough to put on our street clothes, settle our account with the motel, and head for the next booking. The desk clerk did not question our hasty departure; five guys, one girl.

A problem for any brass quintet is finding a horn player who plays strongly enough to balance with the forward-facing brass instruments. The horn points back, away from the group. We would try to compensate by having the trumpets and trombone point their bells across the stage rather than directly into the audience, which helped a little. But we also found it desirable to devise a folding sound reflector to go behind the horn. We did that by finishing some light quarter-inch plywood so it looked nice onstage and fashioned piano hinges on eight panels eight inches wide.

Then we could position it whatever way we felt best benefited the horn in our concerts. When folded, it lay in the bottom of the trunk of the car. It became a very useful item on the tour by giving us more flexibility in the various concert halls we were faced with. Now, I think most groups tour with a reflector for horn made out of clear plexiglass so that it is hardly visible.

Our American tour was very successful and became the first of many. The tour was four weeks long and most of us were pretty exhausted by the time we got back to New York. I had two telephone answering services and an answering machine on my phone at home, so my upcoming schedule was full.

FIRST EUROPEAN TOUR—MAY–JUNE 1963

In arranging for the quintet's first tour of Europe, Bob Nagel made contact with a European agent who, from his office in Amsterdam, booked an unforgettable tour. We received some valuable support from the Martha Baird Rockefeller Foundation. Our performances included evening concerts, school performances, and radio broadcasts. We began the tour in London, then played in Brussels, Hilversum (Netherlands), Enkhuizen (Netherlands), Copenhagen, Oslo, Paris, Berlin, Bonn, Frankfurt, Cologne, Stuttgart, Zurich, Munich, Essen (Germany), Scheveningen (Netherlands), and Kiel (Germany).

We arrived in London and left the hotel in the early morning for a radio appearance. All the restaurants and hotels had placed their garbage bags out on the sidewalks for trucks to pick up. We were surprised to see that every one of those garbage bags was purple, the very same color as my gig bag, which was made for me back when I was in the circus by the wardrobe department. I became very self-conscious at that moment and the other members of the quintet were amused. We looked like four musicians plus one extra guy hauling a bag of garbage.

We performed that evening in London and premiered the Malcolm Arnold *Quintet for Brass,* which was written for our ensemble. In our audience were both Sir Malcolm Arnold himself and the now-legendary Philip Jones, who had just started a brass quintet and was eschewing the tuba in favor of using two trombones—he didn't feel that the tuba would really work in a brass quintet. But the newspaper the next day had a very interesting headline on its review: "Selfless Tubist Steals Show." That did not go over too well with my colleagues, but I am proud of the review. And, as Philip Jones wrote in his memoirs, hearing our group perform that night persuaded him that a tuba would indeed work in a brass quintet. He started looking for a tuba player and was fortunate to come across the great John Fletcher, who carved a position for himself in the music world. I always liked John's playing because I felt that his sound and my sound were as close as any other tubist I had ever worked with or heard.

We were each allowed a weight of forty pounds on airplanes. The tuba, with cloth cover, only weighed about twenty-five pounds. Carol always had the least weight and this allowed us some flexibility for the extra weight of music and items picked up when touring Europe. We did have one tense situation in an airport. One of the quintet members pointed out that we were overweight and that since I had the tuba, the heaviest instrument, I should pay the extra expense. I replied, "No, that's OK. I will stay here and you can do without the tuba in the next concert." Obviously this put the situation in a new light and there were no more problems.

One of the more memorable stops was Enkhuizen, Holland. Enkhuizen at one time was on the sea but is now inland due to Dutch ingenuity. They built dikes and kept pushing the water out farther. Some of the buildings in the city of Enkhuizen still have Spanish cannonballs lodged in the walls from an attack by the Spanish Armada several hundred years earlier, back when the city was directly on the water. Now the cannonballs would have to travel twenty-five miles to hit the same mark.

In Enkhuizen was a wonderful thirteenth-century domed church. After a brief look around, we set up our instruments to try the hall before we went back to our hotel to change into our concert attire. We were fascinated because the pitch of the sound stayed right as it echoed throughout the church; in most venues, the pitch would drop as it faded. But there was something about the way the cavernous church was constructed that held the pitch true. We were so fascinated by this that we spent a long time playing different chords and listening to them ring. Then we played through some of our pieces and listened as the final chord echoed for several seconds. Then we would play the last chord again. Finally we realized we had a concert to play and had to cut short our experimentation. That was an incredible experience.

Most of our European bookings were concerts at America Houses or national radio stations. Those were live concerts which were also recorded and played again later.

We were pleased to have Roger Bobo meet us for lunch while we were in Amsterdam. He won the audition for the Concertgebouw Orchestra while still a student at the Eastman School of Music, where he was destined for a career as a soloist and orchestral tubist. After a fairly brief time in Amsterdam, he moved to the Los Angeles Philharmonic, where he stayed until retirement.

When we were in the Amsterdam airport to fly to Oslo we had a bit of time to spare. We split up and Carol, of course, went to the famous duty-free shops. She evidently became engrossed in the shopping experience and lost track of time. In the meantime the rest of us had caught the bus out to the plane, which was sitting on the tarmac. We got on the plane and nervously waited—no Carol. Just before the door was to close she rushed in, her face red that she had forgotten the time and barely made that flight. I wrote a poem about the event (and had the passenger in front of me pass it up to Carol):

WHERE'S CAROL?

The tour was going just fine,
all having a wonderful time
London, Brussels, Amsterdam, Enkhuizen
So much to see, no time for snoozin'
We left Amsterdam on our way to Oslo
We had seen all the sights and were ready to go
We arrived at the airport, and no one was late!
We were all overjoyed (there was no overweight)
Some of the boys went to buy tax-free booze
Dry Oslo on Sunday could bring on the blues
The last bus to the plane was ready to go
So we all jumped aboard, win, place, and show
Then we all looked around, but no Carol could we find!
She must be on the plane, she'd be the first in line
Old Ted said that Carol was efficient and sweet
She was on board the plane saving Harvey a seat!

Then we got on the plane and again looked around
We were all much surprised when no Carol could be found
The Captain was warned, but just shook his head
Then on staggered Carol, her pretty face red
From now on we hope she will stay close at hand
We don't want to leave her in some strange foreign land

In Oslo, we played a morning concert at the radio station—the Malcolm Arnold and the Gunther Schuller brass quintets—and an evening concert at the Sonja Henie Auditorium. I also played Ralph Vaughan Williams with the Radio Orchestra. We were amazed at how long the daylight lasted. At 10 PM we saw buses arrive full of high school students who were celebrating their graduation. The celebration didn't start until midnight and it was still light as day.

From Oslo it was on to Paris, and I'm certain that the hotel where we stayed had accommodated the lowest rank of the German army during the Second World War. It had a beautiful long bar on the ground floor; I've seen few to rival it anywhere. But when Carol and I checked into the hotel it took five tries to find a room whose odor we could live with. We settled into our barely manageable quarters and went downstairs to visit the luxurious bar, where we found John Barrows and Ted Weis, who had wisely (or unwisely?) chosen to experience the bar before the room choice.

We were puzzled when the people who managed the Paris concert tried to talk us out of performing the Eugene Bozza *Sonatine* that night. We still haven't figured out their rationale; Bozza was on faculty at the Paris Conservatoire. We performed the piece anyway and it was one of the best performances we ever did of his work. By that time, we had performed the piece so many times that it was a piece of cake.

We had hoped that Eugene Bozza would attend our concert but he didn't appear. When we returned to New York I sent Bozza a letter with a copy of the recording containing his *Sonatine*. He wrote back some time later enclosing the solo part for *Concertino for Solo Tuba and Orchestra* and the quintet piece entitled *Bis* (*Encore*, or *Again*) he had written for the New York Brass Quintet.

From Paris we flew to Berlin with a free day before a concert. The building of the Wall was very much in evidence and of course the city was not accessible by normal driving routes. The Wall was not yet finished, only four to five feet high, and big rolls of razor-sharp wire were being placed alongside it. Some East Berliners were jumping out of buildings over the Wall to escape.

In West Berlin we were very happy to check into a first-class hotel which was centrally located. The city was clean and orderly, but many war-damaged buildings were still in disrepair. We sought out good restaurants and found two, one of which featured a famous German dish, eisbein, which is the hock of a pig. The eisbein was incredible, with snow-white outer skin and reddish-pink meat. We have never had such a classic dish served better. The other restaurant was Chinese, which I chose although Carol had some objections: "We should eat German food while we're here. Besides, they won't have good Chinese food in Berlin." I reminded her that people immigrate all over the world and surely some enterprising Chinese would have seen Berlin as a fresh market to open a Chinese restaurant. I was right, of course. She agreed.

On our second day off, Sunday, we rented a car and decided to visit East Berlin with Bob Nagel, Ted Weis, and John Swallow. We drove and parked at Checkpoint Charlie, where we had to empty our pockets and itemize all our money. Bob, John, Carol, and I had been careful to leave our money in the hotel. But Ted had held on to his money and in emptying his pockets, the lady itemizing his funds became a little perturbed at his mess of American dollars, British pounds, Belgian and French francs, Dutch guilders, and Danish kroner. When just half of Ted's money was documented, she, in Russian army attire and with one eye very bloodshot, looked up at him and barked, "You got too much monya!" If only it were true.

We finally got through Checkpoint Charlie and entered East Berlin. There were no cars in sight and very few people on the sidewalks. When we did come to a traffic light, there would always be three or four children looking for candy or other Western gifts and adults asking for cigarettes. In the course of our sightseeing, I wanted to see the opera house and admire the shell of prewar architectural splendor. From the outside, it looked serviceable. On the inside, it was gutted. I was driving slowly so pictures could be taken, when suddenly, with their alarm horns loudly announcing their presence, we were pulled over and pinned to the curb by six members of the Volkspolizei ("people's police"), who were commonly called VoPos. I, being the driver, was ordered out of the car.

While this was going on, an elderly German lady with a cane, shopping bag, gray coat, and black mushroom hat, came walking by, saying what were obviously insults to the VoPos. One of them barked something back to her and she ended the conversation with "Ja, ja, ja . . . ," mocking the policeman as she walked away. The VoPos asked us if we had money and everyone said no, but I had one West German mark, worth twenty-five cents at that time, in my pocket. I showed it to the police and the one in charge said, "That's a traffic fine." Whereupon I had the nerve to demand a receipt, and got it (we still have it). The guys were pretty scared after that so we left and re-entered West Berlin, back through Checkpoint Charlie. We all had to get out of the car while VoPos searched it, tearing the rear seat loose, looking for possible escapees. We left with the back seat barely reinstalled. Ted claimed his money and we went back to the hotel to rehearse, preparing for our recording at Rundfunk Radio the next day. This was the only station that paid us royalties—for several years to come.

In Cologne we recorded a piece of Henry Brant's written so that there were multiple ensembles, one group of two trumpets and trombone and one of horn and tuba, and we were required to move around to create a variety of antiphonal effects. We had to take our shoes off so the microphones wouldn't pick up our footsteps. John Barrows, who hated moving around, was upset by all of this. But the piece went over very well with the Cologne radio people, and we packed up our instruments in satisfaction. It was then that I noticed that John's sheet music was still in his case—he had improvised his part for all of those different choirs that we were playing, just to show his objection to having to get up and move around in that fashion. John was one of a kind.

After Cologne, we had a few days respite from performing. I don't know where John Barrows went, but Ted Weis went to Rome, sightseeing by himself, and Carol, Bob Nagel, and I rented a car and drove down into Switzerland. John Swallow's wife Wendy had been visiting her parents at their home in England. She joined John for our three-day intermission somewhere in southern France and they drove into Switzerland. Now, we were driving along a very narrow mountain highway in Switzerland when we saw another car coming, so we pulled over to give them lots of room. Surprise—it was John and Wendy! And we just happened to be at a very famous spot where there are seven waterfalls and a restaurant with an outdoor balcony and dining deck where you can see mountain flowers and the waterfalls and enjoy a repast.

Later that day we went through Liechtenstein just to say that we had been to the smallest country in Europe and then it was on to Vienna, where the next concert was scheduled. Carol and I were to meet up with Ted Weis, who was flying in from Rome the next day and had no idea how he was going to get into the city from the airport. We decided to surprise him and watched him from afar as he picked up his luggage and hesitated to decide what his next move would be. In the meantime, we snuck up behind him and, in my deepest voice and best German accent, I said loudly, "Herr Weis!" He stiffened up and turned around quickly, expecting some Austrian authority figure who was looking to deport him. But his apprehension quickly turned to boyish relief when he realized that it was Carol and me.

We returned to the hotel where Bob Nagel was waiting; he and Ted decided they wanted to attend the opera in Vienna that evening. Carol and I agreed to go with them. We had decided that we would spend the afternoon driving around Grunewald. It was a beautiful area, famous for its homemade wine. According to tradition, the owners of palatial houses would put green twigs on their doors if they had wine to sell and they would serve the wine in elegant settings in the backyards of their homes. We stopped at a gorgeous house with the telltale twigs and were greeted as though we had been lifelong friends. We were escorted to the garden in the back of the house and ordered red wine and cheese. The wine was so good that we ordered a bottle of white wine, which was delicious and made us recall how much we liked the red wine. This game continued through the afternoon. We didn't visit another house. Carol is a terrific dancer and I dance like a farmer (anytime I went to a dance, I was playing!). The waiter turned out to be a terrific dancer as well, so he and Carol danced half the afternoon away between our wine-tasting efforts.

I must say, we were alert enough to keep an eye on the clock and left in time to get back to the hotel, change clothes, and go to the opera with Bob and Ted. But this orderly plan had to be altered considerably for, although we did somehow manage to get back to the hotel without incident, we did not change clothes for the opera but fell asleep until awakened by Ted calling on the telephone saying, "Meet us in the lobby. We're going to the opera tonight."

Carol said, "I don't think we're going to the opera."

Ted said, "Where's Harvey?"

"He's here . . . some . . . where," replied Carol. We continued to sleep and Ted and Bob made contact with us again, after the opera. We were able to join them at that time.

The next night's performance was Alban Berg's twelve-tone opera *Wozzeck*. It surprised me to find that there were so many young people there who were obviously dating and would consider *Wozzeck* a worthy date. The sophisticated music culture of Old Vienna runs very deep.

We performed our final concert in Kiel and went our separate ways. Carol and I chose to visit Rome, Madrid, and Lisbon before returning to New York. Since it was our first visit to Rome we felt it appropriate to see all the usual tourist spots: the Vatican, the Spanish Steps, the catacombs, the Forum, the Coliseum, and so on.

We saw all of the fountains that inspired composers to preserve them forever in music. We set out on the Appian Way and, after a few miles, started coming in contact with way stations. People lived in these structures and almost all of them had wine for sale, again signified by the evergreen twigs on the door. Carol and I stopped at one such rest stop and were shown inside where the people lived among two huge barrels of their homemade wine. We purchased a bottle of red wine. At the next village we went through, we bought some Italian bread and cheese. We were having a wonderful time, enjoying the Italians, the countryside, the villages, and their traditions, when suddenly Carol said, "I don't think we should drink this wine. There could be something wrong with it. I'm dizzy." She related a story she had read in the *New York Times* just before we left the States, of several bums in the Bowery of New York who had drunk wood grain alcohol and some of them had died from it. Not wanting the wine to go to waste should it prove to be good, we gave it to some guys working on the road. Looking in the rearview mirror as we drove off, we saw they were still waving and smiling.

In Madrid I had my luggage opened and searched and was made to unclothe my tuba, whereupon I asked if the customs officers had some favorites they wanted me to play for them. They didn't. I was ready to embarrass them. They were probably hoping for me to offer them some kind of bribe. Perhaps I was emboldened by our experience with the VoPos, because I wasn't going to give in.

From the Lisbon airport we arrived downtown by taxi and checked into a charming little hotel recommended by our travel guidebook. We spoke to the hotel concierge about where to rent a car, and he recommended a rental agency close by and called to confirm that a car was available. We walked the few blocks to the agency and rented an English "Herald" bright red convertible, which was fun to drive. According to our travel book the best restaurant in all of Portugal was a five-star restaurant in Cascais. We checked the map and decided that driving to Cascais would be a pleasant experience. We arrived at the beach there and parked the car. Strolling on the beach, we were fascinated watching the fishermen arrive with small, colorful, fish-laden boats. Their catches were readied for auction as their happy families made the occasion into a party. While they were tidying things up, Carol took pictures with a Polaroid camera and handed the undeveloped film to her subjects. They were captivated, watching the photos develop. This caused a near riot on the beach. They had never seen Polaroid pictures. Everybody wanted pictures taken. Carol complied until she ran out of film.

After the frenzy of picture taking, a gentleman came up and introduced himself as a reporter for a Lisbon paper. He asked if we had ever attended a fish auction. When our response was negative he invited us to accompany him. The fish auction proved to be an exciting event. It moves at a much faster pace than American auctions. Strategy for getting the best price for the fisherman has the auctioneer start by announcing and posting the highest possible price for each item. The auctioneer lowers the bid until someone buys. The first bid buys the fish. There is no second bid. It seemed to me that there was no conversation and anyone who made a sound was considered to have bought the fish. The atmosphere of anxiety is more charged than at traditional auctions, where a higher bid is always possible. At the fish auction, bidders were nervously trying to assess the actions or potential actions of other bidders. The star of this auction was a huge tuna.

After the fish auction we were anxious to go to our five-star restaurant. We told our new friend where we were going and asked him what he thought. He said "Oh, I've got a better restaurant for you; it's where all of the fishermen eat. It may be the best restaurant in the world." We decided to take his recommendation and invited him to come along. He thanked us but he had professional commitments. He told us how to get to the restaurant and accompanied us for the first couple of blocks. On our way there, we passed one of the handicapped people of Portugal. In both Spain and Portugal, the government gives jobs to handicapped people. In Spain, for example, we pulled into a no-parking space when there were no other spots available. For an agreed-upon amount, a handicapped person took the responsibility of watching our car, making sure that the police didn't put a crab claw on one of the wheels. The crippled man we encountered in Cascais was selling lottery tickets. He had quite a few tickets left on a roll. Through the reporter I asked him how much each ticket cost and how many did he have left. I bought all the rest of his roll of tickets. He was exuberant! I thought that having sold all of his lottery tickets, he would go home.

We went on to the restaurant. They seated us in a booth by a window at street level. When we looked up we saw the crippled man's face and his happy toothless smile. He had followed us. I think he was in awe of Carol. For at least the first half hour of our meal every time we looked up he was there, smiling. Finally he was gone; we ate longer than he could stand. We began our meal with grilled sardines and some bouillabaisse. We hopscotched through the menu; it was a feast. The food was just unbelievable. Eventually, the waiter started coming over, trying to tell us we couldn't order any more (which had happened in other restaurants). "You can't have more, don't order anything more." We would say, "Let's have more of this." Then we'd order another course. Finally, we were finished. I called the waiter over and asked for the check. I assured him this was the best meal we'd had in Europe and I was giving him a choice: I would tip him generously or he could have this roll of lottery tickets. His eyes got big and he chose the tickets. We hope he won and retired on the coast, but I guess we'll never know.

From Lisbon, Carol and I flew back to New York, but it wasn't long before we were again rehearsing and performing with the quintet.

The tour was very successful and we were especially proud of the large audiences we reached through various radio broadcasts. We were also proud that we were able to bring something new to European audiences—they had never heard anything like our group. There were no brass quintets or brass choirs in Europe at that time except for the Philip Jones group, which was just getting started. But many of the composers whose music we performed—Purcell, Pezel, Gabrieli, Susato, Holborne—were Europeans. So, in a way, we were taking their own music back to them and presenting it in a new light. We did another European tour in 1965 that was also very successful. Now, of course, there are many wonderful and successful European brass quintets.

BACK IN THE U.S.A., JUNE 1963

Back in New York, the quintet had a few days to visit relatives and friends before driving to Madison, Wisconsin, where we presented a concert and master classes at the University of Wisconsin. We traveled in separate vehicles. John Barrows was riding with Carol and me. Our first son, Jesse, was traveling with us but we didn't know it at the time. Our parakeet, Campbell, was also with us. En route to Madison, we were booked for a NYBQ concert in Escanaba, Michigan. We traveled via the new Interstates to the bridge over the Straits of Mackinac. The toll of $7.50 to access Route 2 was a surprise but it also gave us access to smoked chubs, a delicious fish consumed with cold beer, purchased along the way, which we had in the trunk of the car. It was a refreshing rest stop, with another hundred-plus miles before we arrived in Escanaba.

Our first clue that this would be an historic visit was that we arrived at the hotel our agent had scheduled for us and found it boarded up with a sign reading "Closed" placed prominently across the front entrance. A local citizen, on inquiry, said the only other hotel in town, located on the end of a main street, looking south onto Lake Michigan, was the House of Luddington. At this time we were joined by Ted Weis, Bob Nagel, and

John Swallow, who were traveling together, and we motored to the House of Luddington. Luckily, they were able to book us for what would be an unforgettable stay of three days. We all registered and went to claim the rooms assigned. Unfortunately, John Barrows found his room obviously still occupied. John, in a bit of a huff, walked down to the desk, showing as much control as he could muster. He told the desk clerk he doubted if the person who already had the room would welcome his moving in and did they have another—unclaimed—room. The elderly woman manager, supporting the efforts of the young clerk, told John the clerk only had this position for two weeks. John said, "I've only been here twenty minutes and already I know the hotel better than she does." They weathered the storm and all was peaceful again, after John had his room, of course.

Our concert that evening was at 7:30. It was now 5:30 PM. We were all tired and hungry and decided to forego checking the hall before the concert, choosing instead to have dinner. The restaurant didn't officially open until 8 PM, but I volunteered to check with the busboy what fare on the menu might be available for a quick evening meal. On consulting with the chef we were told we could have anything on the menu, and have their exclusive attention. Over the phone I took orders from the other quintet members and conveyed this information to the chef. The dining room was beautifully appointed with linen tablecloths, real silverware, designer glasses, and fresh flowers. The room was empty until we took our places at the table. Dinners were delivered at the same time and the food was out of this world, so good in fact that, before we left for the concert hall, John Barrows hastily visited the kitchen and palmed a $10 bill into the chef's hand. We gave a great concert and afterward were ready to relax.

As we approached the bar, we were announced by the lady manager, who had heard the concert. The chef, sitting at the end of the bar, imbibing, introduced himself as Al Hayes. He said this was the first time somebody had come in and tipped the chef. "And you didn't give me time to tell you that I own this hotel, so your drinks are on the house." We got better acquainted with other patrons and employees after that initial exchange. We looked forward to the next day, a Saturday.

We were introduced to the judge, made locally famous for his role in the book and movie *Anatomy of a Murder,* starring Jimmy Stewart. He said he backed his car into Escanaba every weekend so he would be pointed in the right direction when he went home. He reminded us that the score for this film was written by Duke Ellington. When they conversed, Ellington referred to him as "Judgey." So, he said, "I called him Dukey." Stories were told, some exaggerated I'm sure, and some sweetened by pleasant memories. Whether or not the stories were actual fact, they were entertaining.

Al Hayes was a very interesting character. He had been one of Eddie Rickenbacker's World War I fighter pilots. He was proud that once a year the King of Sweden visited the House of Luddington for a feast, and that John F. Kennedy had visited the hotel during his 1960 presidential campaign—he showed us actual menus of their visits. Hayes told us that all of his staff, including waitresses, were from Ireland, and that once a year he offered three of them free trips to Ireland. He promised that if we could be in the dining room for brunch at 10:00 the next morning he would make us special eggs Benedict.

One of the ladies we met introduced herself as Zasu Pitts. None of us had seen Zasu Pitts in movies for years and we never did find out if she was the real thing. When the bar closed at midnight, the quintet was invited to her home for nightcaps. Bob Nagel played Irish songs on her piano as background for a heated series of cribbage games between John and Zasu, until John caught her cheating, which brought a quick end to the cribbage game. We arrived back at the hotel at 2 A M.

The next morning Bob Nagel and I visited the local music store and picked out some sheet music of Irish songs, which we shared with the other members of the quintet, and from which we played a special session for the employees. These nostalgic melodies brought tears to the eyes of the staff of Irish ladies with some laughter and homesickness. It was a satisfying experience.

On Sunday our two cars departed Escanaba bound for the University of Wisconsin. Alec Wilder was in Madison to meet us, having traveled by train, his favorite mode of transportation. Alec got all excited when we told him about our experience in Escanaba, and he visited there himself at a later date. The quintet was scheduled to do a concert on Tuesday evening to show our appreciation to John Barrows, who now taught at the university, for making the European tour with us. The concert—on which he played—

made a big hit with the faculty and students of the University of Wisconsin. Composer Eugene Anderson, then a sophomore tuba major, was there. He said much later he thought Harvey Phillips was the best tuba player he'd ever heard and he's still waiting to hear anyone better.

Everybody, except for John Barrows and myself, went home to New York. I had committed myself to do two weeks of master classes for high-school-age tubists at the University of Wisconsin's extension division directed by Dick Wolf.

ALBUM 1

Above. One-room school in Marionville, Missouri, 1937–1938. Harvey Phillips, farthest left, second row; his sister Georgia, middle of last row.

Left. Harvey Phillips, age twelve.

Harvey Phillips's high school graduation picture, *left*, and at age twenty, with sousaphone, *below*.

Homer Lee, bandmaster and Harvey's high school tuba teacher.

Johnny Evans, left, and Harvey Phillips, tubists in the Ringling Bros. and Barnum & Bailey Circus Band, late 1940s.

Harvey Phillips arrives in New York City to
attend the Juilliard School of Music, 1950.

THE NEW YORK
BRASS ENSEMBLE

F. SCHMIDT   E. PRICE   H. PHILLIPS   W. LINDSKOOG   R. NAGEL

"superior performance"
— *New York Times*

"the acme of artistry"
— *Washington, D. C.*
Evening Star

"each a virtuoso"
— *Kansas City Times*

New York Brass Ensemble, 1953. From left: Frederick Schmidt,
Erwin Price, Harvey Phillips, Wes Lindskoog, Robert Nagel.

Paul Lavalle conducts brass in his Cities Service Band of America, 1954. From left: Don Butterfield and Harvey Phillips, back row; Harry London and Albert Corrado, front row.

The Sauter-Finegan Orchestra, 1954.
Harvey Phillips between trombone and guitar.

Above. Harvey Phillips during intermission
of a concert for children by the New York
Brass Quintet, Baltimore, 1954.

Facing top. New York Brass Quintet,
original members, 1954. From top left, John
Glasel, Robert Nagel, Harvey Phillips,
Frederick Schmidt, Erwin Price.

Facing bottom. New York Brass Quintet,
1966: Robert Nagel, Allan Dean, Harvey
Phillips, Paul Ingraham, John Swallow.
Dean joined in 1966; Phillips left in 1967.

Darvel-Phillips Vows Are Read In New York

Miss Carol Darvel, daughter of Mr. and Mrs. Alexander Darvel of New York City, New York, became the bride of Harvey G. Phillips, son of Mr. and Mrs. J. E. Phillips of Marionville in an impressive candlelight ceremony solemnized Monday evening, February 22 at 7 o'clock in the Christ Methodist Church on Park Avenue and 60th street in New York City.

The single ring ceremony was performed by Dr. Sockman before an altar decorated with white lilies. The organist played a program of nuptial music.

The bride was given away by her father. She was attired in a floor length gown of pale blue satin and chantilly lace. Her hat and shoes matched the gown.

The bride's sister served as maid of honor. She wore a gown of pink.

The best man was Eddie Brown, roommate of the groom.

A reception was held following the ceremony at the home of the bride's sister.

Movies and three dimension pictures were taken.

A bridal suite was reserved for the couple at the Roosevelt Hotel in New York. They left in a few days for a honeymoon trip.

Phillips graduated from Marionville high school in 1947 and has since made a career of music. He has played with such musical organizations as the "Voice of Firestone," "Band of America," Lucky Strike Hit Parade," Show of Shows," "The Orchestra of Leopold Stokowski," the RCA Victor recording orchestra, as well as numerous other musical organizations, including the Ringling Brothers Barnum and Bailey Circus band.

Engraving by TASOPE.

Facing. Harvey and
Carol Phillips dance
during a stop on a 1956
New York Brass Quintet
tour. Harvey put this
picture on the cover
of his *Legacy* album.

Facing. Harvey was delighted to return to his place in the orchestra of *Candide* on Broadway, 1956, and find Richard Rodgers sitting in his chair, with his hand on Harvey's tuba.

Harvey Phillips falls asleep while practicing his tuba in London during a New York Brass Quintet European tour, 1963.

Above. At Christmas 1964, Harvey Phillips holds his firstborn, ten-month-old Jesse, while visited by his best friend, Alec Wilder, left, and his revered teacher-mentor Bill Bell.

Left. Alec Wilder, who wrote more music for Harvey Phillips than any other composer. Photograph by Alec's friend Louis Ouzer.

Facing. Harvey Phillips with son Jesse, 1965, at a swimming pool in Saratoga, New York, where Harvey played in the orchestra for the New York City Ballet's season there.

Above. Have suitcase, ready to go on the road, 1966: Harvey Phillips and son Jesse, age two years and three months.

Facing top. Harvey Phillips in a C. G. Conn publicity photo, 1966.

Facing bottom. Stan Kenton, left, brings his band to play for students at the New England Conservatory in 1967. Many years before, he had offered Harvey Phillips a position in his band, which Harvey had to refuse because he was being drafted.

CHAPTER TEN

Family, Friends, and Summer Activities

WHILE IT WAS IMPOSSIBLE to divide my busy musical life into clearly identified sections, there were some events in the 1960s that brought about major changes, most importantly the birth of my three sons, Jesse (1964), Harvey Jr. (1966), and Thomas (1968), and starting Twentieth Century Innovations with Gunther Schuller.

In 1959, Julius Bloom, executive director of the Carnegie Hall Corporation, requested that Gunther—himself one of America's most important composers—select, organize, and present a series of modern chamber music. The concert series would be presented in Carnegie Recital Hall and repeated at major colleges and universities when possible. With our attorney, Gunther and I established Twentieth Century Innovations, Inc., with the goal of giving contemporary composers a venue to have their works performed. Gunther was the president and I was vice president, but in reality this meant that Gunther was the conductor and I was his tubist, personnel manager, and manager of the small budget from Carnegie Hall (or occasionally, Gunther was the boss and I was the lackey!). We featured the music of Luigi Nono, Joseph Arrigo, Charles Ives, Iannis Xenakis, John Cage, Ned Rorem, Ralph Shapey, Harvey Sollberger, Milton Babbitt, Gunther himself, and many others who in general were not your typical household composers. Nobody in New York was performing this music. After only six concerts in three years, this series had presented more twentieth-century compositions than any other chamber ensemble in the world.

For my part, I was intrigued by this new music and by the composers who took it so seriously. I compared it to a special meal prepared by a gourmet chef. You might not like it at first taste but it was still a gourmet dish and had to be respected as such. Gunther Schuller is, in my humble opinion, one of the best examples of a true musical genius in our time. He was principal horn of the Cincinnati Symphony at age seventeen and joined the Metropolitan Opera as first horn at nineteen. He coined the term "third stream" to describe the contemporary blending of musical styles, specifically the jazz and classical disciplines. You can listen to him lecture on the music of Duke Ellington or John Lewis of the Modern Jazz Quartet as though he were born in the jazz idiom, but the next moment he will switch to Bernstein, Beethoven, Mahler, Wagner, or Mozart with astonishing virtuosity. I consider him our most important living American musician.

Gunther has lived every facet of the music profession, always operating at the highest level, with maximum results. His ears were incredible, too. He could hear a twenty-note chord with twenty different instruments and tell you which notes were sharp or flat. It's as if we have always known each other and worked together as a team.

Working as Gunther's personnel manager was a demanding job; there were some compositions that simply couldn't be performed adequately without certain individual musicians. That sometimes posed problems, because the best musicians were busy all the time and it meant we had to schedule rehearsals at odd times, like 5:15 to 7:45 PM so they could do a 2–5 recording and an 8:00 concert. We also had to make sure that everybody was free and not passing up more lucrative work to play for us, because we didn't want musicians to lose money on our account. If we were unable to get the musicians we wanted, we found that it was generally better not to perform the piece at all rather than present a lackluster, second-rate performance. This was sometimes hard to get across to the contemporary composers who were writing extremely difficult music.

Around 1962, we were premiering a Charles Ives work discovered and completed by Gunther Schuller, *Chromatimelotune*. Gunther had rehearsed the work with the ensemble and scheduled it for performance. But when it was time to go onstage, one of our clarinet players hadn't arrived. As personnel manager, I was in trouble! The Recital Hall is on the third floor of Carnegie Hall and the pay telephone (the only telephone) was in the first-floor lobby. Trying to locate the missing clarinetist, I raced up and down the stairs several times to use the telephone (the ancient elevator with operator was too slow). Finally, the clarinetist arrived, with apologies. A previous engagement had run overtime, then unfavorable traffic and weather conditions were also problems. We accepted his apologies and were relieved and happy he wasn't in an accident. In any event, he went onstage with the other musicians.

Gunther and I were about to go onstage when I noticed the tuba part was not on my stand. Embarrassed, I confessed to Gunther I didn't have the tuba part. Gunther didn't panic, but hastily extracted some manuscript paper from a nearby violin case and, holding the paper on the wall, began to scratch out the tuba part from memory. As he wrote he said, "I don't have time to write in the rests. I'll cue you." I had no choice but to go onstage and be alert for cues from Gunther. Luckily, but to my further embarrassment, my music was rolled up in my tuba and I found it when I removed my mute. Gunther saw the whole thing and gave me one of his understanding grins. The performance went well and we gathered in the Carnegie Tavern following the concert. At that point, I took out my tuba part and compared it with what Gunther had hastily scratched out from memory. Every note, every accent, every dynamic, and every slur was there. There were no rests, as promised, but everything else was perfect.

On January 17, 1963, I premiered Gunther's *Capriccio for Solo Tuba and Chamber Orchestra,* which he wrote for me. It has since been retitled *Concerto No. 1 for Tuba and Orchestra.*

While managing musician personnel for Twentieth Century Innovations, the Symphony of the Air, and numerous other freelance orchestras and chamber ensembles since 1957, that area of my work came to the attention of Julius Bloom, executive director of Carnegie Hall and manager of a special concert series for Rutgers University, where he also taught a course in logistics. In 1966 Mr. Bloom engaged me as his administrative assistant. He respected the multiple and divergent priorities of my busy professional life, and so I was allowed to manage my own schedule in successfully achieving and/or resolving whatever task he assigned to me. I had no set schedule of days or hours but we made personal or telephone contact as often as needed. I was assigned a secretary and office next to Mr. Bloom's office at Rutgers in New Brunswick, New Jersey. I also worked from my studio in Carnegie Hall. I had to allow an hour and a half travel time from New York City and one hour from my home in Englewood, New Jersey. A busy freelance performance schedule forced me to make the most of every moment. I don't think any university could have given me a better course in management than I got from Julius.

I had a reel-to-reel tape recorder placed in my car and whether en route or stalled in traffic, I spoke with very few pauses into a lapel microphone. Not a minute was wasted. I spoke about whatever came to mind; even fleeting thoughts were recorded. When I arrived in New Brunswick, I gave the tape to my secretary to transcribe. I told her, "It doesn't have to make sense to you; just transcribe what you hear." Through those transcribed tapes, I accomplished more in 1966 than I could otherwise have ever imagined. I didn't know it at the time, but this was my last year living in the New York area. I had no intention of ever leaving but fate moves mountains.

Major schedule changes over which I had no influence started to evolve in the mid-1960s. In 1966 the weekly *Bell Telephone Hour* broadcast over NBC went off the air. It featured the last corporate-sponsored network orchestra. This was sad news for me because it added to an ever more frustrating year. Many of my closest associates and professional accounts were leaving New York City for more fertile Hollywood: Patrick Williams, Quincy Jones, Billy Byers, Fred Karlin, and Dick Cary, among others. There were also priority shifts within the recording industry, which was moving away from chamber music and classical symphonic recordings to small rock groups of dubious distinction. Some of America's finest symphony orchestras were signing contracts with European record companies.

STRAVINSKY

I did several recordings with Igor Stravinsky after being engaged by personnel manager Loren Glickman. The most important of these recordings was *The Rite of Spring*, conducted by Stravinsky, a landmark recording of 1964. At the first rehearsal, Stravinsky stepped onto the podium, lifted a flask out of his inside coat pocket, and drank a toast to the orchestra before we started.

On the second page of the tuba part, Stravinsky called for "more tuba." I was playing what I thought was a good *ff* and making a support for the other brass. John Barrows, playing first horn, put his head in his hands and said, "He'll be sorry." We went through it again; I played louder and must have satisfied the Maestro. He said nothing more. On the recording, I played the way he wanted.

I remember shaking hands with Stravinsky on that occasion. Being close enough to feel the essence of a person of the stature of Stravinsky or Casals or Stokowski can paralyze you. You never know what to say. A minute can seem like an hour and an hour can seem like a minute.

When you consider the acceptance of Stravinsky's music today, it's impossible to conceive of the angry near riot that occurred at the premiere of *The Rite of Spring.* Suppose those people had been right in their reaction to Stravinsky's music! Today we would have heard very little about Stravinsky. But as it turned out, the opposite came to pass and nobody today remembers the name of even one individual who hissed or threw rotten fruit.

Because of the success of Twentieth Century Innovations and the influence of Milton Babbitt and Gunther Schuller, in 1966 Stravinsky's publisher appointed me as personnel manager for a string of concerts in Washington, D.C., Princeton University, and New York City. That concert series included several landmark recordings and gave me opportunities to have relaxed conversations with the Maestro and his wife in their Hotel Pierre apartment. Of these recordings, Stravinsky was especially pleased with and excited about the recording of *Apollo.* He had made several unsuccessful attempts to record *Apollo* to his satisfaction. Three standout performers on that recording were Gloria Agostini (harp), Samuel Rhodes (viola), and Robert Sylvester (cello).

One of the Washington performances included Stravinsky's ballet *Card Game.* We had only one bus from New York City, so the orchestra was small, almost a chamber orchestra. I was so busy making sure that all the percussion equipment was unloaded and in place and all the music was there with the librarian that I forgot to unload my own instrument. By the time I remembered, the bus was long gone. I made several attempts to locate the bus driver, who had taken the bus to have it serviced and refueled but, in this age before cell phones, I had no luck. So I called my friend Bob Pallansch, who had been my stand partner when I was in the U.S. Army Field Band. I asked him if he had a CC tuba that he could bring down to the theater. I told him to wear a black suit so that he could walk through the stage door inconspicuously. He sat with me while I played his tuba and got a pretty big kick out of the excitement of the performance and watching Stravinsky on the podium. This story illustrates how personnel managers put themselves last!

Stravinsky was always cordial and his mind very sharp despite his advanced years (he was eighty-four in 1966). One evening, sitting with Mr. and Mrs. Stravinsky, I enquired about the possibility of a concerto or other work for solo tuba and orchestra. At this time, one can imagine how many commissions awaited his attention. Nonetheless, Stravinsky was warm to the idea. His wife Vera, who managed their affairs, did some figuring and said, "For him to break free for enough time to write this piece, it would have to be for a commission no less than sixteen thousand dollars." In my opinion, that was very little for a Stravinsky commission but it was unfortunately out of my league. If only our tuba organization had existed at that time, that moment might have marked the birth of the major work of the century for our instrument.

I also approached Aaron Copland about a piece for tuba and have a letter expressing his regrets but his career had evolved into guest conducting appearances. Samuel Barber was also approached, but he said he had too many commissions to squeeze another one in. After I had played in the pit orchestra of *Candide* I asked Leonard Bernstein for a solo composition for tuba. He said, "Why don't you get your friend Schuller to write it?"

ALEC WILDER

I had heard about Alec Wilder when I first arrived in New York. He was already a well-known composer, popular with performing musicians. I played his octets with Sauter-Finegan in 1953, but my initial direct contact with Alec was the first time I spoke with him on the phone. One day in 1959 I answered the telephone and a low, guttural voice said, "Harvey Phillips?

This is Alec Wilder." I thought to myself, sure you are. . . . He said, "I was having lunch with John Barrows, and I told him about a brass quintet I had written for the New York Philharmonic brass, but they haven't had time to give it a reading. John suggested that you might be able to arrange something."

I said, "Gee, Mr. Wilder, if I could get the score and parts, I can have the New York Brass Quintet take a look at it, and perhaps have you up for a rehearsal session." He was enthusiastic. It turned out that his copyist, Stanley Webb Jr., was a friend of mine, so I picked up the score and parts and took them to one of our quintet rehearsals in my Carnegie Hall studio.

Alec's *Brass Quintet No. 1* (the first of eight) immediately captured our interest because it was so different from the rest of the brass quintet repertoire. There were six movements, a solo feature for each instrument, and one for the entire ensemble together. We recorded his quintet on an LP entitled *Two Contemporary Composers*. The other quintet was by Don Hammond, a composer who was also a terrific flute player and woodwind doubler. It was a spectacular album.

Alec soon became an important part of my life and that of my family. As it turned out, he became my closest friend and a bona fide family member. We met often for lunch or dinner at the Algonquin Hotel or in our apartment, a restaurant, or a supper club. It seemed that years before we met we had shared friendships with many of the same musicians. Many people who had personal friendships with Alec considered the friendship a private treasure that he or she did not want to share. From childhood, Alec seemed to develop such friendships.

Alexander Lafayette Chew Wilder developed an early interest in music and studied composition privately with Herbert Inch at the Eastman School of Music. His father was a respected banker. There is still a Wilder Building in downtown Rochester. His mother apparently didn't approve of Alec's interest in music and treated him harshly. Probably as a result of this, Alec liked few women during his life. Notable exceptions were Fran Miller, Lavinia Russ, Arlene Bouras, Marian McPartland, Peggy Lee, Eileen Farrell, Mabel Mercer, Marlene VerPlanck, Barbara Lee, Carol Phillips, Lottie Phillips (my mother), Judy Bell, Helen Ouzer, and a very few others.

Alec talked for years about writing *American Popular Song,* a book of critical appraisal and analysis. When, in 1968, he enlisted James Maher as editor, Maher wrote a grant application to the Avon Foundation, which was funded by Jerome Hill, the wealthy filmmaker. A three-year grant of $102,405 was awarded. When I was vice president of the New England Conservatory, I worked on securing a matching grant (from the Rockefeller Foundation) to the conservatory, which was administering the grant to Alec and Jim Maher.

A group of five loyal friends who were students at the Eastman School of Music and later became famous are Louis Ouzer, Goddard Lieberson, Mitch Miller, John Barrows, and Alec Wilder. It has been my privilege to know all of them and to count them among my friends. I will especially be forever grateful to John Barrows for initiating my first contact with Alec. There now is an Alec Wilder Reading Room in the Eastman School Music Library. From our first telephone conversation, Alec's and my mutual regard and concern for one another grew. As a result of our success with the recording of *Brass Quintet No. 1,* other collaborations followed. *Sonata No. 1 for Tuba and Piano* was written for me and recorded on my *Harvey Phillips in Recital* album.

I commissioned George Kleinsinger to compose "Tubby the Tuba Meets a Jazz Band" as a sequel to his famous "Tubby the Tuba." We recorded it in 1960. The personnel were the Charleston City All Stars—Pee Wee Erwin (cornet), Kenny Davern (clarinet), Lou McGarity (trombone), Moe Wechsler (piano), Cliff Leeman (drums), and Chubby Jackson, who had a children's show on ABC (narration). I played tuba. I needed a companion piece for the other side of the record, so I asked Alec to write an appropriate tuba solo. Some weeks later he called me and said, "Well, I think I have something for your children's record."

"Oh great, Alec! What is it?"

"It's six movements about a charming little elephant named Effie."

My heart sank. I was fed up with solos for tuba that had the instrument depicting lumbering, oversize animals.

The first time I read through *Effie (Suite No. 1),* however, I knew it was a classic. *Effie* became Alec's top-selling piece of chamber music. The order of the movements was arranged to take Effie through a day that started with energy and capriciousness, "Effie Chases a Monkey," and ended with a smile and hypnotizing lullaby. On the original recording, in addition to tuba and piano, drums and xylophone were used in "Effie Joins the Carnival" and vibraphone was added in "Effie Sings a Lullaby." I was so pleased with what Alec had written I asked that he score it for solo tuba and symphony orchestra and I fashioned a narration for each movement. The premiere of this version of *Effie* was with the University of Colorado Symphony Orchestra, conducted by Ozzie Lehnert. I played the tuba and did the narration, the only time narration has been used with the orchestra version.

For the New York Brass Quintet, Alec wrote three quintets and a quintet with strings. In 1963, the Quintet was on a Midwest tour and one of the scheduled appearances was at the University of Illinois's Allerton estate. Alec presented me with another new suite, simply entitled *Suite No. 2 for Tuba and Piano.* Alec came to a reading I did with a faculty pianist there and we were disappointed; it just didn't work. So it was set aside.

On February 14, 1964, Carol and I had our first son and, on the day of his birth, Alec began a four-movement *Suite No. 3, The Jesse Suite for Tuba and Piano.* On September 16, 1966, Alec began *Suite No. 4, The Little Harvey Suite,* and on September 23, 1968, Alec commenced *The Thomas Suite for Tuba and Piano.* In 1970, plans were made to record an album entitled *Harvey Phillips in Recital for Family and Friends.* A new, one-movement solo for tuba and piano titled *Song for Carol* was added to the family suites. Rehearsals in New York City were scheduled with pianist Bernie Leighton. At one of these rehearsals I asked Bernie if he would mind reading one more suite so we ran through *Suite No. 2,* which had been disappointing at the Allerton estate. Surprise, surprise! It was terrific. The only thing missing had been Bernie Leighton. I suggested to Alec, and he concurred, that it be dedicated to our dear mutual friend, poet and philanthropist Ethan Ayer.

I find it interesting to reflect on my attitude concerning first performances. It is based on the strong feeling of commitment I have to composers who deserve to hear their compositions as early as possible. When Melvin Culbertson told me he wanted to do a recital in Carnegie Recital Hall—which I helped set up—and would like to premiere something, I suggested he do *The Jesse Suite*. If I had waited to give the first performance myself, it would have been a year or more before its premiere. I later performed it many times and recorded it.

I don't know how Alec did it. Each suite is a remarkable reflection of each son's personality; maybe the boys grew up to reflect the music that Alec had written for them. The amount of music Alec wrote for me was astonishing. Aside from the five tuba and piano suites, there was also a *Suite for Tuba, Bass, and Piano* written for Gary Karr and myself, and a second sonata which was dedicated to my mother, written in 1964. He wrote ten tuba duets, ten tuba trios, and ten tuba quartets. Then there came *Concerto for Tuba and Concert Band,* which I premiered with the Air Force Band, Colonel Arnald Gabriel conducting.

I performed with him many times, notably once with Doc Severinsen and the Air Force Band's first trombonist, Larry Wiehe. The band's arranger wrote *Concerto for Three Brass* for us to play with the band. Another time, I did "Tubby the Tuba," with actor Tom Bosley narrating.

When I was confined to the hospital, Alec wrote a *Convalescence Suite* of six movements for solo tuba, and repeated the gesture on the two other occasions I was hospitalized. The eighteen total movements of those three suites can be played in any order or selected as a suite of four or more movements. All of this was typical behavior for Alec—he never wrote music just for the sake of writing music; everything he wrote was for a friend or some occasion. He would often write a sonata or other work for a friend and leave it on that person's piano.

In 1963, Clark Galehouse called Alec and told him that he thought Alec should write something for John Barrows and me, since he heard similarities in our phrasing. The result was *First Trio for Horn, Tuba, and Piano*. John and I recorded it with his wife Tate Barrows on piano. The success of this trio prompted *Suite Number Two*. This trio was the last solo recording of John Barrows and was recorded in 1974, when John was losing his battle with Hodgkin's disease. With pianist Milton Kaye (long-time accompanist for Jascha Heifetz), John and I drove out to the Golden Crest Records studio on Long Island. John sounded fabulous but Milton and I noticed how tired he was becoming. We might wish to do a phrase over again, but John very politely said, "I can't do it, fellas. Let's go on." I released it on an LP I entitled *Tribute to a Friend.* John sounds strong and vital and the listener would never guess that it was done under any kind of duress. To show my love for John, I commissioned Bernhard Heiden to write a work for solo tuba and nine horns, which was also on that recording. This reflected well our relationship, for John had organized the Valhalla Horn Society, nine horns and my tuba.

One interesting quirk about Alec: although he read voraciously, he never bought a paperback book. He bought all of his books, hardcover, at Scribner's on Fifth Avenue. When he finished a book, he would either leave it at the house where he was a guest or hand it to a total stranger if he finished it in a railroad station: "Would you like a book? It's a very fine book!" If no one was there, he would simply leave it on the seat. He was not a collector of anything.

Alec despised the atmosphere of the Brill Building. That was the building on Broadway near 49th Street where songwriters would write their songs and large record companies would immediately buy the rights to the songs, making thousands of dollars when they had paid the composer a few hundred. Alec always distrusted corporations.

Like an ivy plant, Alec never really put down roots. He lived in the Algonquin Hotel in New York City for more than fifty years. When he returned from his travels, he would take whatever room was available. Although his family was affluent, he lived mostly off his own royalties. Another resident in the hotel was the author Thornton Wilder (no relation). But one day a lady came in and started telling Alec how much she admired him: "Mr. Wilder, oh, you're just so terrific!" This puffed up Alec's ego considerably, until the doorman unpuffed him by saying, "Alec, you know she thought she was talking to Thornton Wilder!"

Alec said his daily routine was contacting the newspaper stand and having a copy of the *New York Times* brought to his room. He turned immediately to the obituaries. If his name wasn't on the list, he would get up. I used to accuse Alec of dividing his jacket pockets like a filing cabinet: A–F in the left lower pocket, G–L in the right pocket, M–S in the upper inside right pocket, and T–Z in the left inside pocket of his sport coat. Of course this was nonsense, but I was impressed that he always seemed to know which pocket to reach into.

Alec frequently accompanied the New York Brass Quintet on short tours or clinics. In 1963, after a summer session at the University of Wisconsin, Alec drove with Carol and me to Missouri to visit my mother. Alec fell in love with Mom immediately. Since my mother was strict temperance, she didn't approve of drinking, and smoking was a begrudged concession to her husband, who smoked a pipe, and sons-in-law, who smoked. Of course, Alec was a smoker, and he also brought a fifth of vodka (which he said was not noticeable on the breath) and hid it in the woodpile in the back of our chicken house. He would slip out and have a drink in the evenings. While we were there, he started a second *Sonata for Tuba and Piano*, dedicated to my mother. Each night, after everyone was asleep, he would go out and study the stars. Alec loved relaxing in the total nature environment—whether it was the sky or a blossoming locust grove. On our way back to New York, we got about eighty miles north of Marionville when Alec suddenly sat up erect in the seat and said, "We've got to go back. We've got to go back to your home. I left the vodka in the woodpile." I said, "Alec, there's no way a seventy-four-year-old woman will be scratching through the woodpile." I don't think my mother ever found the vodka, luckily for Alec (and his reputation).

Contented to know Mom wouldn't find a vodka bottle, we rode in silence for a time. Then Alec said, "I've got a song for you" and passed up a postal card containing a song. It was his only country song, "If I'd Only Done What Mother Told Me To," which prompted me to say to him, "So I see you compose both kinds of music, country and western."

INTO THE HOT, 1964

Following Gil Evans's involvement with Miles Davis's *Birth of the Cool*, Gil lent his name as the presenter of *Into the Hot*, which featured the music of John Carisi and pianist Cecil Taylor. Gil Evans had been the arranger in the Claude Thornhill band and he added two French horns and a tuba to Thornhill's orchestra. Miles liked the sound and collaborated with Gil for the album *Birth of the Cool*. *Into the Hot* in 1964 was not meant to be a follow-up to the 1950s' *Birth of the Cool* but was more a clever play on words. The instrumentation was brass quintet: John Glasel and Doc Severinsen, trumpet; Jim Buffington, horn; Urbie Green, trombone; Harvey Phillips, tuba; Gene Quill and Phil Woods, alto saxophone; Barry Galbraith, guitar; Milt Hinton, bass; Eddie Costa, piano and vibes; and Ossie Johnson, drums. It was recorded in Webster Hall on East 11th Street, where many original Broadway cast albums like *Hello, Dolly!* and *Fiddler on the Roof* were done.

The sound enhancement provided by the two horns and tuba added important new colors to the usual swing band sound. John Carisi and Gil Evans were very good friends, both very particular with their writing, and both, like Bill Finegan, very slow writers. Gil Evans would write a whole score and throw it away. He would use Bobby Blake's Carnegie Hall studio from midnight until 6:00 in the morning. There would be score pages in the wastebasket as he changed his mind. John Carisi had done a Far East tour with Dizzy Gillespie's band before the Vietnam War. In the jungles of Cambodia, there is a place called Angkor Wat which has many ancient temples. It made such an impression on John Carisi that he wrote a composition called "Angkor Wat." It was one of the tunes we rehearsed on Monday nights in Dick Cary's loft and it became the lead composition for *Into the Hot*.

STUDENTS IN NEW YORK

Three of my favorite students during this period were servicemen Don Waldrop, Dan Perantoni, and Jim Self. Jim Self once came to town for an afternoon lesson and I invited him to sit and listen in the pit during a ballet performance that evening. I told him he would have to wear a dark suit in the pit. So he went out and bought one that afternoon. That impressed me.

I told Dan Perantoni that he could become a great college teacher. He taught at the University of Illinois, then went to Arizona State University. He succeeded me at Indiana University when I retired in 1994.

I never charged a serviceman for a lesson. Oftentimes, I would have a lesson scheduled with a student, but in the interim I would have booked a recording session. I would have the student meet me at the recording studio and he would be invited to sit in the booth while we recorded. If he should be attired in a black suit, he could also attend an evening ballet performance, sitting in the pit, while we performed *Petrouchka* or other ballet repertoire. After the recording session, sometimes there was time for our lesson and dinner before the evening ballet performance.

On New Year's Day, 1959, the ballet orchestra went by train to Albany, New York, to perform Hershy Kay's arrangement of *Stars and Stripes* for the inauguration of Nelson Rockefeller as governor. Some of the orchestra members were upset because we were leaving immediately after playing. I took the time to stop at the reception. I walked up to the lady who seemed to be in charge and told her the orchestra was leaving right away and wouldn't have time to enjoy the reception. She was very gracious and said, "Please take some wine," and helped me fill my tuba and cover with eight bottles. She gave me about forty small cups. Fortunately, entering the train car was convenient: I put my tuba in the back seat and waited until the train was moving. People were still complaining about not having had a chance to drink some wine. I quickly emptied all the bottles, while strolling the aisle. This attracted a good bit of appreciation from the orchestra players. I had proven once again the old adage, "Ask and you shall receive."

PRIVATE HIGHWAY

In 1965, Alec and I made a Saturday morning visit to meet Clark Galehouse at Golden Crest Records to edit the recording of Alec's *Trio for Horn, Tuba, and Piano*. Our sessions with Clark were always very pleasant and without pressure. Alec knew I had a 2:15 matinee performance with the New York City Ballet Orchestra and that Huntington Station, Long Island, which we were near, was an hour's drive from the city. Our casual editing session concluded later than we had planned and we left for the New York State Theater shortly after 1 PM. Alec said, "You'll never make it! What are you going to do?"

I said, "Don't worry; we have our own private highway." I had noticed in the newspaper that on Sunday, the next day, Governor Rockefeller would be appearing at a ribbon-cutting ceremony to open the last stretch of the Long Island Expressway. This meant the expressway was complete and ready for public use, though not officially open.

You can imagine Alec's surprise as I drove around the police stanchion and onto the highway entrance. Ignoring his alarmed cries of "What are you doing?!" I sped in excess of ninety miles per hour down the deserted expressway. I took the Flushing exit and, to avoid extra delay, drove across the grass median to the street leading onto the 59th Street Bridge. We proceeded to the parking garage near the State Theater. It was 2:10. Leaving the car in the middle of the one-way street, I got out quickly and told Alec, "I have to run to make the performance—I'll see you later!" As I passed the parking attendant, I told him my car was number four, and would he take care of it? He said he would.

After the performance I called Alec to assure him I had made it. He said, angrily, "Well I didn't! You left me in the car with the motor running and no instructions. Then a strange man got into the car and told me I would have to get out; he had to park the car. I'm here at the hotel in bed with the covers over my head."

I once mentioned to Alec that I was going to give a clinic in Kutztown, Pennsylvania, and he said, "Oh, I have to go with you; that's where I had my flower garden!" It was at the house of friends of his, Eddie and Helen Finckel, and I suppose Alec tended the garden whenever he was in town. At first I was doubtful but Alec directed me and obviously knew the streets well. As we approached the residence, he was so excited that he was almost unable to breathe. He told me the whole front yard of this house was full of flowers like morning glories and roses. But when we arrived, the garden was gone. Alec was crestfallen and I saw a few tears roll down his face. It had been some time since his last visit and he probably knew that the garden would be gone. If it had still existed, that would have meant that his friends had maintained it for him in his absence and he probably would have been even more affected.

When I first met Alec, I discovered he had written a wealth of popular songs, almost exclusively published by the Richman Organization. Very little of his chamber and instrumental music was published and it was scattered throughout the country. One day, Alec was informed that all of his published octets stored in a warehouse stockroom were destroyed for lack of sales—the space was needed.

Being an enterprising person, I took on his problem as my own and spent the better part of five years trying to get all his chamber music into a central location and then set about attempting to get everything autographed, printed, and published. In 1964 I convinced Alec we should form

Wilder Music, Inc. I wish I could have had more time and energy to devote to this project.

Autographers left us in midstream. I purchased two music-writing typewriters. The person who was so grateful for my setting him up for a career in autography decided to change his career direction. Alec was very patient and had faith in my abilities to win the fight. The age of computers had not yet arrived; what a blessing that would have been. In 1965 I moved my family to Englewood, where I built shelves in the basement, enough to hold Alec's music in good order. He looked at the shelves, came upstairs, and said to Carol, "My God, you could put elephants on those shelves."

FAMILY LIFE

Before we moved to Englewood, Carol used to take Jesse to our local Elmhurst, New York, playground where he, at age one and a half, would admire the bigger kids and their tricycles. They wouldn't let Jesse touch their tricycles. One day on the way home, when I came through Long Island City, I stopped at a big bicycle shop on Queens Boulevard and bought a tricycle. At the playground, Carol saw me coming up the subway stairs carrying the little tricycle. Jesse's eyes bugged out when I set it down and told him it was his. The Christmas after we moved to Englewood, I put a red light, a green light, and a bell on it. Jesse would ride his little tricycle up and down the sidewalk. Once he met two black men. He stopped his tricycle, looked at them, and said, "I gotta wed light and a gween light, and you gotta chocolate face!" They broke out in laughter.

Jesse would get upset when I was absent. I remember in particular the time I went to Pittsburgh for the Mideast Clinic to premiere Alec's *Concerto for Tuba and Concert Band* with the Air Force Band. On my way home, I stopped at a cash register at the airport and saw a display of little wind-up toys: a cop, a cowboy, and a soldier. I bought one of each and brought them home to Englewood. Jesse was watching TV. I said to Carol, "Watch this!" Standing in a place where Jesse couldn't see me, I wound up the three toys and set them down so that they walked in between him and the TV set. I thought he would scream and come running out to greet me. But he didn't. What did come out were the three little toys. He got off the couch and turned them around so they walked right back out of the room. That was his way of telling me that he was upset with me for going out of town. He was only two years old at the time.

ASPEN AND GUNNISON SUMMERS

In the early days of the Aspen Music Festival, there were three brass faculty: Bob Nagel, trumpet; Keith Brown, trombone; and Phil Farkas, horn. In the summer of 1962 the Aspen Faculty Brass Quintet was formed with the addition of John Head (principal trumpet, Atlanta Symphony Orchestra) and myself on tuba. I was asked to come to Aspen for that specific purpose, and I was more than happy to oblige. I had been successful in establishing tuba faculty positions at university schools of music by playing quintets with their brass faculty and giving clinics and master classes, as well as performing recitals and/or appearing as soloist with their bands, wind ensembles, or orchestras to illustrate what the tuba could add to a music program. I saw similar opportunity in going to Aspen.

Carol and I drove our white, blue-leather-seat, Buick convertible (in which I had air conditioning installed en route) first to Bloomington, Indiana, to visit Bill and Aggie Bell. I was disturbed that the School of Music never gave him a rank beyond associate professor—which he probably considered unimportant. We were very unimpressed with the appearance of Bloomington's downtown area. Dr. Thomas Beversdorf and his wife Norma hosted a lavish party for us at their new home east of town. Their hospitality did much to improve our initial impression.

We next stopped to visit my mother in Missouri, on the way to Beaumont, Texas, for a music education conference. On our return, we picked her up on the way to Manhattan, Kansas, for clinics, then on to Aspen for the summer season. She spent a week with us before being returned home by my sister Sue. At my mother's home we picked up as many hickory sticks as we could get into the car, along with the luggage, the Sauter-Finegan library, the George Williams Big Band library, a tuba, and a sousaphone. We were so overloaded that we had to replace two tires on our way to Aspen. Once there, I put the sticks in five-gallon tubs of water so they would smoke but not burn as I barbecued ribs, chicken, pork loins, steaks, and bratwurst. Aspen had a wonderful butcher shop called Tom's. You could almost find our house by the smoke from the daily barbecue. I found mint growing behind Bob Nagel's house and transplanted some to the spring-fed stream that ran alongside our rental. Our guests enjoyed mint juleps and barbecue all summer.

We rented a vacation house from a family who had eight kids with another on the way. The house, half an A-frame, slept twelve comfortably. There was a counter with a surface of ceramic tiles in the center of the downstairs. It was a good party house. I emptied the house of furniture and, using a hose and a scrub brush, I cleaned the entire downstairs. There were two gray Naugahyde love seats which magically became white. Carol scrubbed the small pink tiles of the center counter, which was crusted with jelly, tomato seeds, etc. After we left, I got a letter from the owner thanking us for taking such good care of his house.

When it became generally known I would be appearing at Aspen the summer of 1962, I was invited to the Gunnison Music Camp (also in the Rocky Mountains of Colorado) to perform as tuba soloist on a concert with its jazz band. On this program I performed "Carioca" plus two new compositions by Manny Albam: *Music for a Monday Afternoon* and *Phillips' Manner*. (Manny had lived across the Hudson River in New York from an antique estate called Philipse Manor, and knew I would appreciate the pun.)

After my return to Aspen from my performance in Gunnison, Gunther Schuller visited Aspen to give a lecture and hear a performance of his *Quintet for Brass*. I got very upset at the Aspen Music Festival management when they refused to sponsor a reception for Gunther. I had asked Norman Singer, head of the festival, if the festival would arrange one, but he responded somewhat disdainfully, "We can't be giving receptions to just anybody that comes in." Boy, did that strike a sour note with me. I went directly to the Copper Kettle restaurant, at that time the nicest place in town, spoke with the management, and arranged a wonderful reception for Gunther and all of our friends. I did not invite Norman Singer.

Peter Schickele rode his motorcycle out to Aspen that summer and put together a fundraising pops concert. Out of all the swing music I had brought along we used only two Sauter-Finegan charts, "When Hearts

Are Young" and "Midnight Sleigh Ride," and one from George Williams's arrangements, "I Can't Get Started" (made famous by Bunny Berigan). It took thirteen in the woodwind section to cover all the doubling (by five players) in the Sauter-Finegan arrangements.

On our way back from Aspen we stopped for gas in western Kansas on a very hot day and I asked the attendant to fill my gas tank and check my oil while I went to the restroom. He had me pop the hood and he screamed, "Gol dangit, you got ice on your motor!" Air-conditioned cars, especially convertibles, were few and far between at that time.

I had been working at Aspen for expenses only, no salary, as a favor to Bob Nagel and Keith Brown so there could be an Aspen Brass Quintet. When Singer called to engage me for the next summer, I was still annoyed at him for his snub of Gunther so I told him it would be impossible for me to return. I suggested Bill Bell instead and negotiated a contract for him. Mr. Bell loved Aspen and eventually brought Abe Torchinsky to play with the orchestra and help with the teaching.

The summer of 1963, I went to Gunnison as the third member of the Directors Band tuba section with Bill Bell and Arnold Jacobs. All the members were conductors and teachers; it was an incredible gathering. Many well-known conductors were in residence, including Bill Revelli, Frederick Fennell, Colonel Santelmann (conductor of the Marine Band), and Commander Brendler (conductor of the Navy Band). For the final concert of the season, Arnold Jacobs, Bill Bell, and I performed and recorded Paganini's "Perpetual Motion" in unison, except for the harmonious last chord. That was one of the most memorable experiences of my life. Can you imagine, there were rumors going around among students that Arnold Jacobs and Bill Bell didn't get along. On the contrary, they were the closest of friends.

Every night there was a party of some kind. There was a cabin out in the woods where there was an annual men's party. People who were there for their first year had to keep the fire going at night to keep it warm. The next year, in honor of completing their first summer as fire tender, each person got a beaded belt, Native-American–style. Ed Kleinhammer and I were the fire-tenders in 1963, but we never got our beaded belts because that summer was the final year of the camp's existence in Colorado. In 1964, with state funding sources no longer available for the summer program, Robert Hawkins moved the camp to Morehead, Kentucky, where he continued a Directors Band comprising great wind, brass, and percussion musicians and with renowned conductors.

UNEXPECTED EVENTS IN BUFFALO

In 1963, the New York State Schools of Music Association (NYSSMA) held its annual conference in Buffalo and I was a featured clinician. On this occasion, Carol and Alec flew to Buffalo with me. Alec had written some new music for tuba that he was anxious to hear. I had been assured that a piano accompanist for me would be no problem. (Often I would send music a month ahead and get there to find the pianist opening the music for the first time, with the attitude that anything the tuba could play, he or she could play.)

After a few unsuccessful attempts to rehearse, I realized the problem with the pianist was hopeless. In an effort to show the pianist diplomacy I made the decision to say that what NYSSMA really wanted me to do the next day was to discuss tuba techniques and the teaching of those techniques. I excused the pianist and thanked him for his time. Carol, Alec, and I retreated to the hotel cocktail lounge, ordered some drinks, and awaited the arrival of tubist Ron Bishop, who was to meet us at 10:00, after his orchestra concert. When Ron arrived, he found a rather morose trio. I told Ron about my experience with the pianist and he informed me that one of the finest accompanists he had ever heard had played a concert that evening with singer Jennie Tourel. He took a program from his pocket and said the pianist's name was Charles Wadsworth.

This got me excited for I knew Charles Wadsworth as director of the Chamber Music Society of Lincoln Center. I went to the desk clerk, verified that Charles was staying at the hotel, and left a note for him. I asked if he could meet me for a 7 AM rehearsal and a clinic/concert at 9. He called me at 3:00 in the morning to tell me he had just arrived back at the hotel after a party and that yes, he would be there for a 7:00 rehearsal. There was no time to get word to Alec but he was pleasantly surprised to hear his music at my NYSSMA clinic.

THE CASALS FESTIVAL

When Francisco Franco, a fascist, came to power in Spain, the great cellist Pablo Casals, who had been born in El Vendrell, Catalonia, Spain, in 1876, vowed never to set foot in Spain until Franco had been removed. Casals resided in southern France, where Alexander Schneider, violinist in the Budapest String Quartet, convinced him to lend his name and stature to a music festival. The results were so outstanding that it was decided to move the annual festival to Puerto Rico, which had a Spanish-speaking populace and many Spanish traditions. The festival that bears his name began there in 1957 and included a full symphony orchestra that presented a several-week season. In 1962, I was invited by personnel manager Loren Glickman to join the orchestra but was unable to because of long-standing commitments. I recommended Arnold Jacobs, who of course had a name known to all brass players. Arnold and his wife Gizzy enjoyed Puerto Rico and wondered why they were never called back! The reason is that my schedule was open in subsequent summers. My first involvement was in 1963 when I played a recording session in New York City with the Festival Casals Orchestra. There was no festival in 1963.

Carol and the kids loved the festival; it was like a vacation. That first summer, 1964, Jesse was four months old and was carried about in a nip-nap wherever we went. The Casals Festival usually lasted three to four weeks and then there might follow concerts at Carnegie Hall in New York. The primary conductors were Casals himself, Zubin Mehta, "Sasha" Schneider, Victor Tevah, and Mstislav Rostropovich. The musicians were all top-notch. Sidney Harth was concertmaster one year, Felix Galimir another year. We played much of the standard orchestral repertoire. One day, we were rehearsing the Dvorak *Cello Concerto* with the great cellist Gregor Piatigorsky, who had played in Heifetz's quartet. Piatigorsky looked up at Zubin Mehta, who was conducting, and said, "My God, what an orchestra. How I'd love to do *Don Quixote* with this orchestra." The next morning, *Don Quixote* was on the music stands, replacing the Dvorak. They had ordered it flown down from New York overnight and they hired Ronnie Ricketts of the Minneapolis Symphony to play euphonium.

Another year, Casals was playing the Dvorak *Cello Concerto* and John Barrows played the opening statement of the first theme in the first movement. After John played the opening solo, at the rehearsal, Casals stopped the orchestra and insisted that they would not go on until he heard that horn solo again because it was so beautiful. John murmured something under his breath, but he reluctantly played the solo again, just as beautifully.

Yet another year, I remember taking the last flight in with our boys because the next day's program was *Till Eulenspiegel,* which I could play in my sleep. I met Earl Chapin and John Barrows on a final trip to the rental car to bring up our last piece of luggage. Earl said, "Oh, did you get the program change for tomorrow?"

"No."

"We're doing *Pictures at an Exhibition.*"

Yikes! Once I was inside, I put a pillow in my tuba and practiced for about three hours that night, focusing on the notorious "Bydlo" solo. We did two rehearsals and three performances, which illustrates the quality of the orchestra. Casals was entering his nineties when I first started playing in his orchestra. When we rehearsed with the Maestro, it took two people at least to help him get on the podium. He would sit on a little stool, hunched. When it was time to start, he would sit up, his eyes would brighten, and he was a changed man, waving the baton and singing enthusiastically.

One time, we finished rehearsing and his two assistants came to help him off the podium, but he pushed them aside and began walking through the orchestra. He walked past the cello and viola sections and every person would stiffen out of respect for the Maestro as he approached. He finally arrived in the back of the orchestra and stopped at my chair. He gave me a kiss on the cheek and told me how good it was to have me back in the orchestra again that year.

The Casals Festival afforded me my first opportunity to hear Itzhak Perlman play. I remember glancing over at the violin section during the first rehearsal and there he was, sitting in the back playing along with the section while he was waiting to rehearse his concerto. At the concert, he performed the Mendelssohn *Violin Concerto* and the audience went wild and demanded an encore. He turned back to the string section and said, "Pick a number from one to twenty-four." One of the violinists said, "Fourteen!" He turned and instantly played Paganini's *Caprice No. 14* from memory.

Another time, when Maestro Mstislav Rostropovich was guest conductor, he invited me to his room. He had a garden apartment at the Caribe Hilton in Puerto Rico. He was very cordial. There were hors d'oeuvres on the coffee table, so I assumed there would be others arriving soon. I thought I was there to discuss the music we would be playing. There was vodka and a bucket of ice. But it was just me and the Maestro. Over a drink, he told me that he respected me tremendously and that he thought what I was doing for the tuba was what Casals had done for the cello. That was one of the best compliments I ever received in my life—and I received the same compliment from cellist Janos Starker, years later.

There was one time when Little Harvey had a high fever in Puerto Rico. He was about seven years old at the time. Carol thought it was heat stroke or indigestion, but since I didn't feel any strength in his arms, I was concerned. So I took him to the hospital. They said it was his appendix, which was wrapped around his intestine and had to be removed. They performed an emergency operation on him. I had to sleep with him in the nurses' break room because the hospital was so full. That was a scary episode but luckily he pulled through, and in fact his appendix was such an unusual example that it was preserved in alcohol as a reference for medical students.

Our last year at the Casals Festival was 1978. Casals himself died in 1973. But I did return to Puerto Rico in 1982 at the invitation of John Barnett, who had been conductor of the National Orchestral Association, where I had served as brass coach. He was then conductor of the Puerto Rico Symphony. On the first half I performed the Bernhard Heiden *Concerto for Tuba and Orchestra,* which I had commissioned, and on the second half, the Ralph Vaughan Williams *Concerto for Bass Tuba and Orchestra.* The audience and orchestra wanted an encore. I quieted the audience and first acknowledged some of the Puerto Rican musicians in the orchestra who had played with the Festival Casals Orchestra. I told the audience what a great pleasure it was to make music again with these musicians. The audience felt rapport between the orchestra's musicians and me. I thanked the audience for its reception and said I had no encore prepared but I had something to play for my Puerto Rican friends in the orchestra and the audience was welcome to listen in. I played "Spanish Eyes," softly, very softly and unaccompanied. It was very quiet when I stopped playing. I looked around and half of my Puerto Rican friends were crying. Then all at once everyone started clapping and cheering again. It was a great evening.

EVERYBODY KNOWS WHERE THEY WERE

Metropolitan Opera star Rise Stevens had decided, with her husband's and her agent's encouragement, to package a Las Vegas–style nightclub show similar to that of Eileen Farrell, another Metropolitan Opera diva ("I've Got a Right To Sing the Blues," etc.). Gunther Schuller was engaged to prepare arrangements for this project. Recording sessions were scheduled and Gunther and I assembled a dream orchestra that included Doc Severinsen, Clark Terry, Joe Newman, Urbie Green, John Barrows, Johnny Hodges, Ben Webster, and Phil Woods. As I recall, we had completed one 2–5 PM recording session on November 21 and had two sessions scheduled for November 22, the first one 10 AM to 1 PM. Since this was Gunther's thirty-ninth birthday, I arranged with the recording engineers and musicians to have the afternoon 2–5 session start late so there would be time to celebrate Gunther's birthday. I had a large birthday cake and iced champagne ready. The morning session went very well and I busied myself getting ready for a short celebration of Gunther's birthday.

At 1:30 I was surprised to see violinist Anahid Ajemian return to the studio crying uncontrollably. I was alarmed and thought one of our musicians might have had an accident. But when she could finally speak, she informed me that President Kennedy had just been assassinated in Dallas. Soon the studio was full of returning musicians, all of them upset about the tragedy. The afternoon session (and any future sessions, as it turned out) was canceled, along with the celebration of Gunther's birthday. Margie and Gunther and our mutual friend John Barrows took the champagne and birthday cake to Carol's and my apartment. We stayed up late watching the drama of the President's assassination on television. Through the course of the evening I believe we each had one small piece of cake, but the mood wasn't right for champagne. Needless to say, we all know where we were when our president was assassinated.

AN ASIDE

In the spring of 1970, I was invited to spend five days as clinician/ soloist with the Glassboro, New Jersey, State College brass faculty to rehearse and prepare a series of concerts featuring the tuba in every way possible. One performance was as a soloist, presenting a balanced recital program with solo tuba and faculty pianist accompaniment. The second presented a clinic/master class on brass/tuba. For the third I served as a fifth member of a quintet, with Glassboro faculty, and we rehearsed and presented a concert. The fourth was with the wind ensemble, and the tuba was featured soloist and gave evidence of the enormously varied repertoire that could be showcased with the other brass instruments.

I met with members of the administration and faculty and outlined the enormous variety of performance and instruction possible with the tuba added to the faculty. My efforts were successful and a graduate student of mine, Owen Metcalf, was hired for the position of applied tuba, brass quintet (chamber music), and pedagogy of the tuba.

Throughout the period when I was personnel manager for Stravinsky's final series of concerts and recordings, I continued working on special projects with Gunther Schuller, John Lewis, Manny Albam, J. J. Johnson, Morton Gould, and others. I felt I had the best of both worlds. Working for Stravinsky opened up more opportunities for me and, had it been my intention, I believe I was groomed and prepared to become a major music contractor in New York City.

CHAPTER ELEVEN

New England Conservatory of Music

IN MARCH 1967 I received a call from Gunther Schuller. He told me he had been appointed president of the New England Conservatory of Music (NEC) in Boston and he was inviting me to work with him as his vice president for financial affairs. I was surprised to hear myself instantaneously accept his invitation. Subconsciously, I reserved putting order into my response for later, not fully reviewing the reasons why I said yes right away. I rationalized that having a traditional academic work schedule would allow me to spend more time with my family. But the primary reason I said yes came from our friendship and long association and from my unbounded admiration of Gunther's achievements. Considering that we had worked on many projects together, it was a quick decision, but certainly not a rash one. At least, that's how I explained it to Carol when I arrived home that evening and told her we would be moving to Massachusetts.

I remembered April 1951, following a New York City Opera performance of Alban Berg's twelve-tone opera *Wozzeck*. In the second act of *Wozzeck* the tuba is featured in an important extended role as a tavern musician in a small, onstage ensemble. After the performance, Gunther and Margie Schuller were waiting at the stage door to congratulate me and the orchestra. Following that evening, I made every effort to attend his lectures and performances.

Gunther Schuller, a complete musician, was exciting to be around and exciting to talk to about music. We had worked together on a variety of recordings and other freelance assignments. It just seems we were ever mutually involved in important projects and our careers intermeshed in countless ways. It felt like each day brought new challenges. It was an exciting time.

Gunther had no musical prejudices. He was an icon for music of every description. Musically, I felt safe with Gunther. Personally, we trusted each other. These connections and deep mutual respect made me vulnerable to giving up part of an established performance career for one heavily mixed with administrative responsibilities.

As I soon discovered, assuming the position of vice president for financial affairs was an awesome undertaking. The conservatory, for all practical purposes, was broke.

In mid-May Gunther called from Tanglewood and asked if I could arrange to start at NEC on June 1 instead of September 1. He felt it was important that someone from the new administration be at the conservatory through the summer months. I agreed with Gunther and although Carol and I hadn't yet sold our Englewood house, we managed to rent a furnished house in Needham, Massachusetts. Evenings and weekends we sought realtor assistance for locating a desirable property to purchase in the Boston area.

Gunther shared with me during a telephone conversation shortly before Donald Harris arrived in August that he had appointed Donald as vice president for academic affairs. I looked forward to meeting Donald Harris—I picked him up at the airport and he got settled before the 1967–1968 academic year began. Meanwhile, I engaged tubist Toby Hanks to do the New York Brass Quintet's summer tour of eastern Europe (which I hated to miss) and the summer season of the New York City Ballet at Saratoga, New York.

On June 1, as I was leaving the house in Needham for my first day at the conservatory, Carol wryly asked, "What will you do when you get there, start opening file cabinets?"

I replied, "Yes, exactly, just as soon as I find the conservatory!" I had yet to set foot in the school.

The guard at the front entrance of the conservatory greeted me the first morning I arrived but on following mornings he made sure that he was in a position where he would not have to say hello. I noticed the same treatment from the maids, who, if they saw me coming, would make sure their backs were turned as they polished a brass doorknob or dusted a windowsill. Apparently, the school's service employees were afraid the new administration might fire them as part of saving the conservatory.

Early on I got to know a student flutist named Jan Gippo. He worked part time at a store featuring select wines. He received an employee discount, which he was able to pass on to me and the conservatory. With his assistance, I preempted the Fourth of July by personally presenting bottles of wine to each of the service employees with whom I had contact. I knew they would enjoy the wine with their respective families and suspected most would not have purchased it themselves. I sent each family a short note wishing them a happy and safe holiday. My morning arrivals went from loud silence to greetings from three or four employees waiting to say, "Good morning, Mr. Phillips!" A smiling guard carried my briefcase upstairs to my office.

Gunther was also quick to show his appreciation for the good work of all conservatory employees. Our combined efforts were to win the conservatory family over. We garnered their loyalty and support for future administrative directives.

The business manager of NEC's administrative affairs was a gentleman named Shelby Harrington. I had several conversations with Mr. Harrington regarding the financial status of the school, and was disappointed to learn that the conservatory was indeed broke. Things were in such a state, for example, that the gentleman running the audio department had to sign out the school's only tape recorder, kept in the business manager's office, and return it on schedule.

The conservatory, established by Eben Tourjee in 1867, was America's oldest conservatory of music. It had been functioning with virtually no endowment, because the founder believed that a school of music should pay for itself. There were only a few named scholarships. During my first few days of research it was depressing to work across the hall from the president's office, still occupied by Chester Williams, the man who preceded Gunther in the position. Chester was a man of considerable stature, totally committed to the New England Conservatory, but perhaps tired from having to manage with insufficient financial support and realizing that what had worked for one hundred years could no longer keep pace with modern music education. Some afternoons, in the privacy of his office, Dr. Williams would break down and be comforted by secretary Anne Davis. At Gunther Schuller's invitation, he had agreed to stay on as dean of students; I don't think Gunther could have found a better dean.

My first eye-opening encounter with the conservatory's trustee executive committee was in the Brown Shoe Company boardroom. It was in June, shortly after my first visit to the school. The committee members were committed to the institution and their loyalty was unquestionable. I gave my full attention to this first meeting as a long list of concerns and projections were reviewed. The most telling incident was when one of the younger trustees asked, "Tell us, Mr. Phillips, what are you and Dr. Schuller going to do to save the Conservatory?"

I thought quickly, paused for a moment, then, choosing my words carefully, I responded, "I believe the manifest which established the New England Conservatory of Music would hold the trustees responsible for saving the institution. Dr. Schuller and his administration have accepted the responsibility of creating a conservatory worth saving. With Gunther Schuller's direction we will do our part and hopefully assist the trustees in doing theirs. The trustees and administration must work together to achieve mutual success."

After a brief silence, executive board chairman Sherwin Badger summed up our meeting as one of candid discussion. He assured everyone that we would continue working together for our mutual cause. Meeting adjourned.

I admired Sherwin Badger's persona, the respect he had earned, and his gift for putting people at ease. At the moment he was the conservatory's most valuable asset, and he had also been the primary influence in securing Gunther Schuller as conservatory president. Sherwin Badger embodied the dignity, warmth, diplomacy, and confidence of an executive committee chairman. A smile from Sherwin was like having Marilyn Monroe throw you a kiss.

The whole conservatory needed physical revitalization. The student enrollment was down and some faculty members feared that Gunther planned to fire them. Actually, he fired none of them. When it was discovered that the conservatory had more than eighty trustees, many of whom hadn't visited the conservatory for years nor considered making a gift to help the conservatory through its difficult times, executive board action reduced the number of trustees to thirty-five.

While morale was low, pride was high. The administrative personnel and the faculty had tremendous pride in their relationship to the conservatory. Unfortunately, pride couldn't be spent as endowment. Too many of the faculty and service personnel had let fear and uncertainty make them as much in need of revitalization as the walls needed paint. I decided to dramatize their apathetic attitude. I ordered two-inch-wide rolls of self-sticking tape with the word APATHY printed on one roll in red on white and IS CURABLE on the other.

I obtained the guard's schedule of inspection rounds for each evening and shared it with two specially selected students; I also shared my key to the conservatory and to my office. I gave the students careful and precise instructions to be quiet and stay sequestered in my office until the guard had started his midnight rounds. Then, wearing sneakers, and following the guard undetected, they were to place self-sticking APATHY signs on all glass and metal surfaces at eye level. It was done.

That night around 2:30 AM, I received a telephone call from an excited and fast-talking guard. "Mr. Phillips," he said, "there are 'apathy' signs throughout the conservatory! I don't know how they got there. Should I take them down?"

I said, "No, it's after 3 AM. We will deal with it tomorrow morning."

Everyone had their own thoughts about the source but they also looked inward and asked if they had been apathetic. The second night the exercise was repeated, with the APATHY signs covered with IS CURABLE across like a Band-Aid. Morale improved in like order.

The third week of July Carol and I purchased a house at 120 Loker Street, Wayland, Massachusetts. It was in walking distance of Loker Elementary School. We were in a good neighborhood, twenty miles from the conservatory and thirty-five miles from the airport.

Anne Davis, executive secretary to president Schuller, had begun interviewing candidates for me. I needed a private secretary who would answer my telephone, take dictation, answer mail, and keep a schedule of both on- and off-campus activities. She called to tell me she thought I should meet one young lady interested in the position. Mary Jo Merseth was a recent graduate of Wellesley College. As a student, she was involved in organizing committees for a variety of causes. I immediately recognized the importance of her qualifications.

One of Gunther's prime interests was to establish good relationships with Elma Lewis and other community leaders in Roxbury, the black district which was neighbor to the conservatory. Mary Jo became a perfect assistant for this endeavor. She was important in establishing student committees that served in outreach and discovery of black talent. In Roxbury, the conservatory had been looked upon as a white castle on the hill. She was a tremendous influence in reaching the black community leaders and convincing young NEC students of our sincerity. Her age and enthusiasm were important factors. Also important in bringing talent from Roxbury to the school was eclectic jazz pianist Ran Blake.

NEC: DAILY ROUTINE

As a freelance musician it was difficult for me to establish and adjust to a set daily routine. My responsibilities demanded flexibility. Most mornings, I would get up at 6:00 or 6:30, have breakfast with Carol and the boys, then drive through Natick to pick up NEC comptroller Wellman Bartlett. When prearranged, I would drive by Gunther's house and pick him up as well. We would expect to arrive at the conservatory by quarter to 8 and be in our offices by 8:00. We would often start the day with a meeting prepared by our secretaries. If we had traveled together, we would already have discussed items on the agenda, taking proper advantage of the time en route. We usually discussed raising funds and improving the visibility and position of the conservatory.

We tried to be creative, to innovate new approaches to funding sources. We wanted to develop allies and not become opponents of our sister institutions. We strived to create funding approaches that utilized our experience as performing musicians, staying informed of the latest trends and sharing that knowledge with others who might also benefit from our efforts. With a little tweaking and refinement, innovative approaches captured the imagination of the music education world and earned the conservatory a place center stage.

I collected printed programs from the Boston Symphony Orchestra, the Gardner Museum, the Boston Museum of Fine Arts, Boston University, Northeastern University, Tufts, Brandeis, Harvard, MIT, and others. These programs listed the levels of giving sustained by individuals and organizations. I memorized the names of donors already committed to supporting the cultural arts institutions of greater Boston. Such information was helpful in explaining why they should also consider supporting the conservatory. Sometimes, after conferring with Sherwin Badger and receiving his blessing, I would make my own appointments to meet with potential donors. I would extol the leadership of Gunther Schuller, the enthusiasm of the trustee executive board, the potential of our student body, and the reasons why I gave up my own performance career to serve Gunther and NEC. I was comfortable with such representation. By the time Gunther could meet with some of these prospective donors, they had been groomed to maximum concern for the conservatory and respect for Gunther Schuller.

I spoke with Gunther on several occasions about the enormous success Frank Battisti had achieved in fourteen years directing the Ithaca, New York, High School music program, including the commissioning of twenty-four works for wind ensemble and band by major composers. In 1967 Frank departed his beloved Ithaca High School Band and accepted the position of director of wind ensemble and bands at Baldwin-Wallace College in Berea, Ohio.

That same year, on February 8, 1967, at a Music Educators National Conference in Boston, I had performed with Battisti's Ithaca High School Wind Ensemble in a world premiere of a work I commissioned, Warren Benson's *Helix* for solo tuba and wind ensemble. This was two weeks before I was invited to join Gunther's administration at the New England Conservatory. The Boston performance stands out in my memory partly because *Helix* was an excellent addition to the tuba's solo repertoire and also because I took Frank and his students, along with other special friends, to dinner at the Union Oyster House. In the middle of that dinner, the restaurant lost its electricity, so we ate by candlelight.

On my way to important clinics in Ohio, I called ahead a few days to ask Frank if he could pick me up at the Cleveland airport and drive me to Youngstown, Ohio. We hadn't seen each other in a while, but Frank was very gracious. On the ride, I convinced him that Gunther Schuller wanted him to be director of the new NEC Wind Ensemble. He was perfect for the position and could exercise freely his concepts in music performance and music education. Frank Battisti started the position in 1969 and, as expected, produced an unequaled program.

One of our goals was to elevate the general opinion about majoring in music education. At universities and colleges, as much as 90 percent of their music student enrollment comprised music education majors. Some Boston Symphony personnel who taught applied music lessons for NEC had a clause in their contracts saying they would not be obligated to teach music education majors. A new contract was prepared, simply stating that students would declare their major during their sophomore year. This gave applied teachers the opportunity to experience the performance potential of their assigned students before a major was declared. Students in the top 20 percent of their class could be accepted as majors in music education, which made music education students the elite of the school. The ploy was to turn out incredible performer-educators. Within two years, the majority of our first-desk chairs in the orchestra and wind ensemble were music education majors.

THE PROS PLAY TUESDAYS

We wanted students to realize that the New England Conservatory was being administered by music professionals. To get this across to the students, we announced that at noon on select Tuesdays there would be a special concert by friends of the administration. On the first Tuesday I performed a tuba recital assisted by faculty pianist Russell Sherman.

The second Tuesday featured Peter Schickele. (His P.D.Q. Bach concert that evening in Symphony Hall, across the street from the conservatory, was sold out.) I had called Peter and told him what we were trying to do. Pete said, "Well, since we're sold out anyway, I'll just move our dress rehearsal from Symphony Hall to Jordan Hall," which he did. For the third Tuesday, Don Harris picked up on the French Radio Orchestra, which was on tour and with which he had connections. The following week, we had Ramanathan, a sitar player second only to Ravi Shankar. The week after that we had jazz tenor saxophonist Zoot Sims and his quartet. We couldn't produce an artist every week, but the students learned to check out Jordan Hall every Tuesday at noon.

I called Clark Terry and asked him if his quartet planned to be in Boston any time soon. He said, "No, why are you asking?" When I explained to Clark what we were trying to accomplish, he said, "Well, how about next Tuesday for me and my group?" I said that would be fabulous. He said he couldn't tell me anything until Monday when he talked to his guys. He called me up on Monday evening saying that he had spoken with his guys and they all had regular sessions booked, "but Harvey, I'll be there." Faculty saxophonist Carl Atkins agreed to play also and recruited the best freelance rhythm section in Boston. Clark came into my office at 8:30 in the morning. I sent across the street for a McDonald's breakfast. Clark slept in my office until a quarter to noon, then walked onto the Jordan Hall stage and, without any rehearsal, tore the place up.

This prompted several members of a group of students who had been walking around with chips on their shoulders, vis-à-vis the new administration, to make an appointment to see me. In the course of our getting acquainted, one asked, "Why don't you have Stan Kenton and his Orchestra?"

"Well, let me know when they're in town."

"They're in town. They're playing at Lennie's on the Turnpike."

I picked up the telephone and, without looking up the number, called the Bradford Hotel, where traveling musicians gravitated. I asked for Stan Kenton's room and, as luck would have it, he answered the phone. After a few exchanges in conversation, I told him why I'd called and that the student body would just go nuts if his band could come and do a half-hour or hour program. He said practically the same thing word-for-word that Clark had said: "I don't know, Harvey, I'll have to ask the guys, but I'll be there."

He called me at 3 AM and said, "All the guys want to come to the conservatory." It blew the minds of the students when the Stan Kenton Orchestra bus pulled up at the side entrance of NEC. Stan and his band played a terrific program for students assembled in Jordan Hall. I gave Stan and each of his musicians an NEC mug. That's all we had to offer them. These Tuesday noon concerts helped to establish the new administration's relationship with a hard-to-win segment of the student body.

There was one Tuesday when we didn't have a performance, but I had my Juilliard and Interlochen friend Van Cliburn just walk with me through the school. Van would look through the window of a practice room and the student pianist would freak out to see Van Cliburn watching him or her.

A jazz department was started by Gunther. Several talented and worthy student musicians were discovered and recruited by pianist Ran Blake, a denizen of Roxbury. Jazz pianist Jaki Byard was brought in by Gunther to teach at the conservatory on a commuting basis.

Lennie Sogoloff, owner for twenty years of the Lennie's on the Turnpike jazz club in Boston, recalls how he met me. He said, "I booked Mel Torme, who insisted on a thirteen-piece band. After the first set, I was called into Mel's dressing room. 'We've got a problem. The tuba player's not making it.' I said, 'I'll find a tuba player.' I didn't know where. I called the Berklee School of Music. They referred me to the New England Conservatory. I explained my problem. I said, 'The guy should read. He should be accurate and have a good tone.' The man on the phone said, 'I think I can handle that.'

"'Who am I talking to?'

"'My name is Harvey Phillips.'

"'You think you can cut it?'

"'I'm pretty sure I can.'

"I believe Mel opened with 'Lulu's Back in Town,' which has a prominent tuba part. Harvey sounded beautiful. Mel looked over and blew me a kiss. Honest to God."

To fulfill my responsibilities at the conservatory, I had to rely on my instincts and my personal experience of managing business affairs within the music industry. Some activities were initiated with Gunther Schuller and some were personally generated. When Gunther was inaugurated president of NEC in formal ceremonial attire in the fall of 1967, the conservatory's enrollment was down to just over two hundred.

The Phi Mu Alpha Sinfonia music fraternity, founded at NEC in 1890, had one of the largest rooms as its headquarters. Some tough decisions had to be made, including the allocation of a smaller space to Phi Mu Alpha Sinfonia. The larger room was needed for ensemble rehearsals. Later, the James Madison University chapter of Phi Mu Alpha Sinfonia, in an elaborate ceremony, made me an honorary member. In 1978, I was awarded the Distinguished Service to Music "Blue Max" Award by the music fraternity Kappa Kappa Psi, at an annual national meeting at which Gilbert Eitch conducted a concert band.

At the conservatory, we discussed the dispensation of faculty members who had lost touch with the profession but had ingratiated themselves socially with important members of the greater Boston community. We did not want to alienate funding sources that might become injured if a faculty friend should lose his or her position. It was a chess game.

Another problem was that NEC had no retirement program and there was no state retirement fund. I suggested we adopt the following program: for an employee who had been there thirty years, NEC would match the monthly Social Security check, and employees who had worked at NEC for twenty years would receive one half the amount of their Social Security check. That was about as far as we could go. Keeping faculty who had lost their fire was untenable and expensive.

With so much to be done, it was impossible to avoid scheduling conflicts. As I recall, two of our first fundraising events had to be held on the same evening to accommodate the busy schedules of important potential donors, the executive board, president Gunther Schuller, and others of his new administration. The first fundraiser was scheduled for cocktails and hors d'oeuvres and held on the top floor of a bank in the financial district. Gunther and I played three movements of Alec Wilder's *Suite No. 1 for Horn, Tuba, and Piano.* Buddy Sherman played piano. We had a very cursory talk-through rehearsal. I knew Gunther hadn't played his horn for at least a year. I was amazed—he sounded glorious. Everyone was impressed, especially Alec Wilder, who was present. Donald Harris was supposed to play the piano part but had no time to prepare it.

A terrible snowstorm started shortly after we arrived by taxi. I left my car in the conservatory garage because parking downtown was a problem. Sherwin Badger hosted the evening and introduced Gunther to several important guests. Despite the early winter storm, the evening was a success. As the conservatory's new president, Gunther was the main attraction.

I reminded Gunther we had promised to show up at a faculty performance in Jordan Hall. I arranged safe overnight storage for our instruments and we headed for the conservatory. We had to run. There was total silence. It was still snowing. There was no traffic—nothing was moving. We arrived at the conservatory as promised and attended the performers' reception. By midnight the snowplows and salt trucks were making main arteries passable and we were able to get home.

On the job, my concern was to attract money for the conservatory. The executive committee made the good choice to hire the additional expertise of a fundraising firm headquartered in Pittsburgh. The company assigned to our service a very skilled and knowledgeable fund development consultant named Ralph Peterson. Serious and dedicated, Ralph had the prerequisites of a consummate financial adviser, including a sense of humor when it was possible to exercise it.

For one hundred years the New England Conservatory was showcased as a member of the Boston arts and cultural scene, especially when companies were trying to attract top officers to the city. One day Sherwin Badger and I were talking in Gunther's office and we were struck with the same idea at the same time: we would coerce funds from corporations which used the conservatory's name and cultural image when advertising the city of Boston to potential CEOs. Sherwin was a master of this tactic; he convinced many important executives that, simply by using NEC for recruiting executives to Boston, they had a moral obligation to support the conservatory. With Ralph Peterson's professional training in fundraising, Sherwin Badger's charisma, my contacts in the professional music world, and Gunther's leadership, we were able to stop the bleeding and get the conservatory back on its feet.

I reviewed with Gunther, his administration, and the trustees our goals for student excellence. We knew we had to commit to funding scholarships. The first discussion with Gunther about scholarships included the realization that we would have to give out more merit scholarships than financial aid and we worked hard to have any funding properly identified. I felt that some institutions weren't making clear the difference between scholarships and financial aid. I suggested that we give full scholarships for a brass quintet, a woodwind quintet, and a string quartet and that there be a minimum requirement of twenty hours of rehearsal a week. Such chamber groups, I felt, would be invaluable to student recruitment and public support.

The first brass quintet that resulted was so good that we were able to assign an important premiere to this group. While I was still with the New York Brass Quintet, I had commissioned Karel Husa to write a work for brass quintet and symphony orchestra. Between my commission and his composition, I had left the NYBQ and moved to Boston. The piece was programmed with the Buffalo Symphony Orchestra and the NEC Scholarship Brass Quintet, conducted by Michael Tilson Thomas. Karel Husa attended the premiere and was very pleased with the performance.

To document Gunther Schuller's successful administration, I suggested that we accept the largess of Golden Crest Records founder and president Clark Galehouse to establish an NEC series of recordings on its own label. Gunther agreed and so it was done. The first recorded example of the outstanding student ensembles was a recording of Richard Strauss' *Ein Heldenleben* conducted by Gunther Schuller.

Underwriters were solicited for a contribution of $1,500, of which $1,200 would pay for pressing and packaging an initial one thousand copies of the LP. The contributor would receive the original painting used on the cover of the LP. To establish the concept, I personally underwrote the first four LPs. Carol and I are proud to display in our home four George Lewis paintings (he was paid three hundred dollars for each), now worth more than my original contributions.

THE FAMILY—ONE FOR ALL, ALL FOR ONE

Jesse was conceived in Paris on the 1963 NYBQ tour and was born on Valentine's Day, 1964, in the New York Hospital. The day after he was born, I left on a three-week national tour with the New York Brass Quintet. I decided it was too long to be away from my family. On my return, I sat down with Carol and we made a rule that I would go anywhere for up to four days, but if a fifth day or more was involved, the whole family went or I didn't go. The one exception was when I went on another month-long N Y B Q tour of Europe, arriving back home shortly before Christmas 1965. In a vain effort to have them with me, I bought family gifts in almost every city we visited: Berlin, Frankfurt, Stuttgart, Copenhagen, Hamburg, Amsterdam, Cologne, and Wuppertal. Our Christmas tree served us well that year.

This five-day policy gave me the license to do a short tour or clinic out of town without feeling guilty and it also transformed long tours into family experiences. The industry accepted my mandate, even when I traveled to Australia and to Europe, when they realized that I was serious about sticking to my policy. They would include the airfare for the rest of the family in my fee. Not many artists had a similar policy, by reason of economics. But money didn't mean that much to me.

Little Harvey was born on September 16, 1966, with his forefinger in his mouth and the biggest eyes you've ever seen. He carried a blue English blanket from the hospital that had a label with a swan on the corner. Little Harvey carried it everywhere with him and, after many washings, it was reduced to the corner. He was so attached to it that when Jesse mischievously hid it from him, he would run to Carol crying, "Jesse stole my corn-yer!"

Jesse had been to the pet store and got a little turtle. He was the only kid on the block who had a turtle and he was very proud of it. Little Harvey was jealous. One day Carol noticed that the turtle was missing. After a search, she couldn't find it and asked Little Harvey if he knew where the turtle was. He said, "Far, far away."

She thought about that for a few minutes and, when Harvey lay down for his nap, she again searched the house up and down. Finally, Carol went through the toy trunk and found the turtle sitting in a little boat in the bottom underneath all the toys. I guess Little Harvey thought the boat was going to sail away.

We had a deck off the east side of the house, as well as a sandbox about forty feet away from the deck. Jesse had some plastic toy soldiers and swordsmen that stood about six inches high. He would go down and put little men all the way around the sandbox, then sit on the deck and pop them off with his BB gun, one BB per man. He was a crack shot.

Our third baby boy was born September 23, 1968, at 9:30 PM in Boston Lying-In Hospital on Huntington Avenue, a few blocks south of the New England Conservatory of Music. Suspecting her baby's birth was imminent, Carol went with me to the conservatory that morning. She walked around the Boston department stores and returned to the conservatory at 5:30, whereupon, entering the NEC lobby, her water broke in front of the imposing bronze statue of Beethoven. With many students leaving after class, she ran up the stairs to my office and told Mary Jo what had happened. I was in a meeting with Gunther so Mary Jo passed me a note. We next took a short cab ride to the hospital.

Carol's first observation of our as yet unnamed baby was, "Oh my, what a big long red tongue." A short time later, I made the very same comment. This was an unusually happy baby; his first reaction to any cuddly attention was unbridled belly laughter. Unfortunately, the hospital didn't respond as affably to the days, then weeks, with no name to put on the baby's birth certificate.

On the date of each baby's birth Alec started composing a new *Suite for Tuba and Piano* named to honor each child. On the title page of the third baby's suite one can see where Alec titled, erased, and retitled, over and over again: Arnold, Jonathan, Alexander, Arthur, Thomas, and other names being considered by us on any given day. Gunther and Margie Schuller, who thought his name was Arnold, sent a Christmas card addressed to Master Arnold Phillips.

Some sixty days after his birth, Thanksgiving Day arrived, as did Carol's family to celebrate the holiday with us. Names for the new baby were reviewed ad infinitum as we celebrated and devoured the traditional dinner. Served with each slice of pumpkin pie was a ballot on which to mark three names—from the list of Alexander, Arnold, Arthur, Jonathan, and Thomas—in order of preference. The name with the most points would be accepted and called in to the anxious hospital. Finally, Alec would have the correct name for his new suite. And, with heavy heart, I would later explain the choice of name to my dear friend Arnold Goldberg, timpanist of the New York City Ballet Orchestra. The winning name was Thomas Alexander.

My family has always been the most important part of my life; I worked to make time to spend with Carol and the boys. I would return home from a recording, ballet, or concert in New York City every night except Friday and Saturday, arriving most nights at Boston's Logan Airport around 12:30 AM. I then drove thirty-five miles to Wayland and arrived home between 1:30 and 2 AM. Carol and the boys would be in the master bedroom, all sound asleep in our king-size bed. Just to celebrate being at home with my family, I would quietly get a music stand and chair, then proceed to practice until 3 or 3:30 AM. I practiced as I would at any other hour but none of my sleeping beauties ever awakened. I was always able to function on a few hours of sleep.

When I left New York and went to the conservatory, I didn't publicize the fact that I was leaving. The calls kept coming in. Radio Registry, my answering service, kept my schedule. Because I was in Boston, I would often have to arrange for someone else to do the gigs. The relationship I had with most personnel managers was that they would call me and say they needed a tuba player for a certain number of dates and I'd tell them which ones I could do. For the ones I had to miss, the contractors just said, "Send us the best player." I knew who was available.

The New York City Ballet Orchestra and the New York Brass Quintet were the two musical ensembles I cared the most about in New York. I had gotten in on the ground floor of both, so to speak. One of my biggest regrets about leaving New York was that I didn't know how well Gunther's new administration and I would fare. Gunther was such a musical genius that he never had time to complete high school. With all of the other great things he did, he had never been the chief executive of a major conservatory of music and I had never been in the position I was in. I could manage lots of orchestras at the same time and I could manage accounts, but I had unproven qualifications for going out and soliciting the kinds of contributions the conservatory needed. The first year of this schedule was horrendous and I had to give up most of the playing on recordings and film scores. The conservatory obviously took first priority. After the Boston Symphony offered me the tuba chair, without audition, and I declined, both Gunther and I thought Chester Schmitz of the United States Army Band should audition. Chester sent a request for a time to audition but was refused a time because he didn't have orchestra experience. Gunther, who was in Berlin writing an opera commissioned by the Hamburg Opera, sent a telegram saying he thought Chester should be heard. I spoke to the orchestra manager and supported Gunther's recommendation.

Chester won the audition. Robert Ryker placed second.

In 1967, when I took my administrative position at the conservatory, Chester Schmitz thought I would be teaching the tuba. To resolve the matter, I consented to teach three young players who had been sent specifically to study with me—David Gannett, Gary Ofenloch, and Morris Black. Students Ellis Wean and David Townsend continued their studies with Chester Schmitz.

My policy of taking my family with me to gigs lasted well into the time when the boys were in college. When they were small, we traveled as a family in our station wagon. We'd put the luggage under the back seat and in a luggage carrier on top of the car and I'd practice tuba in the back seat. In the front seat were Carol and Jesse with Tom in between and in the back seat with me was Little Harvey. Between watching for bumps, the boys would call out requests for specific exercises or etudes, like "No. 19 from the *Arban Method Book*." They would sing along, and we'd play word games, too, a sound-alike game and an opposites game. I taught vocabulary that way.

On a trip to Missouri, Carol was driving and I was practicing in the back as usual. While passing a patrol car that had pulled over another vehicle, the officer motioned for Carol to pull over. I kept practicing. As Carol was handing her license and registration to him, Jesse leaned over to the patrolman and said, "This won't be the first ticket she's ever got." Little Harvey was swinging in and out of the rear car window saying, "You did it again, Mom! You did it again!" Carol had never received a ticket before and we couldn't figure out why the boys would say those things.

I kept practicing.

Feeling sorry for Carol, the policeman said, "Just keep it down, lady." The car with the tuba player and crazy kids must have been the joke of the month at the station house. After we pulled away, Carol attempted to take a swipe at Jesse but totally missed and squarely hit Tom in the face with her elbow. We all laughed! Between the boys and me, we saved her a speeding ticket.

When it came to my boys, we did not have quantity time but we did have quality time together. Whenever possible, I took one of my sons with me to New York for a working weekend. I made sure we had a high floor in the hotel that would have a good view of New York City. I'd play the ballet Friday evening and arrange with Arnold Goldberg to sit Jesse or Little Harvey on a timpani stool in a spot where he could see the stage. Saturday morning, I'd usually take him to a historical museum or the Central Park Zoo. Saturday evening, we'd go to dinner at what they called the cowboy restaurant (the Stagecoach Steakhouse). It had a stagecoach, driver, and real horses on the street out in front.

When I flew in by myself, I would go to Al and Dick's Steakhouse. Their steaks were excellent. On one occasion, the buxom waitress said, "Oh Mr. Phillips, you should have the lamb chops. They're unusually good. If you don't enjoy them, I'll bring you a steak on the house." I agreed. They were wonderful. I came home after that weekend and asked Carol to buy some lamb. She almost fainted, because I never ate lamb before then (except for mutton when I was a child).

The New York engagements continued. One day I played a trick on George Michelmore, the personnel manager of the New York City Ballet Orchestra. I noticed that two new glass-enclosed telephone booths had been installed just outside the musicians' green room at the New York State Theater. I couldn't resist. After putting my tuba in the pit, I stepped into the second telephone booth and, looking through the clear glass enclosure, dialed the number of the telephone closest to the dressing room. I knew George would answer that call and, when he did, I said, "George, this is Harvey. I'm at the 125th Street subway station. The subway is not running on time and I'm having trouble getting a taxi. I wanted you to know. I've called everyone who might cover for me and I suggest you have Bob Biddlecome perform the ophicleide part for *Midsummer Night's Dream* on his euphonium."

George was very upset. He said, "Please, Harvey, get here as quick as you can."

I said, "Of course, George. That's understood. I'll get there as quick as possible."

I waited a polite ten minutes and then walked past George's open office door. I greeted him with, "Hi, George. How's everything?"

He leaped out of the chair but was speechless till he gasped, "Harvey, you're at 125th Street."

I said, "Well of course not, George. I'm right here."

"But you called from 125th Street saying you couldn't make it."

"I didn't come from 125th Street. I came from LaGuardia. It must have been someone else who called you, George. I've been here twenty minutes."

I thought it best not to straighten George out on that one right away. When I did, good sport that he always was, we had a few laughs about it.

UNUSUAL ACQUISITION

I made a rule for accepting gifts to the conservatory. So as not to offend any donor, all gifts offered to the conservatory would be accepted gratefully. Once on the premises, final decisions would be resolved.

One day I entered Gunther's outer office, awaiting the start of an executive committee meeting. Anne Davis, Gunther's secretary, was holding the phone with her hand over the mouthpiece, saying, "Mr. Phillips—there's a lady on the phone from Chestnut Hill who wants to give us a piano."

I asked, "What's her name?"

She replied, "A Mrs. Wattles."

I retorted with, "Oh, isn't that ducky? What is she, some kind of quack?" Anne Davis held out the phone for me to take it; she was laughing so hard she couldn't talk. So I listened to Mrs. Wattles as she told me about her husband buying a piano from his business partner to help him out financially when he had just lost everything on October 29, 1929, the day of the stock market crash. Mrs. Wattles said, "It is an unusual piano, one of a kind. The case is teak, with gold inlay."

"What kind of instrument is it?" I asked.

Mrs. Wattles quickly responded, "Why, I believe it's a Wurlitzer!"

I made note that it was probably a Wurlitzer piano and told her someone would soon call and arrange for delivery of the piano to the conservatory. The instrument would then be appraised and the paperwork recorded for income tax purposes. I thanked Mrs. Wattles again for thinking of the conservatory and told her to expect a call from Frank Hansen, who was in charge of all conservatory pianos.

Frank told me that he didn't want to go out and look at a Wurlitzer. I told him to go because it was a very unusual piano.

The next day I received a call from Frank from Mrs. Wattles's home. He asked me, "Harvey, how do you spell Wurlitzer?" I started spelling the word. Frank interrupted my spelling to say, "This Wurlitzer is spelled Steinway."

The Wattles had the piano tuned regularly but no one had ever played it. In 1930 they had built a special air-conditioned room in their house to protect the instrument. I arranged for the piano to be moved to Gunther's office, where he allowed piano majors to practice on it. Mrs. Wattles was pleased with my arrangement for a five-thousand-dollar tax deduction and a brass plate mounted on the left side of the piano identifying the donor. She was retiring to the penthouse of the Fontainbleu Hotel in Miami.

In general, the conservatory had very tight quarters. The piano department, however, had a complete shop for restoration, with a rig where they could remove the entire metal frame to work on any part of the piano's interior prior to putting it all back together. I suggested we make a deal with Steinway: they could use our piano workshop in exchange for overhauling three conservatory pianos per month. At that time, the average age of our 165 pianos, mostly Chickering, was sixty-five years.

In August 1953, the Willard Alexander Agency negotiated an agreement between Vaughn Monroe's successful *Camel Caravan* broadcasts and the Sauter-Finegan Orchestra, in which they would collaborate on radio broadcasts scattered throughout the United States. By having Vaughn Monroe's broadcasts use the Sauter-Finegan Orchestra instead of a Vaughn Monroe orchestra, *Camel Caravan* saved eighteen salaries. The series of concerts with Vaughn Monroe started with shows at college campuses. On September 28, 1953, at Temple University in Philadelphia, CBS announcer Wayne Nelson of *Camel Caravan* announced that the show would star Vaughn Monroe and the Sauter-Finegan Orchestra. It was aired October

12, 1953. Before I left the band at the end of October, I played the additional run-out concerts: one recorded at Villanova on September 29 and broadcast on October 5, one recorded at Duquesne October 6 and aired on October 19, one recorded at the University of Pittsburgh on October 7 and aired on October 26, and one recorded at Glenview Naval Air Station on October 19 and aired on November 2. A short time later, *Camel Caravan* moved to television and was based in Los Angeles.

I met Vaughn Monroe in August 1953. He used to hang around the Sauter-Finegan Orchestra even earlier, when we were at the Meadowbrook supper club in Cedar Grove, New Jersey. Vaughn Monroe was intrigued by the way Ed Sauter and Bill Finegan wrote for the tuba and by the important role assigned to it. We had several conversations about the tuba and became friends.

In 1968, I received a call in my office at the New England Conservatory from Vaughn Monroe, who lived on Newberry Street in Boston. He said, "Harvey, how are things going at NEC? My wife and I are retiring to Fort Lauderdale and I need to do something about my music and record collection. Do you think the conservatory would be interested in accepting my collection as a gift?"

I said, "Absolutely." Vaughn Monroe's *Camel Caravan* radio show had sometimes broadcast from the conservatory's Jordan Hall. Among his collection of records were some 490 *Camel Caravan* radio programs on huge glassine discs. The collection included some twenty to thirty years of arrangements for his orchestra. Vaughn always used the best arrangers and orchestrators, and there were nineteen filing cabinets containing scores and parts, an incredible documentation of the swing bands of the late 1930s and 1940s. I had the conservatory's carpenters make several trips to move the collection into the faculty lounge, the only place available for short-term storage. I was proud of having played a role in acquiring this important collection.

Several months before that, I had received a call from Harry Sosnik, a composer as well as vice president of music at ABC. He offered the conservatory the entire ABC music archives. I told Harry that there was no way we could accept his library; we didn't have space for it. The archives were contained in music cabinets and included everything that had ever been done on ABC. We helped arrange for Boston University to receive the gift and negotiated the conservatory's access to it.

I called Sydney Beck, the school's music librarian (formerly curator of the Toscanini archives in New York City) to look at the Vaughn Monroe collection, which was now completely on conservatory premises. "I've just accepted a gift in your area," I said, "and it will need cross-filing in the library."

Syd came down and started looking through the files. "Sheesh," he said. "What is this?"

"It's Vaughn Monroe's music collection."

"I didn't know we were interested in this kind of stuff. I just turned down the *Voice of Firestone* library."

I couldn't believe what I was hearing. I told Syd to wait for me; I had to make a phone call. I went upstairs to my office and called the Firestone Tire and Rubber Company in Akron, Ohio. I asked to speak with the vice president for public relations and, after speaking to several people and telling them what I wanted, I finally got on the phone with Jack Scarcliff, Harvey Firestone Jr.'s assistant. I told him I had played in the *Voice of Firestone* Orchestra from 1951–1952.

"Oh, you're the gentleman I was supposed to see at the conservatory, but I had lost the business card with your number on it. I went to the telephone operator at the conservatory, who asked what it was about. I said, 'The *Voice of Firestone* library,' and I was sent to talk to Mr. Beck." Nothing had been done with the library yet, but he said that Harvard had expressed interest in it. I told him that he should visit NEC. I said that I already had a clinic booked close to Akron and I offered to present a clinic at the Harvey Firestone Sr. High School.

Jack Scarcliff was in the audience. After my clinic, he came up and said, "You know, Mr. Firestone would like to have lunch with you." He dropped me off in front of a beautiful house. I was met at the door by the maid, who showed me into the dining room where Mr. Firestone was waiting. The dining room table would seat at least twenty people, but only Mr. Firestone and I were there. We greeted each other cordially and started discussing and reminiscing about the *Voice of Firestone* Monday evening broadcasts. After we began a conversation about the collection, the maid served lunch. I said I had played in the *Voice of Firestone* Orchestra, as had Gunther Schuller's father.

The two of us hit it off immediately—we were both punsters. We went on to develop a very close relationship. I went to Akron several times and also visited him at his impressive Newport, Rhode Island, estate. He and Jack, accompanied by Mr. Firestone's secretary of forty years, Bernice Vigar, came to NEC several times as well.

I told the executive board at the conservatory that I had met Mr. Firestone, and noted that the five Firestone brothers built and endowed the Princeton Library in the name of their father, but nothing of such importance was ever done for their mother. Idabelle Firestone composed the opening and closing themes, "If I Could Tell You" and "In My Garden," for *The Voice of Firestone*. It seemed natural that she should be honored as a composer and that an Idabelle Firestone Music Library at the New England Conservatory was a worthy consideration.

Sherwin Badger said that maybe we should get Harvey Firestone Jr., who was in a wheelchair, as a board member. I told him that he wasn't ready for that. We had a good relationship and I didn't want to spoil it by being too aggressive.

I called my attorney, Joseph Taubman, and his brother Howard, the chief music critic for the *New York Times*, to appraise the value of the collection. The appraisal was $1.5 million. The next week, a big limousine pulled up at the conservatory and out came Harvey Firestone and Bernice Vigar. I showed them not only the visible parts of the school, but also areas that could be available and accessible for a library with renovation and without new construction. Space included a large furnace room, coal bins, and water heaters, and an area that had once been a cafeteria for students, which still had its walk-in refrigerator. We looked over the possibilities of making the entire area into a library to house the *Voice of Firestone* collection and other audio materials. He had me seek out an architect in Boston and plans were made to turn the walk-in refrigerator into a supervault, with fireproof, waterproof, and humidity-controlled special files for big glassine discs.

Before a commitment was made, I visited Harvey Firestone Jr. in the Firestone Suite in the Waldorf-Astoria Hotel in New York City. We had a good time together. His daughter, who was also a composer, had just written a theme song for Nelson Rockefeller's bid to be the 1968 Republican presidential candidate. She called Rockefeller on the phone and sang it to him.

In the course of our conversation, Mr. Firestone learned about my family. After that, he would call at Easter and Christmas, asking how we were doing and wishing us a happy holiday. When my family had a tire blow out on our station wagon in Tulsa, we gave the dealer a number that Jack Scarcliff had given us if we ever needed tire service. They took hours fixing the tire. When I went to the office to complain, the manager said, "Oh, Mr. Phillips, I called the number you gave us and was ordered to replace all five tires on your car. We only had four, so we ordered the fifth from a dealer in Oklahoma City."

"What do I owe you?"

"Nothing. I was instructed to give you the tires as a courtesy of the Firestone Tire and Rubber Company."

I put great value on the special friendship that developed between Harvey Firestone Jr. and myself, including my trips to his estate in Rhode Island, the invitation to a major party and reception at the famous Breakers in Newport, his several telephone calls expressing concern and best wishes to my wife and family at important holidays, and our autographed copy of his book entitled *A Man on the Move*.

The portrait of Idabelle Firestone hangs above the entrance of the NEC Idabelle Firestone Music Library. It is a replica by Mme. Elizabeth Shoumatoff of the original painting by Philip de Laszlo.

Idabelle Firestone loved opera. Each of the *Voice of Firestone* programs featured a renowned opera singer, oftentimes performing arias not in his or her normal repertoire. (Eleanor Steber, who appeared more often than any other soprano, had attended the New England Conservatory.) Because the show began as a radio broadcast in 1928, none of the programs could be filmed in color. Also, the preservation of each program involved protecting huge glassine discs. I had technicians do one experiment using the repertoire from black and white broadcasts, balancing with color taken with today's equipment. The first sample we made was having Gunther Schuller host the content of broadcasts featuring traditional artists who appeared on *The Voice of Firestone;* the first program featured the popular Danish tenor Jussi Björling. By alternating scenes in sharp color with the black and white original kinescope, I was hoping success with such a presentation would open a whole new source of funding for the conservatory.

When Gunther Schuller first started his tenure at NEC, the conservatory was in danger of closing its doors. Such secrets are hard to disguise so we even had pens made with the message, "Save the New England Conservatory." Successfully involving one of America's great industrial fortunes through the enthusiastic support of Harvey S. Firestone Jr. impressed the conscience and helped to open the purse strings of Boston philanthropists. I think my most important achievement during my time at NEC was the relationship I established between the conservatory and the Firestone family.

WILDER MUSIC—ANOTHER CHANCE

Living in Wayland, Massachusetts had given Wilder Music a second chance. When we moved there, I purchased two Ozalid reproduction machines, often used to print architectural drawings and blueprints. One took twenty-four-inch paper and one would take forty-eight-inch widths, to reproduce copies of onionskin masters. I built new shelves for Alec's music. I knew I would be busy working for Gunther at the New England Conservatory but I hadn't a clue as to how busy I would be.

I tried to hire help from employees of the conservatory music library, without success. So for four years I would come home from an evening gig, package music into the wee hours of the morning and fill orders for specific pieces so the music could be played in academic and other important venues. I would run off copies, tape them together, bind them, wrap them in a package, and ship them, paying out of my own pocket for all the music and postage—I had no time to prepare and enclose invoices for payment. Getting the music performed was the priority for the time I devoted to the project. I couldn't divulge all this to Alec and he sometimes wondered why he received a letter from a grateful young musician who had just performed his *Suite for Euphonium and Piano* (or some other work). Following the Wayland Second Chance came Third Chance—Bloomington, Indiana. Still no computers!

To save some money on moving, I rented a covered walk-in trailer to transport Alec's music. I backed the trailer into the carport to load it. I had to carry the music around the house and up a grade of grass to get to the trailer. I started loading the trailer around 8:00 PM and it took me until midnight to finish. I was exhausted so I went to bed. At 8:00 in the morning Carol awakened me and said, "I think you'd better look at the trailer." I followed her direction and discovered that the rear bumper of my new Ford Imperial was sitting on the ground. Alec's music was more than it could accommodate. So I had to carry it all back into the house and leave it for the movers to bring to Indiana. I returned the rented trailer. For us to move from Wayland to Bloomington in 1971 cost more than six thousand dollars.

In Bloomington I rented a downtown office and, yes, you guessed it, built another bank of shelves for Alec's music. I hired a graduate student to service Alec's music but discovered he had his own publishing to do. Since we were in need of space, he was considerate in taking the Ozalid machines and a large papercutter to his basement at home. I never followed up on what happened to the machines. I visited a highly regarded publisher in Lebanon, Indiana, but he was more interested in publishing transcriptions of movie compositions and high school marching band fodder.

In 1978, I was happy to ship all of Alec's music to Gunther Schuller to publish in his Margun Music publishing company. I knew Gunther would be an efficient and responsible publisher for Alec. Since 1995, all of Alec's chamber music can be obtained from G. Schirmer, Inc. Of course I retained the original scores to the music he wrote for my family.

Alec was touched by and grateful for my work to make his music available. He said to Jim Maher, "It is one of the very few unselfish gestures ever to have been made to me in my life."

VIETNAM AT THE CONSERVATORY

One day when Alec was visiting us in Boston, on our way to eat at the Ritz-Carlton Hotel, where he was staying, I drove through the Boston

Harvey Phillips performs in a concert.

OctubaFest is celebrated on the roof of a parking garage in downtown Bloomington, Indiana, 1984. From left: Indiana University chancellor Herman B Wells, mayoral assistant Kathy Weigle (back to camera), Harvey and Carol Phillips, Bloomington mayor Tomilea Allison.

Harvey Phillips, in tan jacket, welcomes students to OctubaFeast during OctubaFest at the TubaRanch.

Harvey greets Indiana University Chancellor
Herman B Wells at an OctubaFeast at the
TubaRanch, 1986.

David Baker and Harvey Phillips, 1970s. David and Harvey
met at a 1959 recording session in New York, and both
eventually joined the music faculty at Indiana University.

TubaSantas in rented suits, in their first year in Bloomington, 1974, to test how Christmas carols would sound played by a choir of tubas.

TubaSantas get a ride on a Bloomington fire truck, from IU to their performance location near the courthouse, 1986.

Tuba players turn out in amazing numbers to play carols on the ice rink at Rockefeller Center, New York City, in the annual (since 1974) TubaChristmas. Harvey Phillips, conducting, established the concerts—now held in many cities—in honor of his teacher, Bill Bell, who was born on Christmas day, 1902.

TubaSanta Harvey Phillips with euphonium and tuba in Bloomington, 1986.

Harvey Phillips takes TubaChristmas to Walt Disney World, where he is met by music lovers Mickey Mouse and Goofy, 1993.

Below. Harvey Phillips, in front of Cinderella Castle, announces the TubaChristmas concert at Walt Disney World, 1995.

Charles Kuralt, host of *CBS News Sunday Morning,* joins Harvey Phillips for TubaChristmas in Rockefeller Center, 1995. Kuralt conducted "Silent Night" and wrote about the experience in his book, *Charles Kuralt's America.*

TubaSantas, invited by Congressman Lee Hamilton of Indiana, on the steps of the U.S. Capitol in Washington, D.C., 1996.

Harvey Phillips, always seeking out young tuba students, here in Sapporo, Japan, 1987.

Piano accompanist Hisako Nakayama, Harvey Phillips, and Chitate Kagawa after the two tubists played a duet at a concert in Sapporo, Japan, 1979.

Phillips family portrait, 1981: Harvey Jr., standing; Carol, Jesse, Harvey; Thomas on the floor beside Tootsie, the dog.

Common, where we saw lots of hippies spread out. Alec said, "Look at them! All out there doing their thing."

"Alec! Haven't you done your thing for your whole life?" I asked.

Alec thought for a moment and then laughed, "You know, you're right!"

Having been sympathetic to the first onslaught of the flower children, Alec asked me whatever happened to the flower children. I told him the seed had turned into weeds.

At NEC, my office windows directly overlooked Huntington Avenue, a main thoroughfare for those protesting the Vietnam War. The pressure was building in light of the recent shootings on the campus of Kent State University in 1970. It was disturbing to look right out of my second-floor window. Crowds shouting "Hell no, we won't go!" would pass by, waving flags in protest. I didn't deny their right to march but was both disturbed and saddened to hear loud broadcasts of angry chants and to see the flags of foreign nations.

I understood their concerns and sympathized with their right to protest the decisions of our top military and government officials. The quagmire in which we found ourselves had become quicksand, leaving no way to exit gracefully. Still, I felt it was counterproductive, perhaps overkill, to wear armbands and chant critical anti-American slogans.

The primary protesting group was a socialist organization called the Students for a Democratic Society. The SDS reached its peak influence right when I started at the New England Conservatory. One of its leaders happened to be a conservatory student who was at an NEC Wind Ensemble recording session of circus music with Merle Evans during an SDS rally. Because he attended his recording session obligation instead of the rally, the SDS wanted the conservatory to shut down as a protest of the war.

The students met in Jordan Hall. They demanded a statement from the administration on where we stood with the protest. Both Donald Harris and Gunther Schuller were offcampus at the time, so it was up to me to respond to the students. I told them, in effect, that the administration had no single opinion. Like them, we were individuals, with our own private opinions, so I could speak only for myself. I let them know that, while I thought the war was wrong, their protest was misdirected. The conservatory as an institution served the art of music. If they were going to protest, they should do it through their art and not join strangers from off-campus who knew little or nothing about our personal and professional commitments. This seemed to satisfy the meeting and triggered a point of interest they had not considered before.

I suggested doing a series of recitals. The idea took hold and a committee of students was formed to organize and manage protest concerts around the clock in Jordan Hall. There were recitals day and night, a solid twenty-four hours each day, for ten days. I played a recital at 2:00 in the morning, in overalls. It was either overalls or pajamas. Our faculty bass professor, Buell Neidlinger, performed a bass recital at 5 AM. When the cast of the Broadway musical *Hair* heard about what we were doing, the idea caught fire with them, and they came to Boston and presented a performance starting at 3:00 in the morning.

A commitment had been made to record an anthology of American circus music, and four LPs were recorded, as it happened, during the time of the Vietnam protests. Circus bandmaster Merle Evans, who was seventy-eight, conducted. The boxed set included a fifth LP of Merle Evans recounting some of his circus experiences. The student circus band (NEC's wind ensemble, plus Harvey Phillips, tuba, and John Swallow, euphonium) was organized and prepared by Frank Battisti and was recorded on an NEC label by Golden Crest Records. The music is now available on CD from Windjammers, Inc. It is a collector's item.

During my tenure at NEC, I was still doing clinics and guest recitals. In 1968, I was about to play "The Carnival of Venice" on a sousaphone that Conn was promoting at the time. Backstage, Arnold Jacobs and I were talking and I was putting a little oil on each valve before I went out. I dropped the cap to the bottle of oil and leaned over to pick it up when the first-valve spring fell out of my sousaphone. They were just winding up the previous number and Jake and I were both down on our hands and knees trying to find this spring in the dark. Just as they were announcing me to the audience, Jake found it. I walked onstage screwing the valve cap down. Things were always close with Jake.

I threw a clambake for the Conn Corporation in 1965, ordering five barrels of lobsters, each weighing about a pound and a quarter but a few weighing more, and fifteen pounds of steamer clams. Carol and I had noticed that when we were in Elkhart, Indiana—and we always stopped there on the way to Missouri to visit my parents—all our meals and lodging were provided as a courtesy. I asked Jim Klapp to locate a pavilion for outside picnics that I could lease for one day. He found a beautiful location and we hired the waiters and bartenders from the Elkhart Hotel. The Conn factory closed early that day. One of the officers of the Conn Corporation had a farm in Michigan, which provided wonderful fresh sweet corn and potatoes, and an order from Chicago provided ample clams on the half shell. The bar included a keg of German Lowenbrau on tap. During the party, Jesse stayed with a professional babysitter at the motel.

Lee Greenleaf, whose family owned the Conn Corporation, said it was the first time a clinician had hosted a party for Conn. I was surprised to discover that several of the wives of the almost constantly traveling salesmen and corporate officers had never before eaten a lobster. One of Conn's vice presidents filmed the occasion, including the presentation to me of what they called Conn's CC Tuba for Harvey Baby, a tuba made with four plumber faucet valves, meant as a joke on me. The Conn employees all wanted to hear the Harvey Baby tuba, so I opened the valves halfway and lip-buzzed some music for them. They were impressed that any sound was possible.

The origin of this affectionate name was an incident concerning my flight into the South Bend airport on the occasion of Conn's annual Christmastime celebration of all its dealers and district salesmen. Jim Klapp's wife Pat persuaded some other wives to join her at the airport to welcome me when I got off the plane with rock star screams and open affection for "Oh, Harvey Baby!" The other passengers and people at the airport had no idea what was happening.

At one party given by Conn, the entertainment was a hypnotist. He "hypnotized" one woman and asked, if she was on a desert island, what one person would she want with her. She said, "Harvey baby."

One time we arrived at Jim and Pat Klapp's house for dinner after I had driven all the way from New York. I went to sleep just as the steaks came off the grill. The next year, Jim served me that same steak. He said, "I saved it for you, Harve."

I stayed with the Conn Corporation because I liked the people so much.

My friends in the New York City Ballet Orchestra were surprised and shocked as they entered the pit for a performance of *A Midsummer Night's Dream* and noticed the instrument I was holding was the unplayable Harvey Baby Conn. I was sitting with the tuba at the pit entrance where it could be seen. My usual tuba was hidden behind the timpani of Arnold Goldberg.

I switched instruments after the overture was being played, just in time to play the ophicleide solo. Most people couldn't see the switch of instruments because they were already giving the music their undivided attention. Paul Ingraham, principal horn, had caught a glimpse of the Harvey Baby tuba and, assuming the worst, was nearly incapacitated in a fit of laughter.

WEST VIRGINIA CELEBRITIES

I received a telephone call from Jim Andrews, state supervisor of music education in West Virginia. He told me about a project planned for the state's 1969 conference on music education—discussing how music outside the schools was affecting kids. He requested my assistance in assembling notable people from various kinds of music to meet with West Virginia music professors and teachers of music. I invited Gunther Schuller, who agreed to be the moderator. I was budgeted to pay each performer five hundred dollars plus expenses.

Also agreeing to attend were Odetta, folk music; Bill Graham, Fillmore East and West, rock 'n' roll; and Vladimir Ussachevsky, electronic music. Duke Ellington, on tour with his jazz orchestra, was booked at the time of the conference in Iowa City for a week. He agreed to appear for one day of the conference, which was held in Clarksburg, West Virginia. The schedule for his appearance required an early-morning flight from Des Moines to Pittsburgh and another flight from Pittsburgh to Clarksburg. He would perform his clinic and return on the reverse schedule back to Des Moines, then by car to Iowa City, where his orchestra was booked to appear from 9 PM to 3 AM The more I thought about his appearance, the more troubled I became about such a rigorous schedule for a man who had just turned seventy. I spoke with Gunther and he agreed it was a lot to ask and suggested I inquire about the availability of Dizzy Gillespie. I called Dizzy and explained the situation, and Dizzy responded as though honored to be asked to fill in for Duke. Duke agreed to the change as well, since no publicity had gone out announcing his appearance. The spirit of cooperation expressed by all the artists promised a successful conference.

ANOTHER INVITATION FROM WILLIAM BELL

In December 1970, I attended the Midwest Band and Orchestra Clinic in Chicago. William Bell invited me to visit his Hilton Towers Hotel room for an important discussion. He told me he was retiring from his faculty position at the Indiana University School of Music effective June 1, 1971. He hoped I would be interested in following him as professor of tuba. He had recommended me to Dean Wilfred C. Bain and told me that I should expect a telephone call from him. Members of the brass faculty also favored my appointment.

At first I was not interested and told him, with regrets, that I was fully committed to Gunther Schuller and the New England Conservatory. He said that he understood but still wanted me to meet with Dean Bain about the possibility. I made no promises.

On my return home from the clinic, I told Carol about my conversation with Mr. Bell. I was deeply concerned by his physical appearance and suggested that we accept his casual invitation to visit with him on St. Patrick's Day, one of his favorite holidays. I was afraid it might be our last chance to see him. His sister Ruth Rankin made a special trip from Perry, Iowa, to prepare the corned beef, rye bread, and cabbage for his special St. Patrick's celebration, to which he had invited some of his favored students and faculty colleagues. Even with his worsening health problems, it was wonderful to see him enjoying himself and to see the adulation and respect in the eyes of students and faculty alike.

While we were in Bloomington, we met with Dean Bain and I told him of my position at the New England Conservatory and my reluctance to leave one of my dearest friends, Gunther Schuller. Somewhere, I had dropped the thought that I wanted to raise my boys in the country. Being a good administrator, Dean Bain took this one positive consideration and stretched it into weekly telephone calls requesting my reconsideration. I could not tell him that Bloomington, Indiana, was about the last place in the world that Carol and I would consider living. It seemed dilapidated.

I represented the interests of NEC with a consortium of seven independent American conservatories. In early May, I was visiting the Ford Foundation along with my counterparts from the other conservatories, negotiating the final proportions of a $12.5 million grant to the seven independent conservatories: the New England Conservatory, Juilliard, the Manhattan School of Music, the Mannes College of Music, the Peabody Conservatory, the Cleveland Institute of Music, and the San Francisco Conservatory. I was just signing the legal documents when one of McGeorge Bundy's secretaries came in and quietly informed me that I had a very urgent telephone call, and that I could take the call in his office because he was not in that day. It was a heady experience, standing behind the massive desk of the president of the Ford Foundation.

On the telephone was Wilfred Bain, who gave me an ultimatum: he had to know my decision about coming to Indiana University and he had to know within a week, for they had to make an announcement to prospective students. I recalled my request for the establishment of a William J. Bell Scholarship to be administered by the IU Foundation and School of Music. He confirmed my recollection. I remembered my conversation with Carol the previous evening about raising our three sons in the country and gave an affirmative commitment to Dean Bain.

That's the only way I can justify having given Wilfred Bain a weak but positive answer to his ultimatum. The two most difficult things I had to do, then, were to tell Carol what my decision meant for our future life together and to tell Gunther Schuller that I was leaving his administration. That was indeed the hardest thing I had ever had to do. But the more I thought about it, the more I realized (for my family at least) that I had made the right decision.

I told my secretary, Barbara Chapin, that I would have more time with my family. She said, "You have to remember one thing, Mr. Phillips. You take yourself with you."

CHAPTER TWELVE

The Search for TubaRanch

BILL BELL, WHO WAS SCHEDULED for the two-week Cumberland Music Camp in 1971, took ill before the camp started. His sister came and took him to Perry, Iowa, where she lived. I stepped in. My responsibilities to the camp were finished on a Friday evening. I had made arrangements by telephone for Carol, the boys, and me to meet with a realtor to show us possibilities for a home in Bloomington, but the more we thought about it the more we wanted to make some excursions on our own without a realtor. I contacted the realtor in Bloomington to reschedule our appointment for a later time. I had decided we should get to know Bloomington before getting confused by realtor assistance.

We drove from the Cumberland Music Camp in Morehead, Kentucky, to Bloomington and, like tourists, got to know neighborhoods and located "for sale" signs. When we passed such a property we would try to talk to the neighbors or people living in the house about the price and availability of homes in the area. The only bad impression I got was when I approached a gentleman and asked if there was any farmland in the area for sale. He tersely answered me, "No, there's nothing for sale, and if there was, you couldn't afford it." On the very next road, Snoddy Road, a gentleman had just taken his Sunday newspaper out of the box and waited patiently for me to pass by. I stopped and said hello and inquired again about farmland. The gentleman I later discovered was named Ervin Deckard and he was very friendly but he couldn't think of any farms for sale. I thanked him for his conversation and started to pull away when he suddenly said, "Wait! Wait! There is one farm where I am renting pasture for cattle." He told us where it was located, around a corner, less than a mile away.

We drove by the farm. The yard was so overgrown with weeds and raspberry and blackberry brambles that the realtor sign was invisible. We got out and looked at the house, which was not much, and looked at the outbuildings, which were even less. We walked the eighty-acre property, which had two ponds, a dense forest, and pasture. We came back to walk the property at all hours of the day and night. We were just in love with it, and still are. We contacted the realtor, Jewel Tieman, and arranged to purchase the place. We bought the farm in August 1971, and decided to name it TubaRanch. When I told my colleagues at Indiana University what and where we bought, they exclaimed, "Way out there?!" When we lived in New Jersey, I commuted thirteen miles to Lincoln Center. When we lived in Massachusetts, I commuted to New York for gigs by plane, so it wasn't a big deal to drive five miles in fifteen minutes to work.

In addition to buying a farm as an investment, our initial plan was to buy a house in town so our children could attend Childs Elementary School, recommended by all of our friends in Bloomington. We had to postpone the luxury of a house in town because we already purchased a farm and our house in Massachusetts wasn't yet sold. When we moved into TubaRanch, our furniture hadn't arrived, so we slept on the floor in the front room because it was the only room with carpet. Hippies had rented the place for a few months before with two big German shepherds who lived in the house all day. We were eaten to bits by fleas that first night.

At the time, there were two homes for sale in Wayland. The first person who looked at our house in Massachusetts offered within $1,500 of the price we were asking. I told Carol I thought we should sell it. She said, "You don't sell a house to the first person who looks at it." That week, a couple of engineering companies in Boston and Concord let all their highest-paid executives go and suddenly there were a hundred houses for sale in the area. We kept paying the bank loan we took out to buy the house in Massachusetts and paying all utility bills for a year.

We went to Festival Casals in Puerto Rico in 1972. We were notified there that the realtor we had turned our house over to had sold it, so Carol and the boys went back to Massachusetts to sign all of the papers and take care of business. I went to Caracas, Venezuela, for a series of concerts and returned to Bloomington a few days before Carol and the boys got there. Carol said that it was the most enjoyable trip she never made, because it was a miserably hot summer and I had just installed central air conditioning in our farmhouse on Harrell Road in Bloomington. After we moved into our farmhouse, our neighbor and realtor Mrs. Tieman asked us if we wanted a pony. She said that she would sell us a Shetland pony named Rusty for one hundred dollars. Annie Flo Owens, an elderly widow who sold us the farm, gave us two ponies—Pepper and another, smaller, untamed pony. We of course accepted her kind offer, because this would give each of our three sons his own pony. Rusty and Pepper were very gentle, used to being with children.

We went roaming the countryside in our car to learn more of our new environment. Carol was driving and Tom was in the back seat standing on the transmission hump. We talked about how Pepper, being the biggest of the ponies, would belong to Jesse; Rusty was Little Harvey's horse, and we hadn't named Tom's pony yet. Carol asked Tom what he was going to call his pony. It had a red mane, a red tail, and a red coat. Without hesitation, three-year-old Tom firmly stated, "Blue. I'll call my horse Blue." The name stuck.

The conversation continued. "Blue has to be broken. How can we break Blue?" I said. "We'll have to find someone to break Blue."

Carol looked up in the rearview mirror to see Tom's cherubic face framed with long, blond hair and tears coming down his cheeks. Carol said, "Tom? What's the matter?"

Through tearful sobs, he cried, "I don't want a broken pony!"

When the movers were moving our belongings into our new home in Indiana, I saw an odd ripple on the pond and sent Jesse down to see what it was. It was a water moccasin. He ran for his BB gun. Even though the snake was in the middle of the pond, Jesse hit it directly between the eyes and knocked it unconscious. We never saw another water moccasin on TubaRanch.

One of the tuba students I inherited from Bill Bell at Indiana University was Don Harry. Bill Bell had told me about him and I went to see him where he lived on Walnut Pike. Don's Native American blood came from the Delaware tribe, and he asked our permission to set up a tepee in the back timber at TubaRanch and live in it while he continued his studies at IU. He and Lon Gormley scraped the bark off about ten or twelve long trees in preparation for the tepee. They took the limbs off and set the tent up at a site they had prepared.

Living outside, wild animals would sometimes get in the tepee scavenging for food. Don, typical of Native Americans, kept a forked stick at the entrance of the tepee to handle animal intruders. Don always sent his big dog in first when entering. One evening, Don and Lon were about to retire to the tepee when their dog jumped out of the tepee and howled. A snake had bitten it. Taking action, Don cut off the snake's head with an axe and buried it. In the meantime, Lon picked up the fifty-pound dog and ran for our house, over a quarter mile away, to borrow our car. After three days at the veterinarian's, the dog came to. I later had Don dig up the snake's head so we could correctly identify it. It was a big copperhead. I coiled the snake, with its head in the middle, then we wrapped it in a clear plastic bag and put it in the freezer.

We had an open invitation to any students to use our property if they wanted to take a walk in the country. We had a tree in the locust grove which had a poison ivy vine growing up the trunk. I would show the students the snake and the poison ivy and tell them to look out for both.

Don Harry is an extraordinary tubist. We enjoyed many hours playing duets, including his transcriptions of Beethoven duets. Since 1973 he has been the tubist of the Buffalo Philharmonic. He has also played in the Eastman Brass Quintet since 1990 and has taught at the Eastman School of Music since 1997.

WHERE'S THE BEEF?

Our first spring in Bloomington, I took the family to the Monroe County Fair. Of course, the 4-H children had their multi-coddled pets up for sale as part of the 4-H tradition. The three boys fell in love with a beautiful, well-curried, gentle steer who had won first prize in its division. I purchased the steer at the 4-H cattle auction. We were leaving the next day for Puerto Rico and the Festival Casals Orchestra. As we were driving home, Carol asked what we were going to do with the steer, since we didn't have any fences or a place to keep it. I told Carol (and the boys were all ears of course) that I had arranged to have the animal picked up, slaughtered, and cut into steaks, ribs, and ground beef. At this point there was silence, then an explosion of sobs and crying from the back seat—Carol was crying, too—and Jesse sobbed, "Gosh, Dad, all my life I've wanted a cow and now you buy one and you're going to kill it."

I said, "Gee whiz, Jesse! I'm only trying to provide for the family, and it's the best thing we can do for your cow, which is really a steer." Carol joined in the empathy and sympathy for our short-lived steer. The boys made like they understood, but I don't think that they slept too soundly. Later, they did enjoy the beef, so we never identified what they were eating.

We had many colorful experiences with our farm. Before the first year was out, we had ten horses, which Carol and the boys had to take care of, because I was busy with the university and clinic appearances. All of our animals (and we had several over the years) became pets, regardless of their type or reputation. There was a Chinese goose named Confucius who loved hearing the tuba as I played outside. He would lead the gaggle of some twenty geese to the source of tuba sounds; they would all squat down and stay, under a big black walnut tree in the yard. He then alone arose and walked directly over to me so I could pick him up and hold him on my lap while I played. One summer, I had put up a hammock and fell fast asleep late in the afternoon. I woke up to find Confucius sitting on my stomach and Carol staring at me.

There were all sorts of animals on the TubaRanch. We had a goat named Baba who ran on a tether that was screwed into the ground like a dog chain. We would move it around to let him graze in different spots on the farm. One time, Carol had to take Little Harvey to town for an appointment and left a note reminding Jesse to move the goat and his screw-tether near shelter if it rained. I did not know anything about Carol's note and was a bit surprised when I came home to find this written on a piece of paper:

"Dear Jesse, took Little Harvey to appt. If it rains, screw Baba up by the house. If you need help, call Dad." We all laughed.

Remembering a comedy recording I did with comedian Eddie Lawrence, Carol named our "raised in the house" pet Banty rooster, Eagle. Eagle loved the pile of shoes just inside the kitchen screen door and would flap his wings to make a show for anyone walking in or out. When he got too messy to be in the house, we provided a small doghouse for him to live in right outside the door. When a car would pull into the driveway, Eagle would hear the gravel under the tires and run alongside the car until it stopped and the driver would get out. He would then attack the driver's shoes. While visiting, Zoot Sims, the famous jazz saxophonist, remarked, "Gee Harvey! You don't have a watchdog; you've got a watch chicken." Jazz trumpeter Dominic Spera came to TubaRanch wearing shiny alligator boots and Eagle fell in love. He couldn't leave those boots alone. To escape the rooster, Dominic ran into the kitchen and announced to Carol, "You've got a crazy chicken out there, chasing me all over the place." Just then, Eagle jumped up to sit on the broken empty window of the aluminum screen door, looking for Dom and crowing. Dom yelled, "There he is, that's the one!"

JOINING THE IU FACULTY, 1971

It was an exciting year to arrive in Bloomington. The same year I moved to town, coach Bobby Knight, Indiana University president John Ryan, trombonist Keith Brown, and famed opera soprano Eileen Farrell arrived. Shortly after coming to the Indiana University campus, I met Chancellor Herman B Wells at the first of many social functions associated with every new academic year. He greeted Carol and me with genuine warmth and concern. He wanted to know about our children and hoped we would enjoy the city of Bloomington and being a part of the IU family. Such a cordial personal interest made a deep impression. I was delighted to learn that he had been a euphonium player in his youth. And his mouthpiece was proudly displayed in a glass case in the hallway approaching his office. (I treasure the photo he sent to me of him with his instrument at age nine.)

The first summer I was at IU, students would come to the studio door with a blue card which had to be signed by a teacher, so I signed them.

I found I had more trombone students than either of the two trombone teachers teaching that summer. One of the three trombone faculty had counselled his students to sign up with me for lessons or forfeit continued study with him. After that experience, I told Dean Bain I wouldn't take any more trombone students.

I would usually start teaching at 8:30 in the morning. Every time a student crossed the threshold of my studio, I'd ask how he was doing in his studies and if he had been in contact with his parents. If a student came in who was obviously troubled, we'd talk about it. Sometimes, something would go wrong in a rehearsal and he'd take it out on himself. I talked about things I never dreamed I'd talk about. I was as concerned about my students as people as I was about them as musicians.

The next thing I would usually ask for was scales and arpeggios, something students live with throughout their studies and after. I would sometimes criticize articulations and call to reference the percussion instruments and the varying degrees of articulation in playing with an imaginary tuba mallet of wood, leather, hard rubber, soft rubber, and felt. We would talk about band rehearsals, orchestra rehearsals, and what was going on in the students' lives. I didn't search for, or overlook, things to criticize, though some students don't believe they are learning if they are not being constantly criticized. During the lesson, I tried to stick to my guns and make sure I got through the lesson that was assigned; they would have that edge for their performance.

My first teaching assistant at Indiana University was tubist Rudolph Emilson. Rudy and I would discuss students' performance assignments (band, orchestra, or other) and made certain those assignments were of major consideration to every student. Rudy was the first student I met whose upper and lower teeth were false. I alternated between building his self-confidence and pointing out some of the problems he faced physically and psychologically. His determination was inspiring and he was a good teacher himself, at the State University of New York, Fredonia, turning out such students as Bill Troiano and Matt Stratton.

For twenty years, 1973–1993, I was a featured guest artist/clinician at the Tennessee Technological University Tuba Symposium held in Cookeville, Tennessee. In 1973 Earle Louder was the featured euphonium artist/

clinician. Earle, Winston Morris, and I had a ball performing and recording some exciting new compositions for tuba trio as well as some superb transcriptions of works by master composers (Wagner, et al.). Our audience consisted of eager young tuba and euphonium players, beginners in sixth and seventh grade through high school and into college and beyond. They were all serious students wanting to improve their performance in all areas: tone quality, range, technique, control, and musicianship. Master classes covering these concerns and others were ongoing subjects for discussion and comparison at all levels. Time was scheduled for solo performances, various ensembles, and, most especially, the symposium's closing mass ensemble involving all euphonium and tuba players in attendance. The audience consisted of parents, teachers, girlfriends, other students, and local supporters.

I have always been impressed with the attention given by Winston Morris to every individual. Winston is always especially concerned with the youngest and least experienced so that nothing is misunderstood. I have observed that his entire student enrollment is committed to the same clarity when serving as extensions of his teaching and direction. In 1978 I was impressed with a very young student who took the seriousness of the annual symposium to heart. He was eager to meet every request asked of him by the faculty and clinician staff. At the 1979 symposium, in casual conversation, I mentioned that in the spring I planned to add significantly to our little TubaRanch farmhouse in Bloomington and that it required the demolition of a two-car garage and an attempt to salvage some of the beautiful native wood that showed through the open studs. You can imagine my surprise when Timothy Northcut appeared with his father, a Baptist minister, with carpenter belts and wrecking tools, ready to help me remove the garage. Their timing was perfect.

Tim Northcut, a superb tuba performer, was scheduled to be a teaching assistant at Indiana University but took advantage of an opening for principal tuba in the United States Army Field Band, my alma mater. He received his undergraduate degree in music education from Tennessee Tech and a master's degree in performance from Arizona State University, where he studied with Daniel Perantoni. He is now professor of tuba at the Cincinnati College Conservatory of Music and principal tuba in the

Dayton Symphony Orchestra. I also have observed his creative efficiency when hosting conferences of the International Tuba Euphonium Association (ITEA), Summit Brass, and the Rafael Mendez Brass Institute.

One time, Winston came up to Bloomington with the Tennessee Tech Tuba Ensemble and I offered to put them up in a motel. Winston said, "No, they'll sleep in the barn loft." Twenty or more tuba players slept on the hay in the barn. Sleeping in a loft was not something they were used to, so they hung out in the barn awhile before passing out. About 4:30 AM, I heard some noise. Eagle, our pet rooster, would crow and I'd hear someone yell, "Shut up, chicken!"

There was another crow.

"Shut up!"

He would crow again.

I don't think anyone got any sleep after 4:30, and some didn't get any before 4:30 either.

A FARMER'S LIFE

At that time we had ten horses and ten beef cattle. Responsibility for our increasing number of farm animals was divided between Carol and the boys, mostly Carol at that time. Jesse had, with his mother, responsibility for the cattle and horses, including saddles, bridles, etc. I was responsible for the building and upkeep of fences sturdy enough that we hoped the cattle and horses would give up and stop looking for escape opportunities. Any farmer or rancher knows that mending and building new fences is an ongoing, daily concern. Harvey Jr. and his mother were responsible for any ducks or geese while Tom was being trained to take responsibility for the chickens, including the feeding and gathering of eggs. Once school started all responsibility was on Carol's shoulders. I would come home from teaching and distribute fence posts, rails, newly made gates, and wire if called for. In the following days I would erect as much fence as possible. It was a slow process and sometimes painful.

One day Carol was working in the barn lot when the barn telephone rang. To get to the telephone she had to pass one heavy creosoted oak gate that was hanging in balance on a hinge. In her haste she somehow managed to dislodge the gate, which came crashing down on her Achilles tendon; it was very painful. She managed to reach the phone and shouted, "Hello!" On the other end of the line the voice said, "This is Doc Severinsen, calling for Harvey." Carol shouted her response: "Doc, this is Carol. A heavy gate just fell on the back of my leg. I'll have Harvey call you back." In her pain, she then managed a hasty conversation with Doc, and over the years he has never stopped inquiring, "How's Carol's leg?"

There was a time when we had quite a lot of fowl, including twenty geese, sixteen ducks, and I don't know how many Banty chickens. On the way home from visiting my mother in August of 1972, we had found, in Lebanon, Missouri, a well-known purveyor of exotic breeds of chickens. I bought some Chinese white silkies, some partridge Cochins, and a couple of other fancy breeds including turkins. When people would come to visit, they would always remark on how beautiful some of our chickens were. "My goodness!" they would say. "I never saw such gorgeous birds!" After the chickens crossbred a few times, though, the comment was more often, "What the hell is that?!"

In our old barn, we had a cow that was going to give birth. Carol called some of the mothers of our boys' friends who wanted their children to see this. We had an old oak tree that had been cut and de-limbed and the tree was lying in the barnyard. The kids and other neighbors were sitting on the tree and on lawn chairs, waiting for the calf to be born. Everyone was excited. The kids were getting a big kick out of seeing this whole thing. There was a limestone step in front of the barn and that was where the cow lay. At that angle, the calf about to be born was going to scrape its head on the corner of the stone, so Jesse guided it as it came out. After the calf was born, I noticed that the cow was still just lying there. I told Carol something was wrong—the cow should be up and licking the calf by now. Then we saw two more hooves sticking out of the cow, and got ready for twins.

When Peter Hirsbrunner, an instrument maker from Switzerland, was visiting with us, he woke up to hear shuffling noises, talking, and people getting dressed to go out at 3:00 in the morning. He opened his guest bedroom door and inquired if there was a problem.

I said, "Peter, all of our cows are out across the road and we've got to get them back in the field."

"Wait," he replied. "That's a problem we're used to in Switzerland. I'll get dressed and help you."

"You see, Peter? We'll do anything to make you feel at home."

It took nearly an hour to get all twelve cows back in. We had breakfast very early that morning.

Each of the cattle had her own personality. Shahee, from her first day of life, was an escape artist. She walked the fence line every day, looking for a way out, and she succeeded a few times. We had just put up a new rail fence on the north side of the house. We kept a halter on her and Carol tied her up on the lawn side of the fence near the house. I was getting dressed in my tuxedo, almost ready for dinner and a performance in town. Carol was standing at the kitchen sink watching Shahee graze when the cow put her head down and slipped through the fence. Carol called me to help get Shahee back. When I finally caught the cow, I got mad and wound up punching her between the eyes. Her knees buckled. I said, "One day I'll lock you in the freezer and you won't get out."

Later, when I was putting my tuba in the car, I noticed that my hand hurt. I talked to Carol and she said that she'd meet me at the emergency room. The emergency room nurse asked me, "Mr. Phillips, what happened to your hand?"

Dressed in my tuxedo, I replied, "I punched a cow." After an awkward silence, everyone in the emergency room broke out laughing. Then they bandaged my hand and put my arm in a sling, and I went and played the performance.

We had a butcher in Bloomington at that time who would come and pick up the cattle. The guy came with his truck and said, "Mr. Phillips, do you have a chute to load that cow?"

"No."

"How are we going to load the cow into the truck?"

I picked up a bale of hay and put it behind the truck as a step. "Shahee, get up on that truck." She did. The man took his cap off and said, "Damn, I wish I could get all my animals to do that."

We bought two Palomino horses: Effie (named after Alec Wilder's *Effie* suite) and Ginger. We had both of them bred with Boots, an Arabian horse.

Jesse's birthday was coming up on Valentine's Day, and we told him that the foal would be his birthday present. He and I went out and slept in the barn, so Jesse wouldn't miss the birth of his new horse. She was born exactly on Valentine's Day, and so we named her Valentine. The other horse was going to have her foal a week or two later and it would be assigned to Little Harvey. He and I went out, joined later by Jesse and Tom, and slept in the barn again, awaiting Harvey's present. It was a stormy night, with a lot of thunder and lightning, so Little Harvey named his horse Flash.

NEC SURPRISE

I received a telephone call one morning in 1971 from Sherwin Badger, chairman of the board of the New England Conservatory, and he gave me the following information: "Harvey, we've come across some unfinished business having to do with your term at NEC. Knowing how you feel about your family, I've just put five airplane tickets in the mail for September 24. Reservations have been made at the Colony Hotel, so that we can rectify all items."

On September 24 we were picked up at Logan Airport and driven by limousine to our hotel, where we checked in and made arrangements to be on time for our meeting with Chairman Badger and the executive committee at NEC. I was concerned about what unfinished business there might be but, as instructed, I showed up at the conservatory with Carol and our three boys.

As we approached the main building, we were struck by a sign stretched over the front entrance: "Celebrating HARVEY PHILLIPS DAY." We were met at the door and taken to afternoon cocktails, a dinner, and a concert. There were many gifts and remembrances from all segments of our conservatory family, including students, faculty, administrators, and trustees, as well as security guards, maids, carpenters, and elevator operators. The Gemeinhardt Flute Company sent me two cases of tequila. The entire ceremony was most impressive.

Alec Wilder wrote a multi-movement suite, *Inner-Office Memos*, for my two secretaries at the conservatory: one was studying guitar, and the other, my executive secretary Barbara Chapin, studied flute. Alec rehearsed appropriate faculty members in the performance of *Inner-Office*

Memos, closing with a final movement entitled "Resignation Rag." One of my former tuba students, David Gannett, accompanied faculty members in the performance.

It was a fantastic experience for me and my family. During the tribute, I had been sitting at a table and was kept in conversation. I felt something going on behind me, and was asked to stand. When I did, I noticed that Gunther was in his presidential raiment. All the trustees had their robes on as well. In a very formal ceremony, an honorary Doctorate of Music was bestowed on me. I will never forget the kindness and recognition shown to me and my family on that occasion.

Sherwin Badger, chairman of the board of trustees, announced that it was the first time the New England Conservatory had bestowed an honorary doctorate on someone who had resigned from the conservatory.

PIANIST DISCOVERED

A most enjoyable aspect of teaching talented graduate students one-on-one was counseling on graduate recital repertoire. It was the student's responsibility to find a piano accompanist available for rehearsals and required performance. At Indiana University, student piano accompanists were not assigned to a particular studio. One day, a graduate student walked into my studio with an accompanist he had chosen for his graduate recital. One piece he had to rehearse contained perhaps the most difficult of piano parts—Paul Hindemith's *Sonata for Tuba and Piano.* My tuba student introduced me to his accompanist, Steven Harlos. He turned out to be the only pianist I ever worked with who played the Hindemith without music in front of him.

I was knocked out by Steve. His playing was fantastic and unexpected. I felt like I had found a winning lottery ticket. The one-hour lesson rehearsal flew by and I asked Steve to stay and talk with me. I suggested that if he would give my studio first refusal for his accompaniment time I would respond by recommending him as "house accompanist" for important festivals and workshops, starting at the end of that semester with the May 22–26 First International Tuba Symposium Workshop. That would be followed by a series of festivals and workshops in Denmark, Sweden, and Finland, plus solo recitals in Carnegie Hall and numerous other clinics and solo appearances yet to be scheduled. Steve's positive response saved me many agonizing hours of searching for a piano accompanist.

Steve was studying piano accompaniment at IU. At the Brass Congress in 1976, in Montreux, Switzerland, in the morning he would bring in the music he had played the night before, pick up the music he would play that day, look it over, rehearse with the soloist that afternoon, and play the recital that evening. He played the first performance of the Matteson-Phillips TubaJazz Consort in Switzerland in 1976. He eventually took a job at North Texas State University and most weekends had steady work as a jazz pianist.

MOONDOG IN BLOOMINGTON

As my career progressed, Moondog, my blind friend from New York, came in and out of my life, always clad in his signature Viking outfit. I couldn't predict when he would appear. Shortly after assuming my position as professor of tuba at Indiana University, I received a phone call from Moon on a Thursday telling me that he would be in town the next day. He was touring the Midwest with a promoter from Columbia Records and asked if I could host a concert for him the next week in Bloomington. I wasn't sure. But since it was early in the school year, I managed to book the Recital Hall in the School of Music for the next Tuesday. I told him that I doubted he could expect to get sufficient advertising for the recital with so little advance notice. He simply said, "We'll get an audience."

When Moondog arrived on Friday, there was no time for advertising. However, I did manage to arrange a short interview with Moondog on a local radio station. Following the interview he asked to be taken into the center of town. There, on the busiest street corner in Bloomington, Moondog positioned himself. Dressed in his robe, laced-up sandals and topped off by his Viking helmet, he took a statuesque pose holding his six-foot spear erect. Telephones at the Bloomington police station started ringing off the hook. Concerned citizens wondered what was going on. The newspaper sent a reporter to investigate why they were getting so many calls. Then a hastily written article appeared in Tuesday's paper about Moondog being a Columbia Records recording artist who would be performing a concert on Tuesday at 8 PM in the IU School of Music Recital Hall. On Tuesday evening, the place was absolutely packed.

On the concert Moondog recited some of his poetry and performed some of his chants. He and I premiered some short pieces that he had written in New York especially for us to play together. One was called *One-Four, Two-Four, Three-Four, Four-Four, and What-For*. It was a great evening. Moondog was a remarkable guy and an unexpectedly fine entertainer. He always had a good sense of humor and never took himself too seriously. My family fondly remembers Moondog's Viking helmet crowning one of our October harvested pumpkins as we relaxed on our backyard patio. Moondog enjoyed life and loved sharing it with friends.

A CALL FROM RUTH RANKIN

Bill Bell had been looking forward to better health following his retirement from IU in June, 1971. He planned to tour the country, visit friends, and give master classes. His health, however, had been deteriorating. In 1964, he had gone out to do a clinic and his wife Aggie got pneumonia and passed away while he was on the road. He never forgave himself for not being with her. He started having serious physical problems around that time. On August 7, 1971, I received the phone call from his sister Ruth Rankin informing me of his passing. I was one of the people he wanted to be notified. I felt like I did when I lost my father and my mother. When you have a close one-on-one relationship, the person is more like family than like a colleague.

That same week, I was doing a solo engagement with Bill Revelli. At a break from our rehearsal of the Ralph Vaughan Williams *Concerto for Bass Tuba and Orchestra*, I mentioned to Dr. Revelli that William Bell had passed away on August 7. He turned to me with tears streaming down his face and said, "Oh Harvey, can you imagine his mother on Christmas Day getting Bill Bell for Christmas?" Bill Revelli had a reputation for being a demanding and impatient conductor of college-age students, but my experience with him over the years convinced me of his genuine feelings for people and music. He was such a generous person. He was always the one to whom the checks went at restaurants, and his students were very loyal to him.

I only had two days between Bill Bell's death and the Revelli concert to schedule a memorial concert and wake for Bill Bell for Sunday, October 3, 1971. Over the telephone in those two days, I commissioned six composers who had meant something special to Bill Bell to write pieces which would be performed in his honor. While they were swamped with work, each composer dropped everything to complete the commissions, a testimonial to the way they felt about Mr. Bell. The service took place in Indiana University's Recital Hall. A wake followed at Pic-A-Chic picnic grounds, a favorite location for Bill Bell's outdoor parties.

The program started off with an original piece entitled "Fanfare for a Great Guy" by Robert Russell Bennett and continued with "Bill Bell March" by Paul Lavalle and "Elegy for William Bell" by Alec Wilder for solo tuba, three trumpets, three horns, and three trombones. Morton Gould wrote a six-movement *Tuba Suite* for tuba and three horns. Warren Benson produced "Piece for Tuba and Hand Drum" and Gunther Schuller's contribution was *Five Moods of Bill Bell,* for tuba quartet. Gunther wasn't able to finish the piece in time for the Bell memorial concert; it was premiered at the First International Tuba Symposium Workshop—also dedicated to William Bell—in May 1973. Piccolo player Meredith Willson sent the duet he and Bill Bell used to warm up before a concert in about 1921.

McSORLEY'S OLD ALE HOUSE

Robert Ryker, when he was the newly appointed tubist with the Montreal Symphony Orchestra, envisioned a formal organization of tubists. He issued a press release acknowledging the influence of Bill Bell's periodic gatherings of students and colleagues at McSorley's Old Ale House in New York City. Observing camaraderie that other instruments would kill for, he proposed an organization to be known as the Tubists Universal Brotherhood Association (TUBA). *The Instrumentalist* and *School Music News* both published his press release. Ryker came up with the name and concept and served as acting president. In ad hoc organizational meetings held at Chicago Midwest music clinics, Winston Morris agreed to prepare and present a constitution and bylaws.

Robert Ryker visited me in my office at the New England Conservatory in April 1968. He informed me that I was one of three honorary life members, chosen along with William Bell and Arnold Jacobs, for membership in the Tubists Universal Brotherhood Association, and he presented me with my membership certificate. In 1978 TUBA awarded me an Honor Award and in 1984 a Merit Award.

I had served on committees in the musicians union and at the ballet orchestra, so I had seen the benefits of organization and I recognized the importance, for tubists, of organizing. Knowing Ryker, I figured he would do it well. And I appreciated his clever title for the organization.

For many years, at Bill Bell's invitation, tuba players would converge on McSorley's Old Ale House. It was an Irish pub at 15 East 7th Street, a few doors from Cooper Union, where Abraham Lincoln gave his only New York City speech. The Carl Fisher music publishing company is located nearby. Musicians frequented the area. They were quick to recognize McSorley's Old Ale House as a place for men to meet and relax (no women allowed). Every spring or fall, William Bell would make arrangements with McSorley's ahead of time for ample supplies of cheese and onion platters, and corned beef and cabbage. That was the fare of the day. Professional tubists, a few students, and some trombonists gathered at the two huge round tables in the back room. We took over. There was one waiter who could carry fourteen mugs of McSorley's Old Ale at a time.

It was a strictly honorary situation. Veterans of the occasion would follow the lead of Bill Bell by putting twenty dollars in the center of the table so everyone could order whatever they wanted. The waiter would take what he needed for food or libation out of the pile of cash. After the event was over, we would tip him generously. If there was any money left, we would assign it to one of our group to safeguard until the next meeting. Bill Bell was riding the crest of his popularity in New York and was truly the number one tuba player and teacher in the world. It was wonderful having this association with him.

FIRST INTERNATIONAL TUBA SYMPOSIUM WORKSHOP

I found myself in Indiana with wonderful memories of my mentor and I wanted to initiate a project that would pay honor to him. I envisioned an event in the same spirit and camaraderie of our old days at McSorley's, except with hundreds of tuba players from all over the world.

In Boston, my schedule, which included performing in New York, meant I was unable to pursue my interests in organizing and implementing conferences and organizations for the betterment of the brass world of music.

After Winston Morris, Les Varner, Dan Perantoni, David Kuehn, Robert Ryker, Barton Cummings, and Robert Whaley invited me to a meeting of their committee creating TUBA at the Chicago Midwest Band and Orchestra Clinic, I shared my dream of a symposium workshop of tubas and euphoniums, with special invitations to composers, conductors, and others who had championed these noble instruments.

A second meeting, at the Chicago Midwest clinic the subsequent year, included about fifty tubists, two of whom were Arnold Jacobs, tubist in the Chicago Symphony, and Jim Self, professor of tuba at the University of Tennessee. On my return to Bloomington, I scheduled a meeting with Wilfred Bain, dean of the School of Music, who gave his enthusiastic support and endorsement to host the First International Tuba Symposium Workshop, where TUBA would be formalized, as the first event in Indiana University's new Musical Arts Center, in May 1973.

The committee was invited to meet at Indiana University to plan the event. We gathered in a very large faculty lounge that the School of Music enjoyed at that time. After much heated discussion about who should be invited and how the event should be organized, I finally excused myself, went to the other end of the room, and on a yellow legal pad suggested a structure for the entire conference.

There was so much to do. Sleeping little, I made one phone call after another. In just a couple of hours, I had invited seventy-two of my composer-arranger friends. Only five could not attend because of other commitments. I made arrangements to pay the expenses of each composer but could not pay any extra honorarium. They all came knowing that.

It was my duty to approve all printed materials before they were distributed, including flyers, posters, brochures, and stationery. The entire conference was dedicated to William Bell, so we put his photograph, of him holding his raincatcher sousaphone, on the cover of the program. I sent special invitations to all tuba and euphonium players, composers, and accompanists who would be participants in performances or panel discussions. The last two weeks were extremely busy. I kept myself awake with black coffee and aspirin and was on a diet of rabbit food.

Classical tuba artists, jazz tubists, composers, and friends came in droves. Philip Catelinet, who had premiered the famous Vaughan Williams *Concerto for Bass Tuba* in 1954, was present. The New York Brass Quintet, Arnold Jacobs, Gunther Schuller, Sam Pilafian, Fred Fennell, Bill Revelli, Karel Husa, Vaclav Nelhybel, Richard Peaslee, Barney Childs, Merle Evans, Arthur Frackenpohl, William Kraft, Bernhard Heiden, Abe Torchinsky, Samuel Adler, Gil Evans, Peter Schickele, Gene Pokorny, and Don Butterfield each agreed to be a part of the celebration. The publisher of *Downbeat* magazine was a special guest, along with Colonel Arnald D. Gabriel, commanding officer and conductor of the U.S. Air Force Band. Dean Bain negotiated the use of a dormitory for attendees who wanted to stay on campus.

I opened the conference at 8:00 on a Wednesday morning with a performance of the Paul Hindemith *Sonata for Tuba and Piano,* accompanied by Dean Charles Webb. The symposium was off to a wonderful start. For me, it was like a festival of friends. Composers, orchestrators, and dignitaries who were friends of mine were unaware of the level of tuba performance available to their compositional pens.

The clinic sessions went very well. Some important topics included predecessors of the tuba, invention of the tuba, tuba design, composers, compositions, repertoire, tuba pedagogy, orchestra tuba, and band tuba repertoire.

There was a composers forum that included sessions like Voids in the Tuba Literature, New Directions and Techniques, The Tuba and the Electronic Studio, and Standard Solo Tuba Repertoire. Some of the composers were very active on panel discussions and were really impressed by the performances and activities. Ed Sauter, Bill Finegan, and Manny Albam were there. I scheduled panels on better tuba design, better chamber music, and orchestra programming. Of course, Alec Wilder, Walter Hartley and Tom Beversdorf were wonderful to have with us. There were so many fantastic people from my life. Alvin Etler approached serving on committees with enthusiasm, talking to players and reviewing publications. He was just a dynamo.

In New York, composers sometimes said to me, "If I write something for you, you'll be the only one who can play it." Now, my mission of getting composers to know the many wonderful tuba players around the world was accomplished!

That first evening I was sitting in the Musical Arts Center with Carol and Alec Wilder, listening to one of the many wonderful soloists. I felt my stomach churning and I started to sweat. Sitting on the outside of the row, I discreetly left the hall. I remember meeting Ellis Wean, the tubist with the Vancouver Symphony, who had just arrived for the concert, and we had a short conversation. I then saw one of the accompanists and asked the young lady if she would help me reach the couch to sit down. I fainted. She went into the auditorium to fetch Carol and Alec. They took me home, where I vomited blood and then went to bed. The next day, at the hospital, Dr. Jean Creek told me that too many aspirin had eaten my stomach lining away, and that I would miss the rest of the conference. During the rest of the event I had worked so hard for, I found myself in the hospital unable to enjoy the fruits of my labors.

It went along beautifully, though. I was impressed by reports from my grad students G. R. Davis and Joe Ray and was assured everything was going smoothly. They took over much of my job. Jumping into the breach with his logical mind and expertise was Winston Morris. Dan Perantoni handled administrative matters and Carol stepped in like a true champion to take my place with the business side of things. When I went to the hospital, I requested that someone bring me the two briefcases I needed to run the workshop. Bob Wachtel, a C. G. Conn Company representative, showed up with one. "Harvey," he said, "You're in the hospital. You only get one briefcase."

Many prominent jazz artists attended the symposium. Some of those present included a legendary Dixieland tubist, Singleton Palmer, from St. Louis; Red Callender, a well-known television session player on bass and tuba from Hollywood; and Howard Johnson, a jazz tubist from New York. Perhaps the biggest thrill of all was the presence of Rich Matteson, the greatest jazz euphonium player ever. An incredible gala jazz concert was held on Saturday night of that week.

In the end, the whole conference was kind of a party bringing together many of the tuba players, euphonium players, and composers I had interacted with over the years. Many of them found time to slip away and visit me for a few minutes at the hospital. I felt I was serving as a catalyst to bring the chemicals of the association together for everyone's betterment. I wanted to encourage the composers to write better tuba parts in their ensemble works and to write solo tuba works as well.

The symposium attracted some three hundred tubists from all over the world but, more importantly, sixty-seven composers turned up to see what the tuba could do. Afterward, not a single one of the composers accepted the check that I had sent to them for their expenses. I received many phone calls and notes from those gentlemen telling me that they couldn't accept money in good conscience for all they had learned about the tuba and euphonium. Every one of those composers wrote at least one work featuring tuba without a commission and even without being directly requested. Some have written as many as ten and fifteen works for tuba because they were so turned on. Since most of our composers today are residents in colleges, universities, and conservatories, they really don't have to worry too much about their next meal. This gives them the freedom to write the kind of music they want to write, which is the way it should be. I would venture to say that as a result of that first symposium, just that one alone, we expanded our literature by five or six hundred works.

TUBA now has over 1,500 members throughout the world and most all of them are very serious performers. People ask me, "What's going to happen to all those tuba players?" I say, "What's going to happen to all the lawyers? What's going to happen to all the doctors?" There are three kinds of people in the world—those who make things happen, those who watch things happen, and those who go through life wondering what happened. If those tuba players are the kind of people who make things happen, they're going to be fine because they'll generate activities for themselves. Those who aren't will hopefully never give up the instrument, but they'll have to find another means of income.

I always hoped that composers would send copies of new compositions using tuba to publishers and to TUBA accompanied with program notes they would write and attach to the music manuscript. I hoped for a central place where the program notes, for printing copies, could be stored. Then, when the piece was played or recorded, the composer's own notes could appear in the program, instead of the inadequate program notes which so often appear.

The International Trombone Association was contacted and its officers were asked if they had any intention of including the euphonium. ITA had no such plans, so euphonium was included in TUBA. Richard Strauss wrote many compositions calling for bass tuba and tenor tuba, so the euphonium is in the right place. The name TUBA was later changed to the International Tuba Euphonium Association, or ITEA.

ANOTHER ASIDE

Michael Salzman was an undergraduate student at IU from New York who was always willing to bring possessions we had left behind. He drove a van and would call before departing Bloomington for New York, where he visited his parents on Long Island. He always asked, "Mrs. Phillips, I'm going to Noo Yauk. Is there anything you want me to bring back?" The first item we asked him to bring was a huge iron cauldron I had purchased at an auction of items used in the early days of our country. I intended to make Brunswick stew in it. We had stored the cauldron with Elsie and John Richardson (Carol's sister and her husband) on their lawn in Armonk, New York. Carol referred to the item as "a black pot." Michael had visions of a cooking vessel and was somewhat surprised when the black pot took up half the space in his van. He brought it nonetheless.

The next item he was asked to bring was a painting of me with my tuba, painted by Ira Schwartz, a commercial artist who did much work for famous women's makeup companies, including Estee Lauder, Lanvan, Fabergé, and a few others. He was a genuine character. He came to all my concerts in Carnegie Hall and was a real supporter of my activities. He was easy to spot, with a long, well-kept beard, and in winter wearing an ankle-length chinchilla coat. He had produced three paintings of me with the tuba, one in white tie and tails, one in tuxedo, and another in Western suede. Carol's sister and brother and their families knew nothing about the paintings, and one afternoon while driving in bumper-to-bumper traffic on

Manhattan's Madison Avenue, which has many art galleries, they passed a window that displayed the largest of the three paintings. Almost in one voice, they said, "Hey, there's Harvey." Of course they parked, returned to the gallery, and got information about the paintings. Ira Schwartz painted from a 35 mm slide projected on a screen. I didn't have to be there while he painted.

One day Ira called. He told us the tuxedo and full dress pictures had sold right away. But the larger painting, on a five-foot round canvas, at a price of three thousand dollars, was slow to sell. The size was unusual; not many people living in Manhattan could spare a wall for it. He offered to send the painting to us and said he would be glad to cut it down and make it square so that it would be easier to ship. We preferred it not be cut down.

The very next day, Michael was right on cue, calling from New York about his return from spring break and offering to transport anything we wanted him to bring to us. Carol said, "Well, there is a painting of Harvey and it's in the Osborne apartment building, which is located at 7th Avenue and 57th Street, across from Carnegie Hall. We will notify the artist that you will pick it up." Michael was, no doubt, taken aback by the size but said nothing until he delivered it in Bloomington. When Carol opened the door to meet him as he came up the walk to the house, his one comment was, "Buoy, you guys never do anything smawll, do you?"

At most recent contact, he still offers to bring items we request. He teaches tuba at Hofstra University and is a coordinator for TubaChristmas in Rockefeller Center every year.

21ST CENTURY BEBOP BAND

I received tenure two years after I started teaching at Indiana University. At IU, I had fewer performing outlets than in New York and Boston and especially missed playing with the brass quintet. I had met David Baker in 1959 on a recording session of John Lewis's music, with Gunther Schuller conducting—the classic LP *The Golden Striker*. He was sitting next to me playing bass trombone, with George Russell and some other people from Russell's group. David and I became good friends. When I arrived at Indiana University, David Baker was chair of the Jazz Department. He was concerned about my not having a core group to play with at IU and created the 21st Century Bebop Band, featuring flute, trumpet or sax, cello, and tuba, with bass, drums, and piano. When Dizzy Gillespie gave a concert at the IU Auditorium, the 21st Century Bebop Band warmed up the audience. Dizzy didn't play with us. But, when the concert was over, Dizzy told David Baker about *Hot House* (which had a very convoluted arrangement), "I'm glad I didn't have to play on that!"

The 21st Century Bebop Band performed the same service later for Maynard Ferguson. David is a very creative composer and one of the fastest writers of music I know. We played standards from jazz and bebop repertoire like "Preacher Man" and David wrote a lot of original tunes as well, such as "PaDoSpe" for Patty and Dominic Spera and "CaHaPhi" for Carol and me.

Another of my prime interests was to have time for activities with the IU Band Department. I appeared numerous times with the IU Symphonic Band, and appeared as a solo clinician with Frederick Ebbs, director of the IU Band Department, at music conferences. When Fred Ebbs left the position, he was replaced by Ray Cramer, who had been one of his assistants.

THE FIRST OCTUBAFEST—STARTING A TRADITION

I realized that all the components of the IU Music School scheduled their students for recitals, most of them in the spring. Early in the fall, the Recital Hall was already being booked for spring dates. I decided I would like to have my students present concerts early in the first semester. I wanted to do five evening concerts, in one week.

The upper class students would perform works they had prepared, to illustrate materials entering students would be assigned later. Newly enrolled students would perform works they had prepared for entrance auditions, illustrating their potential. The idea was for everybody to get acquainted as quickly as possible so they could start helping each other.

It wouldn't bring special attention to these tuba recitals to have them scattered in between recitals for violin, voice, piano, etc., in the spring. I saw in these concerts opportunities to acquaint an audience of community members with the repertoire and performance levels of tuba and euphonium students at IU.

The only time I could get a solid week for tuba in the Recital Hall was the first week in October. So why not call that week a festival? In preparing copy for a publicity poster, I made several attempts about what to call it until finally I wrote "OctoberTubaFestival." Then it struck me. Why not "OctubaFest"? My tuba studio was like the great German Oktoberfest each fall. The Germans celebrated the harvest of crops, and we celebrated the harvest of a new "crop" of freshman tuba and euphonium players at our school. The first OctubaFest took place at Indiana University in 1973 during the first week of October (known to me as Octuba). Some years it has been Septuba.

All five concerts were booked in the Recital Hall, Monday through Friday at 7 PM. I insisted that all of my students appear onstage at some point during those five days. The Friday program featured our tuba ensemble. On Saturday there was a reception at TubaRanch. Freshmen (and everybody else, from IU and the community) were welcomed by my family and the William J. Bell Chapter of TUBA. I had thought about William Bell's incredible musicianship and how much he loved his parties at McSorley's. I wanted to combine the two. Our reception quickly became an OctubaFeast. The reception and the concerts were free. OctubaFest and OctubaFeast had arrived!

We were proud to put Bill Bell's stamp on our OctubaFest. I decided to make these five recitals an annual occurrence, another annual event dedicated to honoring his memory and celebrating his life. Actually, all the things I did were inspired by my respect for and association with William Bell.

At the end of the week, for the OctubaFeast, we ordered a thirty-foot cheese board to be placed on the patio at the TubaRanch. The centerpiece was a round of Danish bleu cheese and after that was a Norwegian Jarlsberg, Swiss Emmenthaler, French Brie, Vermont cheddar, Wisconsin Colby, and a few other special cheeses. As had been the center at McSorley's Old Ale House, we encouraged a platter of cheese with an equal supply of onion. Libations were made available to satisfy the age of each student. *People* magazine came out to write an article on OctubaFest, and published a picture of me near the barn. That week, everything went spectacularly.

Over the years, the OctubaFeast expanded to include the Marienfeld dancers from Germany, Indiana cloggers from Solsberry, a German band—from Germany—and lots of costumes. Sometimes, we gave out door prizes, like fifty dollars' worth of sheet music, tickets to a sold-out Horowitz concert, a complete Western outfit, or a restaurant dinner for two with a chauffeured Cadillac. I was the chauffeur of my own Cadillac.

Because the September and October weather can be rainy, one year we put up a tent at TubaRanch and we put the cheese board inside. One of the cheeses featured was an especially potent German Bierkase. It was raining the day of our feast and we put the sides down on the tent. Just before people arrived, Carol and a couple of the boys went out to roll up the canvas sidewall, which exposed the cheese. The first thing the guests did when they entered the tent was to look at the bottom of their shoes to see if they might be the source of the odor. It was overpowering. The next year we obtained a separate, smaller tent and put that particular cheese in it (alone!).

IU Chancellor Wells, who called himself "an old euphonium player," attended OctubaFest concerts and came out to TubaRanch for each OctubaFeast. When he was in a wheelchair, his driver would help him get from his car to a table. If the weather was too bad, or he didn't feel well enough to sit at a table, we would serve him in the car.

One year, the Cleveland Orchestra had an OctubaFest as a fundraiser. It was very successful and, in appreciation of being able to use the name OctubaFest, a voluntary contribution was made to the Harvey Phillips Foundation by a grateful supporter of the Cleveland Orchestra.

I accepted an invitation for an early morning appearance from Gene Shalit to appear on the NBC *Today Show* in New York with my piano accompanist, Steve Harlos. We were soon joined by host Jane Pauley, a graduate of Indiana University. We had a lively conversation about the tuba and the music being written for it by American composers. This prompted a discussion about Alec Wilder and the special qualities of his compositions. The interview ended with a performance of Wilder's *Suite No. 1 for Tuba and Piano*. Both Shalit and Pauley later accepted my invitations to guest-conduct portions of the annual TubaChristmas concerts in Rockefeller Center.

After the *Today Show*, it was a full day of OctubaFest activities for Steve and me. Our next stop was a 1:00 visit to a Harlem elementary school with a demonstration concert. It was fun to talk about music with some thirty eight-to-twelve-year-old enthusiasts.

That evening at 8:00 we were joined at Carnegie Recital Hall by several of my IU students and New York City IU alumni. The concert was well attended and arrangements were made for a post-concert OctubaFeast at the famous Luchow's German Restaurant.

For three years, from 1983 to 1985, we produced OctubaFest as a joint venture between the City of Bloomington and my tuba studio. I had good relationships with every mayor. The first year of our collaboration, we worked with Mayor Tomilea Allison. On the roof of a big parking garage downtown we had a wine garden, a beer garden, and a kindergarten with games for the children, with qualified babysitters. The music for the celebration was a tuba ensemble of my own students and students from other schools. There was a polka-dancing contest. Fourteen restaurants signed up to prepare special German dishes for the occasion. In cooperation with Bloomington Hospital, we organized a volksmarch, which was a five- or six-mile health walk led by Bud Kohr, president of the hospital, which ended at OctubaFeast. OctubaFest was kind of a big deal in Bloomington!

In German Oktoberfests, the Burgermeister is usually the mayor or other male official of the town. Mayor Allison invited Indiana University Chancellor Herman B Wells to serve as Bloomington's first honorary Burgermeister. That pleased him. His smile was infectious. He was saluted by the Bloomington South High School Band, the Bloomington North High School Band, and the Ellettsville High School Band.

In 1976, my tuba/euphonium class at IU had an OctubaFest halftime show at the football game, adding itself to the IU Marching Hundred, along with tubas and euphoniums from the University of Illinois and the University of Michigan. We had a stage setup consisting of two flatbed trailers. I commissioned the Opera Department to create a backdrop canvas measuring twenty-four by forty feet, depicting a German Bavarian village.

Since that first OctubaFest in 1973, the idea spread all over the world, to more than one hundred college and university campuses.

CHAPTER THIRTEEN

Institute for Advanced Musical Studies

IN MY FIRST YEAR at the New England Conservatory, a young conductor, Daniell Revenaugh, of the Jacksonville Symphony, had come to see me. He inquired about my availability to administer a project establishing an advanced school of musical studies in Switzerland. I was interested in the project but could not become involved because of my commitment to Gunther Schuller and the NEC.

In August 1969, Richard Zellner became program adviser for the division of continuing education at Florida State University, Tallahassee. He worked with Daniell Revenaugh to provide continuing education credit to student musicians performing with the Jacksonville Orchestra. Revenaugh introduced Zellner to Dimitry Markevitch, director of the newly formed Institute for Advanced Musical Studies in Sion, Switzerland. Markevitch engaged Zellner as the American liaison to the institute for the purpose of creating a council of American Music School Deans and to recruit students. In 1971–1973, Revenaugh and Zellner worked on the Electric Symphony Orchestra project in Berkeley, California, utilizing members of the San Francisco Symphony. Zellner continued working to establish the Deans Council and to recruit student musicians for the institute in Switzerland. In 1973 the Swiss-based administration of the Institute for Advanced Musical Studies unexpectedly lost control of its facilities in Sion, and the arrival of students was imminent. The Italian-American philanthropist Pier Talenti, the institute's financial backer, summoned Zellner and Revenaugh to Rome, where Talenti asked them to resolve the situation. They contacted the Grand Hotel of Montreux, which agreed to become headquarters for the Institute for Advanced Musical Studies. Zellner was appointed managing director.

In 1971 I was contacted by Richard Zellner and Richard Wolf, directors of the institute, and they hired me for 1972 as a visiting professor of tuba, teaching and performing with a faculty brass quintet and serving as a consultant.

In June 1972, I went to Switzerland for two weeks at the Institute for Advanced Musical Studies. A faculty brass quintet was formed with trumpeters Gerard Schwarz and Stephen Burns (both New York City), hornist Chuck Kavalovski (Boston Symphony), trombonist John Marcellus (National Symphony), and myself on tuba. Students attended our rehearsals of brass quintet literature, most of which was new to their ears. Music was from the Renaissance and baroque periods.

For the duration of the institute, I flew to Switzerland each year after that to make visits as a consultant and guest artist at the school.

Since successful performing artists have busy schedules, students were in residence and the faculty was transient. For tuba, four of us would follow each other, each teaching for two weeks. For instance, I would be followed by Bob Tucci, John Fletcher from England, and a Czech tubist, Vaclav Hoza.

FIRST INTERNATIONAL BRASS SYMPOSIUM

In May 1974, a workshop met to plan for a brass chamber music symposium, concentrating on the brass quintet and its repertoire. Through Mr. Talenti, we acquired the massive funding it would take to organize such a presentation. The first International Brass Symposium was set to be held in Montreux, Switzerland, in late June 1974. After a few phone calls, the New York Brass Quintet and the Philip Jones Brass Ensemble (quintet) from London agreed to participate. It was also arranged to have a European brass quintet formed especially for the occasion!

The first International Brass Symposium was scheduled with master classes, open rehearsals, student and faculty ensembles, and solo performances. Notices of the symposium were distributed throughout Europe, Japan, and the United States. The response was good. Unfortunately, no one had bothered preparing program content.

Zellner and Wolf called me in Puerto Rico, where I was playing at the Casals Festival, and asked if I would prepare the program booklet and symposium sessions. I agreed to do it and I started the work immediately, using the information they had given me over the telephone. Since I had not received program materials from Philip Jones or Robert Nagel, I opened the program with a recital by Danish tubist Jorgen Arnsted, who had won a competition. For the rest of the Casals Festival, instead of going to the beach with my wife and children, I sequestered myself and worked on writing programs, much as I did for the tuba symposium in Bloomington. It would become very successful.

FIRST INTERNATIONAL BRASS CONGRESS, 1976

Riding on the success of the 1974 Brass Symposium, the institute decided to host an international event bringing together four international brass organizations. Planning for the congress started the day after the International Brass Symposium was over, as it was only two years hence. Richard Wolf had returned to his former position as director of extension programs at the University of Wisconsin-Madison, so Richard Zellner and I scheduled an equal number of clinic sessions, recital performances, and evening concerts to span one week for the upcoming First International Brass Congress.

Interspersed in that schedule would be sessions for the four families of brass instruments. We tried to program the congress in such a way that if someone wanted to go to everything, he or she could do so. The program for the whole symposium was printed in the *Brass Bulletin*. I attended everything.

We made immediate contact with the International Trombone Association (ITA), the Tubists Universal Brotherhood Association (TUBA), and the International Horn Society (IHS). (IHS had decided at the time of its organization to drop the word "French" because the "French horn" was more used by German composers than by French.) New professional chamber music and solo literature for each instrument exploded around the world, through the good works of these organizations. Now that enough time has passed, little quirks have subsided; all brass organizations are run with innovative concepts, getting more music written and, even better, more compositions performed for an ever-expanding audience. All of us who have devoted our lives to the betterment of our instruments can be proud of our achievements.

In 1975 we made note that there was no international organization uniting the trumpets. So I invited Robert Nagel, on tour with the New York Brass Quintet, and Charles Gorham, Indiana University Brass Department chairman, two of the most respected trumpet artists and good friends, to TubaRanch. I suggested it was more proper for them to organize the trumpets than for me, a tuba player, to do so. I also suggested that they call their new organization the International Trumpet Guild (ITG). I shared with them copies of the constitution and bylaws of IHS, ITA, and TUBA to assist in making the ITG compatible with its associate organizations. Their efforts bore fruit and in June 1975, the first International Trumpet Guild Symposium took place in the Musical Arts Center at Indiana University.

Lloyd Geisler, principal trumpet of the National Symphony Orchestra in Washington, D.C., was elected the first president of ITG. I was scheduled to present a keynote address at the luncheon, but on that day was confined to Bloomington Hospital because of an irregular heartbeat. From my hospital bed, I delivered the keynote address via cassette recording. The International Trumpet Guild has since become a model organization with thousands of members.

INTERNATIONAL REVERBERATION, DENMARK & BEYOND

My early recital album on Golden Crest Records had terrific acceptance in Scandinavia and Japan. That recording prompted Michael Lind and Chitate Kagawa, both of whom had jobs and influence at home, to want to study with me. They both wanted to play better and wanted better opportunities for their countrymen.

In the spring of 1974 I received a letter from Michael Lind, a young tubist in Denmark. Michael had several recordings of mine and followed with great interest the First International Tuba Symposium Workshop in 1973, which unfortunately he was unable to attend. He asked about coming to Bloomington to study with me, and I invited him to come at his convenience. Michael arrived in Bloomington a couple of weeks later and his studies began. I explained to Michael that building fences was a perpetual activity at TubaRanch, along with other mundane responsibilities. His lessons would be coordinated with my availability. He expected lessons of one hour each, and there were plenty of those. There were also lessons of two to eight hours, for Michael was most precocious and understood that our lessons with tubas would also involve talking about many subjects as he helped my fence building and other farm duties. These lessons included discussions of solo repertoire, brass quintet, commissioning composers, recital tours, and other subjects pertaining to the tuba. With all of this activity, I had Michael relinquish the room he had rented in town and move into the guest bedroom at TubaRanch. I also suggested he take some lessons with Arnold Jacobs and others, as the opportunity arose. Michael soon became, and continues to be, a part of our family.

At this particular time I would charter a private plane to take me to clinic appearances throughout the Midwest. It was worth it since I gained room for two passengers with tubas. With Michael's exuberant personality and exceptional tuba playing, he won friends wherever any circumstance took us. Michael went with me to a tuba–euphonium symposium at the University of Illinois and a recital by the Midwest Tuba Trio consisting of our host, Dan Perantoni, Lesley Varner, and myself. He also traveled with me to Cookeville, Tennessee, where he met Winston Morris and many other players of tuba and euphonium, and to Baton Rouge, Louisiana, for an important clinic appearance. It seemed that if we weren't sleeping or resting up after a busy day we were having lessons of every description. One morning we sat down with the Kopprasch studies and played through all sixty studies nonstop. In short, Michael was an excellent student; about the only thing I suggested was more variety of articulation. It took him only half a lesson to understand and agree.

I missed him terribly when he returned to Denmark and won the audition for the Stockholm Philharmonic. I presented him as a featured artist at the First International Brass Congress in Montreux held in June 1976.

His performance of Arban's "The Carnival of Venice" received a standing ovation from brass artists from twenty-six countries. In 1977 Michael organized the first Swedish Tuba/Euphonium Workshop, in Stockholm. It was a treat to premiere Torbjorn Iwan Lundquist's *Triplets* quartet there with the composer conducting. Joining me for this performance were Michael, Melvin Culbertson, and Robert Tucci. In 1978 Michael organized the first Scandinavian Brass Symposium, in Stockholm. In 1984 he was featured with the Scandinavian Brass Ensemble at the second International Brass Congress, held at Indiana University. In 1985 the Norwegian Euphonium/Tuba Workshop was hosted in Toneheim, Norway, by tubist Geir Lovold. Featured American clinicians were Brian Bowman, euphonium, and myself, as well as John Fletcher and Michael Lind. While I was in Norway I did a concert in Oslo with the Radio Orchestra. In 1988 Michael was co-organizer at the second Scandinavian Brass Symposium, in Helsinki, Finland.

Michael continues to commission composers, with more than seventy works to his credit, featuring tuba with a variety of ensembles. His recordings represent a level of performance attained by few artists. While setting a fence post in place, Michael might ask, "How do you go about commissioning a composer?" I told him the most inspirational aspect of a commission is the assurance of performances, so tell him you need it for an already scheduled concert. Above all else, music is composed to be heard. Most important to composers is having their music performed. Once a work is written, it may be credited as "written for," "dedicated to," "inspired by," or "commissioned by." Whatever its credits, once a piece exists, it belongs to the music world and is claimed for performances heard by the public audience.

TUBAJAZZ

The Sauter-Finegan Orchestra was one of few venues for a jazz tuba in the 1950s. In 1965, I was at the Midwest Clinic in Chicago and happened to be relaxing at a club after a long day of clinics and recitals. Onstage was an incredible jazz euphonium player sitting in with a group. His name was Rich Matteson, an established musician in Las Vegas and a recent appointment to the jazz faculty of North Texas State University. He blew me away! I had worked with everybody in New York, but I had never worked with a jazz euphonium player. After the set, I apologized to him for not having heard him previously. I went home from the Midwest Clinic and told Carol about Rich. I said, "This guy ought to be known by everybody in the world who likes jazz." Like Doc Severinsen, Rich happened to be sponsored by the Getzen Instrument Company. One day I would discover that Rich and I were doing a clinic at the same festival.

In October 1975, William Winkle, director of bands at Chadron State College in Chadron, Nebraska, hosted a tuba–euphonium symposium in Chadron. (Bill later co-authored with me *The Art of Tuba and Euphonium,* published by Summy-Birchard in 1992.) It was a pleasure to serve as a clinician on the same program with Rich Matteson. All the clinics went well. I got to know Rich and suggested we should play together more often. That night, after the final evening concert, we attended a reception in the student union building. The entertainment provided was the tuba ensembles of William Winkle and Don Little. Don Little's ensemble from northern Iowa, with a rhythm section on board, played the swing standards of a big band.

Because the event was held in a small student union, they put Rich and me in a twin suite. We lay there talking. About 2:00 in the morning, Rich suddenly blurted out, "Hey, Harve, working together is such a ball; there should be something we could play together!"

"Rich, do you want to have a band?"

"What kind of band would we have?"

We had just heard a great group of tubas and euphoniums playing jazz. We talked about them, how well Don had prepared the group and how they really did swing. I told Rich that if we could come up with a jazz tuba group, I'd put it on the program of the upcoming Brass Congress in Montreux, Switzerland. We chose from a group of people I knew would be there.

Two of my colleagues who immediately came to mind were Dan Perantoni and Winston Morris. They were the right people for the group and were already scheduled to be at the Congress. Since we had three tubas, we decided on three euphoniums. Rich wanted to have Ashley Alexander, with whom he had worked at many summer jazz camps. However, he couldn't vouch for another jazz euphonium player. I asked John Marcellus to sub because I knew he was an outstanding euphonium player as well as the principal trombonist in the National Symphony. He agreed to perform with us until he had to go back to his symphony job. Rich and I also agreed that guitarist Jack Petersen would coordinate the rhythm section for any group we put together. He accepted. Steve Harlos, staff accompanist for the Brass Congress, agreed to play piano. From Bobby Blake's combo of five trumpets with rhythm section, we borrowed bassist Steve LaSpina and drummer Jerry Coleman. We had a band.

In the same spirit as OctubaFest and TubaChristmas, I suggested one word that said it all: "TubaJazz." The word "consort" evokes the image of a lofty chamber group, so the full title agreed to was The Matteson-Phillips TubaJazz Consort. I called my attorney and registered the word "TubaJazz."

ARRIVAL IN MONTREUX, BRASS CONGRESS 1976

There was much to do in Montreux before the Brass Congress began. I arrived with my family ten days early to cope with last-minute details and still have one week for sightseeing in Italy. There was only one problem with the timing of our family vacation: it was just one week before I was scheduled to play recitals at the congress and I needed to practice. Dick Zellner had arranged for a rental vw bus for our trip so I asked him also to arrange for me to rent a sousaphone with detachable bell. I left the bell at the rental store and took only the body of the instrument. While Carol drove the bus, I sat in the back and practiced. When we passed through small towns, I would play Italian tunes, folk songs, and opera arias. People in their cars or on the street seemed to enjoy our one-car parade.

Meeting with Dick Zellner and reviewing last-minute details, I was impressed with his efficiency and expertise. My family and I were able to depart Switzerland for Italy a day early. Not knowing in advance what problems might arise for the congress or what time we would leave Montreux, I had made no hotel reservations in Italy. We headed for Turin, arriving happy but hungry around 1 AM. We stopped at the only open establishment at the time, a bar with a restaurant upstairs. The kitchen had just closed but they agreed to feed us. We each ordered a dish, but forgot that northern Italian restaurants feature risotto (rice) instead of pasta, so all the dishes we ordered were rice-based. It didn't take long to satisfy our hunger. It was raining outside and since we were all wide awake and had no hotel commitment, we drove on to Pisa. It was a boring ride since we only saw what the headlights allowed.

When I stopped for gas about 6 AM, I bought bottles of juice for the boys. After their morning juice, they went immediately back to sleep. I witnessed in the rearview mirror what Carol witnessed directly: Thomas, in the back seat, fell asleep while drinking his bottle of apricot juice and poured it down the front of his clothes.

At 8:30 AM we located the Leaning Tower of Pisa, which was surrounded by a high wall. I woke the boys. Taking advantage of a restaurant, Carol got Tom tidied and into clean clothes. I told the guys to go see what was on the other side of the wall. They didn't have any idea we were in Pisa and when they saw it was the Leaning Tower of Pisa, they immediately wanted to climb to the top. Carol was as adventuresome as the boys.

I wanted no part of climbing the steps to the top of the tower. I sat in an outdoor cafe and drank coffee. Thomas took it on himself to arrive at the top first; he ran right to the edge of the tower as he went up the floors. There was no guardrail. Fearing that the surface of the tower might be wet with morning dew, my heart was in my mouth. Carol was also very concerned and berated Tom when she got to the top with Harvey and Jesse. But that was Tom . . . first and foremost.

The day we arrived, the town of Pisa was celebrating an ancient victory over invaders from a neighboring province. Residents dressed in period costumes to re-enact, with weaponry of the past, the turning away of the invaders. We watched with fascination before going on to Rome, where we were a touring American family.

A few weeks before the Brass Congress in Montreux, Anthony Steel, manager of the Adelaide Festival of the Arts in Australia, inquired about my attending the 1978 Adelaide Festival for two weeks of recitals and conducting a mass band plus a concert by sixty or more tubas and euphoniums. He wanted to meet with me but we could never come up with a date when we would both be in the same country. While I was planning the Brass Congress in Switzerland, he flew into Montreux from Liverpool, where he was negotiating an arts festival.

Over lunch at a splendid restaurant, I told him that I didn't think my coming to Australia would work.

"Oh, I read your profile in the *New Yorker*," he said. "We bring opera companies and symphonies to Australia all the time. Bringing a family of five is no problem." The *New Yorker* magazine profile, written by Whitney Balliett, had included the fact that I did not go anywhere longer than five days without my wife and three sons.

While we were in Switzerland for the International Brass Congress, walking along Lake Leman back to our hotel, we heard three brass quintets practicing. Seeing these young people so excited about quintet music was inspiring. In the twenty-five years since we put together the first brass quintet, these groups had exploded in number. Between the New York Brass Quintet and the American Brass Quintet, some 1,500 or more works had been written, plus all kinds of transcriptions. To me, it was the biggest unexpected windfall of my career.

Attending the Brass Congress were musicians from many nations, including performers and delegates from Japan, the United States, Canada, all the Scandinavian countries, West and East Germany, Russia, Romania, the United Kingdom, Australia, and South Africa. Arnold Jacobs, Philip Farkas, Barry Tuckwell, Denis Wick, Ray Premru, Jay Friedman, Slide Hampton, John Fletcher, Ionel Dumitru, and others attended. Switzerland was one of the few locations where Soviet artists and others from Eastern Europe could perform and converse with their colleagues. The world-renowned brass artists Vitali Buyanovsky, horn, and Timofei Dokshizer, trumpet, came from Russia, and were both followed by members of the KGB who tried to listen in on every conversation. We could have a normal conversation with our Russian colleagues only if one of us distracted the spy while the other talked to them. Each chair in the theater where we met had headphones with buttons giving a choice of five languages.

There were sessions on repertoire, pedagogy, and study materials of international scope. Discussions of acoustics, anatomy, and physical analysis were on the schedule. We had more than five hundred of the world's greatest brass players together in the same conference. It was an outstanding first-time event.

The Matteson-Phillips TubaJazz Consort rehearsed each night after everyone else had gone to bed. The reception of the group was questionable in the minds of many of the other brass players who were there. We were to be the last ensemble to play at the congress. At the performance, we started with "Spoofy," an original by Rich. Sixteen measures in, the crowd stood up and cheered. They loved it. They had learned something more about the flexibility of tubas and could spread the word. Leaving Montreux, a bus was transporting musician participants to the airport. We discovered that trombonist Buddy Baker, president of ITA and chairman of the Jazz Department at University of Northern Colorado, and who had previously founded the Indiana University Jazz Department, played euphonium. I asked him to join the TubaJazz Consort. He was ecstatic. Buddy was a veteran member of the bands of Stan Kenton, Woody Herman, and other big bands. His personality and musicianship fit right in with the Matteson-Phillips ensemble. He would play with the group after Marcellus left to continue his position with the National Symphony Orchestra. Each member of our group was a professor at a different university. Rich joked that it cost us three thousand dollars just to get together for coffee. Even so, those guys were perfect for the gig.

The morning after our success in Montreux, I called Anthony Steel in Australia and told him what a hit the Matteson-Phillips TubaJazz Consort had made with those attending the Brass Congress, and asked if he would consider bringing them to Adelaide. Anthony was delighted and said he would book the TubaJazz Consort for two weeks in the Adelaide Festival's After Dark Club at the end of my individual contract in 1978. When we came home to Bloomington, Anthony and his financial manager flew out to TubaRanch to go over details.

To know that the TubaJazz Consort had a two-week engagement in Australia in February of 1978 was a morale booster and encouraged us to book other prestigious engagements. Notable among the appearances was one before the National Association of Jazz Educators (NAJE) in Daytona Beach and again a year later in Dallas, where we recorded our first LP.

On our return from our triumph at the Brass Congress in Switzerland, the TubaJazz Consort's first gig in America was at Joe Segal's Jazz Showcase during the Chicago Midwest Band and Orchestra Clinic, in December

1976. We featured Louie Bellson on drums. In his set, he had so many percussion instruments it looked like a window of a downtown music store. Again, the audience went wild. We were a big hit, especially with exhibitors, because many of them were unable to participate in the conferences until the day was over.

While we were walking through the crowd on our way to the stage, one gentleman put his hand on my arm and inquired about the quality of what was going to happen.

"Is this outfit any good?" he asked.

"No," I replied, "You'd look better in a blue suit."

When we got onstage, nobody could play immediately because we were laughing so hard. We played again at Joe Segal's in 1977, 1979, and 1985.

We did two appearances at the Midwest Band and Orchestra Clinic, in 1977 and 1985; four at TUBA/ITEC conferences, in 1978, 1980, 1983, and 1990; and two at Dante's Club in Los Angeles, in 1978 and 1984. We also played at the National Association of Music Merchants in Atlanta in 1977; the Smithsonian in 1977; the Disneyland Jazz Festival in 1978; Dick Gibson's Weekend Jazz Party in Colorado in 1978; the Second Story Jazz Club in Bloomington in 1984; California State University, Long Beach, in 1984; the Monterey Jazz Festival in 1984; and the Western International Band Clinic in Seattle in 1987. The second album was recorded live in St. Louis in 1981 at the National Association of Jazz Educators. We also played at the NAJE in Washington, D.C., in 1991.

Ashley Alexander, our euphonium player, had a heart attack and died during a morning jog at a jazz camp in 1988. The group performed a *Tribute to Ashley* concert at the National Association of Jazz Educators in Los Angeles in 1989. John Allred, a jazz trombone and euphonium player, replaced Ashley in the group.

Then there was the Spokane Summer Concert Series in 1990, as the Consort was on its way to perform at an ITEA conference in Sapporo, Japan, followed by the U.S. Army Band Tuba/Euphonium Conference in Fort Meyer, Virginia, in 1991. In 1994, at the International Association of Jazz Educators in Boston, we played a *Tribute to Rich Matteson*, who had died the year before. A Japanese euphonium player, Keith Oshiro, who had studied with Rich, played.

The Matteson-Phillips TubaJazz Consort received the International Association of Jazz Educators Outstanding Service to Jazz Education award in 1981 and 1994. I received the International Association of Jazz Educators Award in 1977, 1978, and 1991.

Many times when I did clinics in the States, it was not possible to have my family travel with me. Carol and the boys had to hold down the fort at the TubaRanch. Carol fed horses, cattle, and many fowl, cooked meals, and raised the children. When I think back on it, although I was raised in a farming community, I'd never really been a farmer and neither had Carol. We insisted that we would be farmers, though, and were always pushing the envelope. It was impractical, as busy as I was, and especially considering how much traveling the family was doing. Throughout our life together, Carol always took care of everything inside and outside of our home. She inspired all of us.

AMONG THE AUSSIES

The day my family and I arrived in Adelaide, after traveling for thirty-six hours, Anthony Steel, Mike Coad, and newspaper and television reporters met us at the airport. We were also met by a brass band, with a white fiberglass sousaphone sent by the Conn Company for me to use at one of my concerts. They took me to a room, put it on my shoulder, and I played "The Carnival of Venice," which was recorded for the media. The Aussies who met us suggested we check into the hotel and relax until the next day because of jet lag. But Carol, our boys, and I thought we had no jet lag and wanted to go to a Chinese restaurant. It was our twenty-fourth wedding anniversary and Carol and I arrived at the hotel suite to find it packed with flowers, baskets of fruit, iced champagne, hors d'oeuvres, and outstanding Australian wines. After we enjoyed our suite, we went to the Chinese restaurant recommended. It was as though we were all on steroids. We happily gave our order to the Chinese waiter, but while awaiting the food we all fell sound asleep. The waiter had difficulty waking us up and thoughtfully had already filled our order in takeout containers.

Before our Australian TubaJazz debut, I had three assignments. First, I was to give two solo recitals, one each week, with an Australian pianist.

Second, I was to conduct a big concert band. Third, I would conduct the largest tuba ensemble ever assembled on that continent.

Eighty-six tuba and euphonium players showed up, all from Australia. At the first rehearsal of the mass tuba choir, I became distressed when I heard no second parts in the euphoniums. I was afraid maybe we didn't have any second parts, so I called over my host conductor, Andy Alderslade, and expressed my concern.

He said, "No, mate, I know the problem; no one wants to be a second eupher." He hit the nail on the head, and so with some diplomacy we were able to entice the euphonium players to alternate and play second parts half the time. This was one of the subjects I spoke of during my clinic following our preparation for the concert. The concert band was very good and was assembled to do an extra concert, shared with the Matteson-Phillips TubaJazz Consort. This concert was in a large stadium containing multiple tennis courts.

An apartment had been reserved on a southern beach when we first got to Australia. I had a recital rehearsal the next day and was anxious to have some practice time. Little Harvey went to the beach with me, where we scooped out a place to sit. We put sand on the corners of the music. The beach was deserted, except for one man and his dog about a hundred yards away. I was just preparing to play my first note of practice when the other visitor on the beach cupped his hand to his mouth and yelled, "You're Harvey Phillips, aren't you?!" I replied in the positive, of course. So, instead of practicing, I had an enlightening conversation. As it turned out, he was a former horn player and woodworker who had lost the fingers from his left hand to a finishing saw. He had since that time taken up the tuba and played with the Adelaide Symphony. Meeting new colleagues is always a pleasure but I was a bit upset at having my small opportunity to practice erased.

When my recital and conducting assignments were over—they made a big hit, by the way—and the TubaJazz Consort personnel arrived, we opened at the After Dark Club. One hundred and fifty people packed the place. When we reached the stage, the crowd was excited. The club was so crowded that there were forty people seated at tables behind the stage. Rich got the idea that he would play a chorus on one side of the stage, while Ashley played one on the other. The TubaJazz Consort started into the first number and the crowd went wild. They were wiped out by our performance, and we loved it, too.

Australian musicians and their jazz club patrons, having heard broadcasts from the Adelaide Festival, were enthusiastic about the TubaJazz Consort. We had been elevated to celebrity status by their enthusiasm.

I was able to schedule my rehearsals with Australian accompanists while Carol and the boys made exciting excursions into the outback, each riding a camel. Perhaps their most adventurous excursion was a visit to the opal mines in Andamooka, a two-and-a-half-hour, seven-passenger-plane ride from Adelaide.

While we were in Adelaide, we were invited to an Australian picnic and dance in a humongous wine-aging barn. It illustrated the warm hospitality that can be shared. When we passed by one of the family gatherings in the barn, there would be invitations to have a plate or fill a glass. No one seemed to be in a hurry but all seemed totally relaxed, just having a good time. It was a heartwarming experience.

At the Basement jazz club in Sydney there were so many people that it took an extra half hour to get our musicians into the club and set up to perform. We could not have asked for a better audience. The next evening we played a concert in the Sydney Opera House with much success. From Sydney, TubaJazz traveled to Melbourne for another capacity audience. The concert in Melbourne was delayed by a large jewelry heist across the street from the concert hall. The reception of Melbourne musicians was something to remember.

From Melbourne we traveled to Brisbane, site of the Great Barrier Reef. One of our sponsors was a famous seafood restaurant that, in and of itself, would have been worth the trip. We left Australia with many memories and many new friends. Rich's provoking arrangement of "Waltzing Matilda" for the TubaJazz Consort was a major success. We all had a ball in Australia.

JAPANESE TUBISTS PLAY HOST

Genkichi Harada, tubist with NHK Orchestra and conductor of the Yamaha Band, visited me at the New England Conservatory in 1967 and presented me with pearl cufflinks and tie pin. He asked about my coming someday to visit Japan. Time passed after his visit, and in 1979 I received an invitation for me and my family to visit Japan as guests of a number of Japanese tubists for two weeks, followed by Seoul, Korea, for four days, Hong Kong for four days, and Manila for four days. The invitation was to celebrate my fiftieth year.

We were met at the Tokyo airport by Harada and transported to the hotel reserved for us, directly across from the NKO studios. After checking into the hotel we were ushered to a Chinese restaurant located in the hotel, for a "Welcome to Japan" reception and dinner party. We were greeted by Mr. Sato, "The Bill Bell of Japan," and twenty or so other tubists who served as a platoon of hosts. Mr. Sato was present when the World War II peace treaty was signed. Later he met Mr. Bell when the New York Philharmonic toured Japan. They became great friends.

Our hosts were generous and efficient throughout our visit. There were many parties, as many as three on some days: 6 PM for twenty to twenty-five students, 8 PM for ten to fifteen professional tubist colleagues, and 10 PM for four to five local corporate and business executives, two to three tubist colleagues, one bank president, one newspaper publisher, and three music company executives. The food and libation served at each dinner party was so delicious and plentiful we had to pace ourselves to stay alert.

At a concert with the orchestra in Yamaha's concert hall, Dale Clevenger played a Mozart horn concerto. I played the Vaughan Williams concerto. For our encore, to lighten the occasion, Dale and I played some Dixieland together.

At that time, there was no association of tubists in Japan. Each gathering was organized by one or two tubists who knew the restaurants and sightseeing opportunities—temples, the electronic district, and historical shrines. A young lady, Sanae Osawa, who had studied euphonium with me at Indiana University, volunteered to escort us to Kyoto, Nagasaki, and Osaka.

At Osaka, we went to dinner in a restaurant where the waitresses wore kimonos and patrons were accommodated at counters surrounding pools full of fish. There were walkways across the center of the pools. At one end of the pool, there was a large cutting board, and when someone ordered a certain fish, the waiter would net that fish out of the pool and take it to the cutting board, where the chef chopped off the head and prepared a plate of sushi for the customer. It could not have been more fresh.

Our waitress served us our meal, which we obviously enjoyed. A young man, observing our pleasure, approached us and in excellent English said, "You seem to enjoy Japanese food." We assured him he had made the right observation. He smiled and said to us, "Best Japanese restaurant is in Chicago. Hatsuhanna."

In December, we were in Chicago for the annual week-long band and orchestra clinic. A good friend of mine, Daniel Henkin, president of United Musical Instruments, took a party of twelve to Hatsuhanna. We were told by the head waiter that there would be no table for an hour, whereupon Dan called his wife Mary over to speak to the maitre d' and show him her identification as a member of the Japanese royal family. Almost immediately, we were escorted to our table in a private dining room.

Among other interesting sites we visited in Japan was a stop in the town of Nagasaki, where deer roamed in the park. We boarded a bullet train on our way from Nagasaki back to Tokyo.

Throughout our sightseeing, there were regularly scheduled rehearsals for concerts in Sapporo, Tokyo, and Saitama. At the concert in Sapporo, I was featured with a wonderful Japanese pianist, and a Mozart duet was arranged for Chitate Kagawa and me to perform. The small auditorium at the Sapporo Kyouiku Bunka-Kaikan was packed with local dignitaries. The next day, we traveled back to Tokyo for a dress rehearsal and concert.

Our next stop, after a memorable evening of farewell parties, was Seoul, Korea. Accompanying us to Seoul was Genkichi Harada, who came just to assure our having a good time. After checking into the hotel and getting comfortable in our room, I had a call from the lobby, asking if it would be all right for the tubist of the Seoul Symphony Orchestra to visit with me. We of course had him in and enjoyed talking with him. He was disappointed that I was not performing in Seoul but wanted to help us enjoy our stay. With Genkichi and my family as his guests, he made a reservation for a dinner at 10:00 PM at a Korean restaurant, where we sat on the floor and cooked a bountiful meal over hot coals at our table.

One day in Hong Kong, after a steady diet of Asian food, I was on my way back from the bank to the Hong Kong Hilton when I observed the grand opening of a McDonald's restaurant. I went in and ordered an abundant lunch, two shopping bags' full. All of us attacked that.

For dinner the evening before departing to Manila, we made reservations for a table on the famous floating tourist restaurant in Hong Kong Harbor. We were served a relaxed multi-course meal of epic proportions. We were impressed by the hundreds of family sampans moored in the harbor, cooking, eating, and relaxing.

We arrived safely at the Manila Airport and, after going through customs, proceeded to the Manila Hotel via one of the famous Philippines taxis. Dr. George C. Wilson, director of the National Music Camp at Interlochen, had asked that I make contact with Imelda Marcos's assistant for music and the arts. Madame Marcos loved music, and had consulted with Dr. Wilson about building an academy of music and the arts somewhere in the mountains of the Philippines. When I reached Madame Marcos by telephone I introduced myself and delivered greetings from Dr. Wilson. She invited my family to dinner that evening. I accepted her invitation, and mentioned that I wanted to shop that afternoon for some of the famous Filipino shirts. She informed me that I wouldn't be able to get them, because we would be leaving the next day and the stores were closed for the weekend. She said to give her our shirt sizes, though, and Carol did. By the time we went to dinner at 8:00, the made-to-order shirts were delivered to us.

We ate in the best-appointed restaurant in Manila. We discussed the proposed Interlochen of the Philippines, which I reported back to Dr. Wilson. The restaurant had a quintet of bass, drums, piano, saxophone, and trumpet. They were very discreet, playing in an open room, and their music did not interfere with dinner; it really added something to the meal. What struck us as we were about to have dessert was hearing a voice on the microphone singing "Hey Jude" with the band. The next number was "Yellow Submarine." It was ten-year-old Thomas.

TUBACHRISTMAS

During my New York freelance years, one of my musical heroes was trumpeter Harry Glantz. He was a giant, establishing a standard of performance that paved the way for the exceptional players we have today. Glantz spent nineteen years with the New York Philharmonic and another seventeen years with the NBC Symphony Orchestra. I worked with him for nine years on *The Bell Telephone Hour,* on NBC. In November 1974, a trumpet student at IU had a Glantz trumpet mouthpiece, but didn't know what "Glantz" was. I gave him a lecture. That night, I told Carol, "Can you imagine? What if, in twenty years, tuba players don't know who Bill Bell was?"

Because Christmas day was Bill Bell's birthday, I wanted to gather his students to pay him honor in a New York tribute concert at Christmastime. His students could in turn invite their students, so I hoped for two hundred to three hundred players. I called Rockefeller Center in New York City and asked about the availability of the ice rink as a stage. The conversation went something like this:

"Hello. My name is Harvey Phillips, and I would like to reserve the ice rink stage at Rockefeller Center for a musical tribute to a great musician."

"What is your ensemble?" asked the vice president who answered the phone.

I said, "Well, I don't have an ensemble but I am expecting around three hundred tubas."

The phone went silent. He said very quietly, "Would you repeat that?"

I said that I expected an ensemble of three hundred tubists to honor the man considered to be the greatest tuba player of the century: William Bell, who performed with the Sousa Band, the NBC Symphony, and the New York Philharmonic.

"I don't think so, Mr. Phillips. We've never done anything like that."

I gave him the unlisted phone numbers of some references. Among them were Leopold Stokowski, Leonard Bernstein, Andre Kostelanetz, Gunther Schuller, and Morton Gould, who was then president of ASCAP. He called me back about an hour later. Apparently he was intrigued to know the unlisted numbers of these people, so he had called them.

"This is the vice president of Rockefeller Center," he said. "Mr. Phillips, I have spoken with some of your friends. You can have anything you want, and we will help you in any way that we can to have a successful event."

I decided to call it "TubaChristmas." We were excited about it, but by Thanksgiving weekend, I realized that we had no music to play. I had spent all of my time getting the word out to 342 tuba players about our tribute to William Bell. At the time, Alec Wilder was spending time in Rochester, New York, so I called to tell him what I was going to do. When I asked if he could arrange some music, he said, "Well, Harvey, I can't write music anymore. I haven't been able to write since John died."

In March 1974, John Barrows, a close friend and colleague of his since 1936, had passed away. When Alec lost a dear friend, he took it very hard. It just shut him down as a composer. Alec would go for months without writing a note because of his despondency over having lost a dear friend.

Finally, I got a little rough with Alec on the phone. I said, "Alec, come on. I am not asking you to write music; I am asking you to arrange music. It is already written." He said, "Well, I don't know. I will have to call you back."

The next day he called. He had been up all night arranging eighteen Christmas carols for tuba ensemble and had already taken them to a copyist. By the end of the week, they were on their way to me. When I received the music in Bloomington, I wondered what it was going to sound like. My students played all of the carols with me, and they sounded wonderful. One of America's great composers had arranged these carols for us to play. He wrote them hastily but they were of professional caliber. Alec's musical floodgates opened and he started writing, one composition after another.

After our first few run-throughs of the music, I thought, "You know, maybe we should do a concert here in Bloomington." At that time I had an assistant, Ronald Lee Spencer, a young tuba player from Winston Morris's studio in Cookeville, Tennessee. I asked Ron to rehearse the group a little more and I started looking for a place for us to play in Bloomington. In the meantime, I explored ideas concerning how we could benefit the community with this concert.

During the course of our discussions, Ron and I came up with the idea that the tuba players should dress in Santa costumes for the performance. It would add to the spirit of the event and would attract public attention. Ron and I called all the places in Bloomington that rented Santa suits. We managed to come up with twenty-three suits, and I rented every one for the going fee of seven dollars and fifty cents apiece. After some inquiry, we found that the Firemen's Auxiliary did not benefit from United Way and was trying to raise funds for burned children. (There had been an unusual number of house fires during that year.) That week, we met with the auxiliary and they agreed to let us try to raise some money. Having gone that far, we went to the fire chief and asked him if we could have a fire truck to transport the tuba players from Indiana University to downtown on the square where I had arranged for us to play. I had called Mayor Frank McCloskey and asked if we could perform near the courthouse. He gave his blessing, and attended the concert.

The concert worked out fabulously. After the tuba ensemble performance, the players broke into quartets. Each little group went to different stores and passed the can for the storekeepers and customers to make contributions to the Firemen's Auxiliary. The most generous contributors were the early afternoon patrons of taverns near the town square. One patron requested a tune and contributed ten dollars. We wondered later how he would explain to his wife giving ten dollars to Santa Clauses playing tubas.

Four years later, in 1978, Mayor Frank McCloskey presented me with the Community Service Award from the City of Bloomington.

On that day in Bloomington, December 14, we still did not have a conductor for the New York performance. I contacted Paul Lavalle, then music director for Radio City Music Hall and formerly of the Band of America. He loved Bill Bell and said he would be very excited to do it. The day of the performance, December 22, 1974, more than three hundred tuba players showed up for the first-ever TubaChristmas. Rockefeller Center gave us rooms on the second floor of the NBC Building where we might leave our cases and coats while we warmed up our instruments and prepared for rehearsal.

All they could come up with for a rehearsal hall, though, was a hallway corridor in Rockefeller Center. It was about twenty-four feet wide, and very long, at the bottom of a ten-step staircase which served as a podium. We placed the euphoniums, tubas, recording tubas, and sousaphones in that order. The sound of three hundred tuba players warming up was an incredible cacophony. This many tubas and euphoniums had the potential to sound glorious or awful, which put Alec and me on edge.

A reviewer in *Newsweek* (Hubert Saal) had recently named me "The Paganini of the Tuba," which piqued the interest of Whitney Balliett, noted writer for the *New Yorker* magazine. Alec had invited his friends Fran Miller, Marian McPartland, James T. Maher, and others. I stood near them with Whitney, nervous about how the music would sound. Paul Lavalle walked to the top of the stairs to conduct the rehearsal. He got everybody quiet. Paul lifted his baton and started the first carol in the book, "O Come, All Ye Faithful." From the first note, it sounded fantastic! To have all that lush, gorgeous sound contained in that space was so amazing that everybody started crying or laughing or hugging. With tears in his eyes, Alec looked at me to exclaim, "Harvey! It works! It works!"

After the rehearsal, we had to get everyone onto the ice stage. As we approached the back entrance to the rink, we realized that three hundred tuba players had to get out on the ice through a lone revolving door. At any one time, only two people would be in the door. Guests of a next-door restaurant left their tables to gawk at the novelty that slowly passed near the window.

Out on the ice rink stage, the music was grand. The tubas were below the huge Rockefeller Center Christmas tree and under the statue of Prometheus. The next day, the performance was the centerpiece of every newspaper in New York City. At that time, I had no vision of any performances beyond that one event. I was very pleased and somewhat surprised when they asked us to do it again the next year. Of course we accepted.

In the end, I had created another opportunity to gather Bill Bell's students and colleagues who knew of his warmth and personable nature. The next year, my tuba quartets in Bloomington again passed the hat in taverns and stores, and donated what they collected to the Salvation Army. The second year, we worked with the mayors' offices in Chicago and Dallas to host TubaChristmas celebrations in those cities. Our Rockefeller Center performance in New York continued. By the third year, we had added Los Angeles, and it just exploded. The New York City performance became a sort of legend in its own time. On the sidewalks around the ice rink, almost forty thousand people gather to hear the concert each year. New York musician friends of mine would tell me, "I'll see you at your concert in New York!" Later, they would call to let me know that the closest they could get was a block away.

Through wind, snow, and hail, TubaChristmas continued. One time, the temperature dropped to sixteen degrees and the valves of our instruments were freezing up. Some players mixed antifreeze with their valve oil so they would keep moving. It was especially uncomfortable. Before we went outside for the concert, I made an announcement: "It's sixteen degrees and sleeting. I'll cancel the performance if you want to." There wasn't one person who wanted to cancel it. We have played when snowflakes as big as golf balls were falling. One year, when Jane Pauley of *The Today Show* was conducting, it started snowing right on the downbeat of "O Come, All Ye Faithful." It was perfect.

I did about thirteen years of TubaSanta concerts in Milwaukee's Performing Arts Center and three in Herman B Wells's hometown of Lebanon, Indiana. When he was president of Indiana University, Herman Wells acquired his own Santa costume. When time permitted, during the Christmas season he would sometimes wear his Santa suit and walk through the campus, stopping to linger with students, discussing thoughts of the university at Christmastime or whatever the student wanted to discuss. Students would often come away with feelings of a wise, warm, and wonderful person who could be the real Santa. He told me that if his health had permitted, he would have played his baritone with the TubaSantas.

TubaChristmas celebrations spread across the United States and around the world, and there are now more than 242 of these events worldwide. TubaChristmas proves my point that it takes no more energy to think big than it does to think small. It also proves another of my points: Nothing ventured, nothing gained. There are TubaChristmases in France, Italy, Germany, all the Scandinavian countries, Switzerland, Puerto Rico, and several in Japan. TubaChristmases have been led by distinguished guest conductors in many cities including Anchorage and Baghdad. In New York, we hosted guest conductors like Charles Kuralt and Gene Shalit. I had former IU president John Ryan guest-conduct in Rockefeller Center. Colonel John Bourgeois, conductor of the United States Marine Band; Hugo Fiorato, of the New York City Ballet; Colonel Arnold Gabriel, of the U.S.

Air Force Band; and Roger Kellaway flew in from California to lead the group. Doc Severinsen, from *The Tonight Show,* volunteered to conduct as well. Some fans try to attend as many TubaChristmases as possible during the season.

Chris Donze, president of Ludwig Music Publishers of Grafton, Ohio, organized a 2003 TubaChristmas in Cleveland where two hundred players onstage at Severance Hall wore tuxedos and evening gowns. This celebrated the thirtieth anniversary of TubaChristmas and was the most impressive one I've experienced. It was recorded on CD. And in 2008, the Sacramento TubaChristmas ensemble marched in that city's Christmas parade.

Since our initial performance in Bloomington, the TubaSantas have been hosted by Carnegie Hall, on a split concert with Canadian Brass. We played special programs at Marshall Field in Chicago, played for the Downtown Commission of Indianapolis, and played at various other important venues, as well as at many shopping malls. The first Kansas City TubaChristmas accompanied the lighting of the official tree, and was hosted by Hallmark Cards. Both TubaChristmas and the TubaSantas have gained popularity wherever they have appeared.

The music is especially arranged by Norlan Bewley, a protege of mine. He edited Alec's eighteen arrangements and added another fifteen. This book of 33 selections is used in every TubaChristmas concert throughout the world. Norlan lives in Dayton, Ohio, and returns to Bloomington each year to conduct the TubaSantas.

In 2009 we decided to explore additional occasions that would offer the tuba and euphonium new opportunities for public events. So, in addition to OctubaFest, TubaChristmas, and SummerTubaTime, we are adding HolidayTubas, which can be featured within an established festival on important national and international holidays.

HOMECOMING: HARVEY PHILLIPS DAY

It was announced in February 1976 that Marionville, Missouri, would hold a Harvey Phillips Day to honor me at its Fourth of July Bicentennial celebration. I asked that it be done on August 29, my mother's birthday. When she got the news in February, she started working with a physical therapist to be sure she could walk on the day of the event. I received a telephone call agreeing to my request for late August, but they wanted to do it on Saturday the 28th instead of Sunday the 29th. I complied. Saturday was a better day for their parade, picnic, and concert. The Army sent a band from Fort Leonard Wood in Missouri to do a concert and to march in the parade. There were a few high school bands, too. In the parade were antique cars, fire trucks, tractors, and people riding horses. Tammy Estes, a grandniece of mine who was a baton twirler and a majorette, marched out in front of the Army Band. Sadly, Mom died before the celebration. Carol and I went to her church the next afternoon, Sunday—her birthday—and I played several of her favorite hymns, until I could play no more.

CHAPTER FOURTEEN

Bassed in Bloomington

IN TEACHING AT INDIANA UNIVERSITY, I endeavored to discover each student's strengths and weaknesses. Our job was to work on the weaknesses while not losing any of the strengths. Each student made two columns on a piece of paper and wrote down strengths on one side and weaknesses on the other. The goal was to bring things from the weaknesses column into the strengths column. I would always make assignments based on what I felt were the weakest aspects of a student's progress. Even so, I always made it clear that the priority for each student was the ensembles he or she was assigned to.

At IU, I taught private (one-on-one) tuba, some private euphonium, and a tuba repertoire class, as well as coaching performances. I served on a repertoire committee and would later join the distinguished ranks committee. Sometimes I had as many as twenty-six or twenty-eight students. The load for one-on-one was eighteen, enough to serve the performance needs of the ensembles: four orchestras, two bands, and miscellaneous groups.

One year I told the students that, instead of grading the year, we would grade each lesson, together. At the end of a lesson I'd say, "What do you think the grade should be? I can't give you an A. Maybe a B minus or a C." That got their attention.

AN ASIDE

When Alec Wilder was not on a springtime vacation at Mitch Miller's estate on Grand Cayman Island or Tennessee Williams's home in Key West, he would call up to ask, "Are the locusts in bloom?"

"No, not yet," I would tell him.

"Well, call me when they are."

Alec would travel to Bloomington and would sit in our locust grove writing music, surrounded by the smell of the flowering trees. He would stay for two or three weeks, writing about the innocence of children, the innocence of nature, and the innocence of music. While in Bloomington, Alec would often come to the university with me and sit in the corner of my studio reading a book or writing music while I taught. He attended my sons' school functions with Carol and me. My home office is now in what used to be "Uncle Alec's room."

Alec was always upset that IU didn't have a faculty brass quintet, so he told me once, "Maybe if I write a quintet and dedicate it to the Indiana University Faculty Brass Quintet, they'll make one." So he did. Alec Wilder's *Brass Quintet No. 4* is dedicated to the IU Faculty Brass Quintet, yet it did not bring about the creation of such a group.

One day I received a phone call in my tuba studio. "Hello, Mr. Phillips? Please hold for President John Ryan."

He said, "Harvey, I've been hearing so much about the tuba that I want to learn more about it and I'd like to take lessons!"

I had the Conn Company send a brand new tuba to his on-campus residence. Each week, he and I would schedule a lesson, which would usually be on a Friday in his house. Afterward, we would have a scotch or bourbon and talk about the university and the School of Music. Occasionally he would see me in the audience at a faculty meeting and point me out as one of his trusted advisers.

STARTING THE HARVEY PHILLIPS FOUNDATION, 1978

For years I have added to the tuba repertoire by commissioning composers. They have usually been receptive to my pleas. No matter how busy they are, they listen and are open to discuss anything. Their minds are absorbed with sounds, old and new. I vowed never to give up the pursuit of new compositions from every composer of my acquaintance, and I continue to seek out composers, arrangers, orchestrators, composition teachers, and their gifted students. (I tried arranging, early on, but I didn't have the patience.) I couldn't always offer monetary commissions but usually managed some assistance with expenses of score duplication and extraction of parts. I was also helpful in securing publication, first performances, and sometimes showcase commercial recordings.

Alec Wilder observed that I was spending a lot of money underwriting projects to promote composers, musicians, music, and the tuba. For instance, when Fred Karlin came to New York, sent to me by Arnold Jacobs, it didn't take long for me to realize that he was an exceptional talent. I made other people aware of the talent of Fred Karlin, resulting in an album produced by Raymond Scott, *Jazzbo Collins Goes to the Opera,* featuring jazz musicians playing Fred's arrangements of opera arias. My favorite track was an aria from *Martha* played by Bobby Brookmeyer. Another album, which I produced with Fred doing arrangements, was *Three Examples of Stephen Foster,* featuring Phil Woods. This introduced Fred to record producers and others who could help his career as composer, orchestrator, and arranger, and broadened his contact with movie producers. He wound up in Hollywood.

During one of Alec's frequent visits to TubaRanch he got very angry with me and said, "Harvey, you've got to stop this. You can't keep spending your family's money—it's not your money; it's your family's money. It's your children's education and their future. It's your retirement. You can't continue to spend money this way." He went on, "There are many people who believe in what you are doing but you must provide a vehicle for them to help you. You need a private foundation."

"Would you be an officer of the foundation?" I teased. Alec hated any authority position. I was surprised that he reluctantly agreed, however, and became vice president of the foundation we were to form. Garnett Davis, tuba professor at Vanderbilt, became secretary-treasurer.

To find a name for our new organization, Carol and I stayed up late one night researching other foundations and looking up names in the thesaurus. We came up with more than twenty names we could live with, but we wanted to have Alec's input. A month or so later we were in New York and made reservations for breakfast with Alec in the Algonquin Hotel Rose Room. After we were served coffee and gave the waiter our order, I pushed the list across the table and said, "Tell me what you think."

He said, "What is this?"

"It's a list of names for the foundation that Carol and I can tolerate."

Alec didn't even look at the list. He wadded it up and threw it into the corner. "You have to use your name for the foundation because people who know you will know what it's about. You won't have to explain it."

The Harvey Phillips Foundation, Inc., is a not-for-profit, tax-exempt foundation dedicated to "developing, expanding and preserving the music arts." The foundation's goals are facilitated in part by providing scholarship assistance to selected established institutions offering academic and professional training to talented music students; assisting in the commissioning of new compositions; creating opportunities for public performances of unique ensembles; building public audiences for all music; presenting lectures and clinics which impart knowledge and understanding of the urgent and special needs of the music arts and developing musicians; and offering consultant services and public relations expertise to other not-for-profit music arts organizations. The Harvey Phillips Foundation has continued to commission composers such as David Baker, Warren Benson, Gunther Schuller, Bernhard Heiden, and Patrick Williams. While the foundation accepts donations, it continues to be primarily funded by my personal activities.

At the same time Alec was chastising me for not having a foundation, I received a handwritten letter from Traugott Rohner, founder of *The Instrumentalist*, America's leading music education publication. He said he had never known anyone so successful at promoting his cause. He suggested a foundation be formed to support my efforts.

JUDGE NOT

Chicago Chamber Music hosts an annual chamber music competition, and it has been my pleasure to serve on this committee on three occasions. The second year, I was on a judging panel with Felix Galimir, concertmaster of the Symphony of the Air; Ray Still, principal oboe of the Chicago Symphony; concert pianist Eugene Istomin; and George Rochberg, a composer in residence at Northern Illinois University. We had listened to the first day's competitors, which included a saxophone quartet, a woodwind quintet, and two string quartets. All the groups distinguished themselves, but the saxophone quartet had been especially spectacular. It was a good beginning for the three additional days yet to come. At the end of that first day, we were meeting in the lobby of our hotel prior to a dinner party at the Greek Isles restaurant with the trustees of Chicago Chamber Music. We were standing around waiting to collect all of our judges when I heard Eugene Istomin say to Felix Galimir, "I don't care how well they play—I would never vote for a saxophone quartet over a string quartet."

Carol, all happy, having toured and shopped the city all day, ready to go to dinner, walked up just in time to hear me tell him, "You are a pompous ass!"

Istomin abstained from dinner with the judges. The next morning, he got the attention of all the judges and said that he had thought about it all night and wanted to apologize to the committee. To me, he grew six feet taller with that admission. We all said, "That's okay."

Eugene Istomin was later making a visit to Indiana University to perform and give master classes, and I heard from some of the pianists that there was no reception planned. I had a party for him at TubaRanch. He played my piano and then signed it, and a wonderful time was had by all.

BILL BELL MEMORIAL CELEBRATION

In 1978, someone told Carol that he had stopped to visit Bill Bell's grave in Perry, Iowa, and that the gravestone was very plain, with a treble clef at the top and his name and dates of birth and death, 1902–1971. I visited with Mr. Bell's sister, Ruth Rankin, whom I'd met at Mr. Bell's last St. Patrick's Day party, to tell her what I had in mind for the gravestone. She was very pleased to learn there would be a bronze plaque made the exact size of the gravestone, to be attached following a memorial service. The bronze plaque listed a bibliography of his professional career and quoted Arturo Toscanini, who considered Bell the greatest tubist of the age.

The memorial service was held in a city park downtown. Music was provided by the Air Force North American Defense Band. My assistant at Indiana University, G. R. Davis, contacted the newspaper and mayor of Perry, Iowa, and kept them informed and involved. We provided music on this special occasion for some 120 tuba and euphonium players to rehearse and then perform downtown and in a service at the graveside. I conducted. The Harvey Phillips Foundation underwrote the costs for the first two years of memorial concerts, then passed it on to eager Iowa musicians, who have kept the event as an annual celebration.

DISTINGUISHED RANK

Distinguished Rank (in my case Distinguished Professor of Music) is the highest faculty position at Indiana University. This rank is bestowed by the trustees. It was awarded to me at IU Founders Day ceremonies in April 1979.

A departmental Distinguished Rank Committee considers candidates. It is unusual for more than one a year to be approved. This name goes to the dean of the school, at which time the candidate is notified and asked to submit names of those who might provide outside letters of recommendation. The dean solicits opinions from those whose names the candidate has given to him and adds other names. He makes a recommendation, based on the responses he received, and informs the dean of faculties, who makes a recommendation to the IU president. If he approves, it goes to the trustees.

INDEPENDENCE DAY CELEBRATION

In the spring of 1982 I received a telephone call from the chairman of the July 4 celebration in Evanston, Illinois. I was asked about providing an all-tuba band to appear at the town's annual celebration, which, due to conflicts, was scheduled for Monday, July 5. I agreed to recruit tubists of all ages from throughout the greater Evanston and Chicago area and would provide the appropriate music for our concert. Later, at a committee meeting, it was announced that an important developer of Evanston properties had to resign as honorary marshal to be with his wife, who was seriously ill. I suggested that since they were having a tuba band, the prominent and esteemed tubist of the Chicago Symphony Orchestra would be a worthy replacement. After some discussion, it was agreed and I provided the committee chair with Arnold Jacobs's phone number and address. I then notified Arnold to expect a call. He was called in due course and agreed to be honorary marshal for the parade and concert.

The day of the parade the weather was beautiful and Arnold Jacobs was transported in an antique convertible. Arnold had a great time waving to the thousands of people lining the parade route. I don't think any other Independence Day parade ever had a more distinguished honorary marshal. Basil Wentworth, one of my older grad students, did a great job arranging patriotic music, including George M. Cohan songs. I was proud of our recruited all-tuba-euphonium band. The concert we presented preceded the fireworks display.

Basil Wentworth's career was with the State Department. My first letter from him was from Australia. He and his wife Jocelyn were thinking of retiring to Bloomington, Indiana, so he could study tuba with me. And they did. She always carries a tuba bell through the crowd at TubaSantas concerts in Bloomington, collecting donations for The Salvation Army, and she was Carol's indispensible sergeant in preparing for our OctubaFeasts.

FLYING TUBA

In 1980, I was flying to Chadron, Nebraska, for a clinic and made a connecting flight out of Denver. Bill Winkle, the tuba professor at Chadron State College, was with his tuba ensemble to greet me at the airport when I got off the plane. It didn't happen. Shortly outside of Denver, we felt a big bump and the captain let us know that the plane had hit a goose and that it had knocked out our radar. We would have to land. We touched down in Sidney, Nebraska. Perhaps a dozen of us from the plane were herded into the terminal. I went to the desk to ask when the plane would be leaving and the clerk said that it would be leaving in a few hours, later that evening. A couple in their eighties, traveling to celebrate their fiftieth anniversary, were sitting in chairs in the terminal. The pilot and co-pilot came down the hall joking and laughing and had their maps and overnight bags. I asked the man, "Are you the captain of our flight?"

"Yes."

"What time will the plane be leaving?"

"It's not going out this evening."

I knew that many of us were not budgeted for an extra night in a hotel. In a loud voice, I told the clerk, "You owe every passenger on that plane a hotel room!" Everyone in the room could hear. It was done. The next morning, we got on the repaired plane and flew to our destination.

I took two one-semester sabbaticals during my twenty-three-year tenure at IU. Gary Bird subbed for my first sabbatical and Michael Lind covered the second one. This gave me more time for the family and for clinics. My tuba and I would always fly to these appearances. Sometimes I would charter a flight, because it was cheaper than going commercial and also allowed me to leave at 2:00 in the morning if I needed to. Most times, however, I would travel on an airline. The tuba can be a very delicate instrument and I sometimes worried that it would be dropped like any other luggage. I had very good luck with my tuba and never had any major damage until 1990, when we flew from Japan to San Francisco on our way to Spokane, Washington. I was going to teach and perform at the Festival at Sandpoint in Idaho. When I arrived in Spokane, the tuba did not. My luggage was there, but no tuba.

I went ahead to the festival. I had flown into the Spokane airport for several years running, and got to know the baggage people and airport managers. That evening, I got a call from the baggage master at the airport that my tuba was severely damaged. I had the tuba player from the Spokane Symphony go out and look at the instrument, and he and the airport manager agreed that I didn't want to see it. It had fallen forty feet and had been run over by a truck. The bell was crushed. I had bought the insurance policy that they usually offered, and I ordered my instrument to be shipped directly to Larry Minic, the famed instrument repairman in California. He put everything aside to work on it. He was instructed by United Airlines that $250 was all they would pay. He told them that the owner of the tuba was a friend of his and that he was going to see that justice was done. The airline paid over $6,000 to have the instrument repaired.

When I first started flying so much in the mid-1950s, I could find places on most airplanes where my instrument would fit, in a coat closet or behind a back seat. I had to make sure that the seat couldn't recline and smash the tuba. After that, the airlines made a ruling that passengers had to strap any oversize carry-ons to the seat. Now, this was any seat at first, but then they insisted that it be a window seat so a passenger didn't have to climb over the carry-on. Then the airlines adopted a policy of requiring half fare for the tuba, and later they both charged half fare and required the carry-on to be next to a window.

Many times, someone would say, "Excuse me, I'd like to sit there."

"I'm sorry, but the seat's taken and paid for," I would reply.

The next outrageous policy was that I could ride economy class, but the tuba had to go first class. I appreciated this recognition of the instrument but opposed the cost. They got rid of that quickly enough, so I went back to strapping it to a window seat, paying half fare. I kidded the flight attendants that they should bring me two meals. After all that, I checked my tuba in its case, as baggage.

THE HOAGY CARMICHAEL JAZZ SOCIETY

Hoagy Carmichael died on December 27, 1981. The memorial ceremony for him took place in the foyer of the IU Musical Arts Center in January 1982. Performing were David Baker, cello; George Gaber, percussion; Eugene Rousseau, saxophone; Dominic Spera, trumpet; Harvey Phillips, tuba; Charles Webb, piano; and Sylvia McNair, soprano. In Alec Wilder's book *The American Popular Song 1900–1950*, he identified Hoagy as the most jazz-oriented of all the pop music composers. Born, educated, and buried in Bloomington, Hoagy was always proud of his Indiana roots.

I thought that someone so famous in music should be recognized by his hometown and I formed the Hoagy Carmichael Jazz Society (HCJS) in 1982. The first four artists performing for it were world-famous jazz pianists. Our inaugural concert featured Dave McKenna in the downtown Second Story jazz club. Anyone in Bloomington could come. All of the featured artists, that year and in following years, were good friends of mine and provided their support by appearing at minimum professional fees. They each also provided a master class at the university at no charge.

The second night's festivities, with Dave McKenna, took place at Tuba-Ranch. The entire event went incredibly well. I made sure the piano at the Second Story matched the one I had at home. While in Bloomington, Dave McKenna recorded a CD for Concord Records called *A Celebration of Hoagy Carmichael,* featuring the live performances at the Second Story and the TubaRanch (where we put all the living room furniture out on the deck to accommodate the crowd listening to Dave). The alternate "relief" for Dave McKenna was provided by Bloomington's own Royal Garden Irregulars, featuring Frank Gillis, piano; Jack Ost, cornet; Dave Pavolka, trombone; Harvey Phillips, tuba; Karl Schuessler, clarinet; George Bohrnstedt, tenor sax; Gary Potter, bass; and Ron Brashear, drums. We were fortunate to have obtained the services of my good friend Dave McKenna for this important inaugural occasion.

In 1984, the HCJS sponsored Hoagy Carmichael Festival week, November 12–16. Other artists performing for the Hoagy Carmichael Jazz Society included Dick Hyman (1984), Frank Gillis (1986), Roger Kellaway (who composed and played the closing theme for *All in the Family*) (1987), and trombonist Urbie Green (1984) appearing with Bloomington's own Al Cobine and his band. Marian McPartland appeared as guest artist in 1985. Her popularity demanded a larger venue and this was provided by the IU Auditorium. I set up a luncheon for Marian and leading businesswomen and lady jazz fans at the Irish Lion, a favored pub downtown. The role of hostess was filled by Charlotte Zietlow.

We sponsored the naming of the auditorium at Bloomington High School South for Hoagy Carmichael. Present for this dedication were his son, Hoagy Bix, who joined Mayor Tomilea Allison and other dignitaries. A permanent bronze plaque acknowledging the Hoagy Carmichael Auditorium, donated by the Harvey Phillips Foundation, was attached to the wall of the auditorium.

Another goal of the HCJS was the renaming of Seventh Street to honor Hoagy. Unfortunately, some residents of Seventh Street objected because it made their street address too long. Renaming the street made sense because a childhood home of Hoagy's was two houses away from Seventh and Dunn Streets and one block from Dunn Meadow, where he played as a boy and where the idea for the tune of "Stardust" came into his mind. Hoagy rushed from Dunn Meadow to the nearby Book Nook, which had a piano, on which he quickly composed "Stardust." Also, the Book Nook, a student hangout, is across the street from the IU law school, from which he graduated.

Hoagy had a good ear for music, especially his own. Shortly after graduation, he was engaged by a law firm in Florida. One day he happened to hear one of his melodies coming from a radio outside his office window. It was enough for him to resign his law position and return to music.

When Dick Hyman played at the Second Story, he directed me to turn off amplification of the piano, because of the noisy audience. Suddenly, with the piano heard softly, people who had been greeting friends and loudly ordering drinks began to whisper. Hyman later did a great master class with Luke Gillespie, then a student. They were seated facing each other at two concert grand pianos without lids. Hyman let Luke choose a selection and play the introduction and first chorus. Then Hyman played Luke's solo, almost note for note, demonstrating the importance of "call and response," so important to creative jazz improvisation.

Establishing the Hoagy Carmichael Jazz Society in 1982 was just one of the things I did, *not* because I needed something to do in my busy schedule, but because it was something for the community and should have been done long before. When I observed what I felt would bring the university and Bloomington community together, I shared my thoughts with anyone who would listen. A good listener and good friend in this regard was Mayor Allison. When I suggested a portable stage that could serve Monroe County and the city of Bloomington, "taking programs to the community," Mayor Allison was listening and took action on this suggestion. It is still used today. One group that uses the portable stage is the TubaSantas.

A businessman and good friend, Dick Schmaltz, who understood how overcommitted I was and had spoken to other people about it, recruited a local personality who agreed in a meeting of the three of us at the Schmaltz home to take charge of the Hoagy Carmichael Jazz Society, as president. He was to contact me for the paper records. I never heard from him and there were no more activities by the HCJS.

The president of Bloomington Hospital, Bud Kohr, had an idea to raise money for the hospital with a TubaSantas concert, which raised quite a bit of money. I had served on some committees with the newspaper, bringing in service bands and other things, and made friends with committee members, including Bud Kohr. I took my tuba ensemble to the Rotary Club and gave them some entertainment at their Tuesday lunches. That's how I got acquainted with a lot of local citizens.

EXECUTIVE EDITOR OF *THE INSTRUMENTALIST*

Ann Driscoll, the executive editor of *The Instrumentalist,* came to Bloomington in 1983 to interview me for an article. She asked about my upcoming schedule, which included a trip to the University of Wisconsin-Milwaukee for a concert. She suggested that I meet Traugott Rohner, the publisher, on my way to Wisconsin. She was leaving her position within a year and thought I would be a good source of articles for the magazine through my many professional contacts in the jazz and classical music worlds. Although she didn't say anything, she was thinking of me as her replacement.

I stopped in Northfield, Illinois, as requested, and had a very pleasant meeting with Mr. Rohner and some of the editors. The meeting ended with my being invited to an advisory position with the magazine. I agreed that it was important to have articles by professional musicians to complement and balance articles by middle school and high school teachers. I accepted the position with the understanding that I would be permitted to schedule my visits to *The Instrumentalist* around my professional performing and teaching schedules, to which I was previously committed. I enjoyed the opportunity and the challenge of working with the magazine. Before the year was out, I was made executive editor.

The largest portion of subscribers were teachers. I tried to give broader coverage to academia through professional artists who were invited to contribute articles of mutual interest to the magazine. I served for eight years as executive editor, writing feature articles about friends and conducting interviews that became articles. Two of the articles won publishers' awards. Every time I could arrange a trip to Chicago, I would include *The Instrumentalist* in my schedule. I would meet with the publisher to discuss philosophy, high school music, clinicians, elementary education, and college music. I still serve on the advisory board of the magazine.

ALBUM 2

Right. Harvey Phillips playing
the tuba in a recital, 1977.

Harvey Phillips with his two
greatest heroes, 1968: his teacher
Bill Bell, left, and Merle Evans,
conductor of the Ringling Bros. and
Barnum & Bailey Circus Band.

Facing top. Confucius, the Chinese goose, on
Harvey's lap as Harvey practices his tuba out in the
yard at TubaRanch, Bloomington, early 1970s.

Facing bottom. Attendees at the First International
Tuba Symposium-Workshop, 1973. It was the first event
at Indiana University's new Musical Arts Center.

Above. Merle Evans, conductor of the Ringling Bros.
and Barnum & Bailey Circus Band for fifty years, is
invited to Indiana University to be honored, 1974.
He poses between Little Harvey, left, and Thomas
Phillips. Top row: Harvey, Jesse, and Carol.

Always eager to inspire young musicians, Harvey Phillips performs with a high school band in Kenosha, Wisconsin, 1974.

Left. Doc Severinsen—a friend since Harvey's New York days, on the IU campus in 1974 to give a concert—announces one of the concerts at OctubaFest.

Harvey Phillips conducts at a tuba–euphonium symposium in Chadron, Nebraska, 1975.

Left. Harvey Phillips, wearing badges from each year's TubaChristmas, arrives in Tampa, Florida, for its TubaChristmas in 1992.

Below. Harvey Phillips sings while Frederick Fennell, considered the greatest conductor of wind bands since Sousa, turns from the massed tubas to conduct an audience sing-along at TubaChristmas in Chicago.

TubaChristmas fills a Hilton Hotel lobby in Chicago.

Above. TubaChristmas at CNN Center in Atlanta, 1998.

Facing top. Harvey Phillips interviewing composer Morton Gould for *The Instrumentalist* magazine, ca. 1990.

Harvey Phillips with composer-pianist John Lewis, who composed music which was recorded as *The Golden Striker.* Harvey was always proud of having performed on that recording.

Above. Harvey Phillips, tuba, and Rich Matteson,
euphonium, in Australia to perform in their band,
the Matteson-Phillips TubaJazz Consort, 1978.

Harvey Phillips throws his tuba into the air in front of tuba
students at OctubaFest at the TubaRanch, 1982. *Star* photo
by Jeff Atteberry. Courtesy of the *Indianapolis Star*.

Facing. Chitate Kagawa with Harvey, his tuba, Carol, and
son Thomas, 2004, during a visit to the Phillips family
home. Kagawa, tubist in the Sapporo Symphony, and
the Phillips family forged a bond when in 1972 he came
from Japan to take lessons with Harvey Phillips.

Above. Harvey Phillips and his sons, 1983.
From left: Harvey Jr., Thomas, and Jesse.

Above. Tubists surround a tubist, 2009. Standing, from left: Bob Tucci, Jim Self; front row: Dan Perantoni, Harvey Phillips, Winston Morris.

Facing top. Harvey Phillips and the typist of his memoirs, Mary Campbell.

John Baker, trombonist in the Spokane Symphony, organized and named a series of tuba–euphonium concerts held in various cities in the northwest. The Harvey Phillips Big Brass Bash held its twentieth anniversary in 2006.

Above. Harvey talks with Gwyn Richards, dean of
the Indiana University Jacobs School of Music.

Gunther Schuller, president of the New England
Conservatory of Music in Boston, prepares to confer an
honorary doctorate of music on Harvey Phillips, 1971.
Dean of students Chester Williams stands at right.

Above. Indiana University president John Ryan, right, meets with the newly honored distinguished professors in 1979. Harvey Phillips is standing on left.

Right. The University of Missouri, from which Harvey Phillips dropped out during his freshman year to join the Ringling Bros. and Barnum & Bailey Circus Band, awards him an honorary doctorate of humanities, 1987.

Harvey Phillips's family proudly attends his induction into the Classical Music Hall of Fame, Cincinnati, 2008. From left: sons Thomas, Harvey, and Jesse, and wife Carol. Harvey was the first wind instrument player to be inducted.

Indiana University president Michael A. McRobbie confers the President's Medal, for sustained academic excellence, on Harvey Phillips, distinguished professor emeritus of music, and Denis Sinor, distinguished professor of Central Eurasian studies, right, 2008. It is the highest honor that an IU president can bestow.

During the ceremony in which President McRobbie bestowed the President's
Medal on Harvey Phillips, IU Jacobs School of Music professor of horn
Jeff Nelson, professor of tuba Dan Perantoni, and emeritus Dean Charles
Webb performed Alec Wilder's *Suite for Horn, Tuba, and Piano No. 2*. Wilder
composed it for John Barrows and Harvey Phillips, who recorded it with
pianist Milton Kaye. After the ceremony, from left, Nelson, Perantoni, and
Webb joined Tom Phillips and Carol Phillips in congratulating Harvey.

CHAPTER FIFTEEN

Carnegie Hall Recitals

FOR SEVERAL YEARS, some of my colleagues, both composers and performers, suggested that I do a Carnegie Hall recital. I resisted the temptation because I felt my teacher, William J. Bell, should present one first. In 1961, Roger Bobo, a tubist wunderkind, on his graduation from the Eastman School of Music, presented the first solo tuba recital in New York City's Carnegie Hall. I was unable to attend Roger's concert but I know it was excellent from our mutual friend Alec Wilder. Alec not only attended the concert but wrote "Encore for Tuba" especially for Roger Bobo's recital. William Bell passed away on August 7, 1971, without ever having performed a solo recital in Carnegie Hall.

I did not get around to performing a solo tuba recital until January 1975. That month, I presented five recitals in nine days in Carnegie Recital Hall, sponsored by the Carnegie Hall Corporation. My purpose in doing five recitals was to illustrate the growing repertoire and acceptance of the tuba as a solo instrument. A number of colleagues assisted the performances, but none of the professional players, with whom I worked consistently, would accept payment. Preparation for the nine days consumed sixty-seven hours of rehearsal, some in Boston. One started at midnight with the New York Saxophone Quartet; it was the only time everybody could get together.

One was in Bloomington with IU School of Music Dean Charles Webb, who was my piano accompanist on one of the five recitals.

If the tuba was going to become a solo instrument, we needed repertoire and artists who could sustain it. I had worked with many composers over the years and encouraged hundreds of pieces for the instrument. (But I never tried to tell a composer what to write.) I had a grand scheme in mind that the tuba could be established—not just tolerated—as a solo instrument. How important would the string quartet be if its repertoire, for the first hundred years of its existence, had to suffer the same quality and scarcity of repertoire imposed on the tuba? By the 1970s, we were not playing tuba music; we were playing music on the tuba.

I wanted to include a total of thirty-nine works, including eighteen premieres, over those nine days. I wanted to establish an awareness of repertoire in the eyes and ears of my fellow musicians and the critical press. The recitals did that.

At every recital, I would recognize each composer if he was in the audience. Alec came to every recital and, feigning shyness, would always tell me not to recognize him after I played his piece. He said, "I don't want to bow. Don't make me bow, please." However, after playing one of his compositions, I would announce Alec's presence to the audience and, with the usual gesture, ask him to stand. On hearing his name as he was recognized, he would be up on the stage in a flash, grinning from ear to ear. I knew there was enough child in him never to turn down a bow.

Whitney Balliett of the *New Yorker* was with me at every New York rehearsal, and every taxi ride from rehearsal to concert and rehearsal to rehearsal, for the five solo recitals in Carnegie Hall. In all the time we spent together, I never saw Whitney take a note or record anything. He became a buddy who was with me everywhere I went, and he helped me with my tuba, briefcase, or music as I prepared for the January 5–12, 1975, marathon in Carnegie Recital Hall. His recollection of our conversations in his eventual profile of me was absolutely amazing.

The last concert in the series took place on Sunday, January 12, 1975. After it ended, I went to the Roosevelt Hotel with the Composers String Quartet and played a command performance of David Baker's *Sonata for Tuba and String Quartet* for the Charles Colin New York Brass Conference for Scholarships. We had just premiered the sonata at Carnegie Recital Hall.

The next day, I was scheduled to be at the New England Conservatory in Boston to record the Ralph Vaughan Williams *Tuba Concerto* and Gunther Schuller's *Capriccio for Solo Tuba and Chamber Orchestra*. The recording was scheduled at the conservatory to convenience the student orchestra, all of whom resided in the Boston area. The time reserved was from 7 to 10 PM. Unfortunately, January 13 suffered a blizzard from New York to Boston. We left early. Carol and a student, Ronald Lee Spencer, tried driving but couldn't deal with the icy roads, so I drove. What should have been a four-hour drive turned out to take eight hours, even though we were starting from our recital series headquarters at Carol's sister Elsie's home in Armonk, New York, an hour's drive north of New York City.

We drove through snow and sleet, driving no faster than 20 MPH. There were trucks jackknifed and passenger cars skidded and facing every direction. Carol was especially concerned about our three boys and objected to the chances I was taking. She didn't think all the orchestra would show and thought the recording would be canceled.

We arrived at the front of the conservatory a little before 8:00. Gunther Schuller, all the orchestra players, and the studio personnel were there on time and spent an hour rehearsing sections of both works. It took me a good ten minutes to warm up my instrument and play a couple of scales before we started to record. Somehow we managed to finish on time. Carol and the boys were real troupers and found a warm and comfortable office to relax in. I could never thank those students enough for keeping their commitment with such professional conscience. And I have to include my own family for the enormous sacrifice and understanding.

I felt that my having presented a mini-marathon of five recitals in January 1975 justified presenting ten recitals of selected colleagues, including my own solo recital, at Carnegie Recital Hall in the concert season of fall 1975–1976. My rationale: what valid recognition could there be for the tuba as a recital instrument if only one or two players were exercising the right and privilege? How popular could any other instrument be with limited repertoire and few solo opportunities? I wanted to present some of the outstanding tubists I considered to be soloists. The series opened with Roger Bobo, followed by Daniel Perantoni, John Turk, myself, Bob Whaley, J. Lesley Varner, Barton Cummings, the Tennessee Tech Tuba Ensemble directed by Winston Morris, and outstanding euphonium soloist Brian Bowman, and ended with tubist Floyd Cooley. I felt these soloists and ensembles, and the works they inspired, were a good representation of the tuba family's deserved position as viable solo and ensemble instruments.

This is represented by the musicians' individual choices of repertoire. I premiered Alec Wilder's *Sonata No. 2 for Tuba and Piano,* dedicated to Lottie Phillips. My other concerts at Carnegie Hall featured a number of premieres, including Vincent Persichetti's *Parable* and *Serenade No. 12 for Solo Tuba* and Bernhard Heiden's *Variations for Solo Tuba and Nine Horns,* which I played with the Valhalla Horn Choir. A New York premiere of Thomas Beversdorf's *Sonata for Tuba and Piano,* Ed Sauter's *Eight Random Thoughts for Solo Tuba,* John Downey's *Tabu for Tuba,* Halsey Stevens's *Sonatina for Tuba and Piano,* and Gregory Fritze's *OctubaFest Polka* were heard. A world premiere of Dick Hyman's *Requiem for Pee Wee Erwin for Tuba and Piano;* Steven Harlos's *Legend for Tuba, Horn, and Piano,* written for me, Daniel Katzen of the Boston Symphony, and the composer; Charles Eakin's *Capriccio for Tuba Alone;* Irwin Bazelon's *For Tuba with Strings (Quartet);* and Harris Hubble's *Elegy for Jimmy,* dedicated to the memory of Jimmy Burke, were all included.

I kept playing recitals at Carnegie Hall through the late 1980s, at the rate of one or two every year. I had premieres on every concert. One of those concerts was a tribute to friends who were no longer living: I dedicated pieces to John Barrows, Bill Bell, Tom Beversdorf, Jim Buffington, Jimmy Burke, Pee Wee Erwin, and Ed Sauter. I played the solo tuba piece Ed composed, *Eight Random Thoughts.* Among pieces written for me were a second one for tuba and string quartet (after David Baker) by Jan Bach of DeKalb, Illinois. I played it in Carnegie and we rehearsed it in John Carisi's apartment. We planned to record it but I was without energy that week; we never got back together to record.

My grand plan was to showcase a series of ten tuba solo recitals each concert season, with heavy programming of new compositions with various ensembles. I realized one or two recitals could not establish the tuba as a solo instrument with repertoire equal to that of any other wind instrument. The first set of ten recitals was 1975–1976. There have been thirty-three concert seasons since then, but only one series of ten realized.

The workload for preparing a concert was enormous. I had no budget for advertising, for typesetting and printing, for researching biographical materials of the artists and composers involved, for arranging contracts with the hall, or for locating convenient rehearsal space. I did everything myself. This was in addition to my IU teaching schedule and my clinic appearances, and it was too much for me to handle without considerable assistance. Many new works came about because of this concert series, but if I had had the wherewithal to take care of the countless administrative details, the 2009–2010 concert season would be showcasing the desired yearly ten recitals and would now total 340 recitals. Taking into account the hope of one world premiere for each concert, there would be 340 new compositions to enhance our current repertoire. I think of where we might be today if my intention could have been realized.

It was, and is, my hope that all my tuba- and euphonium-playing colleagues will continue inspiring and supporting commissions of important new works by their composer friends. No instrument can rise above its repertoire.

After meeting David Baker in 1959 on a New York recording session, I commissioned him to write a piece using tuba. We ran into each other at a National Association of Jazz Educators reception in Chicago, and I asked him how the piece was coming along. He said, "Okay. It's coming along okay."

I asked, "What's it for?" He rather wildly looked around, saw a poster on the wall of a string quartet, and said, "Tuba and string quartet." So he started writing his *Sonata for Tuba and String Quartet.*

John Carisi had promised me that he would compose a new piece for the Carnegie Hall recital series but his commitments were such that he didn't get it done. He was embarrassed that he hadn't been able to fulfill his commitment, so he asked if it would be possible for him to come to Bloomington and visit us at TubaRanch while he composed. He was impressed by the David Baker piece for tuba and string quartet and he had decided that that would be the instrumentation of his new work for tuba. We welcomed John to TubaRanch, and he stayed with us in the old house for three weeks writing his *Suite for Solo Tuba and String Quartet.*

I played John Carisi's new piece for the first time in Carnegie Hall at least a year later, on another of my scheduled concerts. On that same concert I premiered another work for tuba and string quartet by Manny Albam. At that concert the Albam and Carisi works were preceded by a performance of Ed Sauter's *Eight Random Thoughts,* composed during the First International Tuba Symposium Workshop in 1973. My schedule was such that I found it impossible to attend rehearsals in New York City with the Primavera String Quartet (Martha Caplin, first violin; Deborah Berlin, second violin; Diann Jezurski Pilafian, viola; and Melissa Meell, cello). My good friend Sam Pilafian rehearsed with the quartet for me and I came in for one working rehearsal and one dress rehearsal. To show my gratitude to Sam I asked each of the three composers on the program to write a duet for Sam and me. In taking a bow at the end of the program, I told the audience what Sam had done for me and as an encore asked him to perform a new work with me for two tubas in three movements, a movement by each of the composers. Sam and I had found time to rehearse the duets beforehand. I dedicated the piece to Sam Pilafian. Manny Albam's title for his work, *The Odd Couple,* was given to all three movements, a heartfelt tongue-in-cheek title.

Melvin Culbertson, who played in the West Point Band and was a student studying with me, presented a Carnegie Hall recital in 1968. I did a duet with him on that recital and he premiered Alec Wilder's *Jesse Suite.*

Some of our fine American brass players, eager to get their careers underway, were attracted to working in Europe, which seemed to offer more professional performance opportunities and had more opera companies with full-time employment than the United States had. American tubists Roger Bobo, Mel Culbertson, and Robert Tucci have been particularly influential in Europe. Roger Bobo won the principal tuba chair with the Concertgebouw in Amsterdam in 1962, and through his recital and master class schedule was a tremendous influence to the low brass players throughout Europe. In 1964 he won the principal tuba position with the Los Angeles Philharmonic and returned to the United States. After retirement from the Los Angeles Philharmonic in 1989, he settled in Florence, Italy, establishing himself as one of Europe's most popular brass soloists. Roger has now moved to Japan and continues to tour throughout the world, giving master classes and solo recitals while he also pursues another career as a conductor.

Mel was an influence through his work in France and Spain, as was Robert Tucci through his work in German-speaking countries. Both established themselves with their personalities and their performances and have toured throughout Europe, giving master classes. Both have unselfishly passed along the American school of performance. Mel teaches at the Conservatoire National Superieur de Musique de Lyon, France, and Bob Tucci, who started in Europe at the Vienna Symphony, Vienna State Opera, and Vienna Philharmonic, teaches at the Hochschule fur Musik in Stuttgart, Germany. Mel performs with the French Radio Orchestra, a position he won by audition in 1976, and Bob performs with the Bavarian State Opera in Munich.

For several years, every time there were orchestral auditions for tuba or horn in Europe, the position was won by an American-trained performer. European horn and tuba players have finally started winning some of their respective country's first-desk positions. Japanese tubists also started winning positions in American and other orchestras throughout the world.

Other American tubists in Europe include Thomas Walsh, Munich; David Le Clair, Basil; and Daryl Smith, Turin and La Scalla. I cannot overlook the Scandinavian countries, which have produced performer/teachers Michael Lind, Jens Bjorn-Larsen, Geir Lovold, and Oystein Baadsvik. All have had careers as soloists as well as in the orchestra.

ALEC

Alec had known Frank Sinatra since the Dorsey days and they were friends. Sinatra even conducted an album of selections from Alec's octets, and also recorded some of Alec's popular songs. Sinatra would call the proprietor at the Algonquin Hotel Tobacco Shop and Newsstand to see how Alec was getting along whenever he realized Alec wasn't feeling well.

In Chicago, while appearing at the 1980 Midwest Band and Orchestra Clinic and presenting TubaChristmas, I received a call from Alec's doctor in Gainesville, Florida, telling me that if I wanted to see Alec, I had better do it before Christmas, because my friend was fading. I canceled my Tuba-Christmas appearances in Dallas and Los Angeles and flew to Gainesville. On the way there I had to go through Atlanta, which was iced in. This delayed my visit with Alec for one full day.

When I got to his hospital room, he saw me and I don't know if he knew who I was. I told him, "Squeeze my hand once for yes and twice for no." As I talked about our strong friendship, he did squeeze my hand a few times. A few minutes before midnight on Christmas Eve, 1980, the nurse came in to give him a shot and I left. Alec passed away that night.

It is a matter of history how much writing Alec did for tuba as a recital instrument. He wrote ten tuba duets; ten tuba trios; ten tuba quartets; eight brass quintets; two trios for horn, tuba, and piano; a sonata for string bass, tuba, and piano; three convalescence suites for solo tuba, of six movements each; "Song for Carol"; a suite of four movements for each of our three sons; *Suite for a Friend* (dedicated to Ethan Ayer); *Concerto for Tuba and Concert Band* (which I premiered with the Air Force Band); and "Elegy for the Whale." There may be others on someone's piano.

The Friends of Alec Wilder group was organized to perform concerts honoring him. The initial concert was held in Carnegie Recital Hall in February 1985, a little over four years after Alec's death (he was born February 16, 1907, and died on December 24, 1980). The program format was to feature, from his multitude of admiring friends, performances that showcased his chamber music and art songs on the Saturday afternoon closest to his February 16 birthdate. Alec was so adored and admired that I thought his friends would jump at the chance to show their affection for him. I was right on all counts. Each year's concert would have a guest host and artists who wanted to participate. The idea was for each host to share with the audience personal experiences with Alec.

I served as host for the first concert—should it be unsuccessful I could shoulder the criticism. Manny Albam wrote a generic arrangement of Alec's "I'll Be Around" that could be played by any combination of instruments. Musicians were invited to bring their instruments. "I'll Be Around" (without rehearsal) closed the first three or four concerts. Gilda Weisberger and Elaine Georges of the Carnegie Hall Corporation were very helpful in securing the dates I required.

In a meeting with Andrew Anspach, manager of the Algonquin Hotel, we agreed that since the hotel was Alec's home for the last fifty years of his life it would be the unofficial home of the Alec Wilder tributes. After the first concert, the audience was invited to the Algonquin for cocktails and hors d'oeuvres in a suite of rooms on the second floor of the hotel. During dinner hour those who had made reservations for a formal dinner party toasting Alec went to the Algonquin's Oak Room.

When I realized how much we were paying for electricians to run the sound system at Carnegie Hall, at the suggestion of Carol Conover I approached Rev. John Garcia Gensel, known as the jazz pastor of New York, about doing the concerts at St. Peter's Church. We moved there. I paid less for the sanctuary, sound system, living room, dressing rooms, piano tuning, and kitchen than I had for Carnegie Recital Hall's sound system, and we had the reception under the same roof. Each concert was unique; one year photographer Louis Ouzer brought photos of Alec from his teenage years. I still typed the programs and folded them. Michael Salzman ran the sound system and brought a birthday cake each year.

The nature of the event and the person for whom it was a tribute filled the church. Before the third Alec Wilder tribute concert, the Algonquin Hotel was sold to Japanese interests. The Friends of Alec Wilder continue to gather on the Saturday closest to Alec's birthday to pay tribute to our dear friend. The Harvey Phillips Foundation underwrote the first nine concerts.

MORE ASIDES

Twentieth Century Innovations and Meet the Composer presented two recitals in Carnegie Hall in January 1980. I played on both and so did the Indiana University String Quartet: Peter DeVries and Karen Chown, violins; David Johnson, viola; and Anthony Ross, cello. The program for January 6 was Persichetti's *Serenade No. 12 for Solo Tuba*, Hindemith's *Sonata for Tuba and Piano*, Halsey Stevens's *Sonatina for Tuba and Piano*, and Jan Bach's *Quintet for Tuba and Strings*. Charles H. Webb assisted as the pianist. The program for January 13 began with Ed Sauter's *Eight Random Thoughts for Solo Tuba,* John Carisi's *Sounds and Silences* for tuba and string quartet, Manny Albam's *Quintet for Tuba and Strings,* and Wilder's *Sonata No. 1 for Tuba and Piano.* Frederick Moyer was the pianist. The Bach, Carisi, and Albam pieces were premiere performances. Maureen Meloy served as liaison between the producers and the Harvey Phillips Foundation in producing these programs.

While in the Navy in Washington, D.C., Don Waldrop was studying with both Don Yaxley on bass trombone and myself on tuba. Halsey Stevens was one of Yaxley's closest friends, so Halsey was asked if he would write something our mutual student could do on either instrument. Halsey Stevens said of course he'd be happy to do a sonata or something.

Don said, "What will this commission cost me?"

"Two dollars," Halsey replied. It was agreed. Some time went by before Yaxley received a package with music from Halsey Stevens. Don got all excited and put two one-dollar bills and a note thanking his composer friend in an envelope and immediately mailed the letter. With a speed some remember from the post office, Yaxley received an envelope containing a one-dollar bill and a note that said, "It's only a sonatina."

I met Pat Williams in the recording studios in New York City in the early 1960s; we knew a lot of the same people. Pat was a graduate of Duke University and while he was a student inherited the directorship of Les Brown's Band of Renown, which had been a regular on Bob Hope's radio show. Pat had an arranging style all his own and I admired his talent. Somehow we hit it off and became good friends. One of our mutual friends was Marion Evans, a very busy and successful arranger. He was so successful that he bought a chair on the New York Stock Exchange and curtailed his arranging assignments. Pat invited me to work with him on many exciting projects, some of which were successful, some nearly successful, and all of which were ahead of their time. We collaborated on projects at Duke University and in Atlanta, Denver, and New York City.

Pat wrote the score for the movie *Breaking Away.* The film was based on Indiana University's Little 500 bicycle race, which takes place in April each year. Pat's score was nominated for an Academy Award. In 1980, the year after the movie had become a success, it was screened again in Bloomington for the anniversary of its release. As people were walking into the Town Theater for another showing, my tuba ensemble played themes from the movie, arranged for us by Pat with Sammy Nestico's help.

In the movie, the main character falls in love with one of the sorority girls and serenades her with his guitar from underneath her sorority house window. To commemorate the film, Tom Hirons, a publicist in Bloomington, had me go with my tuba to the same sorority house. I played themes from the opera *Martha,* just like in the movie. The sorority girls came out to watch and swoon and the whole event was filmed and shown on local television.

Victor Ruthig, the organizer of entertainment for the Indiana Pacers, heard about all the things I had been doing with tubas and was intrigued. I received a call in 1980 requesting an all-tuba marching band for the opening of the Pacers season. I recruited by invitation some forty to fifty tuba players from throughout the state to participate as an ensemble I dubbed TubaCompany. After a quick rehearsal immediately before the show, we marched all the officials from the Hilton Hotel to the Market Square Arena. Owner Mel Simon led the parade of officials wearing tuxedos and their wives dressed in formal gowns. The TubaCompany was attired in blue bow ties and red NBA-logo vests ordered by the promoter. We also provided halftime music during the basketball game and it turned out to be a spectacular event.

The following year, the NBA Finals were coming to Indianapolis. I recruited a group more than twice as large as the one before. When the show was over, I asked the promoter what he was going to do with the vests and light blue bow ties. He had no plans for them, so I said I wanted them. We sewed a "TUBACOMPANY" patch over the NBA logo on the vest and the TubaCompany had its permanent uniform. Two CD recordings later, the TubaCompany still plays important engagements and was a featured group at the Festival of Hope in Hope, Indiana, each September until 2008.

On June 21, 1983, after a circus-theme concert in Fort Meyer, Virginia, Colonel Eugene Allen, conductor of the United States Army Band, Pershing's Own, presented honorary memberships in the band to conductor Merle Evans and me. I think we were the fourth and fifth people to receive honorary memberships in the Army Band, after John Philip Sousa, Arthur Pryor, and Frederick Fennell.

Often at clinic presentations I would meet musicians with intriguing interests. In 1980, at a clinic in Virginia, a young saxophone player named George Wolfe introduced himself to me. We spoke about the *Double Concerto for Alto Saxophone and Tuba,* written by Walter Hartley for Donald Sinta and myself. George suggested that he and I perform the work at the Third International Saxophone Symposium sponsored by the Navy Band, being held in Washington, D.C., in 1981. I agreed. A short time later I was contacted by Dale Underwood on behalf of the United States Navy Band. He inquired if I could also perform a work with the U.S. Navy Saxophone Quartet. I agreed and suggested the legendary Ed Sauter be invited to attend the conference and that I would like to perform his *Suite for Solo Tuba and Saxophone Quartet.*

George also arranged for a performance at his alma mater, Mansfield University in Pennsylvania. I was already scheduled to present a recital and clinic for Donald Stanley, professor of tuba at Mansfield. We performed George Heussenstamm's *Dialogue,* a piece for saxophone and tuba. I was reminded that George Wolfe had served as graduate assistant to Eugene Rousseau, distinguished professor of saxophone at Indiana University. So with a tip of the hat, we performed the first (and only) SaxTubaFest. On our program were Hartley's *Double Concerto for Alto Saxophone and Tuba* as well as the world premiere of *SaxTuba,* written by Northwestern University composer M. William Karlins. It was written for alto and soprano saxophone (played by one player, doubling), tuba, and percussion and it was conducted by Travis Hatton, who had studied conducting with Gunther Schuller. As a special encore, George Wolfe had arranged the infamous "If I Give Up the Saxophone, Will You Still Come Back to Me?" The tuba part was a special addition. Regretfully, no one had a copy of the lyrics.

THE FESTIVAL AT SANDPOINT

For years, Gunther Schuller served on a triumvirate at Tanglewood: Bernstein, Ozawa, and Schuller. In 1982, Gunther left Tanglewood to spend his summers as artistic director of the Festival at Sandpoint in

Idaho. My long association with him was rekindled with his invitation to head up the brass chamber music program at the festival. A variety of national and international artists were featured. The Foothills Brass, a professional brass quintet from Calgary, Canada, came down to play three years in a row. I coached student brass players, rehearsed the Foothills Brass, and was featured as a soloist with them. This activity prompted the Foothills Brass to host with me five OctubaFests in Calgary. I also presented master classes for local students, amateurs, and professionals.

Each summer, Neil Tuttle, dean of the Tokyo College of Music, would send a student brass quintet to Sandpoint for coaching and concertizing. The students were gifted and a joy to work with. It was a beautiful location for vesper-time concerts overlooking Schweitzer Mountain, Lake Pend Oreille, and gorgeous sunsets. I headed the brass chamber music program from 1988 to 1994, when, for budgetary reasons, that program ended. A minimum five-hundred-dollar donation from the Harvey Phillips Foundation prompted each programming of numerous chamber music works by Alec Wilder.

When I accepted the position at Sandpoint, John Baker, bass trombone player in the Spokane Symphony, organized a series of tuba/euphonium ensemble concerts in downtown Sandpoint and at the park in Spokane. In its sixth year, John requested permission to call the gathering "The Harvey Phillips Big Brass Bash." Over the years, policy has been to hold this celebration at a selected college in the Pacific Northwest for two years (and then at another college for two years, and so on), taking advantage of repeated use of facilities and publicity. Celebrating its twentieth anniversary in 2006, the Bash traditionally occurs the weekend following the Fourth of July. The Bash continues my philosophy of being open to all ages of players. It includes clinic sessions on performance technique and solo competition for each age level.

SPAIN

Throughout our married life, I accepted opportunities to travel with my wife and family while serving the cause of music and the tuba. The first ten years of our marriage were childless, so Carol was free to attend concerts and to travel as opportunities arose through my performances and workshops.

In 1982, we were invited to Spain by Edmon Colomer, a graduate conducting student at Indiana University, who was establishing a Spanish conservatory and had recruited a few IU professors to teach there during the summer season. Keith Brown, trombone and conducting; Jerry Sirucek, oboe; and I, tuba, were regulars, usually teaching three weeks each summer. The school was initially in the town of Valencia.

Our relationship with the students in Spain was very relaxed and enjoyable. The sixteen Spanish tuba students were exceptional and they practiced diligently. I gave each student a nickname. One was director of his TUBA chapter, so I called him "El Presidente." One tried to run everything and I called him "El General." One had a tremendous high register and showed off with it all the time. He wanted to be the first at everything. I dubbed him "Primi." Miguel Morino was one of the few who spoke enough English to make up for my lack of being able to speak Spanish.

The first year I taught in Spain, we flew into Valencia and we were staying in a motel in the country. Between Valencia and a smaller town, Bunol, was the city of Lliria. All roads that approached Lliria had signs that said "LLIRIA—FAMOUS FOR MUSICIANS." The Lliria Band had existed since 1807 and was the oldest band in Spain. There were times when the two top bands of Lliria would play at one concert, alternating in a sort of battle of the bands. People would cheer for the band they liked best, but the Lliria Band was always the winner. The band owned a building that housed a restaurant, movie theater, concert hall, and rehearsal and recording studio, and these businesses produced enough revenue to support the band's out-of-town activities. The restaurant was on the main floor, complete with a back room filled with card tables and checkerboards. Above was a two-story rehearsal hall with a recording booth topped by a balcony accommodating listeners invited to observe. It was one of the few buildings that I remember seeing in Spain that was built and credited to the dictator Generalissimo Franco.

They had a full-time conductor who trained beginning bands, intermediate bands, an advanced student band, and a professional band. The rehearsals were run with the strictest discipline. Once an audience member set foot in the balcony, you made no sound. You could not even whisper, or you would be asked to leave. When someone in the band had a question, he raised his hand, and when he was recognized, the conductor would stop the ensemble and the player would stand and ask a question. The two would then have a discussion about how that particular passage would be played. Then rehearsal continued. It was the most disciplined rehearsal I have ever experienced. Their schools did not have music programs, but the town bands taught very young musicians. Exceptional high school players were pulled into the ensemble. They were serious about music.

Each summer I taught in a different city. The degree of public support shown in each city would be considered when making the decision about the location for the potential conservatory building. Other cities hosting the conservatory for a year or two included Tarragona, Escorial, Santiago de Compostela, Madrid, Vitoria, Santander, Seville, Granada, Cuenca, and Vigo. They eventually chose Cuenca for the conservatory.

TUBAEASTER

Back home, planning with Andy Miller of the Salvation Army, we decided to have a TubaRanch/TubaEaster egg hunt for underprivileged children. We knew the Salvation Army would provide one or two busloads of children. We planned our TubaEaster egg hunt for the Saturday after traditional Easter, a very important religious holiday but also one with established traditions of the Easter Bunny and the Easter egg hunt.

We prevailed on local merchants to contribute unsold candy and chocolate Easter eggs, to be claimed on the Friday after Easter. We asked for discounts on packaged hot dogs, hot dog buns, sodas, clear sandwich bags, napkins, and boxes of balloons. We called my friends in the mayor's office before calling Fire Department Chief Gose to arrange for a ceremonial fire truck with driver and Smokey the Bear, in costume.

On the Friday after Easter, Indiana University tuba students were invited to a chili supper at TubaRanch, after which they filled sandwich bags with candy and chocolate eggs. They also blew up balloons and filled them with special prizes inside. The balloons were placed on the barn as targets for darts. On Saturday morning the tuba students returned and distributed shopping bags filled with bags of candy eggs throughout TubaRanch. A special level yard area was reserved for children in wheelchairs.

The party started at 2 PM with outdoor games, sack races, and throwing darts at prize-filled balloons. Game time ended with the beginning of our Easter egg hunt. Because the eggs were scattered throughout our property, all the way back to the spot where Don Harry had his tepee in 1973, the kids all ended up there. While they ate their candy eggs, a campfire, prepared earlier, was lit to take the chill off this beautiful spring day.

Suddenly, to everyone's surprise and delight, Smokey the Bear came walking up from the ravine and greeted the excited children. He welcomed visitors to his woods and told the children about the many wild animals also living in the forest. Smokey called attention to the comforting warmth of the campfire and the smells and tastes of outdoor cooking. Smokey also instructed the children on how to make certain all campfires are properly extinguished. He asked the children to get buckets of water and sand from behind neighboring trees and instructed them to pour water around the outer edge and into the center of the campfire, then follow with sand and make sure all coals were smothered and no wind could restart or scatter the coals.

Smokey then led the children out of the woods and into the field, where a Bloomington Fire Department ceremonial fire truck welcomed them to climb aboard for an exciting ride back to the house with sirens screaming, lights flashing, and bells ringing. Some children were still eating their troves of candy Easter eggs. When they arrived back at the house, they were served hot dogs and sodas prepared by Carol and volunteer women from the Salvation Army. It had been a busy four-hour party. The children boarded their buses and departed TubaRanch tired and happy. No one departed hungry and, according to reports, everyone slept well.

TRUMPETS

One day in 1981, a young instrument maker, David Monette, showed up at the Indiana University School of Music and sought advice and assistance from our trumpet faculty, particularly Charles Gorham, Brass Department chair. Charles Gorham suggested he contact me about his problem. Monette's trumpets were highly regarded. He rented space in the area near Walnut Street and Hillside. Not having all the equipment to make an instrument from scratch, some parts of the instrument he had designed were produced at various instrument companies that possessed all the equipment to produce what was needed. An example of a possible way to do this: one company would make the bell to specifications provided by Monette, another company would produce the leadpipe (tapered tubing) and mouthpieces, and a third company was producing set clusters of three valves, additional tubing of the correct bore size, braces, and water keys.

For some reason David wanted to change his source of valve clusters from Bob Getzen of the Allied Supply Corp. He had been unable to negotiate the matter. I soon received a telephone call from David, who confessed he felt he should have called me earlier. To help David, I took it on myself to invite him and Bob Getzen to my house for discussion. I had a lot of confidence in the whole Getzen family and their multiplicity of instrument manufacturing and supplies and we were able to work something out. Since David had no attorney of his own I suggested that Al Beaver, a practicing Green Bay, Wisconsin, attorney, be engaged to work out all the details between David and Bob Getzen. It was agreed. In the meantime, Al Beaver, at David's request, was working to locate factory space along Wabash Street in Chicago. There were additional instances of my representing the interests of David Monette with the C. G. Conn Corporation and other individuals who could help his cause.

Hoping to resolve all details in David Monette's best interests, we scheduled a strategy session with David, Al Beaver, and myself. The week before our conversation, scheduled in Chicago, Carol and I paid a visit to our good friends G. R. and Carol Davis at their home in Chesterton, Indiana. The evening before our meeting I was restless and in great pain and the next morning was taken to the hospital, where I was told I had a big onslaught of kidney stones. Nonetheless, with Carol driving our car, I lay on the back seat in pain, determined to make my meeting with Al Beaver and David Monette. The meeting was held in the offices of the Chicago Pizza and Oven Grinder restaurant owned by Mr. Beaver. All aspects of the Monette Instrument Company were discussed and resolved. Monette was satisfied to the extent that, since he had no capital for such matters, he stated that he would allocate 15 percent of Monette Instrument Company to me if any business resulted from our discussion. I don't expect resolution of this matter.

As David progressed with his concepts and his instruments appropriately improved, he commenced seeking endorsements of his products from established professional artists, most particularly Doc Severinsen, trumpet virtuoso and conductor of the band on Johnny Carson's *Tonight Show*. Such an endorsement by Doc could be translated into profit. Before Doc moved from New York City to the West Coast, I often worked with him on commercial recordings in New York. Two other artists who became critically interested in Monette instruments were Adolph Herseth, principal trumpet of the Chicago Symphony Orchestra, and Charles Schlueter, principal trumpet of the Boston Symphony Orchestra. Another important artist to be wooed and won over was Wynton Marsalis. Marsalis and Schlueter have become champion endorsers for the Monette trumpets.

GROWING BOYS

Our sons Jesse, Harvey, and Thomas, were relatively easy to raise. They seldom acted out, were bright students and good travelers, and were content to do their chores at home. None of them ever asked me for help on schoolwork. They all went to Indiana University and they never asked to live anywhere other than at home during their college years in Bloomington.

On his graduation from high school, Jesse, the oldest, was in a quandary: he had been offered a football scholarship at Purdue as well as at Indiana University. He had to decide whether he would attend Purdue, training for the veterinary profession, or IU, training to be a physician and surgeon. I am proud to say he made the decision himself to attend IU, but only after giving Purdue in-depth consideration. In the second semester of his junior year, Jesse made an appointment to see Coach Bill Mallory and with regret he gave up his football scholarship. He had come to realize that the attention demanded by his MCAT examination left insufficient time to devote to football. He told me later it was a tearful meeting and Coach

Mallory could not have been more understanding: "Jesse," he said, "your future life in medicine is far more important than one more year of football." When Jesse, after getting a degree in chemistry from IU, graduated from IUPUI Medical School, Coach Mallory and his entire staff attended Jesse's graduation party. A nice letter welcoming Jesse back to Bloomington (to practice medicine) was received from legendary Chancellor Herman B Wells. Jesse maintains a successful practice in otolaryngology (ear, nose, and throat), and Jesse and his wife, Kim, proudly produced three sons: Jesse IV, Connor, and Reagan.

Harvey Phillips Jr. pursued multiple interests: while serving as a cheerleader for IU football and basketball, he learned the art of being a fine trapeze artist. For our outdoor parties in the summer and for OctubaFest, a trapeze and safety net were set up in our arena south of the barn. Harvey got through double somersaults and was about to try for three when his interest was diverted to singing and acting. He performed in IU's production of *The Best Little Whorehouse in Texas* and was cast in Cole Porter's *Jubilee* as Mowgli, singing "When Me, Mowgli, Love." What spare time he could devote to extracurricular activities was taken up with the study of classical guitar, an interest he still pursues. In the meantime, four years of demands placed on him by IU successfully earned him a Phi Beta Kappa in chemistry, biology, political science, and French. Then he earned a law degree. But after practicing law for a summer in Indianapolis for a firm that specialized in defending doctors in medical malpractice suits, he decided to become a doctor and he is now devoted to his career in gastroenterology in Jacksonville, Florida. Harvey and his wife, Alison, give their full attention to their son, Riley.

Thomas, the youngest, took an interest in the United States Navy and spent four years in San Diego and the Pacific Ocean, aboard the USS Vancouver. In all the countries he visited, there was only one city—Pattaya Beach, Thailand—that he hadn't already been to with his family. After his return from the Navy, he managed restaurants in Philadelphia and Indianapolis. Thomas now serves as executive vice president for the Harvey Phillips Foundation, Inc.

Our family continues to grow as former "adopted" students visit us at TubaRanch and share with us their successes in life. I am proud to have served as a surrogate father, friend, and colleague to many devoted students.

Sometimes, wishing to escape the four walls of a confining dorm room, students would call and ask if there was something that needed doing at TubaRanch. One winter, Owen Metcalf was out at the house working with me, when I suggested that it would be fun to build a snowman in the middle of the hard-frozen pond. The bus that brought our boys home from school always drove right past the pond and it would be quite a surprise for them to see a snowman there. Owen and I rolled up the base of a snowman and, by pulling and tugging, got it out to the middle. Then we rolled up a second ball of snow and got it over to where the first ball was. We were trying with all our might to get it on top. The ice started to groan. Remembering that we each weighed more than 250 pounds, I said, "Owen, you head that way; I'll go this way." We scrambled for opposite sides of the pond. That snowman never got built.

CLOSER TO BRAHMS

Two of the fine musicians I met at the Casals Festival were Ozzie and Doris Lehnert, a violinist and pianist duo, resident artists at the University of Colorado. Like Carol and me, they always brought their family with them. By 1983, the Lehnert Duo was well-known, and they invited me to join them for a string of performances. We played the Brahms *Trio* and the Lehnerts were featured in a Strauss violin/piano duo. In Bloomington, New York City, and Boulder, Colorado, we received rave reviews. Our tour culminated in a fourth performance in the Library of Congress in Washington, D.C.

The Library of Congress had received a very generous gift that allowed prestigious composers to premiere new works in a small auditorium. Gunther received one, and I played two or three concerts there with the New York Brass Quintet. I was awarded a recital and the Lehnerts agreed to do it with me. It was the first and only tuba recital ever given there. The recital included the premiere of *Introduction and Allegro,* which we had commissioned Charles Eakin, composer from the University of Colorado, to write for us. We also played what we called the Brahms *Tuba Trio.* It was the *Horn Trio,* of course.

At a reception afterward, a musicologist sourly remarked, "What gives you the right to think you can play the Brahms *Trio* on tuba?"

"Well, I feel close to Brahms when I play his music. And you know, I'd rather be close to Brahms than any musicologist I've ever known."

MORTON GOULD

There were several freelance projects I did with Morton Gould. Maurice Peress, Leonard Bernstein's assistant, was working with the American Symphony Orchestra League to honor Morton on his seventieth birthday in 1983. They celebrated with a special evening program in the Grand Ballroom of the Palmer House Hilton Hotel in Chicago. They let Morton choose his program and performers. I was flattered to be chosen and I performed his *Tuba Suite,* a six-movement work for solo tuba accompanied by three French horns. Phil Farkas recruited two other horns to perform the piece with us.

SUMMIT BRASS, RAFAEL MÉNDEZ, KEYSTONE

The outstanding performance of the Scandinavian Brass Ensemble, heard at the second World Brass Congress at Indiana University, was most impressive. The ensemble's excellent performances inspired David Hickman, Regents' professor of trumpet at Arizona State University, to organize Summit Brass, America's first large brass ensemble. Founded in 1986 at the Keystone Ski Resort in Keystone, Colorado, the all-star ensemble attracted a large number of top college undergraduate and graduate students to its program of coaching, teaching, concerts, and recordings. The philosophy was to draw faculty personnel from a pool of outstanding brass players from America's symphony orchestras and brass clinician soloists. The resort put up a large music tent with good acoustics. Helpful to these early arrangements was Richard Zellner, then manager of the Denver Youth Orchestra, who had contacts with management of the Keystone Resort. It was my honor to be chosen in 1984 as board chairman for this new organization.

David secured the library of Rafael Méndez, who, as a child, was cornet and trumpet virtuoso in Pancho Villa's band in Mexico and later a star in Hollywood and radio. He taught his twin sons to play trumpet and performed trios with them. When the library was installed at Arizona State University (which, after 1992, was also the home of Summit Brass and Summit Records), a banquet was held to celebrate the occasion and several Hollywood stars attended. David renamed the Keystone Brass Institute the Rafael Méndez Brass Institute.

The institute continues the high level of musicianship demanded by the top-level faculty. The performing faculty has included such musicians as Joe Alessi, Tom Bacon, Brian Bowman, Bill Caballero, Allan Dean, Donald Green, Lowell Greer, Allene Hackleman, Marty Hackleman, David Hickman, Melvyn Jernigan, David Krehbiel, Mark Lawrence, Carl Lenthe, John Lofton, Ray Mase, Fred Mills, Michael Mulcahy, Dan Perantoni, Anthony Plog, Gene Pokorny, Sam Pilafian, Jeffrey Reynolds, Fred Rizner, Ronald Romm, Michael Sachs, Ralph Sauer, Milton Stevens, Larry Strieby, Bob Sullivan, and Gail Williams.

Méndez's two sons are renowned doctors of urology and take a keen interest in the development of the Rafael Méndez Brass Institute, honoring their father.

My Ringling Brothers and Barnum & Bailey Circus band mentor, Johnny Evans, who had also played in the Sousa Band (1929–1932), toured a few more years with the circus and then went to Las Vegas to play in a gambling casino called Circus Circus. I put in a word for him to play in the Guy Lombardo Orchestra, which he did for a couple of years. Johnny played the World's Fair in New York before retiring to Page, Arizona. In June 1989, following a lively session with Summit Brass at Arizona State University, I spoke with Dan Perantoni, who was teaching at A S U, about doing a special concert to honor Johnny Evans. Dan took it from there.

Carol and I took a holiday trip to San Diego to visit my sister Mildred and pick up our son Thomas, who was on leave from the Navy. In Los Angeles we visited Jim and Jamie Self as well as Doc Severinsen and the Tonight Show Band. After that we headed for Las Vegas to relax and enjoy being together. After a few days we drove to A S U just in time for the recital concert. We flew Johnny and his wife Reba down from Page and checked them into the top floor of a hotel.

The concert featured Dan's students plus a duet by Dan and myself. Johnny and Reba were seated in the first row, center. As each musician entered, they strode to front center stage and bowed respectfully to Johnny before performing. Johnny and Reba were feeling wonderful and proud and Johnny told us they had never been treated so well.

Sadly, Johnny and Reba both died within weeks of that magical evening at ASU. All efforts to telephone and wish Johnny well, near the end of his life, were negated by instructions to the hospital from his son, a Southern preacher.

LON NORMAN AND THE FOX

Back in 1955, Major Chester Whiting, commanding officer, asked if I had any solo material in which I could be featured with the United States Army Field Band. I liked "The Peanut Vendor" and "Yuba" but felt they had both been victims of overkill in performances. In talking to staff arranger and jazz trombonist Lon Norman about it, he asked me if I knew "The Carioca." I did not know it at the time but soon picked up on it when Lon performed it for me on his trombone. He arranged it for me and I performed it with the Field Band. After leaving the Field Band and doing many solo clinics, I performed it on practically every concert I gave. It always made a hit with the audience.

I got a letter one day in the mid-1980s from Lon, writing from San Quentin. He was voluntarily serving time for a crime he claimed to have committed: killing his wife on a trip they had made to Las Vegas. He detailed the location where he had buried her, when they were both consumed by drugs. Despite intense searching by police, no body was ever found. Lon's letter said he had always respected me and he wanted me to know why I hadn't heard from him.

He did arrangements for *The Jackie Gleason Show* when it was broadcast from Miami, then went to Los Angeles to write film music. George Williams, who had done arrangements, several recordings, and other work for Gleason in New York, bought a house in Fort Lauderdale after Gleason moved to Miami. After George moved his family to Florida, Gleason went to California. George Williams became music director for the largest church in Fort Lauderdale. George was known as "the fox" for his skillful and creative arrangements for the Gene Krupa Band, *The Jackie Gleason*

Show, and myriad other well-placed assignments. In 1963, while on a tour of Europe with the New York Brass Quintet, I came across a beautiful brass door knocker that was the head of a fox. I presented it to George, and he was impressed and grateful.

Lon's letter said he had one year to go on his sentence and he missed being in music. I sent him a Hoagy Carmichael songbook along with appropriate manuscript paper to arrange Hoagy Carmichael's music for my performances with concert band, symphony orchestra, and stage band. He did many of Hoagy's most famous tunes, starting with "Riverboat Shuffle" (which Hoagy wrote for Bix), as well as arrangements of "Stardust," "Skylark," "Georgia on My Mind," "The Nearness of You," "Up a Lazy River," "Rockin' Chair," and "Ole Buttermilk Sky." These arrangements came into regular use for my bookings with Columbia Artists Management, Inc. If I was doing concertos and other serious fare, I would use Lon's arrangements of Hoagy's familiar music for an encore. If I was doing a pops concert, it most likely would be all Hoagy.

I tried as best I could by mail and telephone to stay in touch with the many wonderful friends who entered my life with their musical artistry and creative talents. There are always rewards in friendship and admiration.

JAPAN TUBA (HETA)

In 1971, I had received a letter from Chitate Kagawa, tubist with the Sapporo Symphony Orchestra, inquiring about studying with me in the fall of 1972. He came with his wife, Sachiko, and studied with me for two semesters. They took a furnished apartment in Bloomington and we had lessons every week. Chitate was an excellent student and a joy to work with.

I gave the first full tuba recital by any foreigner in Japan, arranged by Chitate, in Sapporo in 1979. Musicians who talked with me afterward created the Hokkaido Euphonium/Tuba Association (HETA), with Chitate as president. HETA has held a tuba and euphonium music camp yearly since 1981. Since 1984, HETA has sponsored the Harvey G. Phillips Solo Tuba Competition, and many of the winners are now professional tubists. I have the winners' plaques made in Bloomington every year and send them to Sapporo to be displayed at the HETA camp.

In 1987 Chitate invited me to the H E T A camp as a guest artist and I performed *Concertino for Solo Tuba and Winds,* composed by Hiroshi Hoshina and commissioned by Chitate Kagawa. In 1990, we held the International Tuba–Euphonium Conference in Sapporo, Japan. During the five days of the conference there were clinics, master classes, recitals, and ensemble performances. The Matteson-Phillips TubaJazz Consort performed several times in the evenings. We performed on regular programs and did extra concerts.

Two works were written for me. One was *Celebration,* celebrating my birthday. It was for three euphoniums, three tubas, and solo tuba, which I played.

The first tuba concerto competition in Japan was held in Tokyo. I was a judge there and at the Hokkaido competition, held at Tiene Ski Mountain Resort. In Tokyo, all players had to play the same composition. It felt like I heard that piece ninety-six times. Hokkaido gave prizes for different ages: over fifteen, over eighteen, over twenty-one, etc. If there was no first prize given, then there were no prizes given in that category. In 2008, no prizes were given in any category; sponsors are trying to keep the competition at a very high level.

CONCERTO COMPETITION—GENEVA

In 1990, I was invited to be a judge for the International Competition for Musical Performers, which was having its first competition for tuba players in Geneva, Switzerland. There were required pieces to play and a required concerto by a Russian composer. Jean-Pierre Mathez had a luncheon for the judges, at the end of which he delivered to each judge a fifth of cognac bottled in the year of the recipient's birth. However, they could not find a 1929 bottle for me, so I received one from 1928. Everyone wanted to try the oldest, so mine was first to be opened. Jean-Pierre Mathez was founder and publisher of the *Brass Bulletin* and BIM publishing company in Switzerland. He provided the program for the First International Brass Congress in 1976, and an edition of his magazine was dedicated to the Brass Congress. There was one judge each from England, France, and Hungary, two from Switzerland, and myself. I had no personal connection with any of the other judges but we got along well and mostly agreed on the decisions made.

We agreed on a Danish and a Norwegian player as first and second. The other judges didn't want to acknowledge a contestant who was fifteen years old as third, because he was young. I thought it was wrong to deny him recognition because he was young and talked the other judges into naming him third in the first round. After that he went back to France to his teacher, Melvin Culbertson, who asked, "What are you doing here?" He said that he didn't go to win; he went to be accepted. His teacher then replied, "Get your butt back down there." He didn't come back and play but he won every competition he entered after that.

The winner of the final round was Jens Bjorn Larsen, from Denmark, who is now playing with a major orchestra in his home country. Runner-up was Oystein Baadsvik from Norway, who is pursuing a very successful career as a soloist.

SOME AWARDS

While I was in New York in 1990 for TubaChristmas, at a reception boasting the best hors d'oeuvres of any press reception I'd ever attended, the Goebel company presented me with the first Hummel Tuba Player. It holds pride of place in a glass-fronted cabinet in the foyer of our home, along with other tuba figurines, most of them gifts from friends.

A tribute concert was given for me on August 18, 2000, by the Houston Symphonic Band, conducted by Robert McElroy. My dear friend Rex Sagle played tuba in the band. We met in 1955 when he was in the Air Force Band and I was playing with the U.S. Army Field Band. A handsome plaque presented to me in Houston at that time states: "A Tribute to Harvey Phillips in Recognition and Appreciation for dedicating his career to bringing THE TUBA into the forward consciousness of the concert-going public throughout the world."

The U.S. Army Field Band honored me by inviting me to be soloist for its fiftieth anniversary concert at the American Bandmasters Association conference being held in San Antonio, and of course I complied. I commissioned Manny Albam to write a work especially for the occasion. After the concert, Colonel John Bourgeois announced the American Bandmasters Association's election of me to the Academy of Wind and Percussion Arts and presented me with a medal and scroll.

The Sousa Foundation held a banquet at the Hilton Towers Hotel in Chicago, during its annual meeting in 1994, and bestowed on me the Medal of the Order of Merit—the Sudler Award.

Other band awards include the Association of Concert Bands' First Mentor Ideal Award given to me in 1994, and the First Legion of Honor from the Goldman Memorial Band in 2002.

OCTUBAFEST IN GRAND CENTRAL STATION—1993

A promoter from New York, Michael Leavitt from MPL Productions, called me in 1993 to say how impressed he was with TubaChristmas and OctubaFest. He wanted to host a tuba event in New York City and inquired as to what we might produce together. We settled on an OctubaFest celebration in Grand Central Station because there was an overabundance of Christmas events. His primary sponsor was Jose Cuervo tequila. I had Norlan Bewley arrange a book of Herb Alpert's Mexican tunes and we settled on a date, Octuba 29. The week before we were to perform, I assigned Marcus Rojas, a New York City tubist, to put together tuba quartets which would advertise the event in designated bars and restaurants that excelled at serving tequila. The Jose Cuervo people were very helpful. We couldn't recruit anyone younger than twenty-one.

The upcoming performance was written up in newspapers and advertised in subway cars and on restaurant tables, so by the time the mass ensemble arrived at Grand Central Station, lots of people showed up. I thought the sound of nearly 150 tubas would produce a continuing echo but the acoustics were perfect. I picked thirty players to be in the TubaQuilas, and Don Butterfield took on the task of finding sousaphones for them. We had custom-made bell covers for these instruments provided by Jose Cuervo to spell out the product's name. Warren Deck, Sam Pilafian, Eddie Bert, and Wayne Andre were there. It was a wonderful group. I gave a tuba lesson to the president of Jose Cuervo and also to Al Roker of NBC. One commuter missed four trains listening to our ensemble and finally had to run to not miss another.

Some of the New York players were concerned about our performance, because it was a call-in and was not contracted through the union. Their fears were quickly assuaged. I called and received the blessing of Johnny Glasel, my colleague from the NYBQ, then president of Local 802. I also called Bill Crow, the tuba player who had long been writing articles for the union's monthly publication. In addition, Local 802 had awarded me with an Outstanding Achievement and Service award in 1985.

I had the same problem in Chicago with TubaChristmas—the union said that I'd have to file a contract. Again, I called the president of the union chapter, Charlie Guse, the tuba player with the Lyric Opera and president of Local 10, Chicago, who knew what I was trying to do. His coming to conduct killed the complaints.

CHAPTER SIXTEEN

Indiana University Retirement

IN FEBRUARY 1972, I received a call from Mason Jones, personnel manager of the Philadelphia Orchestra. He told me I had been recommended by the orchestra search committee for the tuba position being vacated by Abraham Torchinsky and that Maestro Eugene Ormandy had asked him to contact me and negotiate an agreement. There would be no need for an audition and I could discuss salary with him. I told Mason I appreciated his call and I would give every consideration to the position.

But I decided it would be improper to resign from Indiana University after only one year. A couple of days after receiving the call from Mason Jones, I called and told him to pass along my respects and appreciation for the offer but that I had decided to honor my agreement with Indiana University.

In March 1972, trumpeter Fred Mills and tubist Chuck Daellenbach of the Canadian Brass quintet chartered a plane and flew to Bloomington to ask if I would consider managing the Canadian Brass. During my stay at Indiana University, several other schools approached me about administrative positions, including the Oberlin Conservatory, the Manhattan School of Music, the North Carolina School of the Arts, Arizona State University, the Peabody Conservatory, and the New England Conservatory. I was also invited to follow Ed Birdwell as director of the music division for the National Endowment for the Arts. I went to Washington for an interview with Frank Hodsoll, chairman of the NEA. But I had no quarrel with the way I had been treated by Indiana University and the community of Bloomington. I had good relationships with the president, the chancellor, the dean, the faculty, and my community contacts. I co-sponsored activities with the mayor's office from time to time and shared sponsorships for concerts with the local newspaper.

The closest Carol and I came to moving was when I was approached by Arizona State University to become the dean of fine arts. I was invited to lunch at the Harvard Club in New York City by the president of Arizona State. The vice president of ASU flew to Bloomington to talk to the president, the chancellor, the dean, and the mayor, as well as the publisher and editor of the newspaper. He spent several hours during each of two days waiting to see the dean of the School of Music. Somehow, the dean always knew he was there, and would quietly escape out the back door.

Carol and I had decided to take the job if they came up with the salary we requested. They came close but, in the end, were not able to secure the funds. We decided to stay put in Bloomington, and Arizona State hired the former director of the Carnegie Hall Corporation for the position. A few years later, he left. The ASU vice president again called me, letting me know that they had come up with extra money, and hoped I was still interested. I thanked him for his call and told him that my attention had been diverted to other interests. I had decided to stay at Indiana University.

I eventually retired from Indiana University in June 1994. However, it was not a typical retirement year. On New Year's Day of that year, Carol and I and Carol's sister Elsie left for Greece and Spain for two weeks. Also, I presented clinics and made solo appearances in Boston, Chicago, Cleveland, New York, Kentucky, Burlington, Canada, Spain, and Greece. The stream of activity depended only on available time, which was devoured by projects kept on the back burner while students had been my first priority. I mended fences and built a new barn and shop building at TubaRanch. My consulting work increased and I was more able to involve myself in good conscience. I would fly into an airport, meet quickly with the client in an Admiral's Club room, and would be back on the plane.

My students held a concert and a reception for me at the Indiana University High School Auditorium. We had a retirement party at TubaRanch as well as a day of clinics and ensembles. Many colleagues attended, including Arnold Jacobs, who had retired as tubist of the Chicago Symphony Orchestra. He got up to give an impromptu tribute, which moved me very much. Tubist Roger Bobo congratulated me on "one of the most remarkable musical careers the world has ever seen."

When I joined the faculty of Indiana University, I was happy to be greeted by Thomas Beversdorf, a long-time friend and multi-talented professor of trombone and composition. His *Sonata for Tuba and Piano* (1956) was eagerly received by serious tubists, and missed by only a few weeks being the first sonata for tuba; Hindemith wrote the first. Some of the other works Tom wrote for me were *Suite for Tuba and Piano: Of Walruses, Cheesecake, and Morse Code; Concertino for Solo Tuba and Orchestra Winds;* and *Suite for Solo Tuba and Three Horns.*

Also, shortly after my arrival in Bloomington, I met composer Bernhard Heiden. Bernhard had written for my long-time friend and colleague, horn virtuoso John Barrows. He wrote several works for me including *Concerto for Solo Tuba and Orchestra* (also scored for solo tuba and wind ensemble); *Quintet for Brass; Four Fancies for Alto Saxophone, Tuba, and Marimba; Duet for Tubas;* plus several other works. We became close friends. Bernhard and his wife Cola invited us several times to visit them on the beautiful Greek island of Mykonos, where they spent their summers and as much retirement time as possible. In January 1994, we were finally able to accept their invitation.

MYKONOS

Carol's recently widowed sister Elsie was invited to travel with us. On arrival in Mykonos, while waiting for our luggage, a young man who had been on the plane with us walked up to me and said, "You're Harvey Phillips, aren't you?"

"Yes," I replied. "Who am I meeting?" He was a young tuba player from San Francisco on his honeymoon.

Cola Heiden met us at the airport. Since no cars are allowed in downtown Mykonos, she had arranged for a baggage handler on a bicycle with a front cart to transport our luggage and my tuba to our hotel. Bernhard joined us there for lunch in a convenient and very special little restaurant. Over lunch we made plans for the duration of our visit. For many years the Heidens had used their summer house, which was near the island's magnificent windmills. They suggested we take a trip in the country and visit a beautiful public beach. We rented a van early the next morning.

On the way to the beach we stopped a few times to sightsee. Of special interest were an antiquated Greek Orthodox Church and farmland with mile after mile of stone fences to which large flat stones had been added over centuries. After delivering the bathers to the beach, I drove the van up a hill. I parked discreetly and practiced my tuba while sitting on one of the stone fences. The Aegean Sea was royal blue with a light cooling breeze coming across the water, tempering the warmth of the sun. It was a perfect day. I could see the beach from where I sat. My interest was diverted by two large, newly finished buildings that looked like twins, side by side, up on the hillside. Judging by the paved access, one structure was obviously a large home and the other a guest house to accommodate many guests.

After practicing a good forty-five minutes, I was approached by a young couple who were very cordial and friendly. The young lady spoke like an American tourist. She said that she and her husband had enjoyed listening to my tuba playing and asked if I'd like something cold to drink. I answered in the affirmative so she invited me to join them for an afternoon repast. I told her I appreciated the invitation very much, that I'd be honored to accept. As we walked, our conversation turned to the Greek islands, the beautiful Aegean Sea, and their place in history.

Soon we reached the entrance gates to the first house. I was fascinated by a rather large swimming pool. From the house it looked like it was overflowing into the sea. I was told it was ever thus, because the pump kept circulating water from the sea. We then went up about six steps to sit on the covered patio. At the head of a large outdoor dining table that would seat as many as sixteen diners, I was introduced to our host, a gentleman named Giorgio.

He was wearing only a swimsuit and a long, pencil-thick gold chain around his neck, the heaviest gold necklace I have ever seen. Giorgio didn't speak English very well, but much better than I spoke Greek. The maid was ordered to bring some mid-afternoon hors d'oeuvres. They had finished lunch only a short time before but Giorgio was in the mood for a leisurely repast. He asked if I was alone, and I told him about Carol, her sister Elsie, and the Heidens. He said they were also invited.

I positioned myself so the four of them could see me and understand my "come hither" wave. It took them about half an hour to gather their things and join the party. By this time, Giorgio and I, with the help of some excellent Greek ouzo, were singing Italian songs like "O Sole Mio" and "Funiculi, Funicula," he in Greek, I in English—it didn't matter. I played some selections on the tuba for him, some requested, some volunteered, so it was a rather charming display of new friendship witnessed by the Heidens, Carol, and Elsie. Giorgio's wife and the young couple who had invited me had thrown an impromptu party for us.

I discovered that the young lady lived in Chicago and her parents owned one of the popular Greek restaurants we had frequented on Halsted Street. Giorgio, through his niece, our interpreter, asked how long we would be in Greece and how long we would be in Athens. He invited us to stay at one of his hotels, but I advised him that our reservations had been made from stateside far in advance. Before leaving Athens, however, we made time to visit the top floor of one of his hotels for a sumptuous meal next to a rooftop swimming pool.

As we were saying goodbye, Giorgio urged us to join him and his family the next day, for it was his mother-in-law's birthday and they were having a party for her. He had asked the captain of his fleet of fishing boats to come cook a special fish that lives only in the Aegean Sea and is considered a delicacy. There would be octopus and other fresh seafood, of course. It would be a big party. We left Giorgio in time to relax and enjoy the colorful sunset in downtown Mykonos. The next day, we visited as Giorgio's guests and had an unbelievably great time.

I promised to send Giorgio a record, *A Greek in Dixieland,* that I had made two years before with arranger John Carisi. It featured clarinetist Gus Vali and brass players John Glasel, trumpet; Urbie Green, trombone; myself on tuba; drummer Mousey Alexander; and guitarist Barry Galbraith, plus a half dozen mandolin and balalaika players.

We had one memorable home-cooked meal prepared by the Heidens. Bernhard was a master chef, which we knew from our many visits to their home in Bloomington.

In Athens, for three days, Carol and Elsie went to the Parthenon and made the usual tourist inspection of Greek architecture and history. I sat in a park with a cool drink and a Greek salad. We had such a wonderful time that we were reluctant to leave Greece, but we had a date to keep in Spain.

SPAIN

We arrived in the Madrid airport around noon and drove through the beautiful and lush mountains of central Spain on our way to Cuenca, a proposed site for the new permanent conservatory. As we approached the city, we were amazed and curious about how houses and restaurants were clinging to the sides of perpendicular mountains. We checked in with the conservatory administration and ate in one of the clinging restaurants. It had obviously been in business for many years so we were not apprehensive.

The next morning we were bused to the outskirts of the city, where we would do most of our teaching. We were again impressed by the talents of our Spanish students. The three Americans on the faculty—Jerry Sirucek, oboe; Keith Brown, trombone; and myself—had discussions with the conservatory administration about the pros and cons of the different cities we had tried over the previous years. We tried to be helpful but not interfere.

Across the road from the Cuenca facility was a huge green field, I would guess as much as forty acres. The day we arrived, almost centered in the field was one golden sunflower. The next day there were perhaps as many as ten sunflowers. And on the third day the field had exploded with golden sunflowers straining to keep their faces in the sun.

PORT TOWNSEND 1996

In 1996, Ed Birdwell, long after he retired as head of the National Endowment for the Arts music division, booked me for an appearance in Port Townsend, Washington. I had rehearsed an Alec Wilder trio with the first trumpet of the Seattle Symphony and Anne Clevenger, horn.

Port Townsend, a very beautiful area, is where *An Officer and a Gentleman* was filmed. It is a peninsula, only approachable by ferry. The concert, with several soloists, was on a Sunday afternoon, and Carol's nephew and his wife and daughter came from Seattle. I donned my concert attire and had my instrument ready to perform when I realized I was losing blood, as sometimes happens to those on blood thinners. I told Carol to call Ed Birdwell and tell him I was unable to play. Carol's nephew called paramedics when I fainted in the doorway. A Port Townsend doctor informed me that they did not have enough blood to treat me and they would have to get me to Seattle. The traffic to the ferry was bumper to bumper and moving very slowly. Luckily they were able to call in a medical helicopter, which was already in the area.

When we arrived at Virginia Mason Hospital in Seattle, I was still unconscious. Fortunately, my son Jesse, being a doctor, had prepared a pocket-size copy of my medical records for me to carry. The records showed that, six months earlier, I had suffered an attack of diverticulitis while in my office at *The Instrumentalist*.

Lying in my hospital bed, I thought about what I was putting Carol through. I kept trying to remember the lyrics to "Day by Day," the song from which Doris Day took her stage name, made popular by Jo Stafford in the 1940s. I sang aloud.

> *Day by day, I'm falling more in love with you,*
> *And day by day, my love seems to grow.*
> *There isn't any end to my devotion.*
> *It's deeper, dear, by far, than any ocean.*

I could only remember one verse. I called Carol and asked for the rest of the lyrics. She said, "Harvey, it's 5 in the morning. I'll be there at 8."

I kept singing for awhile and eventually fell asleep. When Carol came in, she sang "Day by Day" with me. Then we heard a voice from the other side of a curtain chime in with the rest of the lyrics. I didn't know there was another patient in my hospital room. The poor fellow had suffered through my singing all night and hadn't said a word. We pulled back the curtain to meet author Jack Olsen. He signed one of his books for us, *The Night of the Grizzlies*.

After three weeks I was anxious to get out of the hospital. Arthur Statter, long-time friend and former first trumpet with the New York City Ballet

Orchestra, arranged for us to sublease a furnished apartment in a land-mark round apartment building overlooking downtown Seattle and Puget Sound. We stayed there two weeks, for two more medical checkups, before being discharged by doctors, with permission to travel. It was good to be "back home again in Indiana."

BILLY TAYLOR AND CHARLES KURALT

I had known jazz pianist Billy Taylor for many years in New York. He was selected by Charles Kuralt to be the interviewer for musician features on the CBS *News Sunday Morning* show because of his commitment to music education and live performances. Billy and I had recorded with Quincy Jones in the late 1950s and we both served on panels for the National Endowment for the Arts, the West Virginia Music Educators, and the jazz panel at the Smithsonian Institution, where I performed several selections with Billy's combo. It was this activity that prompted Billy to invite me on Charles Kuralt's TV show.

Billy Taylor's crew came to Chicago to tape my rehearsal with the North Shore Concert Band, directed by John Paynter, in a performance of the Strauss *Horn Concerto No. 1*. They also taped some of the TubaJazz Consort performances at Joe Segal's Jazz Showcase and at the Midwest Clinic. I went to New York and spent an afternoon with Billy Taylor in an interview setting. He spoke about our activities together and my work to popularize the tuba.

Several weeks after the broadcast had taken place, on the morning of the twenty-first annual TubaChristmas, Charles Kuralt interviewed me at his office on 57th Street for his upcoming book, *Charles Kuralt's America,* which chronicled special places to be in America at certain times of the year. After the interview about TubaChristmas was taped, I invited him to come with me to Rockefeller Plaza to guest-conduct "Silent Night" on our 3:30 PM concert. He feigned fear and insecurity as a conductor, but I assured him everything would go well. I was delighted when he accepted my invitation.

He wrote about it in his book, describing how, because "Silent Night" is in three-quarter time, he just kept making emphatic triangles in the air. Then he "held the last note an extra beat or two, and those [four hundred] tuba players, bless them, held it on cue and ended in unison."

TRIBUTE TO A BANDSMAN

In 1948, Paul Lavalle had organized for N B C his forty-eight-piece Cities Service Band of America. The band was to perform on thirteen successive Monday evenings, on radio and T V at the same time, sponsored by the Cities Service Oil Company. The broadcast became a favorite of band musicians of every age throughout the United States and was continued through the summer of 1956, when it was canceled. There was much disappointment expressed at that time by the large, loyal audience, but N B C had made an irrevokable decision. Paul Lavalle continued his involvement with American bands with his famous McDonald's Marching Band of 100, which featured two high-school-age musicians from each state. He was later the music director of Radio City Music Hall.

Texas, which ranks in the top five band states (the states having the most bands), organized concerts in tribute to Paul Lavalle. When I was doing a solo clinic in Arlington, Texas, in 1996, Rex Sagle was there to hear the concert and invited me to play "The Carioca" on one of the Paul Lavalle tributes. I accepted. The next tribute concert was in Friendswood, Texas, by the Pasadena Memorial Band. I said that in addition to playing the "Carioca" solo, I would like to play in the band, on a BB♭ sousaphone. Rex borrowed one from instrument collector Mike Lynch.

I had been in the Band of America and had chosen Paul as the conductor of the first TubaChristmas concert in Rockefeller Center in 1974. On the day of our tribute, heart surgeon Dr. Grady Hallman had a luncheon at his home in Houston for the Pasadena Memorial Band. He is also a euphonium player and has made his own solo albums. I had first met Grady when the New York Brass Quintet was on tour.

It was known that Paul was in poor health. I was given the privilege of calling him at his home in Harrisonburg, Virginia, about our concert. About the sixth ring, Paul picked up the phone and in a weak, husky voice said, "Hello."

I said, "Paul, this is Harvey Phillips and I'm calling from Texas to tell you that this afternoon I will perform on a concert with the Pasadena Memorial Band, paying tribute to you and the Band of America. I have you on speakerphone and all the musicians send you their best greetings. I thought you might like to give them some words of encouragement." I could sense Paul's adrenaline start to flow. He wanted to know what we were doing on the program and was happy to learn that we were playing the Band of America music. He rose to the occasion and paid his respects to all the band, wished them a great concert, and said he was honored by their tribute. It was the last time I had the opportunity to speak to Paul. Everyone involved with the concert was emotionally affected by Paul's words.

We played the entire "Band of America March," which was used to bring the band onto a broadcast on NBC radio for eight years and to close the programs. It was very difficult because it went through several keys. Paul was very pleased that we played it. It was a concert we would all have been proud to have had Paul attend.

PARKINSON'S

I kept up a rigorous schedule until the development of Parkinson's disease became obvious. I have a sister with Parkinson's and I suspected I had the condition. One day, when I held the last note of a performance with the intent to have the sound disappear without alteration, I heard and felt a vibrato which I didn't want and couldn't control. Visits to my doctor confirmed I had the disease. I decided then, in 1997, to stop performing. I have been fortunate to have a loving and understanding family and devoted friends and colleagues.

HONORS

In the years after I stopped playing, I was fortunate to receive many honors.

A former student, jazz tubist David Gannett, in 1998 presented us with a stained glass window, five feet five inches by twenty-one inches, depicting my Conn CC tuba. David said it celebrated my "remarkable life." It is now my front window.

The International Brassfest-Summit Brass awarded me the Outstanding Service and Support Award in 1995. Three years later, I received a Lifetime Achievement Award from the Rafael Mendez Brass Institute.

The United Musical Instruments (formerly twenty-six independent companies) awarded me with a Lifetime Achievement Award in 1996. The owner, Dan Henkin, was my best friend at the University of Missouri, where we had a Dixieland jazz band consisting of clarinet and tuba. The person presenting the award dropped it and the crystal top of the award broke off. Onstage, as he handed it to me, he said, "This is one of two awards you will be receiving." The broken one was replaced later, and both make very prominent bookends.

In 1999, at the University of Georgia, Fred Mills, who played in the New York Brass Quintet and is one of the founding members of the Canadian Brass, presented me with the Platinum Piston Award for lifetime achievement. The award is to express recognition for having taken leadership in pioneering and establishing the brass quintet as a viable medium for musical achievement and for career development in brass chamber music.

I was surprised in 2003 to be informed that Harvey G. Phillips was added to the American Legion Roll of Honor, "For Distinguished Service, Indiana Service Veteran."

George Mason University in Fairfax, Virginia, honored me in 2006 with a concert of music taken from my entire career, accompanied by a narration entitled "The Difference One Man Can Make."

I was included in the Marquis "Who's Who in America," "Who's Who in American Education," "Who's Who in Entertainment," "Who's Who in the Midwest," and "Who's Who in the World" more than thirty times.

John Mellencamp called and left a message, asking me to improvise something on top of a recording that John had already made in his studio in Brown County, Indiana. I did it. About a year later I received a framed LP platinum record commemorating one million copies sold of *Mr. Happy Go Lucky*. It is still displayed in the foyer of my house.

In the year 2000, I was invited to Vigo, Spain, for a special tuba celebration honoring me. Appearing would be many students from my eight years of visits to the National Spanish Youth Orchestra, directed by Edmon Colomer. Even though the orchestra has only one tuba player, who earned his position via audition, an additional ten to fifteen Spanish tubists were added to my class each year. I developed great affection and admiration for the personae and level of talent exhibited by these special students.

Before the trip to Vigo, Carol and I were invited by Mel Culbertson to visit him and his wife Sue in Bordeaux, France. Their invitation was especially meaningful to us because of our long relationship with Mel. While a member of the West Point Band he studied with me in New York, and later he transferred to Boston. He was an outstanding musician. For his Carnegie Hall concert, we performed a duet transcribed from the works of Italian composer Marco Bordogni. Mel spent weekends with us at our home in Wayland, Massachusetts. In 1975 I was in Sweden for the first Swedish Brass Symposium, hosted by another former student, Michael Lind, principal tubist of the Stockholm Philharmonic. Melvin was also invited to attend the symposium in Stockholm. I asked him how French tubists were responding to his winning the tuba position with the French Radio Orchestra, and he said they had declared a strike, which would be resolved by his many French students. He was right. He held the position until he retired. Melvin is an excellent teacher and solo tubist.

While we were in France in 2000, Melvin asked me to judge the tuba class finals at Conservatoire National Supérieur de Musique et de Danse de Lyon, which I did. On the way to Lyon, we noticed life-size wooden statues of people killed in car wrecks beside the roads, at curves, intersections, etc., where you would suspect there might be an accident. After a week in France, we left for Vigo, where there were mornings and afternoons of special performances at the conservatory. I taught a class and prepared the final concert. Much later, in 2009, Eduardo B. Nogueroles, the man in charge of the Vigo conservatory, who had been one of my students, sent me a piece of music for solo tuba and band, "La Tuba de Harvey."

THIRTIETH ANNIVERSARY OF TUBA (ITEA) FOUNDING

In a concert hosted and organized by Daniel Perantoni in Auer Hall at Indiana University in 2003, the ITEA honored me and acknowledged the thirtieth anniversary of the First International Tuba Symposium Workshop. The program opened with Don Butterfield (in his eightieth year) performing William Bell's arrangement for tuba and piano of Bach's "Komm, Süsser Tod," "Air," and "Bourrée." R. Winston Morris conducted an ensemble of ITEA members. At the first International Tuba Symposium Workshop, Don had conducted "Komm, Süsser Tod" with some three hundred attendees. Other pieces performed included: "Variations on 'The Carnival of Venice'" by Jean-Baptiste Arban, arranged by Bell, performed by Tony Kniffen; "Nessun dorma," from *Turandot* by Giacomo Puccini, arranged and performed by Tim Northcut; "Selections from *Serenade No. 12*" by Vincent Persichetti, performed by Jeff Anderson; "Selections from *Family Suite*" by Alec Wilder, performed by Ted Cox; "Song for Carol" by Alec Wilder, performed by Dan Perantoni; "Andante and Rondo" by Antonio Capuzzi, performed by Brian Bowman; "Meditation," from *Thaïs* by Jules Massenet and "Flight of the Bumblebee" by Nicolai Rimsky-Korsakov, both arranged and performed by Pat Sheridan; and "Send in the Clowns" by Stephen Sondheim, performed by Pat Sheridan and Sam Pilafian. Piano accompaniments were provided by Ashley Toms, Barbara Young, and Charles H. Webb.

The concert featured various aspects of my performing and teaching career, from my circus beginnings to brass quintet, military band, symphony orchestra, Sauter-Finegan, TubaJazz, etc. A dinner followed the concert and entertainment was provided by Sam Pilafian, Pat Sheridan, Norlan Bewley, Dan Perantoni, and Winston Morris, who conducted Symphonia, a group of seven euphoniums and eight tubas.

FIFTIETH WEDDING ANNIVERSARY

For our fiftieth wedding anniversary in 2004, Carol and I were just going to have some champagne with Thomas and any family members who wanted to come. For Tom, this wasn't enough. He wanted to celebrate his parents' fiftieth wedding anniversary with a party and to invite my IU colleagues and friends in town. He called Jocelyn Wentworth, who had helped with OctubaFest. She said, "I'd love to help."

He sent e-mails, made phone calls, did shopping and cleaned the house; everything was spic and span. He made the best menu of hors d'oeuvres I'd ever seen. He called G.R. Davis about providing some music for the occasion. On Saturday, G.R. arrived from Nashville, Tennessee, with Romey, popular vocalist with swing band repertoire. They played till 1 AM in Nashville, grabbed a few hours of sleep and drove six hours to perform. G.R. played bass with Romey's pianist Phil Rugh to back up this wonderful singer.

People who received Thomas's invitation put aside whatever they were doing and came to celebrate with us. Jocelyn baked and decorated a three-tier wedding cake and served as hostess, assisting Tom in myriad ways. More than 150 people signed our guest book. It started at noon and went all day until 8 PM. Many people from IU and the community came.

Fifty years went by too fast for both Carol and me. The first ten years, we didn't have children and went everywhere together. The second ten years, once we started our family, my five-day rule (for the family traveling with me) went into effect; this was marked by trips to Asia, Europe, Australia, and Puerto Rico. I always said that I had quality time with my children. Spending hours on long flights over the ocean and on tour with them brought us together. As much as possible, I tried to attend my sons' football and Little League baseball games. Students enlarged my family by their number. I moved to Bloomington essentially to have more time with my family but I found it was something you had to work at. I remember what Barbara Chapin, my secretary at the New England Conservatory, said when I told her how much extra time I'd have to devote to my family in Indiana: "Mr. Phillips, you have to remember one thing. You take yourself with you."

I was so busy and kept myself so full of work and projects that the days just ran over each other. I find it very difficult now to be seventy-seven years old; I never thought I'd make it.

THE FIFTIETH ANNIVERSARY OF THE NEW YORK BRASS QUINTET

The first Brass Chamber Music Forum, held from October 21–23, 2004, was conceived, organized, and hosted by William L. Jones, trumpet professor of the Hayes School of Music at Appalachian State University in Boone, North Carolina. He was a brass chamber music participant and enthusiast, and a long-time admirer of the New York Brass Quintet, the first professional brass quintet in the world. Jones was inspired to recognize the fiftieth-anniversary year of the New York Brass Quintet's debut performance in New York City's famous Town Hall on June 11, 1954, which was booked by artist manager Erminie Kahn.

In three lively days there was talk about brass music, playing of brass music, critiques of student players, and anecdotes from the early days of NYBQ concerts and touring. The forum began with Eric Ewazen's "A Western Fanfare" played by the Bay Street Brassworks, a brass quintet based in Baltimore that formed in a class at the Peabody Conservatory in 1995, now touring and doing educational concerts. Bill Jones then introduced a fourteen-member panel, comprising musicians who had played in the New York Brass Quintet during its thirty years of concertizing; the current American Brass Quintet, none of them original members; a trombonist from the Annapolis Brass Quintet, which existed from 1971 to 1993; and an educator, Frank Battisti, to talk about the amazingly brief history of brass quintets. We appreciated that both the Band of the Air Force Reserve Brass Quintet and the American Brass Quintet also performed to honor us.

Reminiscing, horn player Paul Ingraham recalled an ice storm in Massachusetts in 1963 that caused the concert to start with the musicians who were on time—a trio. He also told of a 10 AM recording session in Denmark. "They scheduled a half-hour of warm up for us and told us, 'We are a small country. We don't splice.'"

Quintet No. 1 for Brass by William G. Harbinson, who composed it to commemorate the fiftieth anniversary of the New York Brass Quintet, was played at the final concert, by the American Brass Quintet, joined by Bob Nagel and Toby Hanks.

An Account Contributed by Gunther Schuller

"I was very happy to be able to attend the conference to help celebrate the New York Brass Quintet, which was the first really permanent brass quintet and which, besides playing a lot of marvelous concerts beautifully, commissioned a lot of brass quintet music. They spawned other brass quintets just by their influence—the Empire, the Canadian, and the American among them. I have written for the New York and American brass quintets, by the way. It was wonderful nostalgia for me, to see brass-playing friends. I was a French horn player for twenty-five years on the New York scene. To go back half your lifetime is quite an emotional experience. Also I felt it was educational for a lot of younger or not quite so involved brass players who were also there, to hear some of the history, in terms of the repertoire that was written for the New York Brass Quintet and others. There are probably 250 brass quintets in the United States now. All that repertoire is now with us and some of it is very good. Some is dross, perhaps. There is only going to be a small percent that will last through the centuries. We hear too many cliches showing up, triple tonguing, and I must have heard 120 pieces that are in 12/8 time and have triplets flying by.

"In every kind of music—string quartet, orchestral, lieder, in every period, since the beginning of the twentieth century—there are maybe half a dozen really great composers who add to the development of music. Maybe twenty or thirty write damn good music and the rest maybe competent but don't write anything you want to hear many times. Brass quintets can't get away from that. That's human nature, human creativity.

"It was wonderful to see Harvey Phillips. His personal and artistic integrity shines through whenever he speaks. It was also amazing for me to hear how fantastically well Robert Nagel plays at eighty, just as he played forty years ago. As a brass player, that is not supposed to be possible, physically or psychologically."

Added Impressions by Robert Nagel

"Bill did a great job of organizing and presenting this first Brass Chamber Music Forum. Spirits were high, and, speaking on behalf of everyone involved with the NYBQ, we appreciate the honors and recognition bestowed on us, especially that of the American Brass Quintet, which attended—and performed—in our honor.

"I feel that having leading composers of brass music, Gunther Schuller and Eric Ewazen, plus Frank Battisti—champion advocates of new brass ensemble and wind ensemble music—in active participation was a real highlight of the Forum.

"Overall, I believe the Forum aptly demonstrated that dedicated musicians, both here and abroad, have contributed to the development of brass chamber music over the years. They have accomplished much for the art of brass music and furthered significant traditions of repertoire and performance for future generations."

Celebrating the NYBQ's fiftieth anniversary, a CD was made of the quintet's first two recordings, released in 1959 and 1960.

CHAPTER SEVENTEEN

Renaissance of the Tuba: A Summary

IN DISCUSSIONS WITH FRIENDS and associates, I would occasionally hear, "Harvey, you take the tuba too seriously." When appropriate, my response was, "The tuba is my vocation and my avocation; it houses, clothes, and feeds my family. Don't you think I should take it seriously? If everyone took their profession more seriously, their life with their families and friends would be more fulfilling." I'm just as serious about what I do, about my instrument, as my two sons, who are surgeons, are about their scalpels! We try to work with the same precision, the same artistic concern for the patient, for those who will listen to us, and hopefully learn to admire what we do. As Bruce Duffie, a Chicago radio personality, said, "The surgeon works on the physical body; the musician works on the immortal soul!"

As I look back on my life as a dedicated tuba player and musician, my proudest achievement is the role I have played in helping to elevate the quality and abundance of tuba repertoire in all music disciplines and styles. I have prompted many composers to be aware of the tuba as a principal instrument in the symphony orchestra, to recognize its potential in brass quintet and other chamber music combinations, to include it in their compositions, orchestrations, and arrangements, and to be familiar with the world's great tubists, gain their acquaintance, and know their individual qualities and special sphere of activities.

I have conceived public events that welcome performance participation of bass tubists and tenor tubists (baritone, euphonium) of all ages and expertise. These events are performed for the public audience free of charge.

An example of perseverance to achieve an intended goal was set in the late 1700s by Johnny Appleseed, who planted apple seeds across the land. He knew the seeds would grow into mature trees bearing apples for the populace. I endeavored to plant seeds for tuba repertoire. I knew they would bear fruit eventually and give tubists a bountiful library.

TUBISTS' ACCEPTANCE OF SUBSTANDARD LITERATURE

Before 1950, the tuba as a solo instrument played sea chanteys and polkas—themes with variations and characteristic novelties, destined to be played, if at all, on a program of "a summer band concert in the park." They were at best a curiosity, an entertaining feature, a light distraction from the "real" band selections on the program. In fact, hardly a solo for brass existed that was *not* a theme and variations. Every piece was worked under the same formula: theme, cadenza, variations, and closing. One of the most popular is "Solo Pomposo," which is often the first tuba solo challenging the developing high school tubist. It was mine.

I find it surprising that apparently none of the great tubists of the late nineteenth and early twentieth centuries took the initiative to commission new solo repertoire from the great composers of their time—they were already writing challenging and rewarding orchestral tuba parts. Tubists would have been coming into contact regularly with music by Prokofiev, Tchaikovsky, Rimsky-Korsakov, Igor Stravinsky, Johannes Brahms, Bela Bartok, Aaron Copland, and many others, but apparently never approached these composers about stretching their treatment of the tuba into serious solo literature. Speaking from my own experience, I will forever find it difficult to believe that great tuba musicians could be satisfied by solo repertoire about the devilish Beelzebub and pachyderms. Thankfully, and mercifully, the pattern was broken in 1954.

I'm proud to say that I was one of the New York musicians who championed the listing of the performing personnel on commercial recordings, years after tubist George Bouje was not credited on the most famous recording of "Tubby the Tuba." This action improved, especially at West Coast companies, but was not embraced by many record companies. The Burke-Phillips All-Star Concert Band recordings listed personnel and instrumentation on the front of the first LP and inside the folding cover of the second.

On June 4, 1954, the Ralph Vaughan Williams *Concerto for Bass Tuba and Orchestra* was premiered by tubist Philip Catelinet. I got a letter from Philip that said he was preparing it for a concert with the London Philharmonic Orchestra and, in his British humor, made little of it. In point of fact, Philip, a composer himself, was disappointed with the Vaughan Williams work. I don't believe that he recognized the importance of breaking new ground with composers throughout the world, especially one with the stature of Ralph Vaughan Williams. One year later, in 1955, Paul Hindemith, another prominent composer, wrote his *Sonata for Tuba and Piano*. Diving into the work with enthusiasm, I realized that we tubists had gained the influence of two of the world's most respected composers. I tried always to remember this and use the information when approaching other composers to write for our instrument.

It is regrettable that 119 years had to pass after the tuba was patented before the first serious concerto for tuba with orchestra was written. All tuba players will forever be indebted to Ralph Vaughan Williams and Paul Hindemith for their respectful tips of the hat to our instrument. These two pieces helped to open the floodgates for commissions of new solo literature. But neither of these works was written for a particular player. No tuba player asked these composers to write these pieces.

The fuse for the explosion of solo works for tuba that I instigated was lit in 1950 with Vincent Persichetti's observations, advice, and encouragement to me, an admitted "fixer." Before 1950 the priority of most tubists was winning a position with an orchestra or symphonic band. Technique was the most important asset. The range of tubists rarely ventured above middle C. Novelty numbers were the only considerations given to solos for tuba, with the exception of a few transcriptions of Bach, Beethoven, Handel, and Schumann.

Over the course of my career, I commissioned, inspired, coerced, or did whatever it took to generate new works for the tuba. I learned quickly that composers, whose lives are made of sounds—timbres and harmonies in unique combinations—were always interested in using instruments in new ways and were often sympathetic to my cause. I am proud to take credit for more than one hundred solo works, with more to come.

Sadly, Alvin Etler, who had promised me a concerto, passed away before he could write it. I was again disappointed when my good friend Morton Gould passed away in 1996 before he could compose the concerto for tuba and orchestra I had commissioned from him. I was told by his assistant that she had never seen him more excited about a commission. I tried for years to get tubists to join together and pay for commissioning new works for tuba, but I finally gave up trying and accepted the status quo, which was that I commissioned composers on my own. When I found myself too busy to premiere some of these compositions, I passed them on to others for premiere performances. Roger Bobo recorded a work written for me with cello before I had time to play it.

To me, it doesn't matter if a work says "commissioned by," "inspired by," or "dedicated to." Each work is a testament to a relationship between the tubist and the composer.

The growth of solo repertoire has happened at an astonishing rate since Vaughan Williams wrote *Concerto for Bass Tuba and Orchestra* in 1954. Today there are more than one thousand compositions written for an ever-increasing number of outstanding tuba soloists. Tubists and composers throughout the world have "discovered" each other. I was certainly not the only tubist who took the initiative to commission new works. My former student Michael Lind has commissioned more than seventy compositions from Scandinavian composers. And we should not fail to mention the Hollywood studio tubists, led by Jim Self and the late Tommy Johnson, whose technical virtuosity allowed film composers to break new ground in brass writing. Tommy Johnson played the shark music in *Jaws* and Jim Self musically portrayed the aliens' mother ship as it communicated with

Earth in *Close Encounters of the Third Kind*. Both are John Williams scores; he also wrote a concerto for tuba and orchestra.

I encourage my students and all serious-minded tubists to seek tuba literature from even young composers. I have discovered that if we wait until a composer has reached renown, he may be too old, too committed, and too expensive to write for our instrument. In 1929, Vincent Persichetti, age fourteen, composed *Opus 1*, for combined woodwind and brass quintets. It was published by Elkan Vogel in Philadelphia. At that time there were no acknowledged woodwind or brass quintets.

I had the best luck with composers who were also friends—they knew I had no financial support outside of my own tuba playing, so they were willing to work for modest commissions. Vincent Persichetti, for example, agreed to accept a case of Beefeater gin for his *Serenade No. 12* for solo tuba. But my firm policy was that composing wouldn't cost them anything. Sometimes their commission was a clean set of parts ready for publication. I wouldn't want to deny a composer even one opportunity to have his music played.

Some composers tell me that writing for the tuba advanced their careers in ways they didn't expect. All seemed to be grateful for the chance to write for the tuba.

ELEMENTS OF THE RENAISSANCE

A renaissance doesn't happen overnight. Elements that started the Tuba Renaissance included:

1. The recognition of tuba as a principal chair in the orchestra
2. Increase of the major orchestras' seasons from 32–36 weeks to 52 weeks, including a vacation period
3. The acceptance of women and minorities in the orchestra
4. The steady growth of brass chamber music, including tuba
5. The innovations of the tuba in modern jazz
6. The explosion of solo literature for tuba
7. The increase in full-time tuba faculty positions at colleges and universities (in 2002–2003 there were 737)
8. The improvement in instrument quality

9. The presentation of public events showcasing the tenor-bass tuba choir
10. Establishment of the International Horn Society, International Trumpet Guild, International Trombone Association, and Tubists Universal Brotherhood Association (now International Tuba Euphonium Association)
11. The worldwide interest in international brass symposia and the unprecedented forum for exchange of ideas that happen there
12. The increase in solo recitals and featured soloists with orchestra, band, and wind ensemble

I felt it important that great new solo compositions be widely heard by audiences and so I endeavored to create public performances of them whenever possible. Some of the more fruitful of these performances were the recitals that I presented in Carnegie Hall. My logic in presenting five recitals in nine days, rather than one recital, was to create a sense of permanence of the tuba as a solo instrument in a variety of instrumental settings.

All my life I've been a fixer and organizer. If I experienced or observed the need for new music I set about commissioning works that would fill the void of repertoire. I've told students and my colleagues to generate compositions for the tuba with established chamber ensembles such as a string quartet, woodwind quintet, saxophone quartet, or other concert ensemble that has already established an audience and repertoire. This presents the tuba to an unknown audience, and as the old saying goes, you are judged by the company you keep.

In the 1950s I served on orchestra committees and joined others in improving the status of music. I played an instrument that has taken more than its share of abuse and misunderstanding from both the public and professional communities. Tuba players were especially isolated by their lack of numbers in any kind of music ensemble. One of one hundred instruments in the orchestra is a tuba. In the concert band of fifty players, there would be three to four tubas and two to four euphoniums. In the British brass band there are two E♭ and two BB♭ tubas, two baritones, and two euphoniums.

SYMPOSIUM ACCOMPLISHMENTS

What has been accomplished by brass workshops and symposia? So much that it's overwhelming. There have been opportunities for discussions of mutual concerns about the quality and quantity of solo literature, chamber ensemble literature, new organized memberships, new directions, better instruments and accessories, visibility, and public and professional awareness. These gatherings let the performers know what instruments and pieces of music are available, and point out the shortcomings of instrument manufacturers. The most important thing is that they bring people together to share all aspects of playing their instruments and to network and learn from one another. One thing I always dreamed of doing is combining an official meeting of a composer organization (such as Meet the Composer) with a brass conference.

It is distressing to scan through a roster of memberships and discover that some of those who benefit most from an organization's purpose and objectives withhold their membership and support. I'll never understand how a professional artist can accept, without conscience, the expenditure, time, and energy of his or her professional colleagues. I saw the need early on to have things organized among tubists. We were denied a lot because we were denying ourselves.

I got involved with a musicians union and became an orchestra committee chairman of almost every orchestra I was involved with. I thought it was important to have other opportunities, which is why I fell into the brass quintet with my total energy. I felt the need for musicians of common interest to get together on an organized basis to improve the profession. All the brass symposia have had tremendous success because they were organized with specific goals in mind. Brass conferences have helped people appreciate where they stand in the world of performance. What all the meetings have given us are opportunities to work together for common goals.

I wanted composers to provide program notes for every solo work and major chamber music work that involved tuba and send them to TUBA. For deceased composers, when possible I would have another composer of his generation or a closely involved student provide program notes, so that the notes impart information, not opinion. I thought we had a lot of catching up to do. I passed this idea on to one of my students, Gary Bird, who proposed program notes as the subject of his doctoral thesis. When a committee turned that down, he wrote about the use of predecessors of the tuba in nineteenth century orchestral music. Later, he wrote a book, *Program Notes for the Solo Tuba,* which was published by Indiana University Press in 1994. I wrote the foreword.

What yet needs to be accomplished? Loyal audiences for our music. To maintain that audience, you need a high quality of performances. At this time, every audience and every member of an audience wants to be entertained, not educated. The Canadian Brass knows this and makes sure its audience has fun. Early on, formal performance by the New York Brass Quintet paved the way.

A SENSE OF COMMUNITY

At Indiana University I always made an effort to include the public audience. I wanted to interact with the community with all of our activities, including OctubaFest and TubaChristmas. I knew that scholarship support someday might come from the private sector. The private sector learned of our serious commitment and our serious intentions and shared with us some of the pleasure and enjoyment we derived from making music. I am a little unhappy when I hear of an International Tuba Euphonium Conference where the only people who attend any of the events are those who are there as participants and the local communities are totally unaware of the week's activities.

Perhaps this happens because the public has not been invited, or hasn't had its excitement piqued enough to come to a tuba concert. There needs to be conversation among the business community, the college community, and the general public. Musicians go to a retirement community to perform because the residents can't come to us. That's why a portable stage, with sound equipment—which Bloomington, Indiana, has—is a good idea. People may have a preconceived notion about the tuba, or perhaps no one has challenged their assumptions about the music that we make. We can never extend too many invitations.

Recently I was involved in an activity of this kind, and I asked the director of the event, "How large is the auditorium?" I was told it seated just a little over a thousand, but, as usual, it wouldn't be filled. I said, "How big is the city?"

"Well, a million and a half at least."

I said, "You mean to tell me that there aren't a thousand people out of a million and a half who would enjoy hearing some of the greatest brass players in the world perform in concert?" There is something wrong with our efforts if we don't popularize our instruments and the music they produce with the general public. Without an audience, a performance is just a closed rehearsal.

Leon Barzin, born in 1900, was principal chair violist with the New York Philharmonic at age eighteen and played on a famous recording of *Ein Heldenleiben* conducted by Willem Mengelberg. Once, Toscanini was conducting a rehearsal and had to leave the stage for a time. He handed the baton to Barzin, who had studied conducting with Eugene Ysaye. Barzin waited for Toscanini to leave the stage. Then he told the musicians that he expected the same from them that they gave the Maestro. He was telling them the music is the same, no matter who is conducting.

Barzin left the Philharmonic in 1930—to the surprise of many colleagues—to found the National Orchestral Association, the country's first training orchestra. Barzin's concerns, for more American-trained musicians in American orchestras, opened the door wide for musicians of every race and gender. The training of top conservatory and school of music students has raised the professional level of all orchestras and emboldened the second, third, and fourth tiers of the orchestra hierarchy. Barzin was magic as a conductor. He did things with a baton I never saw another conductor do. I performed the Ralph Vaughan Williams *Tuba Concerto* in 1956 with Barzin conducting the National Orchestral Association, the only time I performed it in Carnegie Hall's main hall.

When I began playing, auditions were often conducted by the maestro in his hotel room. Five tuba players showed up for the audition in New York for the Minneapolis Orchestra, for conductor Antal Dorati. Only two of them were qualified to do it. I went to the audition to see what it was like because I had never been to an orchestra audition. I was offered the job and turned it down, because I was enrolled at Juilliard on a draft deferment from the Korean War.

Sometimes, a conductor would prefer taking the recommendation of an established performer rather than to bother with the expense of an audition. In the early 1950s, some conductors would take someone from the orchestra with him and go to several major cities to hold auditions.

Some orchestras were able to extend their seasons by doing park concerts or light summer programs. The best illustration of this is Arthur Fiedler and the Boston Pops and the summer residency of the Boston Symphony Orchestra at Tanglewood. The New York Philharmonic has presented mini-summer seasons at Lewisohn Stadium. The Philadelphia Orchestra plays at Saratoga in the summer.

In the future, tuba players who also compose will be properly trained by professional pedagogues of composition as well as of the tuba. They will not be misdirected by incorrect notions of the limits of the tuba's potential, as described by Walter Piston in his heralded textbook on orchestration. There will continue to be new challenges, as-yet-unrealized new techniques consistently upgrading the potential of the tuba. Composers are no longer afraid to write important passages for the tuba. In the nineteenth century, tuba players apparently chose to write their own solos, two or three minutes long, within a large work, rather than request established composers to expand on their orchestral writing.

Right up to today, the renaissance is still going on. Today we have tuba players who are writing works for the tuba, such as John Stevens at the University of Wisconsin. He received a commission from the Chicago Symphony Orchestra to write a concerto for tuba, which was premiered by Gene Pokorny. Other tuba players who are serious composers, including Gregory Fritze, Eugene Anderson, and Jim Self, are receiving requests and commissions from fellow tuba players.

Today, professional bands are best represented by the military bands in Washington, D.C. Some of them travel, filling the voids left by now-defunct civilian professional bands. The demise of the Goldman Band, a New York cultural gem for over fifty years, was no less than tragic.

For years, musicians spoke of the "Big Five" orchestras in no special order: New York, Boston, Philadelphia, Cleveland, and Chicago. Tuba players in the Big Five orchestras may have careers of thirty or thirty-five years. Arnold Jacobs performed for forty-five years in the Chicago Symphony.

Giovanni Manuti was in the Met Opera Orchestra for forty-five years. We figure there will be an opening twice a century.

If you see you can't be in the top five and you want to have a career as an orchestral tuba player, don't look askance when opportunities arise for the second-, third-, and fourth-tier orchestras, because the music you play is the same. The lower-tier orchestras pay better now than they used to and their concert season is more assured. If you play *Petrouchka* with your school orchestra, you will be playing the same notes as you would in the Chicago Symphony or the New York Philharmonic. And the music should be approached with the same integrity.

It depends on what lifestyle you want, too. If you want to live in the country, a good orchestra for you might be Nashville, Jacksonville, Des Moines, Minnesota, etc.

It's possible today that the brass sections of Los Angeles, Baltimore, the National Symphony, St. Louis, Detroit, Dallas, San Francisco, Houston, Atlanta, Minnesota, Seattle, Denver, Pittsburgh, Indianapolis, Toronto, Montreal, even Sarasota—the so-called "second-tier" orchestras—could give the Big Five a run for their money.

The standards set by Pryor, Mantia, Helleberg, and Bell, which remained as an established plateau for many years, have now been surpassed considerably and there is no turning back. International solo and ensemble competitions are coming to the fore all over the world. Each of these competitions reveals wunderkinds and inspires composers to write new and ever more challenging works. When symphony orchestras today announce an opening for tenor trombone, bass trombone, or tuba, as many as two hundred applicants may respond, and half of them (or more) are qualified for the position. When the major service bands announce an opening for euphonium or tuba, they expect one hundred or more applicants for each instrument.

It should also be mentioned that the tuba and euphonium have been embraced by exceptionally gifted women performers, who have won important teaching and performing positions. Most notable is the first celebrated woman tubist, Constance Weldon, who performed with the Kansas City Philharmonic in the 1950s and taught for many years for the University of Miami. More recently, an exceptional performer, Carol Jantsch, won the coveted tuba chair of the Philadelphia Orchestra. Soon, there will be many other female tubists winning auditions and leveling the artistic playing field.

With each generation come unique artists who have worked hard to raise the standards and create opportunities. The Tuba Renaissance could not have happened without the work of artists including Winston Morris, Dan Perantoni, Floyd Cooley, Don Harry, John Fletcher, Michael Lind, Roger Bobo, Mel Culbertson, Bob Tucci, Gene Pokorny, Sam Pilafian, Daryl Smith, David LeClair, Jens Bjorn Larsen, Tim Northcutt, Chitate Kagawa, Koji Suzuki, and others. But the first credit is due to William Bell's attempts to transcribe music of Bach, Handel, Schumann, etc. The other players of his generation weren't even doing that.

I'm all for transcriptions. For years you couldn't hear a tuba player playing Mozart. But when a Mozart horn solo is transcribed and a tuba player plays it, then he or she must be judged by the same criteria as a horn player. If a violinist plays a great solo and a tubist plays "Solo Pomposo," you can't compare them. You need two pieces with the same musical integrity. I've always said the tuba needs literature good enough that other instruments want to borrow it. For example, the "Romanza" movement of the Ralph Vaughan Williams *Concerto for Bass Tuba and Orchestra* has been transcribed for cello.

When I play something in an orchestra by a well-known living composer and he writes well for my instrument, that's an invitation to ask him for works with a more involved tuba part. I want the composer to be astute enough to know what a particular instrument or player is capable of.

Most of the playing that's done in the symphony orchestra is chamber music. Each performer must be sensitive to intonation, dynamics, and blending of the instrumental colors. Sometimes the instrumentalist you need to blend with is sitting a fair distance away from you.

There are moments when the whole orchestra is just roaring and then there are other moments when the whole brass section is roaring, but for the most part it is chamber music. I think of Prokofiev and *The Prodigal Son* or the *Fifth Symphony,* which is the closest thing to a tuba concerto he ever wrote. There are passages with tuba, bass clarinet, flute, and violin, and those musicians are sitting twenty-five feet apart. In the second movement of Mahler's *Symphony No. 1*, the little trio starts with the contrabass and then the bassoon and then the tuba. Those musicians, sitting twenty-five feet apart, have got to blend and match sound level. That's chamber music personified.

Other challenging composition techniques include unison. Example: When I first arrived in New York, a passage in Wagner's *Die Meistersinger* was often referred to by other tubists as a tuba solo. It's not a solo; it's really tutti. Wagner was smart enough to add tuba. The basses and bassoons couldn't define the passage nearly as well as when tuba was added. It's also one of those parts easy to play too loud.

Symphony orchestra tuba players have accepted playing chamber music partly because it enhances, to varying degrees, their professional income as tubists. Playing a week with a symphony orchestra gives you lots of free time. What are you doing on Monday, on Tuesday afternoon, on Thursday morning, when you are not in rehearsal? If you are comfortable with different styles and chamber ensembles, you could be making commercial recordings, giving school demonstration concerts, or putting together recital programs.

I have already discussed in detail the circumstances surrounding the formation of the New York Brass Ensemble and the New York Brass Quintet, but the importance of these two ensembles to the Tuba Renaissance cannot be overstated. In particular, the prize-winning Gabrieli recording of the New York Brass Ensemble caught the attention of many important musicians and conductors and paved the way for a new level of brass chamber music. Prior to 1950, the brass chamber ensemble repertoire was almost nonexistent. But by 1954, the New York Brass Quintet was firmly established as an important chamber ensemble and began researching and discovering brass chamber music and commissioning new repertoire. Every new piece written for a brass quintet was a chance for a composer to write for the tuba in a performance setting that had not yet been considered. Many great works were written with excellent tuba parts, including the Bozza *Sonatine,* the Malcolm Arnold *Quintet*, Alvin Etler's *Quintet for Brass Instruments,* and Gunther Schuller's *Brass Quintet*. Another important piece is Ingolf Dahl's *Music for Brass Instruments.*

The growth of brass quintets provided ample performance opportunities for tubists. Led by the New York Brass Quintet, the American Brass Quintet (with bass trombone), the Canadian Brass, the Empire Brass, the Los Angeles Brass Quintet, the Philip Jones Brass Quintet, the United States Army Brass Quintet, and others, the quintet quickly became an accepted chamber medium. And with this acceptance came further acceptance for the tuba. The establishment of brass quintets throughout the world has done more to elevate brass instrument performance than any other medium including symphony orchestra, wind ensemble, and concert band. I could list some of the prominent new brass quintets of the last twenty years, but they are too many to count! Their growth in numbers and proficiency has been impressive. Adding a brass quintet to the chamber music program (woodwinds, strings, etc.) also increases the number of students whose interest and development warrant a chance at a professional career in their chosen medium.

Furthermore, the brass quintet represents a good opportunity for tubists because of sheer economics. The playing opportunities are proportionately greater for tuba players in chamber music than in orchestral playing, and the creation of a new professional brass quintet provides an equal employment opportunity for the tubist compared with horn and trombone. Moreover, the forming of a brass quintet, compared with that of a new symphony orchestra, has a significantly smaller budget! The highest-paid tuba player in the world is not in the Berlin Philharmonic but in the Canadian Brass Quintet.

One of the things that helps me justify using massed tubas and euphoniums, in TubaChristmas for example, is that people see and hear tubas, which means they can see and hear them in their minds. Then, when they hear a commercial on the radio and it includes a tuba, they recognize what it is.

Eighteen to twenty students are assigned to each applied professor of a given instrument at Indiana University. If there are one hundred violin majors, there will be at least five teachers of violin. Having five hundred tubists show up for TubaChristmas in big cities means that some young ones will choose to pursue a career in music. TubaChristmas gives a youngster an opportunity to broaden his understanding of his instrument—it is the only opportunity that eleven- and twelve-year-olds have to perform in the same ensemble with established professional artists, enthusiastic amateurs of every age, serious conservatory and school of music students, and high school students preparing for college study. And the audience is the public, people who appreciate and enjoy the massed choir of tenor and bass brass instruments.

Because it takes so long for a string player to develop performance skills, many high schools have active band programs instead of orchestras. Junior high school teachers tell me that, before the creation of TubaChristmas and OctubaFest, for years they would have to assign their overabundance of trumpet students to play tuba and euphonium. Now, on the day that students are recruited for their junior high band program, they come to the director and tell him or her that they want to play tuba or euphonium.

For years, university schools of music didn't have a tuba teacher. One teacher taught trombone, euphonium, and tuba. By generating people's interest in playing the tuba and euphonium we increased the number who wanted to enroll for study, which in turn justified each added teaching position. Colleges and universities, which before about 1970 generally hired brass teachers only as adjunct faculty, became increasingly attracted to the idea of a faculty brass quintet. This required them to hire full-time professors for each position. Suddenly the tuba teacher at a university saw his title change from brass instructor to artist-in-residence.

With tuba faculty positions come increased solo opportunities in the form of faculty recitals and concerto performances with the school orchestra and wind ensemble. This has the added benefit of demonstrating to the tuba students from the very beginning of their careers that the tuba has a natural and well-earned position in solo and chamber music, as well as in band, wind ensemble, and orchestral music.

A beginning tuba student must have the strength to manage the size and weight of the tuba, have even teeth (there are exceptions), and be in general good health. He or she should be old enough to participate actively in music ensembles. Ideally, a student will have enthusiasm for music, talent, desire, an outgoing personality, and leadership ability. A wimp will not make a good tubist.

The human voice is the most physical of all musical instruments. Brass instruments are the second-most physical. Both generate sound with vibrations of vocal chords or vibrating lips. Both resonate within the human body.

When a student shows enthusiasm for music, his or her interest should be served and guided. When parents inquire about why their child should be in a music program, I tell them, "Music is fun and will enhance the child's total education." Starting with the school's resident teachers, recommendations can be made for regularly scheduled private lessons with a noted player of the instrument chosen. Such guidance is important to avoid bad playing habits which will need correction and hold back a student's progress. Also important is the acquisition of a quality instrument. Parents are cautioned to rely on the private teacher to recommend an instrument that will assist the development of basic skills. An instrument can be rented or sometimes borrowed from a good private teacher, or provided by the school, for the first year. When a teacher feels that the student is advanced enough and the parents feel their child is interested enough, it is time to consider purchasing a quality instrument. While it is not necessary to buy the most expensive instrument you can find, I believe that providing a bad instrument is like giving a student a pencil without a point. Having his or her own instrument will hasten the development of each student. A beginning instrument player shouldn't be blamed for the faults of the instrument he or she is playing.

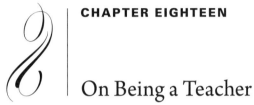

CHAPTER EIGHTEEN

On Being a Teacher

BECOMING A TEACHER of music is a calling equal to that of religion. Teaching personifies a devout life of selfless giving and sharing all that you have with others. Instrumental teaching is like being a parent, a lifetime commitment concerned with every aspect of life. It demands that you continually seek to add to your knowledge and experience so that you have more to give and share. We who teach one-on-one hope our offspring will be good musical citizens, sharing their gifts of talent and achievement with the world in future generations.

Let me quote Phil Woods, friend and colleague of fifty-four years, and in my opinion the greatest jazz alto saxophonist of his generation. In a major magazine interview about the teachers of great jazz players, Phil related the experiences he had with his first teacher, Harvey LaRose of Springfield, Massachusetts. Phil spoke of the profound influence this teacher had on everything he had accomplished professionally. The publishers notified Phil that his interview would not be published because no one connected with their publication had ever heard of Harvey LaRose. Didn't Phil study with a famous saxophone player or teacher known to their readership? Phil's response was perfect, and shared by many: "The unsung heroes of our music profession are often the local teachers who help us discover ourselves through their concern and toil. It was Mr. Harvey LaRose who turned me on to Benny Carter, Johnny Hodges, and Charlie Parker (!) plus he taught me the American songbook and gave me advanced improvisation lessons when I was thirteen years old!"

Like Mr. LaRose, my high school teachers endeavored to teach each student everything they could. They seemed proud and content to live their success in music through their devoted and eager students. I realized some time ago how very fortunate I was to have had the influence of such great teachers throughout my life. Many great teachers are conspicuous by their success and reputation and have the success of students to prove it. We are irresponsible when we ignore rather than adopt and pass on to others the great early teaching we encounter and benefit from.

When I was a beginning and developing student, teachers Alice Hardin and Homer Lee were just what I needed. In their own special ways, they guided and supported me and challenged me to practice diligently and to be proud of my instrument and the music I played. There were no restrictions or microscopic studies of a particular music discipline, and if on my own time I wanted to play melodic lines of any style, I was encouraged to do so. The bass parts I played enhanced the melodies and countermelodies and made me aware of dynamic balance and the blending of tonal colors.

I doubt I could have explained my awareness at the time, but I had heard enough church singing to know that bass voices complemented the melody and countermelodies of singers or melodic instruments. Nonetheless, I was always eager to get all the music I could out of my tuba; I never considered it a "background" instrument. I enjoyed playing in the band at school. At home I continued playing and enjoying church music and country music. One thing is certain: *never* in my life have I been anything but proud of my tuba, my sousaphone, my helicon, my instrument, or my role(s) in music, whatever the discipline. That is a legacy of great teaching.

I give thanks to the splendid musicians who, from the beginning of my tuba studies and early experience with professional circus bands, encouraged me and taught me, often by their examples. I feel satisfaction in being able to impart a legacy enriched by experience.

I tried as best I could to carry on this legacy with my own students. I remembered how it felt to be a student of Bill Bell—every activity together was a lesson, an opportunity to learn something about the music business or about life. When I finished formal studies with Mr. Bell, I was more than just a technically proficient tuba player. I was a musician who was equipped with all the tools needed to make a life in music.

TEACHING AT IU—BASICS

My studio at Indiana University had a good sense of camaraderie. My students often practiced together in our large tuba locker room, the Tuba Basement, and always got along well with each other. Having such a close environment allows students to learn from each other and provide motivation and support. I advised my students, "If you hear someone doing something you can't do on your instrument, you should feel free to go over to ask the person, 'How do you do that?' And if you yourself are asked such a question, you should have the humility to say, 'Sit down and I'll show you.' Furthermore, if you hear someone practicing and they are doing something wrong, politely tell him or her, 'That's not the right way to do that.'"

But the close-knit environment also can create an overly competitive atmosphere. I always told my students that their focus should be on improving their playing, not on trying to alter their playing beyond their skill level. I have noticed that exceptional students tend not to think about competing on a daily basis; they recognize that the only true competition is internal. You compete with yourself and your own benchmarks. Playing an instrument, especially taking an audition, is more like golf than any other competitive sport: you may be in competition with others, but their mistakes will not put your ball in the hole. I always encouraged my students to discover themselves as individuals in life and in music.

I am flattered and honored that so many of my former students recall fondly their experiences of studying with me. In addition to working with them on the basics of tuba technique, I tried to equip them with the secondary skills needed to make a career in the music business. And as they would all come to find out, my door was (and still is) always open to them.

I tried to teach the whole student. I tried always to speak directly to the student, not to someone who was with him/her or someone else who was in my studio already. I think my attitude resembled that of someone who recognized the incoming student as one who was hungry, thirsty, hot, cold, or in pain, and needed help. I tried to balance out a student's priorities of need. If he or she is still chewing on a last meal, then that person is obviously not hungry. If the student is rude and offensive and shows other ill manners, that's something to work on, before scales, arpeggios, technical studies, or other basic performance considerations. One thing all students and potential artists need is to know how to behave, to be a good musical citizen.

I have often been asked questions about pedagogy. My attitude is "keep it simple." In presenting clinics and master classes, the following material has been used, developed, and revised over many years. I hope this material will answer important pedagogical questions.

First prepared for a California Music Educators Association convention, this information has served me well in discussions on tuba technique and pedagogy. For the purposes of this book, I have expanded some of the points and added some additional thoughts on general musicianship. This provides a summary of my approach to teaching, to playing the tuba, and to being a musician. Non-brass players may find this section overly technical, but I hope that anyone who is a musician may find some useful information in the following.

PHILLIPS PEDAGOGICAL PS OF BRASS PERFORMANCE

Prologue: For the better part of my life I have pursued the knowledge and wisdom of musicians and others I most admire and respect. I have learned much from their experiences and candor as we explored subjects of mutual interest. While knowledge fills volumes of texts readily available for research, wisdom is generally in the intuitive minds of individuals who use knowledge with the addition of logic. Since music is the most organized of all art forms, the merger with logic makes perfect sense. The following points are presented for logical consideration by brass players, particularly tuba students, urged always to keep an open mind and to organize their approach to breath supply and control: producing a clear, centered tone with clean articulations; intonation; range; technique; and musicianship, in that order. Of maximum concern is attitude about self-esteem, family, colleagues, audiences, and strangers. Attitude reflects who you are. Attitude is a major determining factor for achieving success in music and life. I tell teenagers that they will have a smoother transition from their teen years to their adult years if they make a positive impression on every adult they meet, from the janitor to the president of their institution.

Piano should be studied by every musician. The piano keyboard is our most organized visual and tonal reference. Intonation, harmonic structure, and form are at your fingertips when you sit at the piano. The piano keyboard is your best reference for personal ear training. Remember, no one can advance in music beyond his/her ability to hear pitch, tone, balance, blend, rhythm, and style!

Posture is the most important basic consideration in organizing your approach to playing a brass instrument. It allows for correct breathing, breath supply, and control, and the development of maximum endurance. Comfort and balance are always important. Stand or sit erect and relaxed, mouthpiece and valves comfortably accessible. If sitting, be comfortable on flat-bottom chair, feet flat on the floor, straight back, relaxed mid-section, arms relaxed, shoulders down, straight neck, open throat.

Note: Being relaxed and comfortable with pliable mid-section is important for correct breathing and endurance.

Placement of the mouthpiece on the mouth: start centered (left to right) with ⅔ to ¾ upper lip and ⅓ to ¼ lower lip. An embouchure is simply a mouth with *firm* (not tight) corners in place, not pushed forward (pucker), pulled back (smile), or pulled down (anchoring). Puffing the cheeks is a bad habit; it blows away the firm corners of the embouchure. Pulling back the corners is a bad habit; it stretches the flesh of the upper lip, causing too much mouthpiece pressure. Bad habits are hard to break. Bad habits avoided never happen.

If you have mastered the art of circular breathing, you must take in breath through the nose while expelling breath through the mouthpiece and the instrument, in which case you will also have learned the importance of keeping control of the corners of your embouchure.

Preparation of breath supply: you must have a good comfortable supply of air in your lungs! Every note at every dynamic must be strong and rich, supported and directed by air, by breath support and control. A good expression to remember: *Fill your lungs with air as you would fill a bucket* *or glass with water—from the bottom up.* This simple reminder will help prevent shallow breaths. A long phrase will require a full supply of air rationed over the length of the phrase. Brass players should never feel they are about to explode from too much air or faint from having too little air in their lungs.

Once during a lesson, when David LeClair, now in the Basel, Switzerland, Orchestra, asked how to breathe, I flippantly answered, "In and out." But it is true. The breath should not be held at the end of the inhalation nor artificially hindered during the exhalation. Just breathe in and out.

Take in maximum amounts of air through the mouth. Take in minimum amounts of air through the corners of the mouth or nose. Utilize all sources of air. Avoid breathing through the instrument. Before every practice session or performance, I encourage students to do breathing exercises that will increase their lung capacity and strengthen their tone, regardless of dynamic. Breath control is of maximum importance for slurring and clean articulation. Avoid the feeling of tension from too much air and avoid the feeling of weakness from too little air. John Barrows (horn) would say, "If you feel tension or nervousness when you go to play a recital, just think of putting twice your weight on the chair." It relaxes everything from the waist up and stops the tension in your shoulders when you breathe in. Once at a clinic, I was asked, "Mr. Phillips, what do you think about breathing?" I responded, "Well, I think it's a good idea." Breathe naturally and without tension, and the rest will take care of itself.

Placement of each note: Like the piano keyboard, each note has only one position on your brass instrument. Pick up your tuba and visualize a vertical piano keyboard directly in front of you. This creates an imaginary "tuba keyboard." Using the syllable "oh," choose the center note of the complete potential range for your choice of tuba (BB♭—CC—E♭—F). That centered note should be the most comfortable note on your instrument, the easiest to produce with a straightforward, focused airstream. Once you (and your teacher) are pleased with your quality of centered tone, challenge yourself to keep that quality as you develop your range in both directions. Be patient. It takes much regular and correct practice time to develop strength in the facial muscles directly related to the embouchure.

You'll find that in the circle of the mouthpiece, if you blow an airstream toward the top of the mouthpiece, your pitch will rise. If you blow toward the bottom of your receptacle, the pitch drops. This is an important tool for managing intonation. On my own CC tuba, for example—the tuba I used for my entire career—the open "G" in the staff is very sharp. So I learned to blow that note on the bottom part of the circle to pull the pitch down. Changing the pitch in this way may alter your timbre slightly, but it is better to have a different timbre than to be out of tune. You will learn the location of each pitch on your instrument by relating it to its position on the "tuba keyboard." Just as a pianist can find a pitch without looking, so too should a brass player be able to find a pitch without fumbling around. If you find yourself missing notes in the upper range, it can be corrected by relaxation. With enough practice, you will become so familiar with the placement of each note that you will be able to picture in your mind, and feel in your instrument, what kind of air column you need to produce for any particular pitch. This will give you the accuracy that the profession requires of you! Note that a baseball player who hits four out of ten baseballs is a hero, while a symphony musician who hits nine out of ten can be *fired*!

Pivoting minimally (and mentally) is very important. It avoids changing embouchures, excessive pressure, moving the mouthpiece up and down, and any other cumbersome motion as you traverse the range of your instrument. Again I compare the pivoting embouchure to a pianist. The piano keyboard is a horizontal row in which all pitches are available. The pianist must use a consistent method of tone production regardless of the position of the keys; he should not strike the keys any harder just because they are extremely low or high. But he must also pivot his body on the bench to reach those extremes of range. It is a necessary motion that prevents reaching or overextending. So, too, must the tuba player adjust his position to avoid overextending or pushing, in the extreme of register.

As I related earlier in this book, I was encouraged to adopt this "pivot system" early on in my career by my teacher, William J. Bell. I have observed the same system in action by many if not all successful brass players I know. Some students shy away from the term "pivot"; perhaps the word conjures an image of jerky motion that precludes any hope of maintaining smooth intervals. In reality the opposite is true; the pivot allows smoothness and flexibility across all registers. Gradual adjustments must be made across the range of the instrument to maintain the quality of sound. Trumpet players may tell you that they do not pivot, but if they play high notes you can watch their bell go up and if they play low notes the bell goes down. A trombone player might tell you that he doesn't use the pivot system and yet he raises his slide when he plays high. Those are examples of the pivot system in action. Note that I mentioned pivoting *minimally;* some players lose the subtlety and rock like Grandma in a rocking chair on her porch. That's overkill and probably not effective.

It is important to understand that the pivot must be *gradual*—this is the only way to prevent gaps in the range. A player who does not pivot is likely to require a different embouchure for each register. I encountered this in many of my students; they would have one embouchure for the middle range, one for the low range, and another for the high range, and would have to "reset" to access each one. This, of course, is problematic in any musical passage that requires large leaps or smooth connections between registers. By pivoting, the player can approach such passages with smooth, consistent sound.

When developing tuba students enter college for advanced instruction, they are often given the option of either altering or retaining their approach to the instrument. These decisions are always in the forefront of the teacher's mind and can be discussed at any stage of development.

Pivot Points: The three pivot points are (1) the upper rim of the mouthpiece, (2) the hinge of the lower jaw, and (3) the instrument itself as it rests on your lap or chair. Remember the three registers you must develop to the maximum: the low register, the high register, and the *cash register*! The cash register is the middle register; most of the income you derive from being a tuba playing musician is earned in the middle register, with bonuses paid occasionally for extreme high and/or low registers. As you ascend into the upper register (focus on the imaginary "tuba keyboard"), gradually (in one octave) change the syllable TAH to OH, let the instrument bell move toward you and the oral cavity (resonating chamber) get smaller as you raise your jaw, make your lips ever firmer toward the center of your embouchure, and project an ever smaller and colder stream of air for each note as you ascend. As you descend into the low register (again focusing on the imaginary "tuba keyboard"), gradually (in one octave) change the mid-range OH syllable to AH, let the bell move away, and gradually enlarge the oral cavity by gradually dropping the jaw and pushing the chin forward, letting the lips become softer and focusing an airstream ever wider and warmer. Never use an EE vowel; this is indicative of the tongue interfering with the airstream. And keep those corners in place!

The concepts behind the pivot system, which Mr. Bell adapted for his own use and teaching, were first codified by trombonist Donald S. Reinhardt in his *Encyclopedia of the Pivot System*.

Pivot Definitions:

1) The hinge of the jaw is the primary pivot. The jaw opens gradually, increasing the size of the oral cavity and accommodating descent into the lower register. The embouchure remains focused, and the airstream gets warmer, moves more slowly, and is directed upward.

2) The upper mouthpiece rim (embouchure contact) acts as a hinge, allowing and accommodating the lower jaw to open, causing the mouth (resonating chamber) and lower lip to enlarge gradually as the teeth part. *Important: The corners of the mouth remain firm and in place—the cheeks do not puff.*

3) The butt of the tuba acts as a hinge minimally and opposite the hinge in pivot No. 2. Approaching the upper register, from the neutral position described above, requires opposite movements.

4) Upper Register: As the range ascends, the jaw is raised (a minuscule amount) while the corners of the mouth become more firm, the muscles of the embouchure become more focused and directed toward the center of the embouchure, and the airstream becomes cooler and is projected downward.

Pivot System Makes Sense: Mr. Bell's explanation and demonstration made logical sense to me. It allowed me to place each note on the tuba confidently over a three-plus-octave range and over a full range of dynamics. Mr. Bell urged me to adopt the system, and I started feeling and hearing positive results immediately. Once it became my natural approach to playing the tuba, I no longer had technical issues interfere with playing music. I had no need to experiment with another search for the right embouchure. I never considered any other approach until I started teaching a lot and had to deal with one homemade bad habit system after another.

Pressure on the embouchure should be minimal at all times, but enough to prevent air leakage. Pressure will increase in the higher register and/or in louder dynamics, and it will decrease in the lower register and/or softer dynamics. At all times there must be minimal contact pressure on the upper lip, which offers a natural cushion for it. The lower lip must be pliable, able to relax as the jaw opens (increasing the oral cavity), tighten as the jaw closes (decreasing the oral cavity), and allow for directing the airstream for pitch (note) placement in a descending or ascending direction and as logically indicated by the imaginary "tuba keyboard." Lower pressure allows for greater endurance.

One good exercise to reduce mouthpiece pressure is to play a moderately high note, such as middle C (above the bass clef staff), and sustain the note while consciously relaxing every part of the body until only your lip remains tight. When you reach this state of total relaxation except for the firmness of your embouchure, you have found the most efficient playing position. Increasing endurance is one of the most important early goals for a young tuba player. I have seen people exit practice rooms after an hour or less with an exhausted look and a hand massaging their lips. They are playing with too much pressure. If you play efficiently and develop endurance, you can practice for three hours at a time instead of one hour, and will therefore improve three times faster!

Production of a clear, centered tone, in the center of your instrument's potential range, is the *first* important achievement for any student brass player. Maintaining consistent quality of tone throughout your potential range requires understanding of breath supply, breath support, and breath control. Remember that tubas are wind instruments *first,* brass instruments *second,* and musical instruments *at all times.*

Pronunciation of every note must be precise, clear, in tune, and exactly in time. There are unlimited articulations to choose from. The choice of articulation depends on the style and musical message you are sending.

Cleanliness of articulation is a virtue for every brass player. I have always objected to using the word "attack" when describing the start of a tone or note; I prefer "articulate." Think about it—when you play *cantabile* on your instrument, do you sing or do you attack? You can "sing" with any number of articulations. *Cantabile* and *staccato* are not mutually exclusive terms. Tuba players need to develop a full range of percussive articulation gradations.

There was a period of several years in Europe when many orchestral positions for horn and tuba were won by Americans, due largely to the German schools' approach to double-tonguing; they thought it was impossible on the horn or the tuba. Wrong! The key to double-tonguing, and all articulations, is control and relaxation. After Americans began winning auditions in Germany, as they played and taught, German players began to win their country's auditions. Dale Clevenger and I agree that most problems with articulation are caused by the tongue. So, in Dale's words, "Get rid of the damn tongue! Keep it out of the way." You can start a note just as loud with only air as you can by putting the tongue between the lips and doing an explosive articulation.

Projection: Every note and every phrase, regardless of dynamic or range, must be projected to the back of the hall and the last row in the top balcony. This doesn't mean loud; it means to project. Send every musical message to that back row, even if there is nobody sitting there. Everyone in the front rows will be sure to get your message!

Practice with Purpose: Plan every practice session. Find the most private place you can to practice. Before entering your practice room, review what you will work on in that particular practice session. Work on techniques you need to improve or new techniques you need to develop. Watch yourself in the mirror and see if you are doing what you think you are doing. Every practice room should have a full-length mirror. The practice room is where you develop good playing habits. When you perform, they should take care of themselves.

Know the difference between practice, rehearsal, and performance. To work on your control, your technique, your range, the clarity of your performance, is practice. Preparing a recital is a rehearsal. I've known people who go to a rehearsal who are still practicing and others who go to a performance who are still rehearsing. Even worse, I sometimes hear people performing who sound like they're still practicing, and people practicing who sound like they're just warming up . . . or showing off.

A daily routine is important because it ensures that all that you have achieved on your instrument remains available to you in whatever playing situation you will encounter. I developed my own daily routine by following Bill Bell's example—he always did scales and arpeggios across the whole range of the instrument in a variety of dynamics and articulations. Some players confuse the daily routine for a warm-up. It's not a warm-up; it keeps you perpetually warmed up. I compare it with having an emergency vehicle in your garage that's tuned up, full of gas, and ready to start on the first turn of the key.

Prepare every assignment, rehearsal, and performance. Review proper interpretation for every selection. Several years ago, I received a letter from a young man, Dennis Cooper, who wanted to know how I approach a new piece of music. This was my response:

1. Learn as much as you can about the composer and his other compositions for whatever instruments, voice, etc. Is the composer American, English, Irish, French, Spanish, Italian, German, Greek, Hungarian, Polish, Russian, Chinese, Japanese, Mexican, or other? Don't play all music like it was written by Wagner! Don't play French music like German music. Don't play Polish music like Greek music. Study music history and know in what period of time the music was written. Know the meaning of a sarabande, courant, allemande, bal, bourrée, etc. If applicable, get to know the particular styles, background, and output of the arranger, transcriber, etc. Your major responsibility is always to present and represent the composer to the audience, in the correct and intended style, with your very personal musical signature. Don't play Duke Ellington like Scott Joplin; don't play Bach like Stravinsky, etc. Learn composers! If you are playing a composition of Bach arranged by Quincy Jones, you must know Quincy and his vernacular. Study the melodic line, harmonic structure, and rhythmic patterns; be aware of tempo suggestions; follow all composer's and/ or arranger's instructions. Learn arrangers! Learn styles!

2. If the music has lyrics, pay attention to their meaning and their message! If the music doesn't have lyrics, add your own! Make each piece of music mean something special to *you* in the established style of the composer and/or arranger. Deliver a message with each performance. Is it silly, frivolous, happy, religious, romantic, tranquil, sad, *what*? Decide what the music means to you!

3. Be conversant in all music disciplines . . . remember, music is *one language* with *many dialects*. Be authentic. Is it baroque, classical, romantic, contemporary, or other (ragtime, traditional, Dixieland, swing, bebop, Latin—rhumba, samba, tango—rock, acid rock, heavy metal, aleatoric, twelve-tone)? Should it swing . . . like Gershwin or Basie and Ellington? Like Parker and Gillespie? Like Dorsey? Like Kenton? Like Goodman? Learn to understand, appreciate, and enjoy all of them!!

4. Recognize the tonality of a piece and determine what key it is in (major, minor, diminished, modal, twelve-tone, aleatory). Review the single line. Take a red pencil and lightly circle every scale pattern, then with a blue pencil, circle and identify every arpeggio, major, minor, diminished, augment, etc. If you know your scales and arpeggios you can determine how much of the work you already know.

Do the same with rhythmic patterns, which repeat themselves in various notations. Keep a personal notebook of difficult passages you have made more different by inversion and repetition. You asked, what is the one major obstacle you must overcome every time you start the task of learning a new piece of music? ANSWER: Personal prejudice toward any music. Remember, prejudice is born of ignorance and unfamiliarity. You also asked, "Is it mental, emotional, or perhaps physical?" ANSWER: All. (1) *Mental:* apply knowledge and experience. (2) *Emotional:* pour yourself into each piece of music you play. (3) *Physical:* concentration and application can be physically draining and tiring or it can be relaxing and *fun.* That's what music is all about. It is to be enjoyed and savored by the performer and the audience. It is always well worth the effort! The most satisfying life you could ever have is a life in music!

Professional and Personal Integrity is essential to success and developing lifelong relationships with professional colleagues. There are three measures expected of a professional musician: (1) integrity, (2) integrity, (3) integrity.

Pride in your instrument and in being a musician is important to representing your instrument, the music, and the music profession with dignity. I have always been proud to be a tuba player and this pride led me to take steps to improve the public profile of the instrument and the state of its repertoire.

Plead with composers, arrangers, and orchestrators to take advantage of the high performance levels of tubists and give them more and better parts in their arrangements and orchestrations as well as in their compositions.

Promote music performances at every opportunity. Always exhibit a pleasant personality to the audience. They are there to be entertained. Remember that without an audience (even if only a few people) there is no performance!

Instrument Balance: The tuba is supported on either the player's lap or chair seat in a comfortable and well-balanced position—not inclined to tip in one direction or another, the mouthpiece placed comfortably on the mouth, the valve caps (or spatulas) easily accessible to the right hand and the upper valve slides easily accessible to the left hand.

Bill Bell really made me think about how I played the tuba. His teaching encouraged order and logic, and practicing with a plan and a balance of techniques. He had observed that my approach to the tuba was to open the mouth in the upper register, seeking a large sound in that range. I had been doing the opposite of Mr. Bell's approach from the eighth grade through the circus. Mr. Bell's gentle but firm guidance changed my approach to the instrument.

OTHER THOUGHTS ON MUSICIANSHIP

Vibrato

There are many factors to consider with vibrato, starting with direction (up or down), width, speed, duration, alternating speed (slow to fast, fast to slow), how much, when to use, when not to use, etc. You can learn to match the speed and width of any other instrument's vibrato. You can go fast and narrow, slow and wide, jazzy (like a trombone's slide vibrato) and all manners in between. Different styles and different musical situations call for different uses of vibrato.

I like to use lip vibrato. It's more of a jaw vibrato; you can easily match the speed another instrument is playing, and any style, too.

Note: Lip trills are made by simply widening the vibrato.

Rhythm—Precision—Subdivision

For the sake of rhythmic precision, subdivision must become a way of life for every musician. I am reminded of the old cliche, "What's worse: a wrong note in the right place or a right note in the wrong place?"

Playing anything out of time is an unforgivable musical sin. You can play a note out of tune or perhaps even play the wrong pitch and it will be forgiven (if not forgotten), but if you play a rhythm incorrectly you risk causing a "train wreck." Do it on an audition and you're likely to hear a terse "Thank you!" from behind the screen.

Coloring Tones

Experiment with the subtle use of vowel sounds that change the shape of the mouth (resonating chamber) and the quality of tone. Vocalize on your brass instrument and become expert at using tonal colors when appropriate. Every color is another tool in your musical toolbox.

Balance

Over the last thirty years, tubists, like locusts and butterflies, have emerged from musical puberty into adulthood. Sadly, too many have chosen to be locusts only. Locusts are incapable of gaining attention with subtlety, grace, and beauty, for they have none. Locusts generally perform at one dynamic: loud.

Over the course of my teaching career, I have witnessed the instrument gradually become a bombastic weapon for many orchestra players. Their dynamics seemed to range from forte to louder. I reached the end of my tether when a student came into my studio to be coached on an orchestral tuba part with "kill" written over a tuba passage. I have always believed that the worst sound of tuba is too much tuba. Remember your responsibility to the music and to the composer: play the right dynamic to balance and blend with your colleagues.

Performance Objectives

When impressed with a student's performance level and his knowledge of style, literature, etc., I'm going to look for other things to teach him or her. Every school teaches theory. I think Juilliard was right when it changed that course title; it is now called Literature and Materials in Music. I think a teacher wouldn't be a good teacher if he or she didn't give students credit for what they know and endeavor to teach them things they don't know.

I wanted to get across to students that communicating with an audience is very important. You walk on stage with a brass instrument and you put it up to your mouth. The only way you have to communicate is through that brass instrument. You don't have the benefit of using speech. You communicate with sound and interpretation. You have to communicate the message that you've received from the composer and your judgment of the composer's message. If you communicate well and know the position of the composer, the audience may get a message they've never heard before. One of my goals was never to play the same way twice. Keep looking for a mood and a message in the music that you haven't yet considered.

I'm reminded of Hoagy Carmichael's "Stardust," which was written without words and played as a jump dance tune. Mitchell Parrish put words to it: "Sometimes I wonder why I spend the lonely nights dreaming of a song..." You can't sing that fast and have it make sense. When playing a melody that doesn't have words, try adding your own words, setting a mood and message that will convince your audience. Cocktail pianists deliver messages through known lyrics, which pop into their listeners' minds.

Hoagy used to sit down at a piano. He'd say he knew there was a great song in that instrument. He just had to find it.

Finding just the right tempo, dynamics, and mood for each selection and choosing the weight and emphasis of each note in a piece of music is tricky sometimes. Persichetti would play something on the piano and have me sing it back to the class. He thought I had some good ideas and approaches for interpreting a given style. Sometimes it would be from an orchestral score, sometimes it would be violin and piano. Persichetti was always trying to get his class to explore mentally.

The Paul Hindemith sonata starts on a low B♭ and has ninths. He has that passage marked "fortissimo." I sometimes hear that and feel it is being attacked, not played. When it is played too loud, there is no musical line. When you make the intervals as small as possible and perform it lyrically, it has a mysterioso sound.

When playing with a string quartet, try to emulate string articulations. When you're playing with other brass instruments, it's essential to match articulation. This is an approach students should consider in homogenizing music played with other instruments in ensemble.

Musical Taste

When approaching a piece of music, consider its particular style and imagine a type of food that goes with that style. When I hear Dixieland, I think of ribs, beer, ham, and all the things they serve with Dixieland jazz. Music should be prepared like a given dish with its own unique flavors. When you play in this style, make sure you are including all of the necessary flavors that give the dish its distinct taste.

When I first arrived in New York, I heard some very new sounds. I heard aleatoric music for the first time in 1950 at a concert at Columbia University and I met Milton Babbitt, Vladimir Ussachevsky, and other modern composers. Although I didn't understand their music right away, I listened to what the composers had to say and determined that they weren't insane. In fact, they seemed to know what they were doing and believed in it very strongly. I compared the experience to eating at a gourmet restaurant for the first time. And so I trusted that some of the more "out there" music did indeed have shape or form, even if I couldn't digest it immediately. If you ever hear something that doesn't go down easily, ask yourself, "Is it really bad music, or is it just an acquired taste?" The average person will probably not appreciate gourmet food if he has been eating junk food all his life, but that doesn't mean that acquiring such a taste is impossible. It just requires an absence of fear and a willingness to learn.

Timbre Distinction

Timbre appears to be an established expectation from a particular instrument. In reality, it is a personal trait with physical, mental, and environmental influences. Whether the tone is always centered (ideal) depends primarily on the preconceived tone qualities established by an early teacher and reinforced by listening to great performers. Tone is also influenced by the quality and condition of a particular instrument or other equipment. In brass instruments, this involves mouthpiece and valve alignment; in woodwind instruments, it's the alignment of the mouthpiece and condition of the key pads. In string instruments, it concerns the bow and strings, and in percussion, the choice of mallets or drum heads.

Everybody gets a sound that's theirs and theirs alone. It's very good for a young player to listen to performances and recordings of other players—but from the very beginning the player should also accept that physical equipment and mental aptitude are going to determine the sound produced. I have known some players of advanced age who are still trying to sound like somebody else. It won't happen. Tenors and sopranos in the Met Opera accept that they can't sound like Caruso or Callas; there is only one Caruso and only one Callas. They are able to sing all the same notes, but they can't produce the same sound. If they try to do so, they may hamper their careers or damage their voices. Their best hope for a career is to find and exploit all of the unique strengths of their own individual voices. You, too, have your own individual voice on the tuba! Do not settle for a cheap imitation of another's sound. Find *your* sound.

Blending

One of our most important responsibilities as tuba players is fitting in with the rest of the ensemble. We must listen intently to the tonal colors that each orchestral section produces and then determine what tonal colors we add or influence when added to that section. We must ask ourselves: what role are we playing in this music? Has the composer assigned it to complement or contrast the section sound? I think the best example of this is what's often referred to as the "tuba solo" in *Die Meistersinger*. It's no solo—the basses all play it, too! Wagner's genius is evident in this passage;

adding tuba to that part gives definition that you can't get with the string bass section alone. That is your role in this particular case: adding definition and articulation. If you can't hear the basses to blend with them, you are not following the wishes of the composer!

No Instrument Has Talent

No instrument has talent! Even the coveted Stradivarius violin (a work of art in and of itself) will remain silent until a human being gives it voice. And, strange though it may appear to some, it can only amplify and enhance the musical and artistic skills of the person who gives it voice. A tuba is made of brass. I could play my tuba and hand it to you and the tuba won't know the difference. It will respond the same way if you give it the same instructions.

Playing Chamber Music

I am disheartened when a student chamber ensemble cancels scheduled rehearsals because one or two members cannot be there. When I was in the New York Brass Quintet, our rehearsals were often on Thursday from 10 PM until 2 AM because of conflicting schedules. It was not uncommon for members to be absent due to other paying commitments. If all five of us made it, great, but if three or four or even only two made it, we still rehearsed. You can learn a lot about the structure of a piece of music by isolating two or three voices.

In a chamber group, it is taken for granted that all members can play their written parts. Their primary responsibility, beyond learning their individual parts, is making it possible for the other ensemble members to play their best. If a member of the quintet has a very challenging part, think through the part with him or her as you play your own notes and it will be easier for that player to blend with you. If all five members of the quintet share this attitude, they will elevate each other's performances.

Reception Etiquette

In the early days of the New York Brass Quintet, we were often invited to post-concert receptions. After realizing that post-concert parties were too often limited to conversations with each other, we decided that visiting with our audience at receptions was really an important extension of each performance. So all of us endeavored to make ourselves available in various room locations, inviting people to approach us and engage in conversation. We adopted the attitude of "never being the second to say hello"!

CONCLUSION

The tuba has finally been accepted for its musical stature and potential. The growth of quality solo literature for the tuba has increased, improving performances. The frequency of solo recitals and the audience for them is constantly growing. Each generation has a responsibility to extend the work of the previous generation. There are more young soloists playing today but it takes many well-performed works to generate an audience that can support and sustain a handful of careers as solo artists on the world stage. Poorly performed works reflect badly not only on the pieces of music but also on the instrument. Teachers must bear the responsibility of choosing repertoire for their students that will enhance, not detract from, the instrument's reputation. The level of technique is never more important than musical content.

Outstanding young tuba players today are bringing even greater recognition and acceptance to our instrument. Raising the level of tuba playing elevates the entire musical pyramid, because we as tuba players are the foundation of that pyramid. Since the year 1950, the tuba has seen unprecedented growth in solo, chamber, and orchestral literature. And most important to me is the fine quality of new literature and the larger audiences for it.

Every tuba player should understand that he or she represents at all times all the others who play the instrument, whether the player is dealing with colleagues or the general public. If you're a good musical citizen and represent your instrument's role with pride, respect, and commitment, you will further the cause of the instrument every time you pick it up.

CHAPTER NINETEEN

Performance Tips

IF YOU HAVE THE OPPORTUNITY to appear on a local or national popular talk show, dress well, look neat, be alert and personable, and, most importantly, be knowledgeable and articulate. Send information about your instrument and your career to the host well in advance. Remember, the listening/watching audience is accustomed to being entertained. Be enthusiastic about your instrument and its roles in music. Select repertoire that shows off the best qualities of your instrument and your artistry. Whatever you choose to play, introduce the music clearly, interestingly, and concisely. Be prepared to discuss the chosen repertoire with your host(s) and always acknowledge any accompanying musicians.

I was on Studs Terkel's radio interview program in Chicago three times. I went on with six other tuba players. I was primary spokesman. We played Christmas carols and talked about the tuba, euphonium, and tuba literature's affording more choices all the time. Studs Terkel was an example of an interviewer who did not try any ill-humored requests. All his questions and inquiries were upbeat and sincere.

But, like some of my colleagues who play tuba or euphonium, I have been victimized by prejudiced or irresponsible writers for newspapers or magazines who copy others' cliches or attempt to create their own clever insults to our noble instruments. I caution all musicians to be on their guard against writers who, before any personal interview, have already determined what they will write. Have a short conversation with the writer before an interview. Ask what motivated him or her to want to do an article. The best foil to a writer's barbs is to be proud of your instrument and its role in music, and to be well-informed and well-spoken about your instrument and its history, fabrication, configuration, techniques, pedagogy, literature, and repertoire.

In a live TV or radio interview, remember that when the interviewer shares the microphone for your response to a question, that microphone belongs to you! If the interviewer makes a ploy for a humorous or negative answer, ignore the question and make a positive statement such as, "Did you know the tuba has the widest range of any wind instrument, over half the piano keyboard!" If the interviewer repeats the question, you might say, "The tuba is one of two solo instruments in the orchestra; the other is the harp." Don't fall for a request to make your ugliest, loudest, lowest, or highest sound. Always display your best sound and be positive, sharp, knowledgeable, and personable.

LIVE RECITAL PERFORMANCE

For a recital, select a balanced program of established and contemporary compositions. If baroque or classical transcriptions are performed, program them early in the recital. Whenever possible and appropriate, communicate with the audience about your program, especially when there are no printed program notes. Many chamber music programs are most enjoyable when informal. Also, remember that when you speak to an audience, your voice is your instrument. Don't *mumble*. Your sound and technique (at all dynamics) and your spoken words must be clear, audible, and projected to the last seat in the room (even if no one is sitting there).

Throughout my career as a professional tubist, I have never received a negative review of a recital, solo, chamber music, or other public performance.

TESTING AND EVALUATING BRASS INSTRUMENTS

Every professional brass player takes a personal approach to testing and evaluating brass instruments of different brands. This is as it should be, for professionals rarely purchase an instrument with someone else in mind. Professional players give attention to every detail and characteristic of each instrument they evaluate and, unlike most students, do not use testing time to audition for everyone within earshot. Professionals are constantly searching for instruments that will improve their performance in whatever music discipline(s) in which they earn their living. Studio musicians will often select quite different instruments from those selected by the exclusive jazz artist or the exclusive symphonic artist. A lead trumpet player may seek equipment different from that sought by a section player. In their personal evaluation of each instrument tested, professionals (and students should follow suit) will play selections from regularly performed repertoire, favorite songs, excerpts, exercises, scales, arpeggios, patterns, licks, chord progressions, etc. This allows them to test the instrument's intonation in every possible musical situation the professional player might encounter.

Each instrument must be judged and evaluated with an open mind. Ingrained preferences and prejudices must be set aside to make a value judgment. Some musical instruments can be quickly rejected, while others require more consideration and are often well worth the time required to gain familiarity.

I will share my personal approach for evaluating quality and playing characteristics. I urge everyone to prepare his or her own checklist when evaluating brass instruments. I also recommend open discussions with professional colleagues about a particular instrument's characteristics.

The design and aesthetic appearance of an instrument can be attractive and unique or just the opposite. Whether old or new, each instrument design deserves to be considered and evaluated. Is the bell in balance with the total design and bore size or is it over- or undersized? Do tapers of the instrument complement the overall design? How often have we played on eighty-year-old instruments and wondered why, in spite of superior design and inherent playing qualities, their manufacturer stopped making them?

Some of today's most popular instruments are "carbon copies" of older models with only the name of the manufacturer changed.

Hold the instrument in your normal playing position. Is it well-balanced? Is it comfortable to hold? Does it want to tip one way or the other? If you place the instrument on its bell (an unwise but common practice), is it easily tipped over? When the instrument is in normal playing position, are the leadpipe and valves comfortably accessible? Are the water keys easily accessible? If you desire access to upper slides, are they easily reached while in normal playing position? Are all the slides, especially the upper slides, removable? Does the instrument have a good center of balance for the way you want to hold it? Some players like to hold the tuba in their lap; some want it to rest on the chair seat; and still others want to use a supporting stand. Can you tolerate changing your habit of holding your instrument? Such change may be necessary and can sometimes be an improvement to proper posture and correct breathing.

Look carefully at the quality of assembly and materials used in making each instrument you test and evaluate. Is the material durable? Can the instrument be dented by simply squeezing the metal tubing? Is the instrument adequately and logically braced? Are the braces strong and well-designed to help avoid damage? In the case of tubas, are the bottom bow and outer tubing well-reinforced with beaded shields? Are the valves well made and of good quality or are they noisy and flimsy? If they are piston valves, can the pistons be turned easily in the casing; do the ports meet correctly; are they quiet; are they sluggish? If they are rotary, is the spatula's mechanism strong and well-braced; do the valves respond quickly when compressed? Check out the valve section with special care. The valve section is the heart of your instrument; make sure it is strong and dependable! Whether lacquer or silver, the finish of the instrument should be spotless and even, and there should be no solder acid leaks. Remember, a well-made quality instrument is not just a purchase but an investment; with proper care it will return steady dividends and never lose its value.

Starting with the middle register, test the response of the instrument. Is there too much or too little resistance? Can each tone be centered with a proper balance of highs and lows? Are you able to articulate from your softest tone to your loudest tone without distortion and with control of pitch?

Explore the upper and lower registers and their extremes. It is important that the instrument have even response throughout *your* range; no dead tones and no thin tones that leap from the instrument. Response will have much to do with the quality of sound produced on any instrument.

Check thoroughly that the instrument allows flexibility to both ascend and descend smoothly during scale passages. It's common knowledge among brass players that a descending line is like a woodworker going with the grain but an ascending line is going against the grain. So, look for an instrument that equalizes, as much as possible, ascending and descending arpeggios and scales. There should be resistance for control of every musical nuance but a thin line separates resistance from stuffiness. A stuffy instrument will impede your efforts to ascend smoothly and effortlessly. No amount of breath support and no degree of breath control can overcome a stuffy response, and flexibility will be greatly curtailed. Test this factor with the flexibility studies from Arban and Clarke.

After thoroughly checking response and flexibility, one should be sufficiently comfortable with the instrument to assess the quality of tone the instrument allows the player to produce. Every brass musician will produce a distinct tone quality. The response of any given brass instrument either helps or hinders a player's tone production. In checking intonation, I suggest that the open instrument be checked first for interval relationships of the overtone series, then the second valve, first valve, third valve, and 1–2 combination, 2–3 combination, and 1–3 combination. Then, with the fourth valve adjusted to personal preference, check the fourth valve overtone series, 1–2–3 and 2–4 combinations, 1–4 combination, 1–2–4 and 3–4 combinations, 2–3–4 combination, and, last, the 1–2–3–4 combination.

All scales should now be checked for diatonic and chromatic relationships. Playing familiar melodies is extremely important to checking intonation and to determining what embouchure, alternate fingering, or slide adjustments must be considered for the best intonation patterns. Finally, once you start to feel familiar with the instrument you are testing, spend some valuable time with a good tuner, solidifying your evaluations.

Four valves are essential; five valves are not. A fifth valve adds from five to ten pounds to the weight of the tuba. Negative: You carry that weight around to every job you play. Some use that fifth valve as a BB♭ valve. Positive: You have a choice of valve combinations. We know that each valve that is added becomes another overtone series.

It is important to determine which instruments will best fulfill your performance commitments and will allow musical growth to continue. That is the bottom line.

DEVELOPING A CAREER FOR A LIFE IN MUSIC

I am often asked to speak to music students about potential careers in music. The following presentation is the core of my message and, when I am present, is followed by a question and answer session. I implore students to seek knowledge that enlightens and assures future careers in music. That knowledge can be gained from books, live performances, recordings, or the minds and experiences of their applied teachers and other established performers. I always tell the students to whom I am speaking that their enrollment as a music major at this institution tells me that they have committed themselves to a life in music. That's great, for in my opinion (and I have my own life to substantiate this opinion) no other career offers equal potential for fulfillment and happiness.

WHAT ARE THE PRIORITIES FOR PREPARING A CAREER IN MUSIC?

These concerns should be uppermost in the mind of every student and teacher. Teachers should endeavor to stay ahead of the current and ever-changing music scene. Foremost in the minds of students and teachers must be the development of new opportunities. Teachers must nurture and mentor the development of each individual student. I never thought it was enough to teach students all the ways to play a tuba and then not do anything to help them find a job. Teachers should be the students' most reliable source of information, but teachers should not be expected to bear the entire burden. Every student must constantly seek and explore all available resources, from books, recordings, and live performances.

Human minds can best be opened by conversations, questions, and discussions. Networking with other students and faculty should be constant. These unlimited resources of information must be tapped by students themselves. A great wealth of knowledge passes by in the hallway each day, in the person of faculty, unapproached and untapped. Think about it!

THREE AVENUES OF MUSIC CAREER PLANNING

As you develop and personalize your music career, it is important that you understand the art, profession, and business of music.

1. **The Art of Music.** Learn all you can about the art of music (the theory and structure of music, the history and traditions of music). This knowledge is your primary source of credibility for a career in music. You will be able to discuss the music art with anyone and they will be impressed with your knowledge. Unfortunately, even an in-depth knowledge of the art of music is no guarantee of a career playing music.

2. **The Profession of Music.** The two major divisions of the music profession are performance and teaching. If you want to partici- pate actively in music as either a performer or teacher, you must learn all you can about every aspect of both. Not only must you de- velop your performance skills to maximum potential but you must understand and learn how to teach all aspects of your instrument. You must know how to avail yourself of opportunities to audition for a performance position and how to get invited for important faculty or administrative job interviews. You must learn about the importance and influence of the American Federation of Musicians and/or the American Federation of Teachers and other governing organizations.

3. **The Business of Music.** If you are to have maximum security in your music career, you must learn all you can about the business of music, all the dollars-and-cents/sense aspects of music: What makes a good contract with an agent, manager, or other employer? What does the chain of performer–composer–publisher–music dealer comprise? What are the dealer markups on music, instruments, recordings, etc.? How do you market talent? How do you market performance? Do you want your career—your potential income from music—to

be always at the mercy of others? You will never have maximum security in music until you understand the **Business of Music** and how it overlaps and intertwines with the **Profession of Music** and the **Art of Music**.

You must be tough to survive as a professional musician. The profession itself can be very fragile. Inept managements not only lack administrative skills, but are losers when it comes to fundraising and public relations as well. Funding for musical concerts, if not endowed, may be impossible to come by without long-range planning. More and more, it behooves professional musicians to gain knowledge of the business of music and become involved with their own destinies.

Training for a performance career is serious business. Several years ago, at a brass conference in Norway, I was asked to present a clinic on how to practice. As I prepared my notes, I realized that before we discussed how to practice we needed to deal with why, when, what, and where to practice. When I asked my audience of brass players *why* we practice, one young man held up his hand and said, "I practice because I want to get better." My response was that getting better was not a reason but a byproduct of practicing. I guarantee you will get better if you practice. Now let me give you my definitions of **why, when, what,** and **where** to practice:

WHY "We want the option of a career in music as a performer."
WHEN "At every opportunity."
WHAT "Everything we cannot do, everything that needs improvement."
WHERE "In the most isolated place available."

Know your strengths and weaknesses. Make two separate lists of your ten strongest and your ten weakest qualities (in order of strength/weakness) as a person *and* as a musician. Endeavor to display your strengths in public, while you work in private to turn every weakness into a strength!

As you regularly evaluate your qualities, avoid competing with your peers. Be aware of their achievements and strive to stay even or ahead. *But,* if you find that no matter how hard you try, you cannot keep up with your colleagues, do an honest review of your dreams and desires and make judgments about alternative directions you should be considering for a career in music. If you are a senior and a freshman arrives and blows you off the stage, you may have some serious thinking to do. Confide in your parents and in your applied teachers; oftentimes your best guidance is there.

Teachers content with just passing on performance skills are doing only half their job. Great teachers inspire their students to excel and great teachers work equally hard to instill self-awareness, self-esteem, pride, commitment, and professional ethics—and to guide their students.

THE MUSIC PROFESSION CAN ACCOMMODATE EVERYONE

Everyone who wants a life in music can have one—it just may not be as a performer. People can live a dream for just so long. No matter how much one may want that special performance career in music, if he or she does not possess the talent or is unable to invest the many, many hours necessary for success as a performer, then it may not come to pass. But one can seek other outlets in the music profession. One may have the knowledge, patience, commitment, and desire to be an outstanding teacher. If one is good at managing personal and professional affairs, it may be possible to become a personnel manager or promoter or serve in other important administrative positions. Such positions may ensure an income beyond that of a performer and provide a very satisfying life in music! We enter music school as young people because we realize or decide that we have a passion for music making. This passion need not diminish if one does not immediately achieve the lofty goal of stardom. Our choice of career should not be determined by, "What is the most prestigious career I can have?" but rather by, "Given my own set of strengths and weaknesses, what career path will allow me to serve the art of music to the best of my abilities?" Our goal should not be to achieve personal glory but to make life better for all musicians and the audiences they entertain.

Thus an important lesson to learn is that all students must strive to know themselves, to know their strengths and weaknesses, and to have the initiative to recognize and courage to seize opportunities when, like a lightning bolt, they strike.

Today, we strive to cope with the phenomenon of more and more sophisticated electronics. As innovations displace and supplant established concepts, we endeavor to imagine how these amazing discoveries will enhance and expand professional opportunities. We struggle to retain and preserve the existing treasury of recorded performances by legendary artists. One thing is certain: the digital revolution has changed and will continue to change our profession, hopefully for the better. Today's young musicians and their mentors must continually combine new technologies with traditions.

Performance and teaching opportunities will also continue to change in the face of improved techniques. If we are truly committed to preserving the best of our art and traditions (as we know them today), we must work diligently to enhance and establish public awareness and support, not just for today's music profession, but for tomorrow's profession. It will not be easy. We must look to the recent past and into the unknown future. We must foresee the disappearance of musical buggy whips and gas lighting fixtures. We must anticipate, innovate, and increase future career options in music and all the arts. Seeking and creating new opportunities must become an ongoing obligation and priority for all who value the future of our musical art. If, in this pessimistic world, you can be an optimist and a person who makes things happen, you very likely can have a happy and successful life in music.

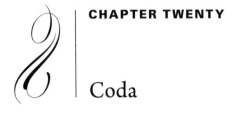

CHAPTER TWENTY

Coda

ALLOWING MYSELF to be put in positions for which I had not been prepared forced me to work an insane schedule when it came to balancing family time, personal time, and professional maintenance as a performer. By that, I simply mean if I had kept my initial priorities, I was first and foremost a player. By 1960–1965, I was at the crest of my playing. The years 1957–1967 had to be the high point of my career as a performer simply because that's all I was doing. I was performing and teaching in my Carnegie Hall studio, accepting only the few students I chose to teach. At times, convenient to my schedule, I didn't work—I played, words of double meaning for any musician.

I took on administrative positions for which I was not trained and so I had to "burn the candle at both ends" to learn the responsibilities which came as a trust from others I admired. Each leap—working for Gunther Schuller at the New England Conservatory, taking on the responsibilities of executive editor at *The Instrumentalist*—was like going into a war zone without a weapon. It's one hell of a job to gain the respect that's necessary to administer important tasks for which you've had no training. It is like an actor who has never played anything but cowboy roles suddenly finding himself playing *Hamlet* without ever having heard of William Shakespeare.

Some of us have always felt how different orchestras would be if there had been a section of tubas as there was of the trumpets, horns, and trombones. But music written for the ophicleide (the instrument preceding the tuba) was the first orchestral music inherited by the tuba—as a section of one. Today we have two basic sections of brass instruments: cylindrical (trumpets and trombones) and conical (horns and tuba). The sound of conical instruments is warmer and mellower than that of the cylindrical instruments.

Great brass instrument performance did not start last week, last year, or even fifty years ago. Great brass playing has been with us for a very long time. It is not possible to hear recorded performances of Jean-Baptiste Arban, but recognizing the pedagogical legacy of his *Complete Method* compels us to consider that he was a tremendous performer. The Arban book, referred to as "The Brass Players' Bible," is still being sold. Edwin Franko Goldman edited the definitive edition of the Arban *Complete Method for Cornet or Trumpet* in 1912.

Other great brass artists established ever-rising standards for their respective instruments. Some of these artists became international celebrities, such as Jules Levy and Herbert L. Clarke (cornet and trumpet). Clarke is reputed to have performed more than fifteen thousand solo performances with the Sousa Band. Other international celebrities include Bruno Jaenicke (horn), Arthur Pryor (trombone), Simone Mantia (euphonium), and August Helleberg (tuba). Although their repertoire was limited mostly to manuscripts they had time to arrange, transcribe, or compose, their tone, style, and technique were not so limited. The 1929 recording of *Ein Heldenleben* conducted by Willem Mengelberg was identified as something very special.

We look with pride at the first celebrated orchestral tubist, August Helleberg (1861–1936). No individual tubists received accolades of notice before him. His son John (whom I knew well), used to say, "Yeah, my father, August Helleberg, was the daddy of 'em all!" As principal tuba of the Chicago Symphony Orchestra when it was founded, Helleberg was geographically close to Elkhart, Indiana, home of the C. G. Conn Instrument Company. He collaborated with this manufacturer in producing instruments worthy of any orchestra and of any performer.

There are no tubists other than Helleberg and Fred "Fritz" Geib, to my knowledge, who achieved recognition or fame in the nineteenth century. Some important early-twentieth-century tubists were John Kuhn, Giovanni Manuti, Fred Pfaff, Jack Richardson, Gabe Russ, Johnny Evans, and others who were made prominent by their work with the John Philip Sousa Band, Bohumir Kryl, the Patrick Conway Band, and other famous touring bands. Others established their reputation through playing the jazz of the period: Joe Tarto (a.k.a. Vincent Joseph Tortoriello), Phillip Cadway, and, to a lesser extent, Joe Park.

THE SHIFTING MARKETS OF THE EARLY TWENTIETH CENTURY

It may seem to the reader that, with the noted exception of Helleberg, orchestral players were kept under wraps and were unknown in comparison with the band performers. Bear in mind that the first thirty years of the twentieth century belonged to the band. Every town of any size had its own local town band modeled after the great touring bands of Sousa, Pryor, Kryl, Creatore, and Conway. Professional touring bands were assured audiences by the popularity of these town bands. The touring circuses also maintained outstanding bands, admired by legions of other musicians. Many recruits for the great touring bands came from the ranks of circus musicians. Since there were few public schools or even colleges with major music programs, the primary market for brass instruments was professional touring musicians, theater musicians (every theater of consequence maintained an orchestra or other ensemble to play for silent films and traveling vaudeville artists), or semi-professional players in town bands. Needless to say, this market inspired competing American instrument companies to produce instruments of superior quality. That is why every tuba and euphonium player searches for instruments made during this period.

Commencing in 1928, three major events brought about a change that could not be reversed:

1. In 1928 Al Jolson was featured in a movie entitled *The Jazz Singer.* This movie had sound on film and was the death knell for theater

musicians and for vaudeville. Almost immediately all theater owners determined that since films were available with sound, they no longer needed vaudeville acts onstage or musicians in the pit.

2. In 1929 the stock market crash caused panic and unemployment. The Great Depression began and people were struggling to provide for their families. There was less and less time for the town band.

3. In 1932, Sousa died and with him the touring professional band. It is speculated that even the Sousa Band could not have survived the Depression.

With the demise of a major portion of their instrument market, American instrument companies set about creating a new market for their products. They turned their attention to establishing music programs in high schools and colleges. They initiated instrument rental programs and in many instances contributed a bass drum and sousaphone as well as the first year's salary of a band director (often an alumnus of the Sousa or Pryor Band). This country now has a music education program unmatched anywhere in the world. In more recent years, the advent of the drum corps and increase in drum corps competitions have weakened some high school band programs.

One unfortunate victim of this was professional quality instruments. In the golden days of the professional band, instrument companies offered as many as fourteen models of tuba (with choices of four-valve top-action or side-action valves—either piston or rotary; varying bore sizes; fixed or detachable bells; clear, brass, or gold lacquer, *or* silver plating in either satin or bright burnished finish). Custom instruments were created by simply ordering individual preferences of these choices, which is why so many "one of a kind" tubas are being discovered in attics and basements. From all these choices (when a professional market motivated the instrument companies) we moved to the choices of a three-valve BB♭ or E♭ tuba or sousaphone, or a three-valve BB♭ upright recording tuba with interchangeable bells, if you were lucky.

The decline of the professional band meant that young players now had to "cut their teeth" in high school music programs and, later, conservatories, and would find their greatest performing outlets in professional symphony orchestras. These players who came to prominence through their conservatory studies and orchestral recognition were led by William Bell. However, although he played in the New York Philharmonic, his allegiance was just about equally spread between the band and orchestral worlds. But to most conservatories, band was just a four-letter word.

Other prominent orchestral players were led by Arnold Jacobs, Phillip Cadway, and Abraham Torchinsky. Coming out of the 1940s, and also conservatory-trained, were Joe Novotny, Don Butterfield, and Bill Barber. William Bell was the tubist with the most established reputation before 1950. I credit him with making an effort to establish the tuba as a solo instrument via his transcriptions of Bach, Handel, and Beethoven. But, then, a tuba solo was usually presented as a curiosity with the band in the park on Sunday afternoon.

WILLIAM J. BELL, ARNOLD JACOBS, AND OTHER TWENTIETH-CENTURY TUBISTS

There would be no biography of Arnold Jacobs if not for Brian Frederiksen, a devoted student. Brian not only published *Arnold Jacobs: Song and Wind,* but has produced and presented numerous lectures and master classes representing the teaching, professional pedagogy, and artistry of a great musician. Arnold was not a writer and was reluctant even to sign checks, except for those he got from the Chicago Symphony. He presented a week of master classes at Northwestern University each year, which were recorded. Brian owns those recordings. Dee Stewart, also a Jacobs student, compiled and had published *Arnold Jacobs: The Legacy of a Master,* which featured recollections of Jacobs by students and colleagues.

The seemingly ageless Joe Tarto represents the many nameless Dixieland and traditional jazz players who maintained the use of tuba in Dixieland jazz in New Orleans. Seeds were planted in the 1940s in terms of attitude and resistance to exclusion from certain activities. In the decade preceding 1950, some young tubists broke out of the classical and romantic stable, embraced swing and jazz with equal grip, and became solo material for music that didn't yet exist.

With the exception of a quintet composed by Ingolf Dahl in 1944, brass chamber music was almost unheard of. Breaking out of this mold began in

1945 with schools of music and conservatories being overrun by returning World War II veterans.

The most significant occurrence prior to 1950 was the exploration of the Juilliard-based New York Brass Ensemble, formed by the students themselves, in an effort to accommodate the performance desires of outstanding brass students. This ensemble earned international recognition by winning the Grand Prix du Disque in Paris for an all-Gabrieli LP recording. This recording preceded the release of the *Birth of the Cool* LP, which was led by Miles Davis and spawned use of the tuba in jazz chamber music. Bill Barber played tuba on both these recordings. Also active in scattering different seeds, the use of the tuba in swing was personified by the writing of Ed Sauter and Bill Finegan for the Sauter-Finegan Orchestra (1952). Another tubist dissatisfied with relegation to concert band literature and who sought a place for the tuba in jazz as well as symphonic challenge was Don Butterfield.

Prominent tubists emerging from the 1940s and early 1950s into the world of orchestral playing were Joe Novotny, Bill Rose, Jay McAllister, Bill Lewin, and Herbert Wekselblatt. This phalanx of tubists eager to put more opportunity on their plates exploded symphonically into the 1950s with the masterful playing of Arnold Jacobs, who rose above all others in this field of performing. When I arrived in New York in September 1950 to commence my studies at the Juilliard School of Music, I was fortunate to have had the privilege of being made familiar with the potential for the tuba. Led primarily by William Bell and Arnold Jacobs, the technical and pedagogical future of the instrument was assured.

AMERICAN CLASSICAL MUSIC HALL OF FAME

In November 2007, on an especially busy day, I received a phone call telling me that I had been nominated for induction into the American Classical Music Hall of Fame and asking if I would agree to be included. The day after Thanksgiving, a letter came, saying they had received my acceptance over the phone and they were sending materials I could share with my colleagues and family. Once I saw the letter and realized its importance, I got excited. I am proud to have been the first wind player so honored. Present for the ceremony in Cincinnati were Carol, Jesse, Harvey

Jr., and Tom; daughters-in-law Kim and Alison; and our four grandsons, Jesse IV, Connor, Reagan, and Riley.

The induction ceremony into the American Classical Music Hall of Fame was most impressive. It started with the world premiere of Gunther Schuller's "Fanfare for Harvey," performed by the U.S. Marine Band Tuba Quartet. "Song for Carol" by Alec Wilder was played by tubist Dan Perantoni and pianist Donna Loewy, who along with Brian Bowman, euphonium, then played "Romanze" by Gustav Cords. Next came *Variety Is the Spice of Life,* a fifteen-minute eclectic program of excerpts from my recordings of works by Handel, Persichetti, Swann, Gould, Bozza, Ellington, and Sauter-Finegan. The award—a heavy gold medallion depicting a lyre and a soaring eagle—was placed around my neck by Trish Bryan, chair of the board of trustees. I wore it the rest of the day.

The program continued with Bach's "Komm, Süsser Tod" ("Come, Sweet Death"), transcribed by Eddie Sauter and traditionally played at every meeting of ITEA, which was going on that week, hosted by Tim Northcut, at the Cincinnati College Conservatory of Music. "Air on a G String" and Sousa's "The Stars and Stripes Forever" were played by the United States Armed Services Tuba Euphonium Ensemble, conducted by R. Winston Morris with Dan Perantoni performing the famous piccolo solo on tuba.

Others inducted the same year were cellist Yo-Yo Ma, the Cleveland Orchestra, and composer Donald Martino.

After the ceremony, in the foyer of Corbett Auditorium, a picnic was held and various groups performed, including the Harvey Phillips Tuba-Company conducted by Norlan Bewley.

THE IU PRESIDENT'S MEDAL

I believed the induction into the Hall of Fame would be the last honor I would ever receive. But in June 2008 came a letter from Indiana University President Michael A. McRobbie saying that he would confer on me the President's Medal, for sustained academic excellence, at a formal dinner in the IU Auditorium on September 5. This is the highest honor that the president of Indiana University can bestow. Denis Sinor, professor emeritus of Central Eurasian studies, also received the President's Medal at that ceremony.

Both the President's Medal and the American Classical Music Hall of Fame medallion are displayed in the foyer of my home.

I was honored to have the opportunity to share this honor with and represent many of my faculty colleagues and associates who are also dedicated to their profession. I realized after fifty professional years why the conscience of a preacher would imagine a life of sin to be unavoidable in a circus. I forgive the preacher who never left the insulation of his small town. I do not think I lived a life of sin, but, speaking tongue-in-cheek, I may have pushed the envelope. Composer Richard Peaslee may have had this in mind when he entitled my commission for solo tuba, four horns, and two percussion, "The Devil's Herald." Though I admit my jokes, tricks, and pranks were devilish in nature, they were not by any stretch of the imagination sinful. I feel I lived a life full of joy and privilege—privilege to be a musician and privilege to have a lifetime of associations with great music makers and, of course, my wonderful family.

FRIENDS AND COLLEAGUES

"While learning an instrument, a musician benefits from hearing an ideal sound in his imagination, which he tries to achieve in reality. My ideal sound is Harvey's, from all the lovely things I've heard him play."

BILL CROW, freelance bass musician

"Leon Barzin used to call him the king of tuba players and say there was nobody like him. From the very beginning Harvey was respected as the greatest tuba player in the world. He played with such style and freedom. It was not just that he played the instrument well but he was such a good musician. He would knock off Fritz Kreisler, much to everybody's astonishment."

HUGO FIORATO, conductor of the New York City Ballet Orchestra, former member of the WQXR String Quartet

"He brought class to the low brass."

CLARK TERRY, New York freelance jazz trumpet

"Harvey was very kind and friendly to me when I joined the New York City Ballet Orchestra. I was only twenty-one. He was generous in his conversation and made me feel like I belonged (something I have tried to emulate in my professional behavior). I always think of Harvey Phillips as a wonderful shining example of what an inspiring musician should be."

ORIN O'BRIEN, double bassist, New York Philharmonic

"He plays his instrument better than anyone else in the world. Phillips's sound is unique. His tuba suggests a graceful trombone, or a horn minus its nasal qualities, or a baritone saxophone of the most velvet persuasion. His technique is astonishing. His arpeggios are glassy and clean, the alarming intervals he sometimes has to play are deft and exact, and his staccato passages are cream."

WHITNEY BALLIETT, *The New Yorker* magazine

"Rehearsals and recording sessions were rescheduled by conductors if Harvey was not available. He was that much in demand."

HERB WEKSELBLATT, tubist, Metropolitan Opera Orchestra

"When Harvey said he would take me places, I thought maybe we'd go to Kentucky, or even Illinois. Then we went all over the world. Every opportunity I've had has come directly from Harvey."

STEVE HARLOS, piano faculty, North Texas State University

"I first met Harvey in 1963 when he came to the University of Wisconsin to perform with the New York Brass Quintet. Harvey was the best tuba player I'd ever heard. Little did I know then that I am still waiting to hear anyone better!"

EUGENE ANDERSON, composer, tubist

"There are very few musicians and human beings whom I admire as much as Harvey. Very few musicians have given as selflessly to their profession as Harvey Phillips; very few have committed themselves so deeply to enhancing the cultural environment in which we toil, and very few have dedicated themselves so completely to training the young, helping colleagues and uplifting audiences.

"He is not only a brilliant performer but, more than that, has taken the tuba out of the underdog category of instruments and has shown the world that the tuba can be an eloquent spokesman for all manner of musical artistic expression. He has been a driving force and initiator in dozens of organizations and projects, all of which are dedicated to improving our cultural climate and our profession. While most musicians think primarily about what they can get out of their profession, Harvey most of the time is thinking of what he can give to it."

GUNTHER SCHULLER, composer and conductor

"So here I am, Harvey, a maturing jazz artist with pencil in hand, contemplating yet another piece for Tuba. Now, I wonder, who could have put such an idea in my head?"

ROGER KELLAWAY, jazz pianist, composer of more than twenty-five film scores

"Some people did not know what was motivating Harvey. I can tell you from endless hours of observation that Harvey was never motivated by ego. His goals were way too sophisticated to be designed to elevate one person's self-esteem. His objective was to do everything he possibly could to create opportunities for the tuba and the tubist and to advance the image of the tuba in the eyes of the music world and the audience at large. It would have been simple for someone of Harvey's intellect and dedication to have focused on his own career. Harvey had a borderline obsession to improve the lot of his fellow tubists.

"When Harvey found out in 1973 that I was hosting an annual Tuba Symposium in Tennessee that involved one hundred or more tuba/euphonium students from a half dozen states, he declared that he would be attending. When I told him that I did not have funding to underwrite his participation he stated that wasn't a concern, that this sounded like a good thing that was happening for the tuba and he would cover his own expenses! Which he did as our annual guest for the next twenty years!

"I was further honored in 1976 when Harvey invited me to join him and Dan Perantoni to make up the tuba section for the newly formed Matteson-Phillips TubaJazz Consort. We would rehearse, thank you Rich, for three to five hours, then do three sets at the jazz club that night. Harvey was playing as strong, after eight or ten hours of playing, as he was after the first hour. Incredible was the only word for it.

"There are scores of people around the globe who feel the same way about Harvey as I do. He makes everyone feel special and he is always interested in what others are doing."

R. WINSTON MORRIS, professor of tuba, Tennessee Tech University

"Harvey has created events that affected the whole community, giving from a heart as big as his tuba."

ANDREW S. MILLER JR., Major, The Salvation Army

"Someone has said Harvey Phillips is the Heifetz of the tuba. Having toured and recorded with Heifetz I certainly agree. I shall never forget hearing Harvey play for the first time. It gave me such sheer joy to hear someone play that large instrument with such delicate precision and musicality."

MILTON KAYE, piano accompanist to violinist Jascha Heifetz

"Sometimes Harvey would need to learn a recital program on short notice and would pull out the pieces he would be playing during my lesson so that we could go through them together. What a blast that was! He was performing this repertoire at such a high musical level, with a real 'go for it' attitude, right there next to me. What a treat!"

JAY HUNSBERGER, tubist, Florida West Coast Symphony

"Harvey's considerable credits single him out as 'Mr. Tuba.'"

COLONEL ARNALD GABRIEL,
conductor and commanding officer, U.S. Air Force Band

"Harvey was one of the most respected guys in the band. Everybody loved him. He was like a big dad even when he was young. He had such a great sense of humor and a ton of energy!"

JOE FERRANTE, lead trumpet, Sauter-Finegan Orchestra

"Harvey would have more original ideas driving between two small towns in Iowa than most of us would have in a year of touring."

ALLAN DEAN, trumpet, professor of music, Yale University

"I formed my own music groups; I started my own private teaching studio; I write and publish my own music. The last thing I auditioned for was college. Harvey Phillips teaches this approach by doing it.

"Harvey was more likely to talk to you about tractors than mouthpieces. He was a gourmet chef. He was much more interested in being with his family then being onstage. It occurred to me that perhaps I should appreciate my own family more, at an age when one doesn't typically think that way."

NORLAN BEWLEY, tubist, leader, composer, arranger, teacher

"I first heard Harvey play when I was a student at Eastman. The New York Brass Quintet came to play a concert. I couldn't believe the sound he was getting out of the tuba; he played it like a cello. I had to meet him. In my next meeting with Harvey in 1963, I was in the United States Army Band. He asked if I would like to have a lesson. I was flabbergasted. I tried to pay him, but he wouldn't take money. I went to New York to study with him the next year. He told me that I could become a great college teacher. I took him seriously."

DAN PERANTONI, professor of tuba, Indiana University

"Harvey Phillips has a brilliant mind, and is the complete clinician of all time. He was a consultant for instrument design with our company. He was always pushing for the finest details for better instruments. He was an advocate for the players, and audiences are the beneficiaries of his efforts."

GARY SIGURDSON, retired director of marketing, C. G. Conn

"I think of you so often. Of all the wonderful gifts you gave me, the most important might very well be the gift of giving whether in a performance, a lesson, or just spending time with my wife. You opened my eyes to what is really important in life, and for that I will be eternally grateful!"

GARY OFENLOCH, principal tuba, Boston Pops Esplanade Orchestra and Utah Symphony, and tuba professor, University of Utah

"Harvey Phillips is a performing artist of the highest caliber with a genuine interest in the music literature of our time. I knew Harvey Phillips as a student in my theory and literature classes at Juilliard. He often sight-read violin parts on his tuba to demonstrate his concept of proper phrase shapes to the amazed string players. He is indeed one of the top brass performers in America. Mr. Phillips brings dignity and scholarship to any music faculty. And there is an optimism and delight about his attitude that is contagious."

VINCENT PERSICHETTI, writing to recommend tenure at Indiana University, 1972

"Harvey Phillips was the finest tuba player anybody ever heard. I always hired him. And he's a wonderful person."

LOREN GLICKMAN, Contractor and Personnel Manager, Casals Festival

"You deserve special thanks for almost single-handedly creating the environment that allowed the tuba world to prosper. Many of the jobs, much of the music, and most of the good will for our instrument is directly a result of your efforts. You have created a Golden Age of the Tuba. I love you for these things and just for being a beautiful, sensitive human being."

JIM SELF, freelance recording and film studio tubist

"Always foremost in Harvey's thoughts was, is there something I can do that will help somebody and bring pleasure to others? He retained the joy that kids have. When they play ball, for instance, they do it full throttle.

"If Harvey has an idea, it is not going to be small and safe. He thinks in huge dimensions. Sometimes he would just get in over his head. The incredible thing is that, in confidently seeking great and noble dreams, he was successful the majority of times.

"Harvey is a very special person and I treasure our friendship. When something needed doing he did it. As a player, teacher, developer of literature for the tuba, editor, and administrator, he has made a lasting and huge contribution to the music of our time. May Harvey and his legacy continue to create, motivate, and inspire!"

FRANK L. BATTISTI, retired director of the
New England Conservatory Wind Ensemble

"Harvey has helped me numerous times with recommendations, advice, etc. He was more of an influence on my life than any other teacher I ever had. I quote him on a daily basis to my students. Much of what tuba playing is about today is due to his influence, but more important, the life lessons he has given his students have made the world a better place to live in."

G.R. DAVIS, professor of tuba, Vanderbilt University

"Harvey could play anything you put in front of him and with the right feeling. He was the most entrepreneurial person I've ever met. I mean that in the best spirit. He was very creative in the way he thinks.

"We were going to start a summer music program for advanced young musicians in Los Angeles, with eclectic music. The timing wasn't the best for us, but the ideas were. Ten years later the ideas came to fruition, to be called the Henry Mancini Institute, exactly what Harvey and I had been trying to do."

PATRICK WILLIAMS, composer and conductor
of recordings and music for film and television

"I can safely say I have never worked with a more penetratingly insightful musician. He has the ability to broaden the musical vistas and draw out the best performances in all those he comes in contact with. He practices the highest ideals of musicianship, scholarship, excellence in all endeavors, and immense generosity of his time and resources, treats others with kingly kindness and grace, and has an unwavering commitment to the betterment of musicians everywhere. Harvey, you've made a difference, and the world a much better place for us all."

RICHARD ARMANDI,
professor at Tritcon College, College of DuPage, and St. Xavier University

"There has been no one like Harvey. I believe he is a genius and deserves that title. You can actually go to a music store now and look through the tuba folder and find music there that was written for the tuba, which you could not do when I was a young man. (I started playing professionally around 1930.)

"I can remember meeting with Harvey after a Chicago Symphony Orchestra concert at Carnegie Hall. Harvey was telling me of his plans, that he was not going to go the route that so many of us did, joining a symphony orchestra, but that he was going to travel a different route entirely and develop the tuba as a solo instrument, as an instrument of much better recognition. I wondered at the time, is this a feasible thing to do?

"Today, you hear solo tuba recitals, tuba quartets, and tuba ensembles. This development and the recognition are due to Harvey Phillips."

ARNOLD JACOBS, principal tuba, retired, Chicago Symphony Orchestra

"I joined an orchestra which, four years later, shut down for a year for monetary reasons. I arrived at IU with very rusty chops and a shattered future. Mr. Phillips had a gift to bring people up rather than tear them down. He helped give me confidence in my own abilities as a player again."

TONY KNIFFEN, principal tuba, Indianapolis Symphony Orchestra

"Harvey, you are one of that rare breed of performer-teachers who, by deed and word, dared to lead your students and colleagues where no tubist had gone before. By not being content or allowing others to be content with what you, they, or others have played before, you have extended the scope of your instrument and its literature, so that we composers are no longer intimidated by the brass behemoth, but have learned and are continuing to learn to love its flexibility, delicacy, and range of capacities."

MILTON BABBITT, composer

"I played duets with a lot of people, but the best person I ever played duets with was Harvey. And he was a lot of fun."

TOMMY JOHNSON, Los Angeles, tubist for John Williams,
Henry Mancini, and others

"Harvey's emphasis on the importance of performers and composers cultivating relationships is something that I promote with my
own students and colleagues. I am proud to play a small part in carrying on the Harvey Phillips legacy, and thankful for the part he
played in starting me on a rich and rewarding life in music."

JOHN STEVENS, composer and tubist, University of Wisconsin

"I was Harvey's student at IU from 1980 to 1984. He was always preaching
the gospel to be diverse in what you do as a musician. There are only so many
orchestra jobs. When I was thinking of a career in arts administration, he
wrote letters of recommendation and helped me get into grad school."

PAUL HELFRICH, executive director, West Virginia Symphony

"Marketing is not a word that is normally associated with musicians and educators, but Harvey Phillips was a great marketer of the
tuba. His promotion of the instrument was global. It is astonishing
how much more he contributed beyond musical performance."

RICH KESSEL, publisher, *JAZZed* magazine

"I started my conducting career by leading the kindergarten rhythm band in Washington, North Carolina, and ended
it fifty-five years later at TubaChristmas in Rockefeller Center,
with no performances in the interim. I am now retired."

CHARLES KURALT, former host, CBS *News Sunday Morning*

APPENDIX

With King Bros., I soon adopted some of the most used and colorful words of circus language.

Advance Man One who travels the route two to three days ahead of the circus, marking correct directions on telephone poles, especially at intersections, with whitewashed arrows pointing the way.

First of May One traveling with the circus for the first time. May 1 is the traditional annual opening of the circus season. ("Don't mind him; he's a First of May.")

Mud Show A circus that travels on roads and highways with motor vehicles (as opposed to traveling by train).

Windjammer Circus musician.

Red Wagon Front Office (managers, owners).

Local Yokel Local citizen.

Hey Rube Altercation between local yokels and circus personnel.

Band Sleeper On King Bros., lower and upper bunks were built into a semi-trailer pulled by a truck cab. Each bunk was equipped with two Army surplus khaki wool blankets (no sheets) and a gray striped feather pillow (no pillowcase). No toilets available; each person had a container.

YMCA Since traditionally there was no specific place to bathe, circus performers often took bucket baths or improvised their own shower setup. Bandsmen, clowns, and others maintained membership in the Sunbury, Pennsylvania, YMCA, which had the lowest annual dues and maximum membership privileges throughout the United States.

CIRCUS TENTS

Big Top The big tent for outdoor performances—performance rings and stages, an oval track (space between seating and rings/stages), reserved seating (either side), bleachers at each end (blues), the cheaper general admission seats.

Side Show Freaks and contortionists, fortune tellers.

Wardrobe Tent Costumes.

Dressing Tents For use by performers, clowns, band, ushers, roustabouts, etc.

Cookhouse Where meals were served (only when the flag was up!). The first tent set up at each venue.

Donikers Tented toilets with honey buckets.

Menagerie tents Untrained caged animals plus trained horses, elephants, etc.

Dispensary Nonprescription medicines, candy bars, etc.

Concession Souvenirs, cotton candy, popcorn, Cracker Jack, hot dogs, cold drinks, etc.

Back Lot Power plant (electric generator), motor homes, house trailers, private autos, service trucks, semi trailer trucks, etc. All vehicles were assigned a number. All tents and other equipment were positioned in a like manner on every lot, their juxtaposition always the same.

(Note: Sunday performances of the circus were banned in many eastern states by "blue laws.")

King Bros. Circus Schedule

JULY

(1)-Waterbury, CT;

(2)-Willmantic, CT;

(3)-Norwich, CT;

(4)-New London, CT;

(5)-Westerly, RI;

(6)-SUNDAY;

(7)-Derby, CT;

(8)-Holyoke, MA;

(9–10)-Springfield, MA;

(11–12)-Bridgeport, CT;

(13)-SUNDAY;

(14)-Pittsfield, MA;

(15)-Northampton, MA;

(16)-Fitchburg, MA;

(17–18)-Worcester, MA;

(19)-Taunton, MA;

(20)-SUNDAY;

(21)-Fall River. MA;

(22)-New Bedford, MA;

(23)-Framingham, MA;

(24)-Athol, MA;

(25)-Greenfield, MA;

(26)-Meriden, CT;

(27)-SUNDAY;

(28)-Asbury Park, NJ;

(29)-Camden, NJ;

(30)-Millville, NJ;

(31)-Dover, DE;

(1)-Salisbury, MD;

(2)-Cambridge, MD;

(3)-SUNDAY;

(4)-Culpepper, VA;

(5)- Front Royal, VA;

(6)-Luray, VA;

(7)-Harrisonburg, VA;

(8)-Waynesboro, VA;

(9)-Lexington, VA;

(10)-SUNDAY;

(11)-Radford, VA;

(12)-Wytheville, VA;

(13)-Marion, VA;

(14)-Kingsport, TN;

(15)-Johnson City, TN;

(16)-Greenville, TN;

(17)-SUNDAY;

(18)-Asheville, NC;

(19)-Spartanburg, SC;

(20)-Greenville, SC;

(21)-Anderson, SC;

(22)-Greenwood, SC;

(23)-Augusta, GA;

(24)-SUNDAY;

(25)-Columbia, SC;

(26)-Camden, SC;

(27)-Florence, SC;

(28)-Sumter, SC;

(29)-Orangeburg, SC;

(30)-Charleston, SC;

(31)-SUNDAY: Depart Charleston, SC, for Missouri and home via passenger train.

1948: RINGLING BROS. AND BARNUM & BAILEY CIRCUS BAND— MERLE EVANS, BANDMASTER

Flute/Piccolo: Max Ring; *Clarinet:* (7) Tony Ramirez, Carl Erickson, Nick Altroth, George Oliva, Fred Dini, Ford Reed, J. C. Colliver; *Cornet:* (6) Jimmy Ille, Al Hiltonsmith, Frank Sering, Joe Browning, Eddie Broz, George Paugh; *Horn:* (2) Paul Davis, Frank Simaner; *Trombone:* (4) Lew Bader, Jack Evans, Rudy Anderson, Andy Grainger; *Euphonium:* (2) John Horak, Clarence Bennett; *Tuba:* (2) Johnny Evans, Harvey "Junior" Phillips; *Snare Drum:* Red Floyd; *Bass Drum:* Rollin Sherbundy; *Organ:* William Sten. (Add five Local 802 musicians for New York City.)

1949: RINGLING BROS. AND BARNUM & BAILEY CIRCUS BAND— MERLE EVANS, BANDMASTER

Flute/Piccolo: Max Ring; *Clarinet:* (6) Tony Ramirez, Everett Gavin, Nick Altroth, Gene Roy, Fred Dini, J. C. Colliver; *Cornet:* (6) Jack Carroll, Al Hiltonsmith, Frank Sering, Joe Browning, Jim Downs, Jack Sparrowhawk; *Horn:* (2) Paul Davis, Frank Simaner; *Trombone:* (4) Lew Bader, Gene Morse, George Roye, Andy Grainger; *Euphonium:* (2) John Horak, Clarence Bennett; *Tuba:* (2) Harvey "Junior" Phillips, *Bob Beatty; *Snare Drum:* Red Floyd; *Bass Drum:* Rollin Sherbundy. *Organ:* William Sten. (Add five Local 802 musicians for New York City.)

*Bob Beatty replaces Johnny Evans

1950: RINGLING BROS. AND BARNUM & BAILEY CIRCUS BAND— MERLE EVANS, BANDMASTER

1950: *Flute/Piccolo:* Max Ring; *Clarinet:* (7) Tony Ramirez, Everett Gavin, Nick Altroth, Gene Roy, Fred Dini, J. C. Colliver, Rudy Bundy; *Cornet:* (6) Jack Carroll, Otis Jones, Frank Sering, Joe Browning, Rusty Bader, W. C. Clark; *Horn:* (2) Paul Davis, Emil Stango; *Trombone:* (4) Lew Bader, Gene Morris, Dominick Tavaglione, Andy Grainger; *Euphonium:* (2) John Horak, Clarence Bennett; *Tuba:* (2) Johnny Evans, Harvey Phillips; *Snare Drums:* Red Floyd; *Bass Drum:* Frank Hoffman; *Organ:* Clarence Woods. (Add five Local 802 musicians for New York City.)

Piccolo	Max Ring
E♭ Clarinet	Martin Hoexter
Clarinets	Everett Gavin, Howard Johnson, Neal Segard, Jimmy Austin, Buck Weaver, Bert Plowman, Harold Hanson, Tony Ramirez
Cornets	Bill Kirkise, Frank Seavey, Phil Garkow, Frank Sering, Joe Steffan, Henry Kyes
Horns	Paul Davis, Pete Staluppi, Burr Holmes, Pete Schmidt
Baritones	Nobel Howard, John Horak
Trombones	Lew Bader, Stanley Czerwinski, Charley Duble, Gene Miller
Basses	Harvey Phillips, Johnny Evans, Bill Bell
Drums	Ray Floyd, Ray Brownell, Rolin Sherbundy
Organ	Pete Heaton

"These are the best musicians who worked for me during the last fifty years. If these musicians could ever have been brought together they would be the best circus band ever assembled anywhere. How they could play a circus program!"

MERLE EVANS, Bandmaster,
Ringling Bros. and Barnum & Bailey Circus Band 1919–1969

FAMOUS TUBISTS: 1850–1950

August Helleberg

August Helleberg (1861–1936), the most renowned tubist of his time, was taught to play brass instruments by his father. He came to America from Denmark in 1878 at age seventeen with his wife-to-be. Helleberg earned his living as a free-lance tubist in New York City. He became the teacher of young Fred Geib. He played in the New York Philharmonic and was the first tubist in the Chicago Symphony, when it was founded in 1891. Helleberg returned to the New York Philharmonic (1898–1903) and played in the Sousa Band and the Metropolitan Opera Orchestra. He designed instruments and mouthpieces for Conn which are still used. Helleberg was an actual voted-in member of the New York Philharmonic, which was a cooperative of musicians at the time. He first appears in the program roster of the 1888 and 1889 seasons, according to Richard Wandel,

New York Philharmonic archivist. Unlike today, each program apparently shows a roster for that particular concert, rather than the orchestra as a whole. The use of the word "principal" is fairly modern. Even the earlier "solo performer" is not used on the roster at this time. The first roster to list tuba is 1854. At that time, tubists were hired for concerts that needed a tuba or ophicleide.

Fred Geib

Born in Germany, Fred Geib (1871–1950) immigrated to the United States in 1886. Young Geib was taught to play tuba by his father. Shortly after his arrival in New York, Geib began private study with August Helleberg. He played tuba in the New York Philharmonic from 1891 to 1898 while Helleberg was in Chicago. Geib played in the Philadelphia Orchestra in the 1904–1905 season and the New York Philharmonic from 1910–1928. He joined the Radio City Music Hall Orchestra at its inception in 1932, retiring from it three years before his death in 1950.

FAMOUS TUBISTS: PERFORMERS AND PEDAGOGUES OF THE TWENTIETH CENTURY

John Kuhn

John Kuhn was a highly respected Sioux Indian of the Blackfoot tribe. He was a terrific tubist and played with Buffalo Bill, then John Philip Sousa. When Merle Evans conducted the final performance of Buffalo Bill's Wild West show, John Kuhn was in it, but not playing tuba: he was on a horse, with a bow and arrow. Bill Bell and John Kuhn played in the Rodeo Band in New York in 1953.

Bill Bell asked me to sit in for a day of performances because he wanted me to meet Kuhn, then eighty-five. He still played well. I've always said the worst sound of tuba is too much tuba. The more discerning musicians, like Bell and Kuhn, made sure to balance with the other sections of the band.

Research continues on this popular American Indian musician.

William J. Bell

William Bell (1902–1971) joined the Sousa Band as principal tuba in 1921 at age eighteen, touring with the Sousa Band until he joined the Cincinnati Symphony Orchestra in 1924. In 1937 he was the third musician engaged by Arturo Toscanini for the NBC Symphony Orchestra and in 1943 he joined the New York Philharmonic. A renowned teacher of tuba at the Cincinnati Conservatory, Juilliard, and the Manhattan School of Music, he joined the Indiana University School of Music in 1961. He was famous for tuba pedagogy built on logic.

Arnold Jacobs

Arnold Jacobs (1915–1998) studied with Philip Donatelli at the Curtis Institute of Music in Philadelphia, graduating in 1936. He played two seasons with the Indianapolis Symphony Orchestra, was the principal tubist of the Pittsburgh Symphony Orchestra from 1939–1944, toured with Stokowski in the All-American Youth Orchestra in 1941, and was principal tubist with the Chicago Symphony Orchestra from 1944 until 1988. His orchestral performances were legendary and his private teaching internationally acclaimed.

1953 TOUR PERSONNEL—SAUTER-FINEGAN ORCHESTRA

Reeds: Harvey Estrin—soprano and alto recorder, piccolo, flute, clarinet, alto sax; Al Block—piccolo, flute, clarinet, alto sax; Raymond Shiner—oboe, English horn, clarinet, tenor sax; Walter Kane—clarinet, bass clarinet, baritone sax; Ernie Bright—clarinet, bass clarinet, tenor sax. *Trumpets:* Joe Ferrante, Bobby Nichols, Nick Travis. *Trombones:* Sonny Russo, Jimmy Thompson, Ed Erwin. *Tuba:* Harvey Phillips. *Piano:* Danny Fenton. *Bass:* Bob Petersen. *Drums:* Mousey Alexander. *Percussion:* Joe Venuto, Spiras Karas. *Harp:* Assunta (Susie) Dell'Aquila. *Guitar:* Mundell Lowe. *Featured Vocalists:* Sally Sweetland, Andy Roberts.

NEW YORK BRASS QUINTET

Attrition and individual professional priorities brought noteworthy changes in NYBQ personnel.

Trumpet:

Robert Nagel	1954–1985
John Glasel	1954–1961
Theodore Weis	1961–1963
Robert Heinrich	1963–1965
Allan Dean	1966–1985

Horn:

Frederick Schmidt	1954–1959
Frederick Bradford	1959–1960
Raymond Alonge	1960–1963
John Barrows	1963–1964
Barry Benjamin	1964–1965
Paul Ingraham	1963–1985

Trombone:

Erwin Price   1954–1956
Keith Brown   1957–1958
John Swallow   1959–1985

Tuba:

Harvey Phillips   1954–1955
Herbert Wekselblatt 1955–1956
Harvey Phillips   1956–1967
Thompson Hanks   1967–1985

MEMORABLE RECORDINGS

Some of the recordings I played on that I most enjoy: *New York Brass Quintet in Concert* (varied program); *Two Contemporary Composers* (NYBQ playing Alec Wilder and Don Hammond); *Baroque Brass* (NYBQ); *Rhythm Was His Business* (George Williams, arranger; Jimmy Lunceford, instrumentation); *Put On Your Dancing Shoes* (George Williams, arranger, New York freelance all-stars); *Into the Hot,* featuring two artists: The first was John Carisi, leader, whose group (John Glasel, Doc Severinsen, trumpets; Jim Buffington, horn; Urbie Green, trombone; Harvey Phillips, tuba; Phil Woods, Gene Quill, alto saxophones; Eddie Costa, vibes and piano; Barry Galbraith, guitar; Milt Hinton, bass; Osie Johnson, drums) played three selections, of which "Angkor Wat" was the most important. Pianist Cecil Taylor was the other artist. Gil Evans is standing on the cover because he wrote Miles Davis's album *Birth of the Cool.*

Music for Band (Morton Gould, composer and conductor)—Bill Bell and Harvey Phillips, tuba section; *Burke-Phillips All-Star Concert Band, Vol. 1* (includes "National Emblem March," "The Elephant and the Fly," "Roman Carnival," etc.) and *Vol. 2* (includes cornet solo, "Lincoln Center March," *Scheherazade,* etc.); *Impressions of Duke Ellington,* Billy Byers, arranger.

Anthology of American Circus Music, Merle Evans, conductor, New England Conservatory Wind Ensemble, four volumes; *Matteson-Phillips TubaJazz Consort, Superhorns,* and *Matteson-Phillips TubaJazz Consort Live* (includes "Spoofy," "Oleo," "Stompin' at the Savoy," "Georgia on my Mind," "Bye Bye Blues," "Waltzing Matilda"); *Music for Organ, Brass, and Percussion,* featuring organist E. Power Biggs, conducted by Maurice Peress; *Swinging at the Opera,* Fred Karlin and His Orchestra; *Peter Meets the Wolf in Dixieland,* (I was the wolf; Pee Wee Erwin, Peter; Kenny Davern, bird; Boomie Richman, cat; Cliff Leeman and Billy Maxted, hunters); *Gershwin in Brass:* Charlie Margulis, lead trumpet, with Paul Whiteman, in the 1930s saved the scores of *An American in Paris* and *Rhapsody in Blue* and played on this album twenty-five years later; *The Happy Dixieland Jazz,* Jimmy McPartland; *Dick Cary and the Dixieland Doodlers,* I did a solo on "Billy Boy"; *John Glasel Brasstet; Charleston City All Stars Go Dixieland,* led by Pee Wee Erwin.

The Sauter-Finegan Orchestra Revisited; Perceptions, Dizzy Gillespie with Gunther Schuller's Orchestra; *Quincy Jones and his Orchestra; Jazz Goes to the Movies,* Manny Albam, arranger and conductor; *Cabin in the Sky,* arranged by Manny Albam with soloist Curtis Fuller, trombone; *Michel Legrand Big Band Plays Richard Rodgers; Duet* by Orchestra U.S.A.; *Juggy's Jass Band; Hello Louis! Plays the Music of Louis Armstrong,* songs identified with Armstrong and with Tony Bennett, Bobby Hackett, cornet; *Have a Happy Jolly Christmas,* the Three Sons, features two tubas, we became friends when they were relief for the Bernie Mann Band and they asked me to get another tuba player so I got Jay McAllister; Buddy Morrow, a beautiful Christmas album, he did the most beautiful trombone playing you ever heard; *A Greek in Dixieland*, Gus Kahn, clarinet, John Glasel, trumpet, Urbie Green, trombone, Harvey Phillips, tuba, Barry Galbraith, guitar, Chet Amsterdam, bass, sections of mandolins and balalaikas, arranged by John Carisi; *Movin' Wes,* Wes Montgomery, leader, I did half and Don Butterfield did half; *Blues, the Common Ground,* Kenny Burrell, leader, Don and I split that one too; *Think,* Pat Williams; *Heavy Vibrations,* Pat Williams; *10th Avenue,* Patrick Williams's New York Band, he had expensive jackets made for us inscribed with "10th Avenue," he was just homesick for New York in 1986; *America the Beautiful,* Gary McFarland, a good recording; *Glass Onion,* Arif Mardin produced; *Virtuosity: A Contemporary Look,* with the Valhalla Horn Quartet, Jim Buffington, Earl Chapin, John Clark, Peter Gordon, a tuba feature was "The Devil's Herald," written for me by Richard Peaslee; *21st Century Bebop Band,* includes "Bebop Revisited," "Hot House," "This One's for 'Trane"; (Al) *Cobine Plays Carmichael,* includes "Stardust," "Georgia on My Mind," "Up a Lazy River."

Morton Gould conducted *Grand Canyon Suite,* and to get the storm scene they took sheets of tin to the balcony and rattled them, New York Philharmonic plus me; *Early Italian Music,* arranged by Stokowski and Lucien Calliet; Calliet and Jimmy Burke conducted *The Burke-Phillips All-Star Concert Band Vol. 1;* I recorded the Berlioz *Requiem* with the Hartford Symphony Orchestra; several recordings with Stokowski; Stravinsky's *Concerto for Piano and Wind Instruments,* Philippe Entremont, pianist; Stravinsky conducted *The Fairy's Kiss* and

Game of Cards; I recorded with a pickup group conducted by Victor Borge; I also participated on a recording of Casals's choral work; while a member of the New York City Ballet Orchestra, we recorded "The Stars and Stripes Forever" and *Western Symphony;* Alec Wilder's *Sonata No. 1 for Tuba and Piano,* with Milton Kaye, plus Alec's *Suite for Horn, Tuba, and Piano No. 2,* with John Barrows and Milton Kaye.

IMPORTANT NYBQ RECORDINGS

New York Brass Quintet in Concert
  (Anthony Holborne, originally on Golden Crest)
Two Contemporary Composers
  (Alec Wilder and Don Hammond, originally on Golden Crest)
Alvin Etler's Music for Brass on CRI
Harold Farberman's Music for Brass Quintet on CRI
Gunther Schuller's Music for Brass Quintet on CRI
Baroque Brass on RCA Victor

THE BURKE-PHILLIPS ALL STAR CONCERT BAND—FIRST LP, 1960

Piccolo-Flute: Andrew J. Lolya, *Flute:* Murray W. Panitz, *Flute/Tenor Saxophone:* Alexander Howard, *Oboe:* William Arrowsmith, *Oboe/English Horn:* Whitney Tustin, *E♭ Clarinet/Clarinet:* Sigurd Bockman, *Bass Clarinet/Clarinet:* Paul E. Howland, *Bassoon:* Loren R. Glickman, *Clarinet/Alto Saxophone:* (2) Alfred Gallodoro, Vincent J. Abato, *Tenor Saxophone/Clarinet:* Albert Klink, *Baritone Saxophone/Clarinet:* Paul J. Ricci, *Clarinet:* (8) Alexander Williams, Bernard Portnoy, Joseph A. Allard, Robert L. Hoffman, Herbert S. Blayman, Charles Russo, Wallace Shapiro, Ernest D. Bright, *Trumpet:* (6) Raymond D. Crisara, Theodore M. Weis, Robert E. Nagel, Harry Glantz, Wilfred Roberts Jr., Manny Weinstock, *French Horn:* (4) John R. Barrows, James Buffington, Earl W. Chapin, Ralph Froelich, *Trombone:* (3) David A. Uber, John W. Swallow, John Clark, *Baritone:* Roger M. Smith, *Tuba:* Harvey G. Phillips, *Percussion:* (2) Bradley Spinney, Chauncey Morehouse, *Conductor/Cornet Soloist:* James F. Burke, *Guest Conductor:* Hunter N. Wiley, *Tuba Soloist:* Harvey G. Phillips, *Production Supervisor:* Eddie Sauter.

HARVEY PHILLIPS AND TWENTIETH CENTURY
INNOVATIONS PRESENTS

Tuba Recital Series 1975–1976, Carnegie Recital Hall 8:30 PM

Sept. 29	Roger Bobo
Oct. 29	Daniel Perantoni
Nov. 29	John Turk
Dec. 22	Harvey Phillips
Jan. 9	Robert Whaley
Jan. 18	J. Lesley Varner
Feb. 15	Barton Cummings
Mar. 13	R. Winston Morris
Mar. 28	Brian Bowman
Apr. 25	Floyd Cooley

INDEX

28; tuba history, 76–83; tuba is dropped, 324; tuba symposium, 281–285; TubaCompany formed for basketball game, 362; two New York Brass Quintet recordings, 168–169; unforgettable Escanaba, 185–187; University of Missouri, 32–34; volunteering with ensembles, 69–72; wedding, 116; working for Julius Bloom, 210–211

Phillips, Jesse Emmett, 3–4, 5, 7, 8, 9; Hudson Super Six, 14–15, 17–18, 33; meets Carol, 127

Phillips, Lottie Amber Chapman, 1–2, 3–4, 5, 6–7, 8, 10, 18; Alec Wilder dedicates *Sonata No. 2 for Tuba and Piano* to her, 219; goes to Aspen, 224; 315–316; meets Alec Wilder, 219; meets Carol, 127; writes to Harvey at the circus, 24–25, 33

Pilafian, Sam, 357, 392, 407

Pokorny, Gene, 405, 407

Prausnitz, Frederik, 73

Price, Erwin, 119

Pryor, Arthur, 55, 82, 157, 443, 444, 445

Rafael Mendez Brass Institute, 372–373

Ray, Joe, 284

Reiner, Fritz, 40

Revelli, Bill, 157, 279

Richardson, Elsie and John, 107–110, 116–117, 164

Richardson, Jack, 444

Ringling Bros. and Barnum & Bailey Circus: Big Blue, 46–47; hall of fame band, 463; 1948, 1949, and 1950 bands, 462; 1948 tour, 47–49; 1949 season, 50; 1950 season, 61; railroad cars, 38–39, 41–46; recording circus music, 61–63; in Sarasota, 35

Rodgers, Richard, 103, 145

Rose, Bill, 42, 52, 447

Rossi, John, 105

Rostropovich, Mstislav, 228, 230

Russ, Gabe, 444

Ryan, John W., *xi*, 314, 318

Ryker, Robert, 150–151; proposes TUBA, 280–281

Sagle, Rex, 377, 388

Salzman, Michael, 286–287, 360

Sauter, Ed: *Eight Random Thoughts for Solo Tuba*, 355, 357, 361; *Solo Tuba and Saxophone Quartet*, 363

Sauter-Finegan Orchestra, 63, 108–111, 113, 130, 146, 252–253, 297, 447; 1953 tour personnel, 465

Schickele, Peter, 225, 240–241, 283

Schmidt, Frederick, 119, 168–169

Schmitz, Chester, 249

Schuller, Gunther, 71, 145; director at Sandpoint, 363; *Little Brass Music*, 171, 172; moderates music education conference, 262, 280, 354; *Music for Brass Quintet*, premiered at Library of Congress, 170–171, 172, 408; plays horn, 243; praised highly, 209; president of New England Conservatory, 233–240, 242–245; *Seven Studies on Themes of Paul Klee*, 170; *Symphony for Brass*, 154, 160, 165, 170; thirty-ninth birthday, 231; writes about Brass Chamber Music Forum, 394–395, 452

Self, Jim, 220, 282, 399, 405, 455

Wilder, Alec, 112, 136, 171, 187, 213–219; *Brass Quintet No. 1*, 214; composes for Jesse, Little Harvey, and Tom, 216–217, 217–219; *Effie (Suite No. 1)*, 215–216; the Friends of Alec Wilder group, 359–360; hears Gunther and Harvey, 243; *Inner-Office Memos*, 276–277, 280, 311–313, 318, 352, 353; list of compositions and death, 359; *Sonata No. 1 for Tuba and Piano*, 215; Wilder Music, 222–223, 257–258

Wiley, Hunter, 69, 105, 158, 167

Wilks, Ralph, 17–18

Williams, Patrick, 211; *Breaking Away* score, 361–362, 456

Wilson, Dr. George C., 15–16, 33, 34, 36, 309

Willson, Meredith, 280

Windjammers, Inc., 260

Woods, Phil, 160, 220, 319, 412–413

Zavarella, Tony, 44, 103–104

HARVEY PHILLIPS (1929–2010) was Distinguished Professor of Music Emeritus at Indiana University Bloomington. World renowned as a tuba soloist and brass quintet leader, he founded and directed OctubaFest, TubaChristmas, TubaSantas, TubaCompany, and the Matteson-Phillips TubaJazz Consort.

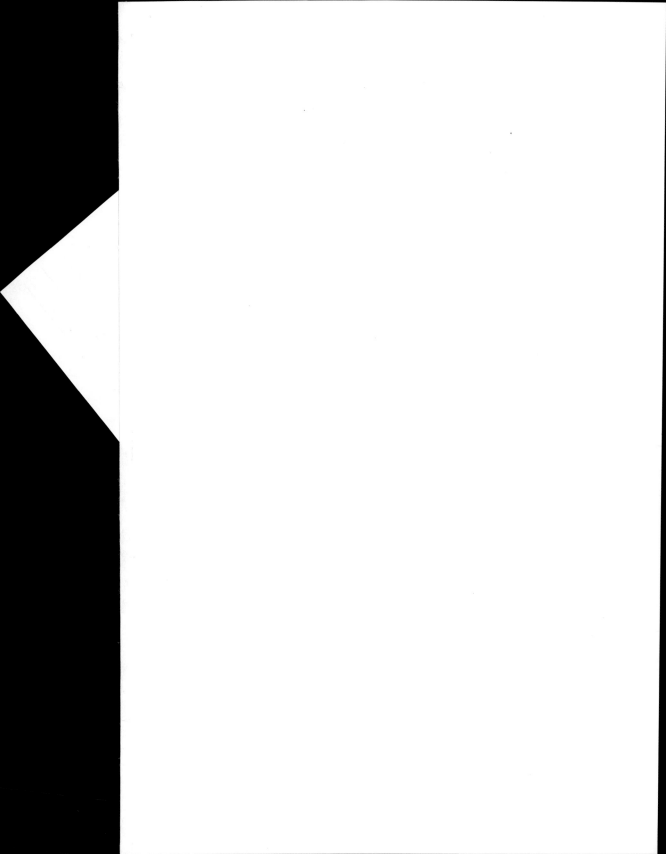

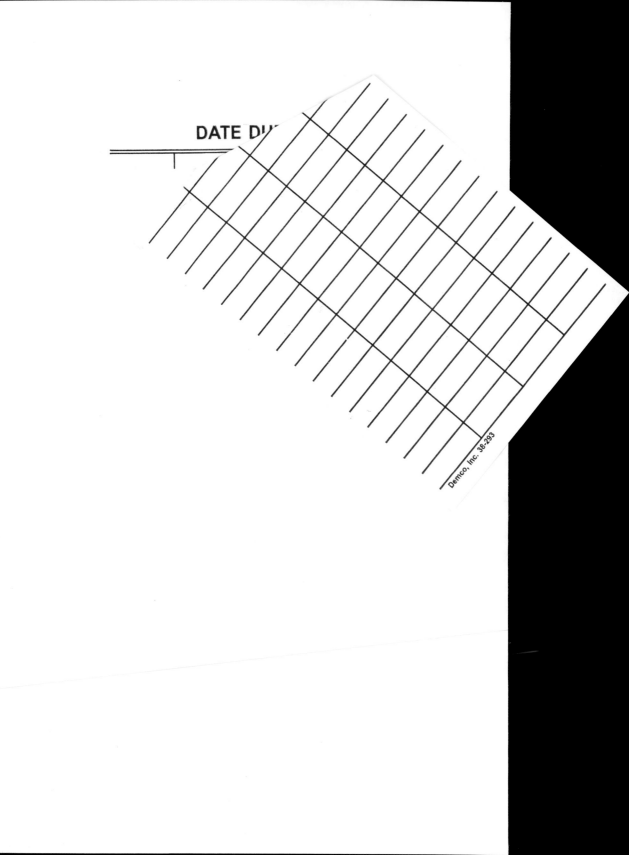

DATE DUE

Demco, Inc. 38-293